AMERICAN ETHNIC GROUPS: THE EUROPEAN HERITAGE

A Bibliography of
Doctoral Dissertations
Completed at
American Universities

by

FRANCESCO CORDASCO

and

DAVID N. ALLOWAY

The Scarecrow Press, Inc.
Metuchen, N.J., & London 1981

Library of Congress Cataloging in Publication Data

Cordasco, Francesco, 1920-
  American ethnic groups, the European heritage.

  Bibliography: p.
  Includes indexes.
  1. European Americans--Bibliography. 2. United
States--Ethnic relations--Bibliography. 3. United States
--Emigration and immigration--Bibliography. 4. Disserta-
tions, Academic--United States--Bibliography. I. Alloway,
David Nelson, joint author. II. Title.
Z1361.E97C67 [E184.E95]   016.973'04   80-28775
ISBN 0-8108-1405-6

Copyright © 1981 by Francesco Cordasco and David N. Alloway
Manufactured in the United States of America

For
Carmela Madorma Cordasco
and
Margie L. Neumoyer Alloway

>Most immigrants said nothing that we can hear, though from time to time, in a letter or a fragment of a diary, in the record of a speech or a riot, they impress themselves on our minds. Their descendants, of course, cannot interpret them: they are merely surprised at their parents' or grandparents' preoccupation with worlds that are not their own. It is for the historian to employ such skill as he possesses to uncover individual stories and to detect patterns in the imperfect evidence. If he judges the effort worth making, it will be because he can feel respect and fascination when confronted by the hardships, the disillusion, the modest achievements of the millions who crossed the Atlantic. Fascination above all: for now and again, from the faceless crowd, there emerge, in Lewis Hine's photographs or the sketches of Jacob Epstein and Joseph Stella, features more striking, more noble even, than those of the generals and prelates, the politicians and magnates, of whom most history is told.
>
>--Philip Taylor, The Distant Magnet (1971)

TABLE OF CONTENTS

Introduction   vii

A Note on the Literature of Dissertations   x

I. WESTERN AND NORTHERN EUROPE
   A. Great Britain and Ireland   3
   B. France, Portugal, Spain, and the Low Countries   25
   C. Scandinavia: Norway, Sweden, Denmark, and Finland   40

II. CENTRAL, SOUTHERN, AND EASTERN EUROPE   59
   A. The Germanies and Austria-Hungary   60
   B. Italy, Greece, and the Mediterranean Basin   90
   C. Poland, Russia, the Balkans, and Slavic Europe   121
   D. European Jewry   142

III. MULTI-GROUP, INTERETHNIC, AND RELATED STUDIES   182

IV. EMIGRATION/IMMIGRATION: HISTORY, POLITICS, ECONOMICS, AND POLICY   238

V. MISCELLANEA   279

VI. A CHECKLIST OF SELECTED PUBLISHED BIBLIOGRAPHIES   333

Index of Names   338

Subject Index   353

INTRODUCTION

The origins of this work lie in our study of minority groups in the United States and in our involvement with a multitude of social needs identified with urban America, particularly during the Johnsonian interventions that constituted the "war on poverty" across the 1960s and early 1970s. It was inevitable that the "new ethnicity" spawned by the black civil rights movement presented itself as a major social phenomenon that invited study and special attention. There is a logical progression from our study of the black minority communities in American cities (Minorities in the American City. New York: McKay, 1970) to our assemblage of a core collection of dissertations dealing with American ethnic groups (American Ethnic Groups: A Collection of Dissertations. 47 vols. New York: Arno/New York Times, 1980). Urban sociology and ethnic historiography coalesce, each indistinguishable from the other, and the amalgam delineates much of the rich texture of American social and cultural history.

The enormity of the resources afforded by American doctoral dissertation literature is staggering. The Comprehensive Dissertation Index, 1861-1972, 37 vols. (Ann Arbor, Michigan: Xerox University Microfilms, 1973) is a guide to over 400,000 doctoral dissertations; it has been compiled from the entries for Dissertation Abstracts International (1938-   ), a monthly publication of abstracts of dissertations. (See "A Note on the Literature of Dissertations," page x, below.) From this enormous resource we have drawn over 1,400 dissertations that deal with American ethnic groups of European origin. We have arranged them in two major geographical areas of origin--I. Western and Northern Europe and II. Central, Southern, and Eastern Europe--and then by nation or region, a framework that does not seriously violate the political and ethnocultural integrity that makes the historical process intelligible.

Our selection criteria have been very broad, and we have accepted even those dissertations whose relationship with ethnic groups, if not direct, was indirectly significant. A dissertation was included if it dealt with any facet of American ethnic experience: to have done otherwise would have gravely imperiled the authenticity of coverage.

Beyond the two geographical areas of origin (each with appropriate subdivisions) our design provides sections on III. Multi-Group, Interethnic, and Related Studies; IV. Emigration/Immigration: History, Politics, Economics, and Policy; V. Miscellanea; and VI. A Checklist of Selected Published Bibliographies. At best, this is a convenient framework that allows the management of hundreds of entries and provides a meaningful measure of differentiation. The Index of Names and Subject Index are the keys to the volume's use; and since the Subject Index is clearly more important, it has been made as complete as possible. The Indexes are keyed to the entry numbers (continuous throughout) assigned to the dissertations, which have been arranged alphabetically by author in each of the sections.

The coverage has been limited to dissertations completed at American universities, although a few Canadian theses have been included. (We have not included dissertations completed at European universities, although these are becoming increasingly important. Two examples may be cited: P. R. D. Stokvis. The Dutch American Trek, 1846-1847. University of Leiden, 1977; and E. Milani. Mutual Aid Societies Among Italian Immigrants in the United States of America: A Comprehensive View, 1865-1977. Istituto Universitario Lingue Moderne, 1977.) The period covered extends from the early 1890s through 1979. Applying the criteria noted above, we have tried to make it as complete as possible; inevitably, some dissertations will have been missed. At this time the volume affords (within its defined delimitations) the fullest guide to dissertations dealing with American ethnic groups of European origin.

The bibliographical information for each dissertation is given as follows: author, title; conferring university (name abbreviated-- e.g., Chicago, and not University of Chicago; name is given in full only when confusion may result); year; pagination; and (when available) the Dissertation Abstracts volume and page number. Most entries include an annotation, and if the annotation is drawn directly from the author's abstract of the dissertation, it is so identified by the designation "(A)." If the dissertation has been published, this is indicated.

Our own annotations for dissertations have been descriptive and not critical; but this is not to suggest that we have been unaware of evolving developments in ethnic/immigrant historiography. It is inevitable that the dissertations reflect the time period in which they were written and that, for a host of compelling reasons, they remain congruent with appropriate historical canons. We basically agree (recognizing the complexity of the issues raised) with the views expressed by Michael M. Passi:

> The dissertation argues that ethnic studies in America has been "ironic" in that it has ignored the persistence of ethnic consciousness in American society and instead has sought to demonstrate the process by which white ethnic communities have been, or are being, absorbed into an homogenous American culture. This, in turn, results from deeply-rooted assumptions about American society which center on the belief that in the New World men were freed from the history, traditions, and institutions of the

Introduction   ix

Old World to recover the ancient freedoms of the "natural"
man. This view shaped interpretations of American nationality from Crèvecoeur to Fredrick Jackson Turner.
Urbanization, industrialization, and mass immigration in
the late 19th century, in the minds of many American intellectuals, seemed to preclude the possibility of further
assimilation of immigrants and threatened to shatter the
presumed homogeneity of American culture. Professional
social scientists in the emerging universities, however,
offered a new synthesis which would make the traditional
view of American society compatible with urbanization and
industrialization. Drawn largely from the rural and small
town, old stock, Protestant middle-class, these professional academics did not challenge the normative assumption that the society ought to be culturally homogeneous.
As new members were recruited into the academic profession, many of them from ethnic backgrounds, the assimilationist position remained unchallenged. In part this resulted from the fact that the concept of assimilation tended
to rationalize the upward mobility of ethnic Americans, in
part because the socialization process in the universities
compelled students to adopt the intellectual framework of
the profession. In the years following World War II, the
work of two scholars from immigrant backgrounds, Louis
Wirth and Oscar Handlin, crystallized the assimilationist
perspective in ethnic studies. Indeed, American scholarship generally affirmed the view of American nationality
with great vigor in the 1950s and early 1960s. Since 1960,
however, the assimilationist perspective has experienced
increasing challenge as American social scientists have
responded to the conspicuous resurgence of ethnic consciousness that emerged in the context of racial strife and
urban crisis in American society [Mandarins and Immigrants: The Irony of Ethnic Studies in America Since
Turner. Minnesota, 1972].

It is a reasoned judgment, provocative and without the polem-
ical fervor that has gripped a still-evolving American ethnic consciousness.

We have incurred many obligations in the preparation of this
volume. First, we acknowledge our indebtedness to librarians at
Montclair State College, Columbia University, the New York Public
Library, and the Library of Congress. We owe a special debt to
Xerox University Microfilms of Ann Arbor, Michigan, and acknowledge their kind permission to publish excerpts from Dissertation
Abstracts International. In those cases where dissertation abstracts
were not available in DAI, we commend the courteous and cooperative assistance of university librarians (particularly at Harvard University and the University of Chicago) who responded to our many
queries.

F.C. / D.N.A.

August 1, 1980

A NOTE ON THE LITERATURE OF DISSERTATIONS

The major source for dissertations is Comprehensive Dissertation Index, 1861-1972, 37 vols. (Ann Arbor: Xerox University Microfilms, 1973), a computer-generated keyword-out-of-context index to about 417,000 doctoral dissertations accepted by some 400 universities in the United States (including Canadian and some foreign universities). It supersedes List of American Doctoral Dissertations Printed in 1912-1938, 26 vols. (Washington, D.C.: Catalog Division, U.S. Library of Congress. Government Printing Office, 1913-1940); and Doctoral Dissertations Accepted by American Universities, 1933/1934-1954/1955. Nos. 1-22 (New York: Wilson, 1934-1956); as well as the Retrospective Index to Dissertation Abstracts International, vols. 1-29, 9 vols. in 11 (Ann Arbor: Xerox University Microfilms, 1970). Within each subject volume of the CDI the listing is alphabetical by keyword. Full citations appear in both the author and subject listings and include title, author's full name, date, university, pagination when available, citation to Dissertation Abstracts or other printed list, and University Microfilm publication number for dissertations available on microfilm. An analysis of the scope of CDI appears in RQ, vol. 14 (Fall 1974), pp. 61-62.

The CDI is compiled from Dissertation Abstracts International (v. 1 [1938]-) (formerly titled Microfilm Abstracts [1938-1951] and Dissertation Abstracts [1952-1968]), which is a monthly register of abstracts submitted to Xerox University Microfilms of Ann Arbor, Michigan, by over 350 cooperating universities in the United States and Canada. Since 1966 Abstracts has appeared in two sections, Humanities and Social Sciences and Sciences and Engineering. An author index appears in each issue, in addition to cumulated author and keyword subject indexes for each volume. The title change from Dissertation Abstracts to Dissertation Abstracts International occurred with vol. 30, no. 1 (July 1969), as the result of the inclusion of some foreign dissertations.

AMERICAN
ETHNIC
GROUPS:
THE
EUROPEAN
HERITAGE

I. WESTERN AND NORTHERN EUROPE

A. Great Britain and Ireland
B. France, Portugal, Spain, and the Low Countries
C. Scandinavia: Norway, Sweden, Denmark, and Finland

A. GREAT BRITAIN AND IRELAND

1. Adams, William F. Ireland and Irish Emigration to the New World from 1815 to the Famine. Yale, 1929. 444p. Published under the same title (New Haven: Yale University Press, 1932). Traces the history of Irish immigrants to the United States, with analysis of the effects of Irish immigration on American institutions and life.

2. Athearn, Robert G. Thomas Francis Meagher: An Irish Revolutionary in America. Minnesota, 1947. 245p. Published under the same title (New York: Arno, 1976). Thomas Francis Meagher (1823-1867) was the epitome of the romantic revolutionary. In 1848 he was one of the leaders of the Young Ireland revolution. After its failure the British government sent him to Tasmania as a political prisoner. Escaping in 1852, Meagher came to the United States and settled in New York City. Athearn discusses Meagher's American career as journalist, lawyer, soldier, and politician. Meagher was the darling of the New York Irish. He led the famed Irish Brigade into combat during the Civil War. After hostilities ceased President Andrew Johnson appointed Meagher Governor of the Montana Territory, but shortly after accepting his new position he drowned in the Missouri River. Athearn judges Meagher's American years as more shadow than substance. His talents never matched his oratory, flamboyance, or popularity. Meagher did little to advance the Irish-American community.

3. Badgley, Robin F. Assimilation and Acculturation of the English Immigrant in New Haven. Yale, 1957. 196p.

4. Barcio, Robert G. Tobias Mullen and the Diocese of Erie, 1868-1899. Case Western Reserve, 1965. 298p. (DA 27:159-A) This biography of Bishop Tobias Mullen, the third Bishop for the diocese of Erie, is also intended to show the development of the diocese during his administration from 1868-1899. Bishop Mullen was an Irish immigrant who served the first 24 years of his priest-

hood in the diocese of Pittsburgh, for which he was ordained by Bishop Michael O'Connor in 1844. His first appointment was to the Cathedral of St. Paul in Pittsburgh, where he remained until 1846, when he was assigned a pastorate in the Johnstown area of Pennsylvania. Here he labored zealously and successfully until recalled to Pittsburgh in 1854 to become the pastor of St. Peter's Church, northside. While stationed at the latter church he became involved in a controversy with local officials of the Pittsburgh House of Correction concerning the right of its Catholic inmates to be given the ministrations of a priest. It was also while still pastor of St. Peter's that Father Mullen was appointed vicar-general of the diocese of Pittsburgh and eventually Bishop of Erie in 1868. (A)

5. Beadles, John A. The Syracuse Irish, 1812-1928: Immigration, Catholicism, Socio-Economic Status, Politics, and Irish Nationalism. Syracuse, 1974. 256p. (DA 36:6888a)
The dissertation is an interdisciplinary examination of the history of Syracuse Irish-Americans from 1812 through 1928, describing immigration, Catholicism, politics and voting, socioeconomic status, and Irish Nationalism. It was written with the determination to gain insight into the social history of Irish immigrants and their descendants, who were on the "bottom" or "bottom middle" of society in a particular Northeastern industrial city during a specific time period. The dissertation, therefore, was designed to be a study in social history from the usually neglected "bottom up" perspective, to make articulate the Syracuse Irish, who have not left behind them letters, collections, or diaries and who were generally not mentioned in the daily press. (A)

6. Berthoff, Rowland T. British Immigrants in Industrial America. Harvard, 1952. 296p.
Published under the title British Immigrants in Industrial America, 1790-1950 (Cambridge: Harvard University Press, 1953). Deals with both cultural and economic adjustment of Scottish, Welsh, and English immigrants in America.

7. Biever, Bruce F. Religion, Culture and Values: A Cross-Cultural Analysis of Motivational Factors in Native Irish and American Irish Catholicism. Pennsylvania, 1965. 283p.
Published under the same title (New York: Arno, 1976). Although American Catholicism has been part of the vast Irish Catholic spiritual empire in the English-speaking world, the pluralistic, American democratic environment gave rise to differences between Catholic attitudes in Ireland and the United States. After studying Irish and Irish-American Catholic opinion in regard to such subjects as the Church's relations to politics, education, the social question, doctrinal communication, clerical-lay relations and ritual, and applying the methodologies of social psychology and cultural anthropology and the techniques of quantitative research, Biever draws clear distinctions between Irish Catholicism on opposite sides of the Atlantic Ocean. He concludes that while American Catholicism is structurally based on an Irish model and

Great Britain, Ireland

that the American Irish have many of the same religious and moral values as Catholics in Ireland, they are much less likely to accept the authority of the Church or her clergy on matters that are not strictly spiritual. They, like other Americans, fear the potential power of institutionalized religion, and insist on democratic and pluralistic controls over the Church.

8. Blake, Nelson M. The United States and the Irish Revolution, 1914-1922. Clark, 1936. 163p.

9. Bolger, Stephen G. The Irish Character in American Fiction, 1830-1860. Pennsylvania, 1971. 194p.
Published under the same title (New York: Arno, 1976). By creating stereotypes literature has always played an important role in shaping attitudes of the dominant majority culture and minority group subcultures toward each other. In many American novels of the nineteenth century the writers portrayed the Irish as agents of alien, authoritarian, and superstitious Popery and as the sources of American urban problems--crime, poverty, and slums. Bolger discusses the role of the Irish as scapegoats for Anglo-American Protestant nativism and as subjects for argument in the slavery controversy that contributed so much to sectional antagonism. Some Northern writers argued that happy, prosperous Irish immigrants demonstrated the superior quality of life in the free states. Southerners countered with the position that blighted Irish urban ghettos in the North proved the benefits of paternalistic slavery in the South. Bolger describes the fictional Irish stereotype as an inferior species: comic, docile, and emotional but essentially harmless, and concludes that perhaps the harmless, humorous stage and fictional Irishman made possible the acceptance of millions of Irish immigrants into the United States.

10. Brown, Thomas N. Irish-American Nationalism, 1848-1891. Harvard, 1956. 206p.
Published under the title Irish-American Nationalism, 1870-1890 (Philadelphia: Lippincott, 1966). An analysis of Irish-American nationalism and its efforts to influence events in Ireland.

11. Buckley, John P. The New York Irish: Their View of American Foreign Policy, 1914-1921. New York, 1974. 203p.
Published under the same title (New York: Arno, 1976). Buckley discusses how the Anglophobia of extreme Irish nationalists like Judge Daniel Cohalan and John Devoy alienated Irish-America during World War I. But in the immediate postwar period, through the agency of powerful newspapers, the Gaelic American and Irish World, they rallied New York and other American Irish opinion behind the Irish war of liberation against Britain. This opinion played a major role in persuading the British government to make an extensive concession to Irish nationalism, and reacted against Woodrow Wilson's brand of internationalism because the President was obviously pro-British and anti-Irish. The 1921 Treaty establishing the Irish Free State was not satisfactory to professional Irish-American nationalists, but to most of the American Irish

Dominion status for 26 Irish counties seemed a respectable symbol of the Irish nation. After 1921 Irish-American nationalism began to fade as a significant force in the American Irish community.

12. Clark, John D. J. The Adjustment of Irish Immigrants to Urban Life: The Philadelphia Experience--1840-1870. Temple, 1970. 284p. (DA 31:5312-A)
This dissertation deals with the social and economic adjustment of Irish immigrants to the life of the industrial City of Philadelphia in the mid-nineteenth century. It describes the social and economic background in Ireland during the period, emphasizing its rural character. The general reaction of Philadelphia to the influx of Roman Catholic Irish immigrants after the potato famine of 1846 is described. The housing conditions and opportunities for the immigrants are examined, as are the opportunities for employment and business activity open to them. The educational and social experiences of the Irish in developing schools and churches are analyzed, and their political and civil organization are evaluated. (A)

13. Cochran, Alice L. The Saga of an Irish Immigrant Family: The Descendants of John Mullanphy. St. Louis, 1958. 275p. Published under the same title (New York: Arno, 1976). Contrary to popular opinion, New England is not the essence of Irish-America. There are as many Midwesterners with Irish heritages as New Englanders who make the same claim. Cochran studies one Midwest Irish family from its beginnings, when John Mullanphy left Ireland in 1792, arrived in the United States, and then pushed on to the frontier village of St. Louis. From the results of her research Cochran concludes that the Midwest Irish were more successful in the United States than their New England counterparts. In contrast to the tight class structure back East, which discouraged social mobility and encouraged ghetto rigidity and paranoia, the Midwest presented a fluid social situation where intelligence, ambition, and hard work resulted in success and assimilation.

14. Coleman, J. W. Labor Disturbances in Eastern Pennsylvania, 1850-1880. Catholic, 1936. 175p.
Published under the title Labor Disturbances in Pennsylvania, 1850-1880 (Washington, D. C.: Catholic University of America Press, 1936). Background and development of Molly Maguires, as relevant to growing trade unionism and Irish immigrants in the Pennsylvania coal fields, with "some justification for their activities."

15. Crocker, Bertram. A Study of the Cultural Integration of a Welsh Community with Its American Environment. Columbia (Teachers College), 1952. 211p.

16. Cronin, Harry C. The Plays of Eugene O'Neill in the Cultural Context of Irish-American Catholicism. Minnesota, 1968.

Great Britain, Ireland 7

(DA 29:2384-A)
Arthur and Barbara Gelb, in their definitive biography of O'Neill,
state that Catholicism, the religion O'Neill abandoned when he
was a young man, was a prominent influence on his writing.
This dissertation begins its investigation with this statement,
along with other selected critical speculations about the influence
of Catholicism on the plays of O'Neill. Catholicism in this dissertation, however, is considered in a different way: as one of
several elements in a rich and complex cultural context. (A)

17. Cuddy, Henry. The Influence of the Fenian Movement on Anglo-American Relations, 1860-1872. St. John's, 1953. 242p.

18. Cuddy, Joseph E. Irish-American and National Isolationism:
1914-1920. State University of New York at Buffalo, 1965.
267p. (DA 26:5991)
During the Wilson era American policymakers tried to lead the
United States away from its traditional isolationism toward a
much heavier involvement in international affairs. The present
study is an analysis of the Irish-American reaction to Wilsonian
diplomacy during the years from the 1914 outbreak of the European War to the final defeat of the League of Nations in the
Presidential election of 1920. During the conflict of these trying
days over foreign policy the Irish played a significant role in obstructing many of Woodrow Wilson's diplomatic efforts. (A)

19. D'Arcy, William. The Fenian Movement in the United States,
1858-1866. Catholic, 1947. 411p.
Published under the same title (Washington, D.C.: Catholic University of America Press, 1947). The history of the Fenian
movement in the United States, its plans to launch an invasion
to free Ireland, and its decline and defeat in 1870.

20. Deye, Anthony H. Archbishop John Baptist Purcell of Cincinnati, Pre-Civil War Years. Notre Dame, 1959. 478p. (DA
28:1368-A)
The present work treats the first 61 years of the life of John
Baptist Purcell (1800-1883), who was bishop (after 1850, archbishop) of Cincinnati for 50 years beginning in 1833. Purcell's
career after 1861 is remembered for his strong support of the
Union during the Civil War, his opposition to the definition of
papal infallibility in 1870, and the crash of the "Purcell Bank"
in 1879. However, in the opinion of the author, the most influential part of his life was the period before the Civil War, when
Cincinnati was the key city of the West and Purcell was the principal Catholic leader west of the Alleghenies. The area of his
importance was religious and pastoral. (A)

21. Dillon, Michael F. Irish Emigration, 1840-1855. California
(Los Angeles), 1940. 240p.

22. Donovan, George F. The Pre-Revolutionary Irish in Massachusetts, 1620-1775. St. Louis, 1931. 158p.

23. Doyle, David N. Irish-Americans, Native Rights and National Empires: The Structure, Divisions and Attitudes of the Catholic Minority in the Decade of Expansion, 1890-1901. Iowa, 1976. 289p.
Published under the same title (New York: Arno, 1976). By the 1890s Catholic America had attained a power and coherence unimaginable only 40 years before, largely in terms of the maturation of its main component, Irish-Americans, who were socially and culturally well equipped to shape a general Catholic response to the issues posed in the wider American society. Doyle tests his thesis in terms of the response of Catholic America to its country's imperialism. He examines the unity as well as the ethnic diversity of American Catholicism and demonstrates that the Irish dominated the Catholic middle class, which led the Catholic community. He emphasizes that the Irish-led Catholic middle class opposed the "New Imperialism" of the Western powers (fashionable amongst other Americans) because it refused to accept the tenets of Social Darwinism. Except for some members of the clergy, who wished an American canopy for their planned revitalization of Cuban, Filipino, and perhaps other Catholicisms, most Catholics followed the dominant Irish-American lead of viewing imperialism as repugnant to their own minority traditions, their position in American life, and their understanding of the convergence of the best Catholic convictions and American loyalties.

24. Eftink, Edward M. The Development of the Legal Status of Catholic Education in Missouri. Catholic, 1971. 268p. (DA 31:6300-A)
This study presents a historical treatment of the relations between Catholic education and the civil government in Missouri from its beginnings until the present day by considering the various constitutional and statutory provisions affecting Catholic education and the political milieu at the time of their enactment. Particular emphasis is given to the decisions of the courts in applying these provisions to specific practices in the field of education. (A)

25. Feldberg, Michael J. The Philadelphia Riots of 1844: A Social History. Rochester, 1970. 250p. (DA 31:3466-A)
The Philadelphia Riots of 1844, which pitted nativists against Irish Catholics, had roots in economic and social conflict as well as religious differences. By comparing the names of rioters with listings in the Philadelphia City Directory, the author found that a majority of the nativist rioters were skilled artisans in such trades as weaving, shoemaking, and ship carpentry. He attributed this preponderance of skilled workers among the rioters to the Depression of 1837-1843 and the fact that Irish Catholic immigrants often proved willing to work for employers in certain trades for less than the prevailing native wages. (A)

26. Fingerhut, Eugene R. Assimilation of Immigrants on the Frontier of New York, 1764-1776. Columbia, 1962. 348p.

Great Britain, Ireland 9

(DA 23:2108)
The domestic effects of the Seven Years' War on Great Britain
resulted in economic problems that drove many Britishers to
America. In Scotland the problems were complicated by a social revolution. Immigrants were also drawn to America by
tales of great opportunities here. About 125,000 people came to
American from Great Britain; approximately 12,500 to 18,500
came to New York, of which about 15 percent moved on to the
frontier. (A)

27. Flynn, Austin. The School Controversy of New York, 1840-
1842, and Its Effect on the Formulation of Catholic Elementary
School Policy. Notre Dame, 1962. 263p. (DA 23:2408)
This dissertation was concerned with a problem in the field of
American educational history. The development of this study required the use of those methods suitable to historical research,
and the data gathered were drawn principally from documentary
sources. The sources for the study include the speeches and
correspondence of Bishop John Hughes of New York, the writings
of his contemporaries, and the public documents and the newspapers of the period. The presentation followed a chronological
sequence and centered on the years 1840-1853. (A)

28. Fogarty, Gerald P. Denis J. O'Connell: Americanist Agent
to the Vatican, 1885-1903. Yale, 1969. 348p. (DA 30:3396-A)
Denis J. O'Connell (1849-1927) was one of the leaders of the liberal movements of American Catholicism in the late nineteenth
century. Ordained in Rome in 1877, he was a favorite of James
Gibbons, who became Archbishop of Baltimore in that year and
who appointed him a secretary of the Third Plenary Council of
Baltimore in 1884 and then sent him to Rome to win Roman approval of the conciliar legislation. From 1885 to 1895 O'Connell
was rector of the American College in Rome, in which capacity
he also acted as agent for the American hierarchy and was on
intimate terms with Pope Leo XIII and with other important Vatican officials. As the liberal movement took shape he became
more and more the agent for the principal members of the liberal party: Gibbons, then a Cardinal; John Ireland, Archbishop
of St. Paul; and John J. Keane, successively Bishop of Richmond, first rector of the Catholic University of America, and
Archbishop of Dubuque. (A)

29. Funchion, Michael F. Chicago's Irish Nationalists, 1881-1890.
Loyola (Chicago), 1973. 263p.
Published under same title (New York: Arno, 1976). Although
nationalism and politics were two ways Irish-Americans expressed
frustration and sought power and respectability, many nationalists,
primarily devoted to the cause of an Irish nation state, distrusted
politicians, who, they claimed, soiled the freedom cause by their
Machiavellian quests for personal wealth and power. In his study
of Chicago's Irish nationalists, at a time when their city was the
center of Irish-American nationalism, Funchion traces the connecting links between nationalism and politics. In the Chicago

of the 1880s Clan-na-Gaelers were prominent in both Democratic and Republican party politics. John Devoy, the nationalist purist, came to Chicago to contest the leadership of the Clan with Alexander Sullivan, a local Republican politician, and to purge Irish-American nationalism of his corrupt influence. The dispute split the Clan and its satellite, the Irish National League of America, and resulted in the gory murder of an articulate Sullivan opponent, Patrick Cronin. Public revulsion against the murder ruined the Sullivan faction, but also dimmed the respectability of Irish-American nationalism, which took a long time to recover from division and violence.

30. Gabert, Glen E. A History of the Roman Catholic Parochial School System in the United States: A Documentary Interpretation. Loyola (Chicago), 1971. 205p. (DA 32:2451-A)
The plight of these schools should be of interest to Roman Catholic and non-Roman Catholic alike. For many years they have provided a significant segment of the population with an education at virtually no cost to the American taxpayer. They have been of inestimable value to the public schools if for no other reason than they helped to keep them more accountable to the general public by offering a viable educational alternative. If public funds are now awarded to private schools or if public schools have to absorb students who would have been educated in parish schools, taxpayers will find significant new demands made upon them. There is much contemporary debate about parochial schools. Some feel that they should be preserved unchanged; others, that they should be radically altered; still others, that they should be abandoned. Yet, what is so surprising, very few persons seem to know anything of the real history of these schools; most see the red brick building next to the church but never stop to ask how it came to be there or why it was built. It is really not possible to plan adequately for the future unless one can realistically assess the present. A knowledge of the recent past makes any such assessment easier. This paper is not intended to be a blueprint for future policy but rather as an analysis of the official policy that has directed the schools to the present day. (A)

31. Genen, Arthur. John Kelly, New York's First Irish Boss. New York, 1971. 350p. (DA 32:1437-A)
John Kelly, the son of poor Irish immigrant parents, was born in 1822 in New York City. At the age of ten his father died and he had to work in order to help support his family. He was educated in the streets of New York and became adjusted to its environment at an early age, becoming a captain of a gang and a pugilist. For more than a decade John Kelly dominated the political life of New York City and New York State. His word decided the nomination of judges, aldermen, assemblymen, state senators, congressmen, and mayors. When Kelly took over Tammany Hall in 1872 it lay beaten and battered as a result of Tweed's corrupt machinations. Within a short period of time Kelly revitalized Tammany and made it the most powerful politi-

Great Britain, Ireland 11

cal force not only in the city and the state, but also a power to be reckoned with in national politics. (A)

32. Gibson, Florence E. The Attitudes of the New York Irish Toward State and National Affairs, 1848-1892. Columbia, 1951. 480p.
Published under the same title (New York: Columbia University Press, 1951). An account of the influence of the strong and politically conscious Irish minority in New York State from 1848 to 1892. Some of the historical events in which the Irish were involved are delineated. Conclusions concerning the group deal with their Anglophobia, their loyalty to the Democratic party, and their extensive activity in American politics.

33. Graham, Ian C. C. Scottish Emigration to North America, 1707-1783. Illinois, 1955. 243p. (DA 15:2180)
Published as Colonists from Scotland: Emigration to North America, 1707-1783 (Ithaca: Cornell University Press, 1956). This study covers the period between the Union of the English and Scottish parliaments (1707) and the Treaty of Paris that ended the American Revolutionary War (1783). The period forms a distinct and intelligible field of study in the story of emigration directly from Scotland to the North American colonies. The Union of 1707 gave Scotland an opportunity to share in the development of the former English empire in America, and of this she took full advantage. Scottish emigration to America in the eighteenth century has too often been confused with the larger movement from Ulster. The Scots and the Scotch-Irish differed in their reasons for emigrating, their patterns of settlement, their roles on the American frontier, the numbers of each who emigrated, the incidence of their peak periods of migration, and the parts they played in the American Revolution. The larger Scotch-Irish movement has tended to obscure the smaller, but equally interesting and significant, migration directly from Scotland. (A)

34. Grozier, Richard J. The Life and Times of John Bernard Fitzpatrick: Third Roman Catholic Bishop of Boston. Boston College, 1966. 243p.

35. Gudelunas, William A. Before the Molly Maguires: The Emergence of the Ethno-Religious Factor in the Politics of the Lower Anthracite Region, 1844-1872. Lehigh, 1973. 208p. (DA 34:1795-A)
Published under the same title (New York: Arno, 1976). In this study of politics in Schuylkill County, Pennsylvania, in the period 1844-1872 Gudelunas argues that ethnoreligious loyalties superseded economic issues in determining political loyalties. Although many members of all religious and ethnic groups were victims of poverty in this anthracite-coal-mining region, class solidarity was not a feature of politics. Irish Catholics and German Lutherans voted Democratic; English and Welsh Protestants, rich and poor, supported Whigs, then Republicans. Political debate more often involved temperance and sabbatarianism

rather than social reform, jobs, or wages. For most of the period under discussion the Irish Catholic-German Lutheran coalition controlled political power in Schuylkill County without much of an improvement in the standard of living for its constituents.

36. Harney, Loyola. The Defensive Action of the Right Reverend Benedict J. Fenwick, S. J. to Anti-Catholicism in New England, 1829-1845. Boston, 1936. 212p.

37. Henthorne, Mary E. The Career of the Right Reverend John Lancaster Spalding, Bishop of Peoria, as President of the Irish Colonization Association of the United States, 1879-1882. Illinois, 1930. 273p.
Published under the same title (Urbana: University of Illinois Press, 1932).

38. Howe, Barbara J. Clubs, Culture and Charity: The Anglo-American Upper Class Activities in the Late Nineteenth-Century City. Temple, 1976. 705p. (DA 37:2358-A)
Art museums, public libraries, charity organization societies, and large social clubs were all products of the time, talent, money, and needs of the upper class in English and American cities in the late nineteenth century. With the growing size and complexity of the Gilded Age city, the members of its upper class, whether parvenu or established, needed some institutionalized means to maintain control of this city and to establish channels for the transmission of acceptable values to the other residents of the city. This study examines Philadelphia, Cincinnati, Milwaukee, and Birmingham, England, in depth to see how their upper class used its resources to establish this control and to pass on its chosen values to new members of its own class, through clubs, and to the rest of the city, through museums and libraries. Finally, it examines business organizations, political activities, and charitable work of the upper class in these cities to see how these avenues were used to enforce acceptable values of thrift, industry, and respectability among the city's residents and to maintain control of the city in the face of rising labor unions and increasingly anachronistic charitable efforts. (A)

39. Hueston, Robert F. The Catholic Press and Nativism, 1840-1860. Notre Dame, 1972. 361p. (DA 33:1646-A)
Published under the same title (New York: Arno, 1976). Anti-Irish, Anglo-American Protestant nativism intensified the inferiority complex the Irish brought with them to "the shores of Americay," strengthening ghetto walls. But nativism also encouraged Irish ethnic consciousness and its ties to Catholicism. In his study of American Catholic press reactions to Anglo-American Protestant nativism Hueston emphasizes that Irish immigration generated anti-Catholic prejudices in the 1840s and 1850s.

40. Jackson, Sheldon G. Henry Dalton: Southern California Ranchero. Southern California, 1970. 240p. (DA 31:2846-A)
The story of Hispanic California is replete with the names of ex-

Great Britain, Ireland 13

tremely interesting personalities who were independent, ambitious and optimistic. Many of these intriguing individuals have been neglected by historians. But when the effort is made to study them, the significance of the role they played in early California history is revealed and their complex personalities provide surprises and information of import. This study traces the life of one of the most versatile of these pioneers, Henry Dalton, an Englishman. (A)

41. Jamison, Edward Alden. Irish-Americans, The Irish Question and American Diplomacy, 1895-1921. Harvard, 1944. 263p.

42. Joyce, William L. Editors and Ethnicity: A History of the Irish-American Press, 1848-1883. Michigan, 1974. 207p. Published under the same title (New York: Arno, 1976). In this analysis of the contents and purposes of Irish-American newspapers, 1848-1883, Joyce emphasizes the two roles of Irish-American journalism: keeping the Irish Irish and making them American. American Irish ethnic journalists tried to construct bridges between the Irish "retrospect" and the American "prospect." Refugees from Irish famine and revolution in the late 1840s made the Irish-American press contentious and divisive. Irish-American newspapers debated Old Country issues--clerical versus anticlerical Catholicism, constitutional versus physical-force nationalism. After 1870 the press debates stopped, and journalists participated in a common effort to use Irish Catholicism and nationalism as instruments to forge Irish-American unity and progress within the American environment. This strategy was enhanced by the domination of Parnell's constitutional Home Rule movement over the direction of Irish nationalism. According to Joyce, John Boyle O'Reilly's Boston Pilot symbolized the Irish-American press effort to keep Irish America emotionally Irish while at the same time adjusting it to the goals, values, and tastes of the general American society.

43. Kane, John J. The Irish Immigrant in Philadelphia, 1840-1880: A Study in Conflict and Accommodation. Pennsylvania, 1950. 270p.

44. Kennedy, Robert E. Irish Emigration, Marriage, and Fertility. California (Berkeley), 1968. 309p. (DA 29:333-A) Published under the title The Irish: Emigration, Marriage, and Fertility (Berkeley: University of California Press, 1973). There is a belief that the word "Irish" is a synonym for "unique" in the field of population studies. While all other European nations increased in population during the last century, the population of Ireland decreased at every census except one between 1841 and 1961. The proportions of persons postponing marriage or remaining permanently single are higher among the Irish than among the people of any other European nation, yet the married Irish have Europe's highest rate of fertility. This work attempts to distinguish those elements of emigration, marriage, and fertility that are indeed peculiar to Ireland from those that Ireland shares, to a greater or lesser extent, with other countries. (A)

45. Killen, David P.　John Spalding's American Understanding of the Church.　Marquette, 1971.　305p.　(DA 32:1065-A)
The purpose of this dissertation is to determine the ecclesial thought of Bishop John Lancaster Spalding from his published, but unedited, works. Spalding's formal essays on the Church have been analyzed and compared with the remaining portions of his writings in order to discover the fuller extent of his ecclesiology. In 1877 Spalding was, at the age of 37, consecrated the first bishop of Peoria, Illinois. His was a relatively long and tumultuous episcopal career involving him in many controversies, both within and without the American Catholic Church. (A)

46. Knuth, Helen E.　The Climax of American Anglo-Saxonism, 1898-1905.　Northwestern, 1958.　348p.　(DA 19:1355)
Anglo-Saxonism became a major influence in America in the period of 1898-1905 as a result of the convergence of a series of events and movements at home and abroad that reinforced America's faith in its national mission and destiny and encouraged the development of Anglo-Saxon prejudice. This thesis explores the roots of Anglo-Saxonism, examines the climate of opinion of the 1890s that provided a favorable environment for the development of the concept, and indicates the ways in which the contemporary economic, social, and political forces in the United States encouraged its growth. (A)

47. Lannie, Vincent P.　Archbishop John Hughes and the Common School Controversy, 1840-1842.　Columbia (Teachers College), 1963.　(DA 24:5170)
Published under the title Public Money and Parochial Education: Bishop Hughes, Governor Seward, and the New York School Controversy (Cleveland: Press of Case Western Reserve University, 1968). Within the context of the general reform movement of Jacksonian America educational reform eventually succeeded in committing the nation to a unique system of free, publicly supported and publicly controlled education. Although religion was not excluded from this emerging common school, it was a nondenominational Christianity that was inculcated within the schools. Both dogmatic Protestants and Roman Catholics challenged this common-core approach. In New York the Catholic attack was spearheaded by the dynamic and militant Bishop John Hughes. For three eventful years, 1840-1842, the battle raged in New York. With the backing of Governor William H. Seward, the Roman Catholics sought public funds to support their private sectarian schools. Arrayed against the Roman Catholic claim stood the Protestant majority, nativist extremists, and the private Public School Society, which exercised a virtual educational monopoly in New York City. During 1840 the Catholics sought relief from the municipal government of New York City. When the Common Council rejected the Catholic request Bishop Hughes continued his fight for two years before the friendlier State Legislature. (A)

48. Loffredo, Carmine A.　A History of the Roman Catholic School System in the Archdiocese of Newark, New Jersey, 1900-1965.

Rutgers, 1967. 506p. (DA 28:1688-A)
Attempts to examine the rise and development of one of the largest non-public school programs in America. Although the emphasis is on the twentieth century, pertinent background material dealing with the nineteenth century has also been included. The main thrust of the dissertation is Catholic education in the Archdiocese of Newark; however, essential historical data relevant to New Jersey as well as the nation has also been included. (A)

49. Lyman, Kenneth C. Critical Reaction to Irish Drama on the New York Stage, 1900-1958. Wisconsin, 1960. 844p. (DA 21:699)
Three primary objectives were established in undertaking this study: to assemble a compact record, heretofore nonexistent, of the critical reaction to Irish drama on the New York stage from 1900 to 1958; with this critical reaction and the length of run of a given production as evidence, to indicate insofar as possible the public reaction to and financial success or failure of Irish drama as presented in New York between 1900 and 1958; and to draw conclusions based on this information regarding the universal appeal of Irish drama with particular reference to the American scene insofar as it may be represented by the New York critics and public. (A)

50. Maguire, Edward J. John O'Hanlon's 'Irish Emigrant's Guide for the United States": A Critical Evaluation. St. Louis, 1951. 243p.
Published under the same title (New York: Arno, 1976). John O'Hanlon was born in Ireland in 1821, but before completing seminary training at Carlow College he emigrated with his parents to Missouri, where he resumed his studies for the priesthood. After his ordination in 1847 O'Hanlon served as a priest in St. Louis for about six years. In 1853 he became seriously ill with bronchitis and returned to Ireland for his health, where he remained until his death in 1905. O'Hanlon wrote a number of books on historical and religious topics, but perhaps his most important writing effort was The Irish Emigrant's Guide for the United States (1851). This manual reflected O'Hanlon's anxiety concerning the fate of the hundreds of thousands of Irish refugees pouring into the United States technologically, culturally, and psychologically unprepared for their new existence. In his Emigrant's Guide O'Hanlon instructed prospective emigrants on how to prepare for the journey and what to expect upon their arrival. He wanted them to stay close to their Catholic peasant cultural roots, which is why he recommended that they farm in the Midwest rather than settle in the cities of the East. In his Introduction Maguire presents a brief summary of O'Hanlon's career and discusses the causes of Irish emigration, tying it to the experience of other Europeans who came to the U.S. He describes the difficulties of the journey across the Atlantic, details the history of passenger acts in the U.S. Congress, and analyzes the impact of the Irish on religion and politics in America.

51. Mahoney, James M. The Influence of the Irish-Americans
upon the Foreign Policy of the United States, 1865-1872.
Clark, 1959. 431p. (DA 20:2879)
The purpose of this thesis is to examine the influence of the
Irish-Americans upon the foreign policy of the United States in
the period 1865-1872. While this work deals with the Irish-
Americans in general, it concentrates upon the Fenian Brotherhood. This revolutionary organization as the most important
body among the Irish-Americans represented their greatest impact upon American foreign policy. (A)

52. Manfra, Jo Ann. The Catholic Episcopacy in America, 1789-
1852. Iowa, 1975. 292p. (DA 36:2389-A)
The 60 men who governed the Catholic Church in the United
States during its formative period faced a situation unprecedented
in the annals of Roman Catholicism. Whatever else can be said
about the prelates, they recognized their peculiar situation, and
determined to build a structure that was simultaneously Catholic
and American. This decision had an external and internal dimension. On the one hand, it reflected pressure from the non-
Catholic society to explain how an "alien" religious organization,
which countenanced Roman political intervention and increased its
constituency each year by welcoming foreign immigrants, could
accommodate itself to American society. On the other hand, the
bishops were not passive objects in the social and cultural developments of the eighteenth and early nineteenth centuries. Their
response to the challenge of the American environment, the ideas
they held, and the decisions they made suggest that they were a
fiercely independent group of men aware of the theoretical and
practical implications of religious pluralism in a democratic republic. The story of the emergence of a Catholic Church in the
United States belongs then to both social and religious history; it
was largely the result of the interplay between certain trends in
the development of the nation and major currents in Catholic life
and thought. (A)

53. Mannion, Lawrence J. The History of the Society of the
Friendly Sons of St. Patrick in the City of New York, 1784-
1835. Fordham, 1958. 265p.
The dissertation is the basis of Lawrence J. Mannion and Richard
C. Murphy, The History of the Society of the Friendly Sons of
Saint Patrick in the City of New York, 1784 to 1955 (New York:
n.p., 1962).

54. Mattis, Mary C. The Irish Family in Buffalo, New York,
1855-1875: A Socio-Historical Analysis. Washington, 1975.
217p. (DA 36:2440-A)
The paper is an analysis of Irish immigrant mobility in Buffalo,
New York, during the period 1855-1875. The investigation generated a descriptive case study of one of the many types of Irish
mobility experiences that occurred in the United States. Data
was derived from the New York interdecile census manuscripts
for 1855, 1865, and 1875, from which a sample of Irish immi-

grants was obtained. In addition, other historical documents were utilized, including marriage certificates, trade and commerce reports, and local histories. (A)

55. McDonald, M. J. History of the Irish in Wisconsin in the 19th Century. Catholic, 1955. 204p.
Published under the same title (Washington, D. C.: Catholic University of America Press, 1955).

56. McGivern, Elaine P. Ethnic Identity and Its Relation to Group Norms: Irish Americans in Metropolitan Pittsburgh. Pittsburgh, 1979. 239p. (DA 40:2965-A)
The persistence of ethnic identity is examined by exploring the relation between group identification and norms. American Irish are examined as an illustrative case. Results of qualitative and quantitative analyses show that, once a political/economic interest group, socially marginal to the American status system, they have lost their marginality. The more secular traditions that define their historical experience, their contribution to American society, may well come to dominate the shared image they hold of themselves as American Irish. While they have not lost their sense of Irish identity as is often claimed, it is clear that they act on this identity in different ways. Those whose Irish self-identity is highly important are more likely to seek validation for it on the basis of religious normative referents over secular ones, while the converse applies to those who attach lesser importance to it. (A)

57. McManamin, Francis G. The American Years of John Boyle O'Reilly, 1870-1890. Catholic, 1959. 264p.
Published under the same title (New York: Arno, 1976). Born in County Meath, Ireland, O'Reilly served as a Fenian recruiting agent while a member of the British army. In 1866 the British government discovered that O'Reilly was a Fenian, tried him for treason, sentenced him to death, commuted his sentence, and sent him to Australia as a political prisoner. In 1869 O'Reilly escaped, arrived in Philadelphia, moved to Boston, and began his career as a journalist. McManamin concentrates on O'Reilly's contribution as editor of the Boston Pilot. He carried his hatred of Britain with him to America and continued to work for Irish nationalism but switched to the forces of constitutional rather than revolutionary nationalism. In addition to his role as nationalist advocate O'Reilly functioned as defender of Irish and Catholic interests, social reformer, and champion of all religious, ethnic, and racial minorities. As a leader of Irish-America he encouraged ethnic cohesion, cultivated an intelligent Irish-American public opinion, and urged his co-ethnics to adapt to the American environment. His popularity among the leaders of Protestant Anglo-America benefited all Irish-Americans. McManamin concludes that O'Reilly, "honored and loved by the Catholic community, and esteemed by contemporaries of different religious and nationalistic backgrounds ... did more than any other man of his generation to help bridge the gulf between Catholics and Protestants of New England."

58. Merwick, Donna J. Changing Thought Patterns of Three Generations of Catholic Clergymen of the Boston Archdiocese from 1850 to 1910. Wisconsin, 1968. 374p. (DA 29:855-A)
Published under the title Boston Priests, 1848-1910: A Study of Social and Intellectual Change (Cambridge, Mass.: Harvard University Press, 1973). The author's purpose was to investigate the ideas of three generations of Boston Clergymen before 1907. It is her argument that however inflexible Boston Catholicism may have become through the centralizing techniques of Rome as applied by Cardinal William O'Connell to the diocese after that date, it was not monolithic earlier. Chancery materials in Boston and Portland (Maine) indicate a number of continually changing mentalities. Clergymen were receiving new impressions from dislocations created by the immigrants, or altering or refusing to alter older genteel values. Social changes brought theological adjustments; ways of piety changed with new needs. A study of myths, popular pietistic literature, and noncognitive needs reveals a segment of hitherto-unexplored intellectual history. Boston Catholicism was not militant or monolithically Irish Catholic, as Handlin has assumed. A powerful Yankee Catholic element affected ideas decisively. Before 1907 the Catholic Church was unsure of itself and experimental. (A)

59. Mitchell, Albert G. Irish Family Patterns in Nineteenth-Century Ireland and Lowell, Massachusetts. Boston, 1976. 409p. (DA 37:1751-A)
Historians of immigration have often concluded that the processes of migration and transplantation had a disorganizing effect on the family. This study explored this assumption. In the case of the Irish, it was discovered that while the family was stable and cohesive in pre-Famine Ireland, unfavorable political, economic, and social conditions exerted disorganizing pressures on the family even before it emigrated. An even more important finding was that, after transplantation in Lowell, the Irish family managed not only to maintain many of the cohesive family patterns that had existed in pre-Famine Ireland, but also appears to have regained ground it had lost during the rural crisis of the nineteenth century. This picture of cohesiveness emerged from a comparison of such patterns as age at marriage, mate selection, sexual morality, parental authority, family loyalty, geographic mobility, and proximity of kin. (A)

60. Niehaus, Earl F. The Irish in New Orleans, 1803-1862. Tulane, 1961. 428p. (DA 22:1604)
Published under the title The Irish in New Orleans, 1800-1860 (Baton Rouge: Louisiana State University Press, 1965). The stream of emigrants from Ireland to New Orleans steadily widened during the first half of the nineteenth century. Although emigration was continuous, the Irish came in three distinct stages: the "old" before 1830, then the "new," and finally the famine refugees beginning in the late 1840s. The "old" members of the middle class in Ireland, bought their own passage on the best ships available; in some instances they became merchants and profes-

sional men. The later arrivals came on the cotton ships returning from Liverpool; in New Orleans they replaced the Negroes as skilled and unskilled workers. The passage of the majority of those fleeing the famine was paid by remittance; many of them became public burdens or victims of epidemics. No reasonably accurate estimate of the number of Irish immigrants who arrived and remained in the city is possible; in 1850, however, one of every five white residents there was a native of Ireland. (A)

61. O'Dowd, William G. The Intellectual Image of the City in Social Commentary and Urban Planning: The Irish Case. Southern Illinois, 1975. 260p. (DA 36:3146-A)
The focus of the study is on the intellectual image of the city in social commentary and urban planning, with particular reference to the implications for urban sociology. The study resolves itself into an examination of the relationship between collective identity, as articulated by intellectuals (including sociologists), and the image of the city. The Irish case is used to demonstrate the nature and extent of this relationship. The influence of the dominant elements of Irish collective identity (i.e., Catholicism and Nationalism) on the social image of the city was examined in a modernizing, urbanizing and ex-colonial context. (A)

62. O'Grady, Joseph P. Irish-Americans and Anglo-American Relations, 1880-1888. Pennsylvania, 1965. 319p. (DA 26:3285)
The purpose of this dissertation is simply to discover what influence Irish-Americans exerted upon Anglo-American relations in the years from 1880 to 1888. Three parallel developments prompted the selection of this particular topic and decade; namely, the growing number of diplomatic disputes which indicated an increasing animosity between the two countries, the unique American political situation in which the narrowness of the balance of power between the two major parties permitted well-organized pressure groups to bargain for favors, and, finally, the dynamic events in Anglo-Irish relations, the work of Charles S. Parnell's leadership of Irish nationalism. (A)

63. Pieper, Ezra H. The Fenian Movement. Illinois (Urbana), 1931. 210p.

64. Robinson, Thomas P. The Life of Thomas Addis Emmet. New York, 1955. 437p. (DA 18:1018)
Thomas Addis Emmet was an important Irish leader from 1792 to 1804. Emmet, according to William E. H. Lecky, was "one of the few really interesting figures" connected with the United Irish movement. Had not Emmet espoused the nationalist cause, he might have achieved greatness as a barrister in Georgian Ireland. As a member of the Protestant ascendancy, the minority that ruled eighteenth-century Ireland, Emmet defied his own social background in supporting the cause of Irish nationalism. Emmet hoped to avoid public life in America, but he never realized that ambition. The Irish immigrant population took vicarious pride in his accomplishments and looked to him for leadership.

Emmet's position among the immigrant population made it impossible for him to avoid politics entirely. He was constantly under pressure to support political candidates. On three occasions Emmet suffered defeat as a candidate for state office. He served briefly as State Attorney General, having been appointed to that office through the influence of Governor Tompkins. A Republican in politics, Emmet supported De Witt Clinton in the factional struggles within the Republican Party. Thus, ultimately, Emmet found himself in virtual alliance with former Federalists, but despite that fact his faith in democracy never wavered. (A)

65. Rodechko, James P. Patrick Ford and His Search for America: A Case Study of Irish-American Journalism, 1870-1913. Connecticut, 1967. 304p. (DA 28:3615-A)
Few studies of Irish-American immigrants, and particularly journalists, have been undertaken. This case study, based primarily on an analysis of Patrick Ford's Irish World, is an attempt to fill the void. Ford, as editor of the World from 1870 through 1913, deserves special attention because he was the most prominent and controversial Irish journalist in America. With a weekly circulation that often rose over 100,000 copies, his paper surpassed those of other Irish editors in the effort to instruct Irishmen. (A)

66. Roohan, James E. American Catholics and the Social Question, 1865-1900. Yale, 1952. 263p.
Published under the same title (New York: Arno, 1976). Roohan emphasizes that although the victims of the harshness of the American industrial system were first the Irish and then other Catholic ethnics, leaders of the church were slow to advocate a change in the American economic system. At first the Catholic hierarchy was too busy building churches and schools and ministering to the spiritual needs of an immigrant population, and too leery of nativist reactions, to speak out on the social question. When they did express economic and social opinions Catholic clerics and journalists were more inclined to praise the virtues and redemptive role of Christian poverty and to blame social problems on the decline of religion than they were to attack the premises of laissez-faire capitalism. Only John Boyle O'Reilly on the left and Orestes Brownson on the right took fundamental issue with the philosophy underlying industrial capitalism. Only after the late 1870s, when the country faced the crisis of strikes and consequent violence, did Catholic spokespeople gradually move to a defense of labor unions, once thought too radical, and suggest state intervention to mitigate social disorder as an alternative to socialism.

67. Ross, Marc. John Swinton, Journalist and Reformer: The Active Years, 1857-1887. New York, 1969. 292p. (DA 30:2468-A)
John Swinton (1830-1901), journalist and reformer, was born in Salton, Scotland. In 1843 the family emigrated to Montreal, and in 1849, to New York City. Having been a printer's apprentice

while in Montreal, Swinton worked, from 1857 to 1860, as a printer for the Lawrence [Kansas] Republican, a free-soil weekly. Back in New York in 1860, he became a member of the editorial staff of the New York Times. Swinton left the paper in 1869, and for the next five years he was variously employed. In 1875 he joined the editorial board of the Sun, where he was employed until 1883 and again from 1892 to 1897. The high point of his career came during the years 1883 to 1887, when he published his own weekly, John Swinton's Paper. Swinton's significance was as a journalist and speaker, in giving public expression to problems and proposals of interest to laborers of America, and in urging workers (both urban and rural) to join together in independent united political action. (A)

68. Scanlan, William G. The Development of the American Catholic Diocesan Board of Education, 1884-1966. New York, 1967. 369p. (DA 28:4463-A)
The hypothesis of the study is that the diocesan board has been serving education needs, cultural needs, and ecclesial needs for the Catholic Church in America. It was the response to these three needs that brought about the foundation of the board and that has engendered its development during its 110-year history. As the priority of need changed, the board adapted itself to the change. (A)

69. Schaefer, Marvin R. The Catholic Church in Chicago, Its Growth and Administration. Chicago, 1929. 181p.

70. Schrier, Arnold. Ireland and the American Emigration, 1850-1900. Northwestern, 1956. 279p. (DA 17:615)
Published under the same title (Minneapolis: University of Minnesota Press, 1958). In the field of immigration-emigration studies in America the emphasis has been heavily concentrated on the assimilation-acculturation process and on the contributions made by immigrants to American society. Little has been done to examine the reverse side of the coin--the impact of emigration on the country of origin. This study is an attempt partly to redress the balance and has been pursued along two major lines of inquiry: (1) an analysis of the impact on Ireland of emigration to the United States in the period 1850-1900, and (2) an analysis of American influences that filtered back to Ireland via the emigrant. (A)

71. Shaw, Douglas V. The Making of an Immigrant City: Ethnic and Cultural Conflict in Jersey City, New Jersey, 1850-1877. Rochester, 1972. 285p.
Published under the same title (New York: Arno, 1976). In this case study of political change in an American city Shaw discusses 30 years of conflict between the native-born Protestant elite of Jersey City and working-class Irish Catholics. The former endowed agencies of Protestant proselytism, rallied to the cause of nativism, and manipulated the machinery of politics to change Irish Catholic cultural identity and frustrate Irish Catholic ad-

vances toward political power. But Protestant nativist efforts and political manipulation intensified and consolidated rather than diminished Irish Catholic identity and political ambition. Finally, in the late 1870s, they took control of the city from their old enemies.

72. Shea, Mary M. Patrick Cardinal Hayes and the Catholic Charities in New York City. New York, 1966. 315p. (DA 29: 550-A)
Patrick Cardinal Hayes, known as the "Cardinal of Charity," had his introduction to the problem of charities in New York City as secretary to Bishop John M. Farley from 1895 until 1911. During this time Catholic charitable activities operated autonomously, lacking financial support and direction from a central bureau. By 1912 Farley, now Cardinal, recognized the problems to be met and attempted to solve them by establishing the United Catholic Works. Working at first as Auxiliary Bishop to Cardinal Farley and later, independently, as Archbishop, Hayes by 1919 had taken several steps that greatly expanded and subsidized Catholic charitable work. Under Cardinal Farley, Bishop Hayes, acting behind the scenes, directed the defense of Catholic child-caring institutions against the charges brought against them during the Kingsbury investigations, 1914 and 1915, and by the Strong Commission, 1916. With Farley, Hayes was responsible for the incorporation of the Catholic Charities Aid Association of New York in 1917. (A)

73. Shepardson, Francis W. A Study of Some of the Scotch-Irish Settlements in the American Colonies. Yale, 1892. 112p.

74. Shepperson, Wilbur S. British Views of Emigration to North America, 1837-1860. Western Reserve, 1951. 264p.
Published under the title British Emigration to North America: Projects and Opinions in the Early Victorian Period (Minneapolis: University of Minnesota Press, 1957).

75. Spalding, Thomas W. Martin John Spalding: Bishop of Louisville and Archbishop of Baltimore, 1810-1872. Catholic, 1971. 528p. (DA 32:2044-A)
Martin John Spalding, Kentucky-born and of Maryland descent, was perhaps the most gifted and influential member of the American Catholic hierarchy in the middle third of the nineteenth century, the period in which the institutions and attitudes that characterized the immigrant Church took shape. His influence was manifested particularly in his roles as administrator, apologist, and legislator. (A)

76. Stack, Robert E. The McCleers and the Birneys--Irish Immigrant Families--into Michigan and the California Gold Fields, 1820-1893. St. Louis, 1972. 736p. (DA 33:1131-A)
This is basically the history of two Irish immigrant families, who came to the United States in the 1820s and early 1830s. The Birney family arrived first and continued their Irish agricultural

experience on farms in Vermont, Lower Canada, and Ohio before reaching southern Michigan in the late 1830s. The McCleer family worked in the mills of Connecticut as skilled craftworkers until they broke away from the East to emigrate to Michigan in 1836-1837. (A)

77. Stivers, Richard A. The Bachelor Group Ethnic and Irish Drinking. Southern Illinois, 1971. 378p. (DA 32:5365-A)
The study centered on attempts to explain the apparent discrepancy between an extremely high rate of alcoholism among Irish-Americans and a somewhat more moderate rate among the Irish in Ireland for the period of 1840 to 1940 and to describe the sociohistorical structure of Irish drinking for the same period. Data were presented that supported the assertion of differential rates of alcoholism for the Irish in Ireland and the Irish in America. Previous hypotheses about Irish drinking were then examined. (A)

78. Szarnicke, Henry A. The Episcopate of Michael O'Connor, First Bishop of Pittsburgh, 1843-1860. Catholic, 1971. 414p. (DA 32:900-A)
O'Connor responded conscientiously to the particular needs of the large German minority within the Catholic population of the diocese. He maintained a good relationship with the Redemptorists who had antedated him in Pittsburgh. He begged Europe for additional German priests and students. He offset a misadventure with the School Sisters of Notre Dame by admitting members of this community into the Diocese. He received the Bavarian Benedictines warmly and induced them to settle at Latrobe by deeding to them two large estates in return for service to the diocese. He argued fairly in a series of controversies with the American founder of the Benedictine monastery and graciously accepted the decisions, mostly favorable to the Benedictines, handed down by the Holy See. He nominated Germans for the episcopacy, including one to succeed himself, and he was generous in his praise of the German religious communities. (A)

79. Tarpey, Marie V. The Role of Joseph McGarrity in the Struggle for Irish Independence. St. John's, 1969. 373p. (DA 31:2326-A)
McGarrity emigrated to the United States in January 1892. A year later he became a member of the Irish-American organization Clan-na-Gael, joining the ranks of many American Irish dedicated to the cause of Irish independence. For in the latter half of the nineteenth there had been a dramatic shift in the source from which outside help would be offered to Ireland. No longer were the Irish people looking to their coreligionists on the continent of Europe for assistance. Attention was focused, instead, upon the New World and the vast colony of relatives and friends who had crossed the Atlantic. As the chief American organization working directly with the Irish Republican Army, the Clanna-Gael became in the twentieth century the most effective channel for aid to the Irish cause. (A)

80. Vinyard, JoEllen M. The Irish on the Urban Frontier: Detroit, 1850-1880. Michigan, 1972. 268p.
Published under the same title (New York: Arno, 1976). In her study of urban frontier Detroit, 1850-1880, which had a significant Irish community, Vinyard shows that the Irish who had the ambition and energy to move west settled in budding cities that offered opportunities for people who were interested in economic and social mobility. The Detroit Irish retained their ethnic identity through the agency of Catholic institutions and, like the Irish in other parts of the country, used political skills to gain influence, but they also worked and associated with people from different religious and nationality backgrounds. The Detroit Irish were a successful ethnic group, and they contributed a great deal to the development of an important urban industrial center. Vinyard's contribution is a revision of the image of urban Irish-America. Her findings on Detroit probably represent the reality in other Midwestern and Western cities.

81. Walker, Mable G. The Fenian Movement, 1858-1872. Ohio State, 1929. 190p.

82. Walsh, Francis Robert. The Boston Pilot: A Newspaper for the Irish Immigrant, 1829-1908. Boston, 1968. 305p. (DA 29:2201-A)
The Pilot, an integral part of Irish-American life in nineteenth-century America, adds a significant dimension to our knowledge of the immigrant's world. Irish opposition to abolitionism and support of the Union in the Civil War become more intelligible when placed in context. The Pilot provides the historian with a rich source of material on the Irish reaction to nativism, politics, reform, the Negro, and attitudes toward other immigrant ethnic groups. Always interested in the working class, the paper became a militant champion of labor's demands during the last quarter of the nineteenth century. (A)

83. Walsh, John P. J. The Catholic Church in Chicago and the Problems of an Urban Society: 1893-1915. Chicago, 1948. 362p.

84. Wangler, Thomas E. The Ecclesiology of Archbishop John Ireland--Its Nature, Development, and Influence. Marquette, 1969. 270p. (DA 31:1885-A)
This thesis attempts to outline historically the ecclesiology of Archbishop John Ireland (1838-1918) of St. Paul, Minnesota, and specifically deals with the interplay of this ecclesiology with American life. The dominant questions in this study therefore deal with the nature of Ireland's ecclesiology, the role that Ireland viewed the Church as having in America, and the extent to which Ireland's ecclesiology may have changed under the impact of American life. (A)

85. Williams, Arthur R. The Irishman in American Humor: From 1647 to the Present. Cornell, 1949. 237p.

86. Williams, Daniel J. The Welsh of Columbus, Ohio: A Study in Adaptation and Assimilation. Ohio State, 1914. 144p.

87. Willigan, Walter L. A History of the Irish American Press from 1691-1835. Fordham, 1935. 193p.

88. Yearley, Clifton K. British Men and Ideas in the American Labor Movement, 1860-1895. Johns Hopkins, 1953. 345p. Published under the title Britons in American Labor: A History of the Influence of the United Kingdom Immigrants on American Labor, 1820-1914 (Baltimore: Johns Hopkins University Press, 1957).

B. FRANCE, PORTUGAL, SPAIN, AND THE LOW COUNTRIES

89. Anderson, Mary C. The Huguenot in the South Carolina Novel. South Carolina, 1966. 264p. (DA 27:3830-A)
The Huguenots, the religious refugees who have figured so notably in both the history and the fiction of South Carolina, have never before been formally studied in their relationship to literature. This dissertation first presents French Protestants as they appear in historical accounts and then specifically shows how they are used by the authors of this state as characters in novels that cover the years 1562 to the present. (A)

90. Avery, Elizabeth H. Influence of French Immigration on the Political History of the United States. Minnesota, 1895. 77p. Published under the same title (San Francisco: R & E Research Associates, 1972). Essentially concerned with the influence of French political thought as transmitted by Huguenot and Catholic immigrants in the United States.

91. Babb, Winston C. French Refugees from Saint Domingue to the Southern United States: 1791-1810. Virginia, 1954. 438p. (DA 14:1689)
This study traces the French refugees from the West Indies, chiefly Saint Domingue, who fled the revolutionary uprisings to the southern part of the United States. In two decades after 1791, 15,000 to 20,000 Frenchmen came into the South. This is a careful estimate, which includes whites, Negroes, and mulattos. Records on them are incomplete or were never made at all. Most refugees remained where they landed and constituted a significant element in these cities. They were a cross-section of French colonials in culture, wealth, and ability. They fled so hastily that they brought virtually no possessions except a few slaves who voluntarily accompanied their masters. (A)

92. Baldridge, Edwin R. Talleyrand in the United States, 1794 to 1796. Lehigh, 1963. 178p. (DA 24:2437)

Charles Maurice Talleyrand de Perigord was one of 10, 000
French refugees who sought asylum in the United States during
the French Revolution. But Talleyrand was not a typical émigré. He had been a leader in the Constituent Assembly and a
recognized authority on government finances. His fame had preceded him to America and his acquaintance was eagerly sought
by leaders both of America's business world and of French refugee groups. Talleyrand's intelligent appraisals of the American
scene show the astute powers he possessed. His quick grasp of
the economic situation in this new country throws a penetrating
light upon life in the United States and serves as an excellent
mirror in obtaining a vivid reflection of the business world at
that time. Furthermore, his acknowledgment of the great possibilities that lay ahead for the United States kindled within him
an interest that periodically appeared throughout his life. That
he never gave up the idea of making money in America is attested by his encouragement to the du Pont family to settle in
America and his financial help to them. (A)

93. Bratt, James D. Dutch Calvinism in Modern America: The
History of a Conservative Subculture. Yale, 1978. 453p.
(DA 39:2481)
A "religious-intellectual" history of an ethnic group in the United
States. Specifically, the study analyzes the cultural experience
of the Dutch subculture of Grand Rapids, Michigan, from 1900 to
1950, looking at the relationship between social and political factors, religious ideologies, conservatism, Americanization, and
conflicts within the community.

94. Bratt, John H. The Missionary Enterprise of the Christians
Reformed Church in America. Union Theological Seminary
(Virginia), 1955. 453p.
Examines the missionary spirit of the Christian Reformed denomination. The details of various missionary enterprises are not
the focus, but rather the development of the church's missionary
consciousness. As a result of the scrutiny of church records
and publications, and printed materials dealing with Dutch immigration to the United States in the 1840s, the study found that a
missionary spirit was one of the motives for the emigration of
the people who would become founders of the Christian Reformed
Church.

95. Bruins, Elton J. The New Brunswick Theological Seminary,
1884-1959. New York, 1962. 223p.
From 1628 until 1784 the Dutch Reformed Church in America was
dependent upon the theological schools of the Netherlands for ministers. During this period the church had the problem of an insufficient number of ministers for its congregations. Following
the Revolution the church established its own seminary. Bruins
presents a history of the seminary, and describes the contribution
that it has made to the Reformed Church, since 1884. He evaluates the school in terms of its service to the denomination and in
terms of its standards and teachings in comparison with those of
the mother church in the Netherlands.

France, Portugal, Spain, Low Countries 27

96. Cabral, Stephen L. Portuguese-American Feasting: Tradition and Change in New Bedford, Massachusetts. Brown, 1979. 263p. (DA 39:5592-A)
This study describes and examines the history, organization and celebration of two patron-saint feasts by Portuguese-American immigrants and their descendants in New Bedford, Massachusetts. The Feast of the Blessed Sacrament was established by four Madeiran immigrants at the Church of Our Lady of the Immaculate Conception in 1915. Four immigrants from São Miguel, Açores, initiated the Festa do Senhor da Pedra at the same parish in 1924. The impact of cosmopolitan and metropolitan influences on rural Portuguese, feasting customs receives special attention. The growth and change of the two feasts in New Bedford contrast sharply. New Bedford residents describe the more popular Feast of the Blessed Sacrament as a "commercial feast" and the less ostentatious Festa do Senhor da Pedra as a "religious feast."

97. Castelli, Joseph R. Basques in the Western United States: A Functional Approach to Determination of Cultural Presence in the Geographic Landscape. Colorado, 1970. 179p. (DA 31: 3472-B)
This study examines two cultures in contact under a specific set of circumstances. It outlines a method of comparison of the cultural groups in order to determine the existence of a cultural landscape created by a small identifiable cultural group within the area of a more "sophisticated" culture. This is accomplished by examining the functions of the two cultural groups, relative to one another, and indicating those functions that identify the smaller group as well as those functions that contribute most to its continued distinct identity. (A)

98. Chevalier, Florence M. The Role of French National Societies in the Sociocultural Evolution of the Franco-Americans of New England from 1860 to the Present: An Analytical Macro-Sociological Case Study in Ethnic Integration Based on Current Social System Models. Catholic, 1972. 396p. (DA 33:5833-A)
Glazer's Beyond the Melting Pot implies that the assimilation model does not adequately describe the process by which ethnic groups have become a part of American society. This study explores the adequacy of an integration model based largely on social-system models presented in recent works of Parsons, Schermerhorn, and Gordon. Specifically, it seeks to find out whether assimilation or integration better explains the process involved in the sociocultural evolution of the Franco-American ethnic group in New England from 1860, the period of the first massive immigration from Quebec, to the present. (A)

99. Childs, Frances S. Refugee Life in the United States, 1790-1800: An American Chapter of the French Revolution. Columbia, 1939. 229p.
Published under the same title (Baltimore: Johns Hopkins University Press, 1940).

100. Chiodo, John J. The Foreign Policy of Peter Stuyvesant: Dutch Diplomacy in North America, 1647-1664. Iowa, 1974. 299p. (DA 35:2166)
Because New Netherland was a territorial grant belonging to the Dutch West India Company, the organization and policies of this colony were unique compared with other early North American colonies. In 1646, when Peter Stuyvesant was appointed Director General of New Netherland, the colony was facing a major problem of checking the expansion of its neighbors, the English, Swedish, and Indians. Chiodo presents a historical study of the development and enactment of the Dutch colony's foreign policy, which was based on the use of diplomacy rather than military force.

101. Condon, Thomas J. The Commercial Origins of New Netherland. Harvard, 1962. 333p.
This study examines and emphasizes two interpretations of New Netherland history. First, the author stresses a commercial framework for the study of New Netherland history. Second, the author notes the similarities between this colony and the New England colonies, suggesting that New Netherland was not the highly institutionalized Dutch society previously emphasized. The study relates the history of the West India Company, examines the role of private merchants in New Netherland, and describes recurrence of private interest in the commercial possibilities of the colony. Covers the period 1609 to 1650.

102. Decroos, Jean F. The Long Journey: Assimilation and Ethnicity Maintenance Among Urban Basques in Northern California. Oregon, 1979. 300p. (DA 40:3541-A)
This is a report on research conducted with the Basque ethnic community in the American West, with special reference to the French Basques and Spanish Basques residing in the San Francisco Bay area. The research was carried out from the winter of 1976 through the summer of 1977. The study has a dual purpose. The first has to do with the application and/or exploration of theoretical postulates dealing with migration dynamics, structural assimilations, and cultural assimilation. Exposure to the relevant dominant subculture of American society is measured in terms of generational sequence, the "institutional completeness" of the subethnic group, age, sex, occupation, and other relevant variables. Attention is also focused upon the maintenance of an ethnic culture and the consequences that this culture has for the assimilation and self-identification of its adherents. The second main purpose of the study is to contribute historical and ethnographic knowledge of one of the older and yet least-studied ethnic groups in this country. (A)

103. DeJong, Jerome B. The Parent-Controlled Christian School: A Study of the Historical Background, the Theological Basis and the Theoretical Implications of Parent-Controlled Education in the Schools Associated with the Christian Reformed Church in America. New York, 1954. 148p. (DA 15:221)

The author's purpose was to study and evaluate the theory behind parent-controlled Christian education as exhibited in the Christian day schools associated with the Christian Reformed Church. He presents a historical background of the church, which has its roots in the Netherlands, and a history of education in the Netherlands and the United States, in an attempt to place the parent-controlled Christian schools within the context of the Dutch and Reformed heritage of those supporting this type of education. The theology of the denomination is examined as the basis of the theory of parent-controlled Christian education.

104. Dennis, Herbert K. The French Canadians: A Study in Group Traits, with Special Reference to the French Canadians of New England. Harvard, 1918. 201p.

105. Dexter, Robert C. The Habitant Transplanted: A Study of the French-Canadian in New England. Clark, 1923. 158p.

106. Dreyer, John R. A Study of the Portuguese Immigrants of Somerville, Massachusetts, with a View Towards Developing a Community-Responsive English Language Program for Adults. Columbia (Teachers College), 1978. 413p. (DA 39:3301)
Like many other American cities, Somerville, Massachusetts, is experiencing a decline in its primary- and secondary-school population while at the same time the number of adults seeking further education increases. Unlike other American urban centers, though, Somerville has a high proportion of non-English speakers, who speak Portuguese, Haitian Creole, Spanish, Italian, Greek, and other languages, in descending order of population. Scholars, professionals, community leaders, and officials at the local, state, and regional level have collaborated with the writer in this effort to perceive accurately and effectively meet the needs of the Portuguese-speaking adults in Somerville who wish to learn English.

107. Dube, Normand C. Guidelines for the Teaching of French to Franco-Americans. Ohio State, 1971. 285p. (DA 32:1378-A)
Franco-American students speak a dialect of French. They must be given the opportunity to perceive those variations in pronunciation, vocabulary, and structure that make their dialect different from and similar to standard French dialect. The writer describes phonetic and morphophonemic differences and similarities between Franco-American French and standard French. He also suggests activities to assist students to perform in standard French. (A)

108. Earl, John L. Talleyrand in America: A Study of His Exile in the United States, 1794-1796. Georgetown, 1964. 243p.

109. Fernandez, Ronald L. A Logic of Ethnicity: A Study of the Significance and Classification of Ethnic Identity Among Mon-

treal Portuguese. McGill, 1978. 212p. (DA 39:2383-A)
Although this dissertation focuses on identities encountered by Portuguese immigrants living in Montreal, its more general relevance is as a study in the organization of cultural meaning. The essential question posed is: how do ethnic labels communicate significance? In simplest terms, the answer given is: proper names of ethnic groups convey meaning because of their <u>position</u> in a classification system.

110. Gehring, Charles T. The Dutch Language in Colonial New York: An Investigation of a Language in Decline and Its Relationship to Social Change. Indiana, 1973. 143p. (DA 34: 6616)
As the Dutch accepted the English government and legal system after 1664 in colonial America, they counterbalanced the accommodation by maintaining a distinct society that preserved their ethnic social traditions. The Dutch language articulated their traditions and was a major part of the Dutch social identity. This study attempts to show the parallels between the assimilation of the Dutch into English colonial society and the linguistic accommodations that developed during the period after 1664 and up to the American Revolution. The decline of the use of the Dutch language is shown in relationship to social changes.

111. Goudeau, John M. Early Libraries in Louisiana: A Study of the Creole Influence. Western Reserve, 1965. 711p. (DA 27:787-A)
Since Louisiana was 100 years old before it became American, Creole culture was well established and became an important influence in the subsequent development of the state. A Creole is a descendant of French and/or Spanish settlers, although some Germans and other nationalities came to the province before the Louisiana Purchase and were absorbed into the French population by adopting the language and Gallicizing their names. Thus, in Louisiana in order to qualify as a Creole one must be descended from a European settler who arrived during the colonial period, 1699-1803. Although the colony was under Spanish domination for more than 30 of those years, the French language and traditions remained dominant. The writer has been primarily concerned with how Creole culture evolved and if it had any effect on libraries. Information about early private libraries was found in inventories of wills and estates and in early Louisiana newspapers. (A)

112. Gray, Margery P. A Population and Family Study of Basques Living in Shoshone and Bocal, Idaho. Oregon, 1955. 250p.

113. Griffin, Joseph A. The Contributions of Belgium to the Development of the Catholic Church in America (1523-1857). Catholic, 1932. 156p.
Published under the same title (Washington, D.C.: Catholic University of America Press, 1932).

114. Grove, Cornelius L. Cross-Cultural and Other Problems
Affecting the Education of Immigrant Portuguese Students in
a Program of Transitional Bilingual Education: A Descriptive Case Study. Columbia (Teachers College), 1977. 407p.
The dissertation focuses on the secondary-level program of transitional bilingual education for immigrant Portuguese youth in a
Massachusetts town. The objective of the research was to discover and describe the cross-cultural problems encountered by
older immigrant youth in the transition from Portugal to the
United States.

115. Guillet, Ernest B. French Ethnic Literature and Culture in
an American City: Holyoke, Massachusetts. Massachusetts,
1978. 383p. (DA 39:2317-A)
This study examines the French literary and cultural life of
French Canadians in New England with emphasis on Holyoke,
Massachusetts, between 1869 and 1940. At the turn of the century French Canadians became known as Franco-Americans; they
tried to maintain their native language and traditions as American citizens in a New England urban industrial setting. (A)

116. Gutierrez, Medardo. A Description of the Speech of Immigrant and Second Generation Gallego-Spanish Speakers in New
York City. A Study in Bilingualism. Georgetown, 1971.
270p. (DA 32:2077-A)
The object of this study is to describe the interference of Gallego-Spanish and English on one another in the speech of Gallegos
residing in Metropolitan New York. The description includes a
contrastive analysis of the phonology of Gallego, Castilian Spanish, and New York City English plus a summary of phonological
influences in borrowing. Borrowings are also classified according to their morphological nature. The group studied consisted
of immigrant and second-generation speakers. (A)

117. Hayes, Mary. Politics and Government in Colonial Saint
Louis: A Study in the Growth of Political Awareness. St.
Louis, 1972. 287p. (DA 33:1109-A)
During Missouri's territorial period the French of Upper Louisiana readily adjusted to their incorporation into the United States
and accepted the responsibilities of their newly acquired citizenship. This study suggests that the history of colonial Saint
Louis, 1764-1803, when Spain governed Upper Louisiana, provides the explanation for the French acceptance of their new
status. (A)

118. Herrmann, Elmira M. Culture in French Bilingual Curricula: An Analysis of Six Title VII Program Designs from
New England and Louisiana. Texas, 1975. 208p.
This study analyzes the cultural content of all of the French-
English bilingual curricula (K through 3). All projects developed
French instructional aids, reading material, and games appropriate for the students. The tendency of writers was to portray the
culture idealistically, not realistically. There were science and
physical-education units developed, among others.

119. Hirst, Arthur H. The Huguenots in South Carolina. Chicago, 1915. 134p.

120. Kenney, Alice P. The Gansevoorts of Albany and Anglo-Dutch Relations in the Upper Hudson Valley, 1664-1790. Columbia, 1961. 248p. (DA 22:1142)
A sociocultural study of the responses of the Gansevoorts of colonial New York to English rule; in a broader frame, the author describes the amalgamation of the Dutch and English cultures.

121. Leder, Hans H. Cultural Persistence in a Portuguese-American Community. Stanford, 1968. 187p. (DA 29:2269-B)
The aim of the study is to describe the degree and kind of cultural persistence evinced by a Portuguese-American community in California, and to identify the processes by which this persistence has been achieved. Underlying this aim is the assumption that the retention by a subcultural group of traditional cultural patterns will affect the manner in which its members adjust, socially and psychologically, to the pressures of acculturatively induced change. (A)

122. Luidens, John P. The Americanization of the Dutch Reformed Church. Oklahoma, 1969. 442p. (DA 29:4431-A)
The Dutch Reformed Church became an American institution through the sporadic stages of a process that was protracted over more than two centuries. This gradual transformation was the result both of a novel environment and of cultural interaction. It began slowly during the brief tenure of the Dutch, was vastly forwarded under the British, and achieved its final form in the early years of the American republic. Through all its permutations the church displayed the stamina and tenacity characteristic of bonds arising from religioethnic sources. After an introductory section describing the European backgrounds of the Reformed Church the nature of the relations between the colonial and mother churches are explained and discussed. The weaknesses of the Reformed Church in America are related to factors of environment and neglect during the Dutch period of New Netherland. (A)

123. Machado, D. A. M. Cape Verdean-Americans: Their Cultural and Historical Backgrounds. Brown, 1978. 383p.

124. McGowen, Owen T. P. Factors Contributing to School Leaving Among Immigrant Children: The Case of the Portuguese in Fall River, Massachusetts. Catholic, 1976. 128p. (DA 37:910)
This study investigated various aspects of the problems experienced by many Azorean immigrant children in the United States who, having reached an age when formal education is no longer legally compulsory for them, drop out of school. It focused on family values, possible influence of a language problem, relevancy of the educational process to these students and the role of peer pressure, seeking to determine how these factors affect the school-leaving situation. (A)

France, Portugal, Spain, Low Countries 33

125. McKinley, Albert E. Representation and Suffrage in New
Netherland and New York, 1613-1691. Pennsylvania, 1900.
151p.
The dissertation is a history (largely political) of the Dutch and
British sovereignty from the period of discovery to 1691.

126. Murray, Jean E. The Fur Trade in New France and New
Netherland Prior to 1645. Chicago, 1936. 321p.
The study is intended as a comparison of the seventeenth-century
commercial activities of the French and the Dutch in the New
World. The author's conclusion is that the resemblances between
French and Dutch trading activities in America outweighed the
differences.

127. Nettinga, James Z. The Church in a Changing Century. A
Study of Social and Economic Influences on the Reformed
Church in America on Manhattan Island. Union Theological
Seminary (New York), 1946. 214p.

128. Newton, Lewis W. The Americanization of French Louisiana: A Study of the Process of Adjustment Between the
French and the Anglo-American Population of Louisiana, 1803-
60. Chicago, 1929. 235p.
Published under the same title (New York: Arno, 1980). This
dissertation traces the relations between the "old" population and
the "new" population to 1960 and explains the process of absorp-
tion of the former by the latter. Newton explains the use of
certain terms. He shows that the population of Louisiana in 1803
was mainly French in derivation and character. This population
was variously termed "old, " "ancient, " "native, " "French, " and
"Creole, " and by these terms it was meant to exclude the few
Anglo-Americans who were then in Louisiana. A Creole was
properly one born in Louisiana of French or Spanish parentage
or remoter descent, and in no sense did it imply a mixture with
Negro or Indian blood. Often the term assimilated to itself in
usage all persons of French descent, whether born in Louisiana,
France, or elsewhere, but Newton has usually employed the word
"French" rather than "Creole" when these latter were included.
Only occasionally is "creole" used to signify anything native to
Louisiana, such as creole cane, creole eggs, or creole cotton;
and then such usage seems to have been derived from the fact
that such things were produced in the land of the Creoles. The
part of Louisiana's population that came from the other states or
territories of the United States or were descended from such immigrants are referred to as "new, " "American, " or "Anglo-
American. " Though Newton recognizes that, strictly speaking,
the French and Anglo-Americans are not separate races, common usage would seem to justify the employment of the word
"race" or "racial" in this study when reference is made to the
peculiar attitudes of these two groups.

129. Ostyn, Paul. American Flemish: A Study in Language Loss
and Linguistic Interference. Rochester, 1972. 374p.

(DA 33:2356-A)
Hitherto studies in bilingualism have concentrated mainly on the direct influence of the source language (Li) on the lexicon of the recipient language (Lii). This influence is manifested by borrowings, loan translations, and semantic loans. These and related problems have been thoroughly investigated for Portuguese, Norwegian, Swedish, German, and other immigrant languages in the United States. This dissertation re-examines the problem of bilingualism on the basis of written American Flemish. (A)

130. Pieters, Aleida J. A Dutch Settlement in Michigan. Columbia, 1923. 208p.
Published under the same title (Grand Rapids, Michigan: Reformed Press, Eerdmans-Svensma, 1923). An overview of Dutch settlement in western Michigan in 1847, causes for the emigration, and patterns of Americanization and assimilation.

131. Pike, Ruth. The Genoese in Seville and the Opening of the New World. Columbia, 1959. 278p. (DA 20:1345)
Published under the title Enterprise and Adventure: The Genoese in Seville and the Opening of the New World (Ithaca, New York: Cornell University Press, 1966). The discovery of America and the opening of trading relations with the new continent was the turning point in the history of the Genoese in Spain. The present study attempts to expose and analyze the participation of the members of the Seville Genoese colony in the American trade during the sixteenth century and to show how they used the capital drawn from this trade to engage in financial operations with Charles V and Philip II. Genoese intervention in other parts of Spanish economy is also described. (A)

132. Post, Ernest H. A Century of Ecumenical and Unionist Tendencies in the Reformed Church in America: 1850-1950. Michigan State, 1966. 301p. (DA 27:2123-A)
The Reformed Church in America is the current name for the Netherlands-originated, Calvinist-bred church planted in New Amsterdam in 1628. Prior to the period of this study it had Americanized slowly and consequently grown rather slowly too. Preponderantly a sectional church located in the states of New York and New Jersey, it still bore some traces of previous factionalism. The Reformed Church in America has evidenced a consistent willingness to cooperate, and even to attempt union with, other denominations, but owing largely to the one union it did achieve in 1850, it probably will never unite again. Nevertheless, the idea of a union has refused to die and since 1962 the church has been negotiating with the Southern Presbyterians. Whatever the outcome of this approach it is unlikely that the church can long maintain both its current distinct identity and its present degree of unity. (A)

133. Potts, Heston N. The Dutch Schools in North America, 1620-1750. Rutgers, 1973. 629p. (DA 34:4279)
This study presents a comprehensive view of those factors that

prevented the early Dutch-Americans from preserving their schools, which were centers of ethnocentrism in an alien country. The author considers the period of early colonial America up to about 1750, by which time the Dutch schools had lost almost all of their Dutch characteristics. He presents a picture of the conditions faced by the Dutch in America and the degree to which the Dutch were successful in dealing with these conditions.

134. Rammelkamp, Charles H. A History of Colonial New York from Its Origin as a Dutch Colony to the Administration of George Clinton in 1743. Cornell, 1900. 38p.

135. Rink, Oliver A. Merchants and Magnates: Dutch New York, 1609-1664. Southern California, 1976. 193p. (DA 37:2384)
The study stresses the commercial relationship between the Netherlands and her colony of New Netherland. The author advances evidence that indicates that the Dutch West India Company played a less important role than previously thought, since the Company was bankrupt by 1640. After this time the colony's economy appears to have been controlled by four Amsterdam merchant families. Through the private trade of these four firms not only was the economy affected, but also the colonizing efforts.

136. Ryskamp, Henry J. The Dutch in Western Michigan. Michigan, 1964. 189p. (DA 25:6106)
Provides a detailed account of the migration of the Dutch immigrants into western Michigan, the growth of this group, and its development as part of American life, with detail concerning the Dutch immigrants' religious background and organization. Sociological and historical point of view relies heavily on those sources dealing with the religious side of the group's life. Along with a historical background the author includes sections on education, occupation, community life, political life, ecclesiastical organization, and assimilation into American culture.

137. Sarrell, Richard S. The Sentinelle Affair (1924-1929) and Militant Survivance: The Franco-American Experience in Woonsocket, Rhode Island. State University of New York (Buffalo), 1975. 490p. (DA 36:6902-A)
The Sentinelle affair involved a group of Franco-Americans (French Canadian immigrants and their descendants) in New England, most notably in Woonsocket, Rhode Island, who in the years following World War I became increasingly disturbed about the state of their ethnic and religious survival in the United States. Led by Elphège Daignault, they decided militantly to defend their nationality's rights. These Franco-American militants identified the Irish hierarchy of the Catholic Church as the principal enemy. They felt that the Church wanted forcibly to "Americanize" Franco-Americans, by limiting the teaching of native language and customs in their parochial schools, and by centralizing diocesan activities, which would threaten the autonomy of individual Franco-American parishes. (A)

138. Sluiter, Engel. The Dutch on the Pacific Coast of America, 1598-1621. California (Berkeley), 1937. 278p.
Studies, in detail, the only three expeditions undertaken by the United Netherlands through the Straits of Magellan to Upper California (1598-1621). These expeditions became a threat to the Spanish, who occupied the west coast of America. Much of this historical study involves conflicts between the Dutch and the Spanish. The introduction attempts to show the relationship between the Dutch activity on the Pacific coast and the Dutch activities on the Atlantic coast prior to 1621.

139. Spurgeon, John H. Body Size and Form of American-Dutch Schoolboys Residing in Michigan. Iowa, 1959. 39p. (DA 20:953)
Intended as a comparative study pertaining to the physical condition of American schoolboys of Dutch ancestry. Three age samples (seven, 11, and 15 years old) were drawn from the schools in Holland, Michigan, during the school year 1957-1958.

140. Stegenga, Preston J. Hope College in Dutch-American Life, 1851-1951. Michigan, 1952. 374p. (DA 12:528)
Published under the title Anchor of Hope: The History of an American Denominational Institute, Hope College (Grand Rapids, Michigan: Eerdmans, 1954). The purpose of this study is to determine the role of Hope College, a denominational institution, in the assimilation of a European national group to American life. Hope College was founded in 1851 in Holland, Michigan, by Dutch colonists in cooperation with the Reformed Church in America. The study places a major emphasis upon the relationships between the college and the denomination. To understand these relationships it attempts to examine the actions, opinions, and influences of the Dutch pioneers, of denominational groups and leaders, as well as those of other groups and pressures outside the church. (A)

141. Stob, George. The Christian Reformed Church and Her Schools. Princeton Theological Seminary, 1955. 469p.
Advances premise that the schools (primary, secondary, and college levels) supported by or closely related to the Christian Reformed Church play a strategic role in the church and that an examination of these schools provides an understanding of the church's relationship to her environment. The dissertation relates the church's educational history, beginning in the late 1800s with the small Dutch-language parochial schools and the schools established for the training of ministers and concluding with an overview of contemporary educational efforts. Source materials include records of the earliest Christian Reformed Churches, school records, and periodicals connected with the denomination, the schools, and the Dutch-speaking American population of the late 1800s and the 1900s. Bibliographical references (the majority of which are related to Dutch-language materials) are included.

142. Taft, Donald R. Two Portuguese Communities in New England. Columbia, 1923. 359p.

Published under the same title (New York: Columbia University Press, 1923). Intended as a study of the Portuguese communities of Portsmouth (Rhode Island) and Fall River (Massachusetts) with notices of Portuguese emigration to the United States.

143. Ten Zythoff, Gerrit J. The Netherlands Reformed Church: Stepmother of Michigan Pioneer Albertus Christian Van Raalte. Chicago, 1967. 269p.
Study of the ecclesiastical background of the Dutch emigrants to America after 1846. It is the author's thesis that the story of these immigrants must be viewed in light of their religious beliefs, which, in turn, can only be understood with a comprehension of the relationship between the Seceded Church in the Netherlands and the Netherlands Reformed Church (the majority of the immigrants being Seceders from the state church). Written in English, but using primarily Dutch-language sources, this study is a critical analysis of the religious conditions in the Netherlands in the early nineteenth century.

144. Ter Maat, Cornelius J. Three Novelists and a Community: A Study of American Novelists with Dutch Calvinist Origins. Michigan, 1963. 241p. (DA 24:751)
This study examines the impact on three contemporary American novelists of having been raised and educated in the highly homogeneous subculture of the American Dutch Calvinists who migrated to the United States in the Middle of the nineteenth century and who settled mostly in Midwest. The three novelists, David Cornel DeJong, Frederick Manfred, and Peter DeVries, were raised in colonies of Dutch immigrants and Americans of Dutch descent in Michigan, Iowa, and Illinois, respectively. Later, as they began to write, these men rejected the confines of the parochial community. (A)

145. Theriault, George F. The Franco-Americans in a New England Community: An Experiment in Survival. Harvard, 1951. 350p.
The Franco-Americans, more commonly known as French Canadians, have constituted a comparatively large ethnic minority group in New England since 1870. Throughout the 80 years that have elapsed since then both friendly and hostile observers have agreed, and studies of them have shown that they have tended to resist assimilation into American culture more strongly than other ethnic groups and to retain with unusual tenacity the language, institutions, customs, and traditions they brought with them from Canada. In the largest sense, theirs is a dual culture, drawing some of its elements from their French Canadian heritage and others from American culture. This study is not concerned either with those aspects of Franco-American life that they share with other Americans or with the consequences that the dualism of their orientation to life has produced in their roles in American life. The primary objective has been, as the title of the study implies, to explore the nature of the experiment they have conducted to perpetuate in a New England setting those aspects of

their culture that are of French and French Canadian origin. To attain this objective the author has made an intensive study of the Franco-Americans in Nashua, New Hampshire, a community that is representative of the old textile and shoe manufacturing industrial centers that first attracted them in large numbers into New England, and of the pattern of conditions and opportunities for la survivance that obtained in many similar communities. In its larger aspects the research has included a study of the history of this community; its ethnic composition and the histories of its ethnic groups, and of the ecological patterns, past and present, found in histories of its ethnic groups; and of the ecological patterns, past and present, found in the community. The study has also involved the investigation in its most salient aspects of the antecedent French Canadian culture, and of Franco-American culture in New England as a regional phenomenon.

146. Trelease, Allen W. Indian Relations and the Fur Trade in New Netherland, 1609-1664. Harvard, 1955. 360p.
The study concerns itself with the dual role of the Indians in the commercial life of New Netherland. The fur trade with the Indians contributed to the colony's economic progress, but the Indians also hindered the expansion of the Dutch settlement and the agricultural colonization of the area by the Dutch. Using a chronological format, the thesis examines three "zones of activity" in New Netherland, each having different problems with Indian tribes.

147. Vander Hill, Charles W. Gerrit J. Diekema: A Michigan Dutch-American Political Leader, 1859-1930. Denver, 1967. 443p. (DA 28:1041-A)
Born in the Dutch-immigrant community of Holland, Michigan, in 1859, Gerrit John Diekema rose from humble origins to the rank of United States Minister to the Netherlands. In addition to being recognized by all but a few commentators as the leading citizen of Holland, Michigan, Diekema's public activities included a host of prominent local, state, and national positions as well as legal, business, and civil contributions. (A)

148. Vicero, Ralph D. Immigration of French Canadians to New England, 1840-1900: A Geographical Analysis. Wisconsin, 1968. 484p. (DA 29:4707-B)
The immigration of French Canadians represented one phase in what Hansen has termed the "second colonization" of New England. Although much has been written about the cultural and social characteristics of this group, many details of the immigration have been treated inadequately from the geographer's viewpoint. The causes, volume and nature of the movement, the numbers and distribution of the migrants through the years, and various aspects of their role in the regional economy have been little known or studied. These topics are emphasized in this study of the French Canadians as one element in the changing economic and social geography of nineteenth-century New England. (A)

149. Wagman, Morton. The Struggle for Representative Government in New Netherland. Columbia, 1969. 359p. (DA 30:2447)
A history of the development of a representative government in New Netherland from 1624 to the end of the Dutch rule in this area. The author divides his study into three basic phases of development. The first phase occupies the years 1624 to 1640, when all property, trade, and government were under the direction of the Dutch West India Company. The second phase, 1641 to 1652, was a period in which settlers accumulated real and personal property and wished to acquire a voice in the provincial government. The years 1653 to 1664 were a period of reform and compromise, in which the community exercised an indirect voice in government but did not form a permanent representative assembly.

150. Wess, Robert C. The Image and Use of the Dutch in the Literary Works of Washington Irving. Notre Dame, 1970. 301p. (DA 31:4799)
Presents a historical sketch of the Dutch people in the Netherlands and in New Netherland; examines the source of Irving's image of the Dutch folklore, cultural specifics, and written histories; describes the manifestations of Irving's image of the Dutch, by tracing the image through Irving's writings; and discusses the purposes served by Irving's use of the Dutch image in his writings.

151. Wilson, Christopher F. An Ethnography of Gypsy-Andalusian and American Aficionado Flamenco. United States International University, 1975. 169p. (DA 36:1834-A)
The purpose of the study was to present an ethnography of traditional Spanish flamenco and American aficionado (fan, enthusiast) flamenco, and to show the changes that have occurred in the cross-cultural transmission of the art. Ethnocentric views of other cultures, as those presented by commercial and American flamenco, decrease intercultural communication. The importance of this study was to present an accurate description of flamenco; and to analyze the relationship between the Spanish and American forms. In so doing, it was intended to aid in a better understanding of the dynamics found in the cross-cultural transmission of this unique art form. (A)

152. Worden, Vincent J. The Influence of a Parent Education Program on Educational Achievement and Aspiration Among Portuguese Immigrant Youth. Clark, 1975. 283p.
Research studies of parental influence on educational aspiration and achievement of children indicates that the parents play a most crucial role in their offspring's planning of the future. The problem to be investigated in this study was an evaluation of the influence of a parent-education program on educational achievement and aspiration upon Portuguese immigrant youth. At the present time some 80-90 percent of the Portuguese immigrant pupils drop out of school before completion of the 12th grade.

C. SCANDINAVIA: NORWAY, SWEDEN, DENMARK, AND FINLAND

153.   Andeen, Gustav K. Trends in the Development of the Program of Higher Education in the Augustana Lutheran Church. Columbia (Teachers College), 1952. 270p. (DA 12:691)
The Augustana Lutheran Church carries on a program of higher education by training theological students at the Augustana Theological Seminary in Rock Island, Illinois, and by conferring baccalaureate degrees at four liberal-arts colleges: Augustana in Rock Island, Illinois; Bethany in Lindsborg, Kansas; Gustavus Adolphus in St. Peter, Minnesota; and Upsala in East Orange, New Jersey. Luther College is also an academy and junior college of the church located in Wahoo, Nebraska. The purpose of the study has been to give the historical background of these schools, to analyze the educational developments, and to note the issues that have arisen, in order to provide material for a current evaluation of their work and to gain historic perspective in projecting the future program of higher education in the church. (A)

154.   Ander, Oscar F. The Career and Influence of T. N. Hasselquist: A Swedish-American Clergyman, Journalist, and Educator. Illinois, 1931. 127p.
Published under the title T. N. Hasselquist: The Career and Influence of a Swedish-American Clergyman, Journalist and Educator (Rock Island, Illinois: Augustana Library Publications, 1931). An account of Hasselquist's work with the Augustana Synod and Augustana College, his many literary activities, and his influence in Sweden and in the United States.

155.   Anders, John O. O. The Origin and History of Swedish Religious Organizations in Minnesota, 1853-1885. Minnesota, 1930. 195p.
Published under the same title (Rock Island, Illinois: Augustana Book Concern, 1932).

156.   Anderson, Arlow W. The Scandinavian Immigrants and American Public Affairs, 1840 to 1872. Northwestern, 1943. 176p.
Published under the title The Immigrant Takes His Stand: The Norwegian-American Press and Public Affairs, 1847-1872 (Northfield, Minnesota: Norwegian-American Historical Association, 1953). The author studies some 20 publications in Illinois, Minnesota, and Wisconsin, noting that the press reflected the conservatism of most Norwegian-Americans.

157.   Anderson, Burton L. The Scandinavians and Dutch Rural Settlements in the Stillaguamish and Nooksack Valleys of Western Washington. University of Washington, 1957. 202p.

(DA 17:1979)
A comparative study between two closely knit ethnic groups, the Hollanders and the Scandinavians from the Stillaguamish and Nooksack river valleys of the Puget Sound region north of Seattle. It investigates the differences in the groups' use of their environment and the possible causes for the differences and analyzes physical and geographic features as well as historical developments primarily through the use of interviews and field schedules. Reveals that Scandinavian rural communities are disbanding and splitting up while the Dutch have adopted a balanced agricultural program and are expanding their rural settlements.

158. Anderson, Verlyn D. The History and Acculturation of the English Language Hymnals of the Norwegian-American Lutheran Churches, 1879-1958. Minnesota, 1972. 380p. (DA 33:4449-A)
During the century prior to the Immigration Act of 1924 at least 750,000 Norwegians emigrated to the United States. Although they were severed from their political environment in Norway, they were free to retain their religious heritage. In America the uniformity of the state-supported Church of Norway did not exist; consequently the forces of democracy allowed the immigrants a variety of religious opinion, especially in church policy, worship forms, and lay-clergy relationships. This caused a proliferation of Lutheran synods among these Norwegian-Americans. Introductory chapters of this study trace the pattern of Norwegian immigration, and these immigrants' effects at transplanting and adapting their religious heritage. After an investigation of worship and music in the Lutheran Church the study narrows to focus on the history and evidences of acculturation in the synodically approved English-language hymnals of these Norwegian-American Lutherans. (A)

159. Babcock, Kendric C. The Scandinavians in the Northwest. Harvard, 1896. 304p.
Published (with additional material) under the title The Scandinavian Element in the United States (Urbana: University of Illinois Press, 1914).

160. Belgum, Gerhard L. The Old Norwegian Synod in America, 1853-1890. Yale, 1957. 466p. (DA 28:3251-A)
From among the earliest of the 700,000 Norwegians who migrated to the United States between 1820 and 1920 a Norwegian-American Lutheran synod was formed. "The Old Synod," begun officially in 1853, was to live through controversy and even schism until 1917, when it united with two more recently formed synods to become the present Evangelical Lutheran Church. (A)

161. Benson, Oscar A. Problems in the Accommodation of the Swede to American Culture. Pittsburgh, 1933. 240p.
Covers both the cultural processes and cultural products of the "cross-fertilization of Swedish and American culture." The author notes that "from this mixture has evolved a distinct Swedish-American culture."

162. Bjorgan, George R. The Success Story of an Immigrant. Minnesota, 1968. 388p. (DA 28:4982-A)
Deals with the rise to prominence of a great American, Knute Nelson, who came to the United States from Norway when he was six years of age. He and his mother were part of the growing emigration from Norway that sought a better life in the New World in the mid-nineteenth century. He came with little to recommend him to his new home except an iron will and the determination to overcome all obstacles in the path to success. Knute Nelson rose to political prominence during a long and illustrious career, which was brought to a climax in 1895, when he was elected United States Senator from Minnesota. (A)

163. Blegen, Theodore C. Norwegian Immigration Before the Civil War. Minnesota, 1925. 413p.
Published under the title Norwegian Migration to America, 1825-1860 (Northfield, Minnesota: Norwegian-American Historical Association, 1931). A classic account, almost totally drawn from primary sources.

164. Capps, Fines H. The Attitude of the Swedish-American Press Toward American Foreign Policy. Chicago, 1957. 304p.
Published under the title, From Isolationism to Involvement: The Swedish Immigrant Press in America, 1914-1945 (Chicago: University of Chicago Press, 1966).

165. Carlson, Carl E. The Adjustment of the Swedish Immigrants to the American Public School System in the Northwest. Minnesota, 1950. 247p.

166. Chrisman, Noel J. Ethnic Influence on Urban Groups: The Danish Americans. California (Berkeley), 1966. 230p. (DA 27:3375-B)
The traditional interest in visible ethnic groups that have a minority status in American society seems to have led social scientists to make assumptions about the nature of ethnic groups that may not be true in the present day. For example, ethnic origin has been considered to be the criterion for membership in an ethnic group, and those sharing that origin have been assumed to be structurally cohesive. Today, although still in existence, many ethnic groups are less visible and less socially cohesive. This being the case, alternative approaches must be sought to accommodate the historical changes that have taken place. This dissertation attempts to provide one alternative approach for ethnic research. Ethnic-group membership is considered to be based upon participation in ethnic institutions of various types. Ethnic voluntary associations, which are the major focus of this study, must be considered within the context of all associations in the city. The associations may be viewed as interest groups, in competition with each other for members. It is essential that these associations advertise, or make visible, their interests so that they may recruit new members. (A)

167. Christensen, Thomas P. The History of the Danes in Iowa. Iowa, 1924. 204p.

168. Dahlie, Jorgen. A Social History of Scandinavian Immigration, Washington State, 1895-1910. Washington State, 1967. 194p. (DA 28:3104-A)
Published under the same title (New York: Arno, 1980). This study, dealing with the Scandinavians in Washington from 1895 to 1910, contends that these people suffered no appreciable cultural shock in settling in the state. In support of this view the study draws on evidence from within the Scandinavian community, principally from the Scandinavian-language newspapers, upon which a heavy reliance has been placed throughout the thesis. Other sources include books and reports by contemporary observers of the Scandinavian-American communities and the materials in the Scandinavian Archives and the Pacific Northwest Collection, both at the University of Washington Library, Seattle. (A)

169. Danielson, Larry W. The Ethnic Festival and Cultural Revivalism in a Small Midwestern Town. Indiana, 1972. 548p. (DA 33:4281-A)
Deals with the Swedish immigrant backgrounds of Lindsborg, Kansas; the historic cultural foci of church and college in Lindsborg life; and the relation of these institutions to the community self-image of the town as a unique and attractive Swedish-American village, of interest to the non-Lindsborg world. (A)

170. Doby, Harry R. A Study of Social Change and Social Disorganization in a Finnish Rural Community. California (Berkeley), 1960. 243p.

171. Dowie, James I. Luther Academy, 1883 to 1903: A Facet of Swedish Pioneer Life in Nebraska. Minnesota, 1957. 384p. (DA 20:4382)
Published under the title Prairie Grass Dividing (Rock Island, Illinois: Augustana Historical Society, 1959). This dissertation examines the religious and cultural context out of which Luther Academy at Wahoo, Nebraska, arose. It seeks to trace the motivation and resulting pattern of Swedish settlement in Nebraska, to survey in a cursory way the church polity of the Evangelical Lutheran Augustana Synod, and to present biographical notes on those church leaders who had a direct influence upon the settlements or the school. (A)

172. Eckstein, Neil T. The Marginal Man as Novelist: The Norwegian-American Writers, H. H. Boyesen and O. E. Rolvaag, as Critics of American Institutions. Pennsylvania, 1965. 283p. (DA 32:4601-A)

173. Eklund, Emmet E. Acculturation in the Swedish Lutheran Congregations of the Boston Area: 1867-1930. Boston, 1964. 339p. (DA 25:3138)

A study of acculturation in the 18 Augusta na Synod congregations of the Boston area between 1867 and 1930. The Augustana Synod was the national body of Lutheran churches founded and maintained for a ministry to Swedish Lutheran immigrants. The study not only traces the process of acculturation but marshals evidence to show that the process in terms of conditions and responses was different for the Boston group from the rest of the Synod. Such conditions as applicable to the Boston immigrants were: urban rather than rural background; difference in the political, social, economic, and religious situation in Sweden at the time of their emigration; and the closing of the American frontier and American urbanization (since most of these immigrants came after 1890). (A)

174. Fevold, Eugene L. Norwegian-American Lutheranism, 1870-90. Chicago, 1951. 243p.

175. Fonkalsrud, Alfred O. Scandinavians as a Social Force in America. New York University, 1913. 127p.
Published under the same title (New York: Heiberg, 1914).

176. Gedicks, Albert J. Working Class Radicalism Among Finnish Immigrants in Minnesota and Michigan Mining Communities. Wisconsin (Madison), 1979. 230p. (DA 40:3566-A)
Finnish immigrants to Midwest mining communities have had a major impact upon the development of radical political and labor movements in the Western Great Lakes region. This dissertation explores a number of questions about Finnish-American participation in these radical movements. The author traces the origins of Finnish-American radicalism in the initial penetration of the Finnish countryside by capitalist agriculture. In opposition to the explanation advanced by the social disease of industrialism theorists, he argues that it is the emergence of capitalist forms of social relations, rather than the breakdown of precapitalist forms of social relations, that accounts for radical predispositions among Finnish immigrants. This hypothesis is tested with data on the agrarian origins of Finnish and Swedish immigrants and their differing political responses in Michigan and Minnesota mining communities. (A)

177. Gemorah, Solomon. Laurence Gronlund's Ideas and Influence, 1877-1899. New York, 1965. 324p. (DA 27:153-A)
There is at present no biography of the Danish-born Laurence Gronlund nor any comprehensive treatment of his ideas and influence. Historians have analyzed the views of this pioneer socialist writer from a specialized perspective. The effect has been a series of fragmented interpretations without any proper study of Gronlund's dynamic and flexible mind. This thesis aims to rediscover and interpret Gronlund's intellectual contribution to the social-reform movements of the last decades of the nineteenth century. (A)

178. Gustafson, Walter W. The Swedish Language in the United States. New York, 1929. 207p.

179. Hale, Frederick. Trans-Atlantic Conservative Protestantism in the Evangelical Free and Mission Covenant Traditions. Johns Hopkins, 1976. 264p.
Published under the same title (New York: Arno, 1979). In this study Hale breaks new ground in interpreting the trans-Atlantic roots of conservative Protestantism in the Evangelical Free Church and the Swedish Mission Covenant Church in America. He analyzes the pietism, revivalism, and scriptural emphasis of various nonconformist groups in Sweden, Norway, and Denmark and their reactions to the evangelistic techniques popularized by Dwight L. Moody and Charles G. Finney, nineteenth-century British and American millenarianism, and German "higher criticism" of the Bible. Two divergent types of Protestantism developed among these Nordic free churchmen in both the Old World and the New--one springing from pietistic Lutheranism in Sweden, the other strongly influenced by revivalistic and millenarian currents of British and American origin. Migration, travel, and cooperation with non-Scandinavian Christians nurtured trans-Atlantic religious continuities. This study of cultural diffusion illuminates several Scandinavian "segments of the intricate mosaic of conservative Protestantism in America."

180. Hamre, James S. Georg Sverdrup's Concept of the Role and Calling of the Norwegian-American Lutherans: An Annotated Translation of Selected Writings. Iowa, 1967. 282p. (DA 28:3254-A)
The primary purpose of this study is to make available in English translation some of the basic works of one extraordinary Norwegian Lutheran immigrant, Georg Sverdrup (1848-1907). Educated in theology in Norway, Sverdrup came to the United States as a professor of theology at Augsburg Seminary in Minneapolis in 1874. At the time the Norwegian Lutherans in America were divided into several parties. Sverdrup soon became a foremost leader of what might be called an "Americanization" emphasis or thrust. He defended the American "free church" system, and, outstandingly, he pressed for the public schools as over against the parochial-school system advocated by other Norwegian Lutheran leaders. (A)

181. Hansen, Judith F. Daniel Social Interactions: Cultural Assumptions and Patterns of Behavior. California (Berkeley), 1970. 186p. (DA 31:7058)
Certain background expectancies and cultural assumptions influence the course of interaction in every society. By explicating such assumptions and by examining them in behavioral contexts Hansen provides understanding of interpersonal relations in a particular culture. In the present study five core concepts and several subsidiary assumptions of Danish culture are explored. Two of these core concepts, hygge and festlighed, are keys to Danish values about the nature of interaction in small groups. Among the subsidiary assumptions discussed in conjunction with these two concepts are the positive orientation, orientations to present and past, the rhythm of enjoyment, the notion of stemning,

and closure. Following consideration of the Danish principle of egalitarianism, the core values of balance, moderation, and inclusion are treated, along with the related patterns of criticism, the positive orientation, the suppression of hostility, and humor. Finally, these concepts and assumptions are analyzed in the context of informal focused interactions among members of a social network. The study is based on one year's residence and research in Copenhagen, Denmark, and several years' acquaintanceship with Danish-Americans.

182. Hasselmo, Nils. American Swedish: A Study in Bilingualism. Harvard, 1961. 237p.

183. Heimonen, Henry S. Finnish Rural Culture in South Ostrobothnia (Finland) and the Lake Superior Region (United States): A Comparative Study. Wisconsin, 1941. 203p.

184. Hemdahl, Revel G. The Swedes in Illinois Politics: An Immigrant Group in American Political Setting. Northwestern, 1934. 211p.

185. Hoglund, Arthur W. Paradise Rebuilt: Finnish Immigrants and Their America, 1880-1920. Wisconsin, 1957. 333p. (DA 17:2254)
Published under the title Finnish Immigrants in America, 1880-1920 (Madison: University of Wisconsin Press, 1960). From about 1850 the retreat from agriculture became noticeable in Finland. Partly under the influence of nationalism, new intellectual aspirations and economic techniques helped break down the confines of a self-contained agricultural society. Different organizations were thus formed to pursue the intellectual awakening or, as it was also called, the Enlightenment. The awakening, however, did not occur evenly in all parts of the country. It predominated in southern Finland, where industrial and urban growth was most pronounced. Consequently, rural areas were slower to share in the fullness of the Enlightenment. Coming mainly from northwestern Finland, most immigrants, who started to arrive in America after about 1865, often had barely experienced the awakening, if indeed they had experienced it at all. As they experienced industrial and urban life in America, they thus really found reasons for the first time to develop associations that bespoke their retreat from rural confinement. Accordingly, they reshaped their oral folklore, essentially rural in character, as the clarion call for the new associative life with its literary overtones. When they developed aspirations in terms of the economic, social, and political conditions, which were unlike those of their rural experiences, immigrants found how readily associations lent themselves to diverse purposes. Above all, through association they expected paradise or a sense of direction to master their new ways of living together. (A)

186. Hoover, Knight E. Organizational Networks and Ethnic Persistence: A Case Study of Norwegian-American Ethnicity in

the New York Metropolitan Area. City University of New York, 1979. 406p. (DA 40:7540-A)
This dissertation discusses the importance of ethnic interest organizations in helping to maintain ethnic persistence among Norwegian-Americans in the New York metropolitan area. According to current concepts of structural and cultural integration, the Norwegian-American population in the New York metropolitan area is assimilated. Nonetheless, Norwegian-Americans maintain viable and, in one instance rapidly growing, ethnic institutions within a metropolitan "community" at a time when Norwegian immigration is virtually at a standstill. The objective of this study is to examine institutional factors that underlie this group's persistence. (A)

187. Houston, Gloria. The Origins, Development and Significance of Atterdag College--A Danish Folk High School in America. California (Los Angeles), 1971. 174p. (DA 32:3653)
This dissertation traces the origins and development of Atterdag College, one of the Danish Folk High Schools established in the United States. Atterdag College was located in the Danish colony of Solvang, California, and classes were held there from 1914 until 1937. The experiences of Atterdag College serve as an example that the Folk High School as an educational institution did not, or could not, adapt to the American milieu. With some accommodation the Danish Folk High Schools might have survived as a part of the educational scene in America. (A)

188. Hove, Haldor L. The Norwegian Immigrant Press, 1870-1890: Purveyors of Literary Taste and Culture. Chicago, 1963. 245p.

189. Hummasti, Paul G. Finnish Radicals in Astoria, Oregon, 1904-1940: A Study in Immigrant Socialism. Oregon, 1975. 449p. (DA 36:4674-A)
Published under the same title (New York: Arno, 1979). In 1920 Finns comprised 1.1 percent of the immigrant population of the United States, 0.1 percent of the total population, and 14.3 percent of the membership of the Socialist Party of America. In Astoria, with its large Finnish fisherman group, the Socialist Party held about one-third of the voting strength, and the Republicans about one-half. It is because of these statistics that the local concentration of Finns is politically significant. "Church-Finns" as well as Socialists lived in Astoria, and they got along together, but the radicals were especially active in social and cultural affairs, in newspaper publishing (Toveri and the women's paper Toveritar), and in politics. They were involved in the socialist-syndicalist controversy and the IWW movement, and they took a deep interest in events in the home country. They never integrated fully with American radical movements. They supported the sovietization of Finland and sent monetary aid to Karelia after World War I, and some of them migrated to Karelia to help build fishing communes--many returning in disillusionment to Astoria. In general, "the young and spirited Socialists of 1904-

1919 had by the late 1920s and early 1930s become older and less enthusiastic Communists. " This detailed study of fishermen radicals complements Puotinen's account of mining radicals in the Midwest.

190. Hustvedt, Lloyd M. Pioneer Scholar: A Biography of Rasmus Bjorn Anderson. Wisconsin, 1962. 506p. (DA 23:1351) Published under the title Rasmus Bjorn Anderson: Pioneer Scholar (Northfield, Minnesota: North American Historical Association, 1966). This study treats the life of Rasmus B. Anderson (1846-1936), a man who rose to considerable prominence as educator, journalist, author, translator, agitator, and politician on the Norwegian-immigrant scene in the Middle West. The biography examines the character and personality of the man himself, explores the historical forces (European, American, and frontier) that influenced his career and views, reviews and in part analyzes the books and articles he wrote, and estimates the immediate and lasting impacts he made upon his society. (A)

191. Janson, Florence E. The Background of Swedish Immigration, 1840-1930. Pennsylvania, 1927. 517p.
Published under the same title (Chicago: University of Chicago Press, 1931).

192. Johnson, Amandus. The Founding of New Sweden on the Delaware with a Chapter on the Religious, Social and Economic Condition of Sweden in the First Half of the Seventeenth Century. Pennsylvania, 1908. 368p.
Published under the title The Swedish Settlements on the Delaware: Their History and Relation to the Indians, Dutch, and English, 1638-1664, with an Account of the South, the New Sweden, and the American Companies, and the Efforts of Sweden to Regain the Colony (Philadelphia: University of Pennsylvania [Americana Germanica, No. 13, 2 vols.], 1911).

193. Johnson, Gustav E. The Swedes of Chicago. Chicago, 1940. 283p.

194. Jokinen, Walfrid J. The Finns in the United States: A Sociological Interpretation. Louisiana State, 1955. 232p. (DA 15:2333)
This study reviews the development of the present demographic status of the Finnish population in the United States and describes and interprets the institutionalized patterns of behavior developed by the Finns. The interpretations are based on data from historical and statistical sources, supplemented by participant observation. Immigration is viewed as a social process involving motivations for migration, the actual transplantation of peoples, and the institutionalization of behavior in the United States. (A)

195. Jonassen, Christen T. The Norwegians in Bay Ridge: A Sociological Study of an Ethnic Group: A Study of the Cultural Heritage of the Norwegian Group in Brooklyn as It Af-

fects Their Behavior and the Character of the Community They Created There. New York, 1948. 341p. (DA 8:153)

196. Karni, Michael G. Yhteishyva--or, For the Common Good: Finnish Radicalism in the Western Great Lakes Region, 1900- 1940. Minnesota, 1975. 416p. (DA 37:532-A)
Approximately 25-30 percent of the Finnish immigrants after 1900 were radicals. They were either radicalized before they left Finland or quickly converted to radicalism once they arrived in America, helped to that position by a strong corps of immigrant agitators among them. After 1913 there was no solidarity among them. At that time the Finnish Socialist Federation was split in the Midwest. Approximately 3,000 members thought joining the IWW (instead of remaining in the Socialist Party) would more clearly reflect their position. This action caused much trouble in the Midwest. Despite the factionalized character of the Finnish radicals, however, it must be recognized that their radicalism was due in large part to the failure of American life to give them what they immigrated for. At their peak the Finns claimed 17,000 card-carrying members of radical movements and an undetermined number of unofficial supporters. (A)

197. Kaups, Matti E. "Suuri Laansi"--Or the Finnish Discovery of America. Minnesota, 1966. 279p. (DA 28:3331-B)
The unique concentrations of Finnish immigrants in the United States have attracted much attention and considerable speculation as to the reason why multitudes decided to settle in the same towns or farming settlements, or at least in the same general area. The assertions that the Finns have settled those areas of the United States that most "look like Finland" and are "most similar to Finland" have been repeated often enough to be accepted as a general truth. In this study the environmentalist thesis is reexamined critically in the light of Finnish-language material bearing upon the problem. Also, the location and concentrations of Finnish immigrants in the United States is reevaluated in spatial and temporal perspectives. The cross-sectional method of historical geography is employed. A series of choropleth maps on national, regional, and local scale depict the changing spatial patterns of the Finnish immigrants in the United States (1880-1920). (A)

198. Kercher, Leonard C. The Finnish-Dominated Consumers' Cooperative Movement in the North Central States: An Analysis of the Factors Involved in Its Genesis and an Appraisal of the Elements of Strength and of Weakness in Its Institutional Expression Today. Michigan, 1939. 187p.

199. Kimmerle, Marjorie M. Norwegian Surnames of the Koshkonong and Springdale Congregations in Dane County, Wisconsin. Wisconsin, 1938. 211p.

200. Kolehmainen, John I. A History of the Finns in the Western Reserve. Western Reserve, 1937. 283p.

201. Lakeberg, Arvid P. A History of Swedish Methodism in America. Drew, 1937. 276p.

202. Landis, Paul H. Cultural Change in the Mining Town: A Sociological Study of Three Mesabi Iron Range Towns: Eveleth, Hibbing and Virginia. Minnesota, 1933. 287p.
Published under the title Three Iron Mining Towns: A Study in Cultural Change (Ann Arbor, Michigan: Edwards Brothers, 1938). An account of Finns in Michigan mining country.

203. Larson, Ralph V. A Study of American Influences in the Finnish Trade Union Movement from 1890 to 1920. Indiana, 1972. 201p. (DA 33:4309-A)
The theory that American industry and unions would contribute to the growth and policies of the Finnish Trade Union Federation was new but was logical because of the emigration. It lacked support, however. Then came Oskari Tokoi, an emigrant to the United States in 1891. His activities and associations reinforced the idea especially when he returned to Finland in 1900 and later when he became active in local labor organizations. After 1907 he became increasingly well known in political and labor circles so that in time he was elected to be a representative to Parliament. He subsequently became chairman of the Finnish Trade Union Federation, an office he held for six years from 1912 to 1918. (A)

204. Lawson, Evald B. The Origin of Swedish Religious Organizations in the United States with Special Reference to Olof Gustaf Hedstrom and the Early Structure of Swedish Methodism. Biblical Seminary, 1937. 138p.

205. Lehtinen, Mari K. T. An Analysis of a Finnish-English Bilingual Corpus. Indiana, 1966. 280p. (DA 27:4224-A)
This study consists of an analysis of a narrative text collected from a third-generation Finnish-American informant. The text is basically in Finnish, but introduced into it are large numbers of English items, some of which are accommodated to the Finnish linguistic system in greater or lesser degree. (A)

206. Lindberg, Duane R. Men of the Cloth and the Social-Cultural Fabric of the Norwegian Community in North Dakota. Minnesota, 1975. 378p.
Published under the same title (New York: Arno, 1980). This historic study of Norwegian immigrant settlement on the Upper Great Plains focuses on the social role of the immigrant clergy in terms of this ethnic group's adjustment to the American environment. The primary task is to investigate the significance of the culture that the immigrants brought with them as a factor in explaining the historic behavior of the immigrant group in response to "threats" from the American environment. This threat is seen in the form of the "American School" and the "American Saloon." As a base for developing the underlying hypothesis, the author has examined 12 novels produced by Norwegian-immigrant

authors that relate to the immigrants' experience in the Upper Great Plains. This germinal hypothesis based on generalizations from this symbolic activity of the Norwegian immigrants is then tested in the light of historical "facts" derived from nonfictional sources and demographic studies, with special focus on a heavily Norwegian universe of counties in North Dakota. Norwegian Lutheran clergy are seen to function as a significant reference elite who reflect the basic goals, values, beliefs, and norms of the various groupings of Norwegian Lutheran immigrants that they serve. Hence, the leanings and actions of these religious leaders are examined in relation to these two areas of conflict with the host culture, the common school and the saloon. Cultural differences among Norwegian ethnics in North Dakota persist throughout the period 1870-1920. This persistent pattern of difference in the cultural fabric of North Dakota is documented by critical studies of language transition in public services, adoption of Sunday school, time given to weekday church schools, voting patterns on the prohibition amendment and in gubernatorial elections, and the organization of abstinence societies.

207. Lindberg, Paul M. The Academies and Colleges of the Augustana Synod in Minnesota. Nebraska, 1946. 246p.

208. Lovoll, Odd S. A Study in Immigrant Regionalism: The Norwegian-American Bygdelag. Minnesota, 1973. 390p. (DA 34:2520)
The social organizations known as bygdelag, which commenced at the turn of the century, grew out of the immigrants' attachment to the old home and were inspired by a strong feeling for family and kinship. They represented the most popular expression of the Norwegian-American organizational urge. Their base was regional rather than national, and they thus differed fundamentally from Norwegian-American groups that spoke for specific interests and projects rather than locale. Membership in these societies was made up of immigrants from given Old Country districts or bygder and their descendants; the bonds of union were dialect, common customs, songs and music, acquaintanceship, and shared traditions. (A)

209. Lund, Gene. The Americanization of the Augustana Lutheran Church. Princeton Theological Seminary, 1954. 244p.

210. Malaska, Hilkka O. A Description of the Nature and Development of Adult Education Among the Finnish Immigrants in the United States, 1880-1930. Indiana, 1978. 236p. (DA 40: 6467-A)
It has been the purpose of this study to determine both the nature and the development of adult education among the Finnish immigrants in the United States from 1880 to 1930. The problem was investigated through a descriptive analysis of written records describing the historical background of the Finnish immigrants and the adult education of these immigrants in three major movements: the religious movement, the cultural movement, and the labor

movement. Within each of these movements the organizations were analyzed according to their goals, policies, programs, and methods. (A)

211. Marzolf, Marion T. The Danish-Language Press in America. Michigan, 1972. 283p. (DA 33:6295-A)
The central theme of the Danish experience in America has been to accommodate and assimilate. Fewer than 400,000 Danes came to America during the past century and a half, but they established their own churches, lodges, and newspapers, two of which are still published. What was the history of this press and what was its role in the immigrants' assimilation? That is what this study tried to find out. The major impact of the Danish-language press was as an aid to the immigrants' assimilation. The press actively promoted naturalization and participation in American affairs, furnished immigrants with vital information, and helped soften the cultural shock caused by uprooting. It also encouraged retention of interest in the Danish heritage, but this was done in the spirit of adding enrichment to American culture. After World War I the Danish-language press experienced a rapid decline. The press during this later period served primarily to unite the ethnic group, but its audience was sharply reduced. (A)

212. Meixner, Esther C. The Teaching of the Scandinavian Languages and Literature in the United States. Pennsylvania, 1941. 231p.

213. Moe, Thorvald. Demographic Developments and Economic Growth in Norway, 1740-1940: An Economic Study. Stanford, 1970. 262p. (DA 31:6259-A)
The basic analytical viewpoint underlying this study is that variations in demographic phenomena, notably births, marriages, and migration, are caused primarily by changes in two classes of factors: economic conditions and demographic composition. The study is carried out with the help of econometric models in which variables describing economic conditions and the age structure of the population in family formation and migratory ages are assumed to be predetermined. The author concentrates on two specific aspects of the study. The first is an analysis of the determinants of aggregate births in Norway before 1865, when internal and external migration was still of small quantitative significance. Thus, the object of this part of the study in effect becomes the successful prediction of births in a closed population. A second major objective of the dissertation is the explanation of the massive emigration from Norway that took place after 1865. In the period after the United States Civil War and up to World War I Norway lost well over 40 percent of her natural increase, the highest national per capita figure recorded during this time period save that for Ireland. (A)

214. Mossberg, Christer L. The Immigrant Voice as American Literature: Scandinavian Immigrant Fiction of the American West. Indiana, 1979. 347p. (DA 40:856-A)

Written by settlers, Scandinavian immigrant fiction, which records the farmsteading experience in the American prairies, challenges descriptions of life in the West provided by mainstream American writers. All that was implicit in the immigrants' flight from the Old World made them receptive to New World frontier concepts of democracy, equality, and independence. But the geographical fact of the vast open spaces--which gave rise to the political and social concepts of the image of the American West--was also a threat to a people with a culture to maintain. Scandinavian-American fiction, unlike mainstream literature of the West, reveals that settling the American West was accomplished at tragic cost. (A)

215. Mulder, William. Mormons from Scandinavia, 1850-1905: The Story of a Religious Migration. Harvard, 1955. 360p. Published under the title Homeward to Zion: The Mormon Migration from Scandinavia (Minneapolis: University of Minnesota Press, 1957).

216. Nelson, Carl Leonard. The Sacred and the Secular Music of the Swedish Settlers of the Midwest, 1841-1917. New York, 1950. 167p. (DA 11:130)
A historical account of the musical activities of the Swedish settlers of the Midwest is provided by this study. The music that they performed and composed was surveyed in an attempt to discover salient characteristics. The nature and scope of the Swedish immigration was reviewed; and the religious, educational, and home and community background of the immigrants was summarized to furnish a perspective for a better understanding of their music. A description of life in the early communities, the first of which was settled in 1841, was included to further this understanding. The musical culture was traced until 1917, after which time immigration and the use of the Swedish language declined. Chief sources were the newspapers, biographies, histories, and music of the pioneers, and more recent historical material concerning these settlers and their migration. (A)

217. Nelson, Eugene C. The Union Movement Among Norwegian-American Lutherans from 1880 to 1917. Yale, 1952. 681p. (DA 27:3508)
The churches established in nineteenth-century America by the Lutheran immigrants from Norway reflected the tendencies characteristic of the religious life in their homeland. Emphases from the highly significant Haugean religious revival clashed with emphases associated with the traditional piety of the Church of Norway, as immigrant groups on the American frontier sought to perpetuate both viewpoints. The low-church Haugeans, led by an uneducated but earnest layman, Elling Eilsen, formed the Eilsen Synod (1846). This body suffered its chief rupture in 1876, when the majority organized Hauge's Synod. The right-wing representatives of traditional Lutheranism, led by well-educated clergymen from Norway, organized the Norwegian Synod in 1853. For a time the latter used the facilities of the German Missouri Synod

to train its pastors. This alliance led the already-conservative
Norwegian Synod to an increased stress on "orthodoxy." By 1870
a clearly defined third tendency was exerting its influence. Individuals
who found the ecclesiastical atmosphere in both the left-
and right-wing segments of the church inhospitable formed two
new bodies, the Norwegian Augustana Synod and the Norwegian-
Danish Conference. (A)

218. Nelson, Frank Charles. The American School Controversy
Among the Norwegian-Americans, 1845-1881. Michigan
State, 1968. 286p. (DA 30:149-A)
The purpose of this dissertation was to trace the controversy
over the American school among the Norwegian-Americans, primarily
the Lutherans of the Norwegian Evangelical Lutheran
Synod and the lay leadership associated with it. Although the
primary purpose of the dissertation was to examine the controversy
over the schools, an attempt was made to show that opposition
to the American common school was not confined to the
Norwegian immigrants alone. There were native-born Americans
who opposed the common school for various reasons. In addition
to looking briefly at the opposition of some Americans to the
common school, four ethnic immigrant groups were traced: the
Germans, Irish, Dutch, and Swedes. (A)

219. Nelson, Leola M. F. Melius Christiansen: A Study of His
Life and Work as a Norwegian-American Contribution to
American Culture. Iowa, 1943. 183p.

220. Niemi, Taisto J. The Finnish Lutheran Book Concern, 1900-
1950: A Historical and Developmental Study. Michigan,
1960. 333p. (DA 21:2304)
The purpose of this study is to present the historical development
of a religious, foreign-language press. The Finnish Lutheran
Book Concern of Hancock, Michigan, an endeavor of the Finnish
Evangelical Lutheran Church of America--or the Suomi Synod--
was selected as the subject for the study because it is one of the
more representative and successful Finnish-language presses in
the United States. It was founded at the early, heavy influx of
Finns to the Midwest and still serves the members of the Suomi
Synod. The years 1900 to 1950, the period of greatest activity
and development for the Finnish Lutheran Book Concern, coincide
with the growth of Finnish-speaking population in the United
States. (A)

221. Ollila, Douglas J. The Formative Period of the Finnish
Evangelical Lutheran Church in America of Suomi Synod.
Boston, 1963. 352p. (DA 24:2159)
The Finnish Evangelical Lutheran Church in America, or the
Suomi Synod, terminated its legal existence on January 1, 1963,
to become a part of the Lutheran Church in America. During
the antecedent period of merger discussions it became clear that
no perceptive history of the Synod had been written. The dissertation
presents a history of the Suomi Synod, tracing its back-

Scandinavia 55

ground in Finland, delineating the growth of Finnish Lutheran congregations in the United States, and outlining the organization and early development of the church body. The chronological scope of the study ends in 1920. (A)

222. Paulsen, Frank M. Danish-American Folk Traditions: A Study in Fading Survivals. Indiana, 1967. 343p. (DA 28: 4069-A)
The purpose of this study is to investigate the extent to which folk traditions survive among a rapidly declining ethnic group in America--the Danes. It is historical in that the development and decline of Danish traditions in America are viewed in terms of historical developments in Denmark and America. It is descriptive in that the cultural milieu operating against cultural conservatism is described and analyzed. It is comparative in that the traditions found among the Danes in this country are viewed against similar traditions collected in Denmark and to some degree with those collected among other ethnic groups in America. Finally, it is critical in that it presents and analyzes five groups of folk narrative, Molbo tales, pastor tales, exempla, legends and eventyr, totaling 135 items, collected from 26 Danish-American informants in Omaha, Blair, and Dannebrog, Nebraska; Kimballton and Des Moines, Iowa; and Los Angeles and Solvang, California. (A)

223. Paulson, Arthur C. The Norwegian-American Reaction to Ibsen and Bjornsen, 1850-1900. Iowa, 1933. 141p.

224. Person, Peter P. A History of Higher Education Among the Swedish Immigrants in America. Harvard, 1941. 310p.

225. Qualey, Carlton C. Norwegian Settlement in the United States. Columbia, 1938. 285p.
Published under the same title (Northfield, Minnesota: Norwegian-American Historical Association, 1938). An overview of Norwegian emigration to the United States, with special attention to the post-Civil War period.

226. Raun, James J. The Danish Lutherans in America. Chicago, 1930. 210p.

227. Reigstad, Paul M. The Art and Mind of O. E. Rölvaag. New Mexico, 1958. 230p. (DA 19:1390)
Published under the title Rolvaag: His Life and Art (Lincoln: University of Nebraska Press, 1972). Though O. E. Rölvaag was born in Norway and wrote in his native language, his seven novels have a distinctly American flavor. Each of them traces a theme basic to his program of cultural conservatism: the need of the Norwegian immigrant to retain the language and traditions of the Old World in order to adjust successfully to the New. Though the novels focus attention upon the difficulties inherent in acculturation, many of his characters make the adjustment successfully and find their places in a dynamic society. (A)

228. Rosenquest, Carl M. The Swedes of Texas. Chicago, 1930. 112p.

229. Schersten, Albert F. The Relation of the Swedish-American Newspaper to the Assimilation of Swedish Immigrants. Iowa, 1932. 127p.

230. Schnackenberg, Walter C. The Development of Norwegian Lutheran Schools in the Pacific Northwest from 1890 to 1920. Washington State, 1950. 267p.
Published under the title The Lamp and the Cross: Sagas of Pacific Lutheran University from 1890 to 1965 (Tacoma, Washington: Pacific Lutheran University Press, 1965).

231. Skardal, Dorothy B. Double Heritage: Scandinavian Immigrant Experience Through Literary Sources. Harvard, 1963. 234p.
Published under the title The Divided Heart: Scandinavian Immigrant Experience Through Literary Sources (Lincoln: University of Nebraska Press, 1974).

232. Sklute, Barbro M. Legends and Folk Beliefs in a Swedish American Community: A Study in Folklore and Acculturation. Indiana, 1970. 834p. (DA 31:4654-A)
Because legends are stories firmly placed in a specific milieu and because they are often intimately associated with the folk beliefs of a group, they are closely connected with a specific locality and its value system. This study concerns the fate of legends and beliefs when they are uprooted from their locale. What happens to these traditions when a group of Swedes from different regions of Sweden moves to America, founds a small town in 1870, continues to attract Swedish immigrants for 50 years, and lives in firsthand contact with Yankees and Frenchmen? What legends and beliefs placed in Old Sweden are retained by immigrants and continue to be transmitted to those born in America, and what changes occur in the process? Which of the old beliefs and legendary models can be transplanted into the new milieu and what happens to them after the transplantation? What new material is absorbed from Yankees and Frenchmen? The data for this study were obtained in New Sweden, Maine, in four fieldtrips during 1964-1967. Some general conclusions are drawn following a survey of New Sweden's history and of its culture in the 1960s, a discussion of the attitudes, lifestyles, and folklore repertoires of some 20 informants, and a detailed analysis of the folklore texts. The analyses are mainly sociopsychological in nature, and they employ comparative data culled from Swedish archives and collections.

233. Stevens, Robert L. Ole Edvart Rölvaag: A Critical Study of His Norwegian-American Novels. Illinois (Urbana), 1955. 340p. (DA 16:966)
O. E. Rölvaag's novels of Norwegian-immigrant life in America are distinguished by perceptive pictures of life on the frontier, by

penetrating character studies, and by a philosophy that was strongly influenced by Ibsen. Amerika Breve (1912), still untranslated into English, concerns the new immigrant in an established society. The view of life given here is that of an orthodox Christian. Lure Golden (1930), a version of To Tullinger (1920), is the story of two persons who have been isolated from Norwegian culture and have found no new culture to take its place. In this novel Rölvaag, consciously or unconsciously, drifted toward naturalism. The two principal characters are convincingly drawn. In The Boat of Longing (Norwegian version, 1912; English translation, 1933), which seems an inferior work in spite of certain poetic qualities, Rölvaag, with his distinction between fearless and timid characters, shows Ibsenian influences.

234. Swansen, Hans F. The Norse in Iowa to 1870. Iowa, 1938. 210p.

235. Swanson, Byron R. Conrad Bergendoff: The Making of an Ecumenist--A Study in Confessionalism and Ecumenism in Early Twentieth Century American Lutheranism. Princeton Theological Seminary, 1970. 417p. (DA 31:4259-A)
It is the purpose of this dissertation to study the relationship between confessionalism and ecumenism in early-twentieth-century American Lutheranism. Within this broader scope the particular emphasis focuses on this relationship as found in the Augustana Lutheran Church, a Synod of Swedish origin. During the second and third decades of the century American Lutherans were forced --often against their will--to answer a disquieting question. Was it possible for Lutherans to support the emerging ecumenical movement, and at the same time remain true to their confessional heritage? (A)

236. Thorson, Gerald H. America Is Not Norway: The Story of the Norwegian-American Novel. Columbia, 1957. 480p. (DA 18:1440)
Although the Norwegian-American novel has assumed characteristics of both Norwegian and American literature, its development stands as a distinct literary movement, growing out of the cultural and social consciousness of an immigrant group seeking its own identity in a foreign land. For this reason, although literary influences and critical standards are not neglected, "America Is Not Norway," in tracing the growth of the novel from its beginnings in 1874, emphasizes the relation of the novel to the life of the immigrant. The study is, therefore, cultural rather than purely aesthetic. (A)

237. Wefald, Jon M. From Peasant Ideals to the Reform State: A Study of Norwegian Attitudes Toward Reform in the American Middle West, 1890-1917. Michigan, 1965. 196p. (DA 27:430-A)
Published under the title A Voice of Protest: Norwegians in American Politics, 1890-1917 (Northfield, Minnesota: Norwegian-American Historical Association, 1971). Earlier studies have

argued that the American immigrants tend to cling to familiar, Old World customs and values, rejecting radical reform in America and distrusting the reformer's pleas for radical innovations in society for fear of disrupting the old social order. Although the Norwegian immigrants have been included in the stereotype of political conservatism, this study argues that the Norwegians became radical reformers in the era of Populism and Progressivism and that Norwegian peasant values and institutions furthered rather than limited Norwegian-American support for progressive reforms and the regulation of industrial-capitalism. (A)

238. Weintraub, Hyman. Andrew Furuseth, Emancipator of the Seamen. California (Los Angeles), 1957. 246p.
Published under the same title (Berkeley: University of California Press, 1959). Furuseth was a Norwegian immigrant.

239. Wheeler, Wayne L. An Analysis of Social Change in a Swedish-Immigrant Community: The Case of Lindsborg, Kansas. Missouri (Columbia), 1959. 387p. (DA 20:2950)
This dissertation is a study of the continuity in the development of the Swedish-immigrant community of Lindsborg, Kansas. The theoretical orientation is largely that derived from the concepts of communal and associational societies as they can be applied to social change. The method is that of the community study plus the application of an ex post facto perspective to ideal types, social structure, and latent and manifest functions. The data were gathered by such techniques and from such sources as official documents and reports, community histories, and interviews. (A)

240. White, George L. Scandinavian Themes in American Fiction. Pennsylvania, 1935. 241p.
Published under the same title (Philadelphia: University of Pennsylvania Press, 1937).

241. Whyman, Henry C. The Conflict and Adjustment of Two Religious Cultures--The Swedish and the American (As Found in the Swede's Relation to American Methodism). New York, 1937. 176p.

II. CENTRAL, SOUTHERN, AND EASTERN EUROPE

A. The Germanies and Austria-Hungary
B. Italy, Greece, and the Mediterranean Basin
C. Poland, Russia, the Balkans, and Slavic Europe
D. European Jewry

A. THE GERMANIES AND AUSTRIA-HUNGARY

242. Anderson, Richard J. The German Vote of Milwaukee in the 1860 Election. Chicago, 1969. 273p.

243. Baker, Louis C. The German Drama in English on the New York Stage to 1830. Pennsylvania, 1917. 168p.
Published under the same title (Philadelphia: University of Pennsylvania [Americana Germanica, No. 31], 1917). Covers the period since 1732, with attention to the dramatic works, productions, casts, performances, and critical receptions.

244. Balogh, Joseph K. An Analysis of Cultural Organizations of Hungarian-Americans in Pittsburgh and Allegheny County. Pittsburgh, 1946. 187p.

245. Bander, Carol J. The Reception of Exiled German Writers in the Nazi and Conservative German-Language Press of California: 1933-1950. Southern California, 1972. 371p.
The purpose of this dissertation is to establish the image of the writer exiled from the Third Reich in the Nazi and conservative German-language press of California. The Nazi press was represented by the California Weckruf; the conservative press, by three weekly newspapers, the Süd-California Deutsche Zeitung, the California Staats-Zeitung, the California Demokrat, and by one journal, Der Deutsch-Amerikaner. The reception of the exiled writer ranged from indifference to antagonism. In order to learn the reason for this attitude a study was made of the political and social conditions surrounding the press and its readers. The Third Reich, through the Reichsministerium für Volksaufklärung und Propaganda, had set up an elaborate system of news agencies and cultural, social, economic, and travel organizations that were to contribute to the materials found in the papers. A direct influence was exerted by some local German groups who tended to defend Nazi Germany. (A)

The Germanies, Austria-Hungary 61

246. Barba, Preston A. Friedrich Armand Strubberg: His Life and Works. Pennsylvania, 1911. 240p.
Published under the title The Life and Works of Friedrich Armand Strubberg (Philadelphia: University of Pennsylvania [Americana Germanica, No. 16], 1912).

247. Barry, Colman J. German Nationality and American Catholicism, 1865-1914. Catholic, 1952. 277p.
Published under the title The Catholic Church and German Americans (Milwaukee: Bruce, 1953). Intended as a detailed study of relationships between the Irish Catholic Church in America and German immigrants, with some notices of other immigrant Catholic groups. Special attention is paid to the movement for German national churches and the Irish hierarchical drive for Americanization.

248. Bauland, Peter M. German Drama on the American Stage: 1894-1961. Pennsylvania, 1964. 444p. (DA 25:2506)
Published under the title The Hooded Eagle: Modern Drama on the New York Stage (Syracuse, New York: University of Syracuse Press, 1968). This study examines the history of the German drama (including the Austrian and Swiss) in translation and adaptation on the New York stage from 1894 to 1961. It discusses the major movements of modern German drama, and it compares the important plays produced in English in New York with their German texts. There is a record of the critical, scholarly, and commercial reception of these plays and a consideration of their relationship to native American drama. An appendix lists pertinent available production information of all recorded plays of Germanic origin to appear in New York during the period studied. (A)

249. Bek, William G. The German Settlement Society of Philadelphia and Its Colony, Herman, Missouri. Pennsylvania, 1907. 104p.
Published under the same title (Philadelphia: University of Pennsylvania [Americana Germanica, No. 5], 1907).

250. Bell, Leland V. Anatomy of a Hate Movement: The German American Bund, 1936-1941. West Virginia, 1968. 281p. (DA 30:645-A)
A history of the Bund from its founding to its disorganization as the result of continued investigation by federal authorities. Analyzes the Bund's anti-Semitism and racial propaganda. Organized in March 1936 at a convention in Buffalo, New York, the Nazi-inspired German-American Bund began its short and stormy existence by seeking to unite the entire German-American community under its direction. The Bund had been preceded by numerous Nazi splinter groups and an organization known as the Friends of the New Germany. The chief distinction between the Bund and its predecessors was the requirement that only American citizens could hold leadership positions in the organization. The Bund also tried to be more circumspect in its relations with Nazi agencies in Germany. (A)

251. Bender, Jan E. Die getrennte Entwicklung gleichen niederdeutschen Sprachgutes in Deutschland und Nebraska [A Comparison of Two Low German Dialects with Their Colonial Derivatives in Nebraska]. Nebraska, 1970. 269p. (DA 31:5382-A)
The purpose of this study is to compare two Low German dialects with their corresponding derivatives in Nebraska. Most informants on both continents belong to the same two families, one speaking an Eastphalian, the other an Eastfrisian dialect. Since their separation almost 90 years ago, each branch has taken its course under a different linguistic environment. A major influence appears to have been the second language of the speakers, American English in Nebraska and High German in North Germany. (A)

252. Bender, Titus W. The Development of the Mennonite Mental Health Movement, 1942-1971. Tulane, 1976. 222p. (DA 37:3180-A)
The development of a social-service delivery system of a minority group is viewed here as being influenced by both the corresponding programs of the larger society and by the culture of the minority group. This historical study traced the blending of the underlying conceptual base and methodologies of mental-health-care programs in the United States with the culture and beliefs of the Mennonites in their emerging mental-health-care program from 1942-1971. A major purpose of this study was to cast some light on the nature and role of a social-service program of minority groups in contributing outward to the corresponding programs of the larger society and contributing inward by appropriating knowledge and expertise from the larger society's programs to develop its own program. (A)

253. Benjamin, Gilbert G. The Germans in Texas. Yale, 1907. 161p.
Published under the title The Germans in Texas: A Study in Immigration (Philadelphia: University of Pennsylvania Press, 1909). An overview of German settlement in Texas with emphasis on the cultural and economic life of immigrants.

254. Benkart, Paula K. Religion, Family, and Community Among Hungarians Migrating to American Cities, 1880-1930. Johns Hopkins, 1975. 255p. (DA 35:3080)
The Hungarian Government viewed the departure of its Magyar constituents with alarm but despaired of using political means to halt the socioeconomic momentum that the migration embodied. Instead, from 1903 until World War I successive Hungarian Prime Ministers supported an extensive program of American Action, which used financial inducements to gain control of Magyar churches, schools, and newspapers in the United States. The chief purpose of the plan was to keep alive the Magyar sojourners' intention to return to the homeland with their American earnings. In addition, Hungarian authorities designed the Action program to prevent American Magyar nationalists from championing

The Germanies, Austria-Hungary

the cause of Hungarian independence and threatening the political structure of the Austro-Hungarian Empire.

255. Bennion, Lowell C. Flight from the Reich: A Geographic Exposition of Southwest German Emigration, 1683-1815. Syracuse, 1971. 385p. (DA 32:5859-B)
The flight of some half-million persons from southwest Germany in the eighteenth century (1683-1815) constitutes a remarkable but neglected chapter in the annals of European emigration. Studies of it have focused on only one of its several destinations--Prussia, the Austrian Empire, Colonial America, or Russia--and on only a few of its manifold source regions. Consequently no panorama of the pattern of flight has appeared, and scholars have offered conflicting explanations of it. This dissertation draws primarily from secondary sources in a pilot attempt to reconstruct the changing geography of German emigration in relation to each receiving region and then for the Reich as a whole. The importance of this geographical-historical approach is increased by the relative lack of information on characteristics of the movers and stayers. Mapping and interpreting the distributions of emigrants at the time of their departure become the major means of determining why they moved--the ultimate aim of the thesis. (A)

256. Bergquist, James M. The Political Attitudes of the German Immigrant in Illinois, 1848-1860. Northwestern, 1966. 463p. (DA 27:2112-A)
As the most numerous immigrant group of pre-Civil War Illinois, the Germans were actively courted by politicians of all persuasions during a crucial period of political realignment. This afforded the immigrant group an unusual opportunity to affect developing party policies. This dissertation traces the Germans through the troubled politics of the 1850s in order to explain their political behavior and define their role in politics. (A)

257. Betz, Gottlieb A. Die Deutschamerikanische Patriotische Lyrik der Achtundvierziger und Ihre Historische Grundlage [The German American Patriotic Lyric Poetry of the Forty-Eighters and Its Historical Background]. Pennsylvania, 1913. 206p.
Published under the same title (Philadelphia: University of Pennsylvania [Americana Germanica, No. 22], 1916).

258. Beynon, Erdmann D. Occupational Adjustments of Hungarian Immigrants in an American Urban Community. Michigan, 1933. 184p.

259. Biesele, Rudolph L. The History of the German Settlements in Texas, 1831-1861. Texas (Austin), 1928. 259p.
Published under the same title (Austin: Press of Von Boeckmann-Jones, 1930). A history of the Society for the Protection of German Immigrants in Texas, with attention to political, social, and economic aspects of German settlement in Texas.

260. Bloomberg, Paula. Hermann Rauschning and the German Emigration. New Mexico, 1967. 154p. (DA 28:1365-A)
The life of Hermann Rauschning is a case study of the German neoconservatives of the post-World War I period who supported Hitler, and ultimately joined the National Socialist Party. Giving up all hope of influencing events in Germany or for Germany's advantage in England, Rauschning immigrated to the United States in 1941 and declared his intention to become an American citizen. He lived the war years in America trying to effect the change from a former National Socialist and expert on Hitler to a more normal role as a citizen in his new homeland. Nevertheless, Rauschning could not give up his involvement with Germany and continued to write and talk about Germany's fate in the postwar world. He became a violent opponent of German rearmament and in 1954 returned for a short time to Germany in a final, futile effort to influence events in his lost homeland.

261. Bole, John A. The Harmony Society, A Chapter of German-American Culture History. Pennsylvania, 1903. 176p.
Published under the title The Harmony Society: A Chapter in German-American Culture History (Philadelphia: University of Pennsylvania [Americana Germanica, No. 2], 1904). A basic study covering the Pennsylvania and Indiana histories of the Society from 1804-1868.

262. Brede, Charles F. The German Drama in English on the Philadelphia Stage from 1794 to 1830. Pennsylvania, 1917. 295p.
Published under the same title (University of Pennsylvania [Americana Germanica, No. 34], 1918).

263. Cazden, Robert E. The Free German and Free Austrian Press and Booktrade in the United States, 1933-1950, in the Context of German-American History. Chicago, 1965. 250p.
Published under the title German Exile Literature in America, 1933-1950: A History of the Free German Press and Book Trade (Chicago: American Library Association, 1970). The literary activities in the United States of exiles from Germany, Austria, and Czechoslovakia who used the German language as a vehicle of communication. A substantial part of the work consists of a detailed historical overview covering two decades up to 1954. The focus is on the various types of periodical publications reflecting the complicated political, national, and religious alignments of the group. Aspects of book publishing, the import trade, and the plight of émigré authors are also examined.

264. Conzen, Kathleen. "The German Athens": Milwaukee and the Accommodation of Its Immigrants, 1836-1860. Wisconsin, 1972. 596p. (DA 33:6834-A)
Published under the title Immigrant Milwaukee, 1836-1860 (Cambridge, Massachusetts: Harvard University Press, 1979). Within ten years of its 1836 founding immigrants constituted a majority of Milwaukee's population; by 1860 Germans alone headed over

half its households. Given such numerical dominance in a new and not-yet-industrialized city of the mid-nineteenth-century frontier, what kind of initial accommodation could be expected of a relatively skilled immigrant population, such as the Germans? This study hypothesizes that Milwaukee's frontier situation, as well as the size, character, and timing of its German immigration, would have permitted the development of a particularly independent ethnic community in the first generation of immigrant settlement. Such a community would then in theory ease the adjustment trauma and economic integration of its individual members while encouraging only limited acculturation and minimal structural assimilation into any kind of "American" life--a situation in which the Germans were neither ghetto residents in the classic sense of the term nor yet participants in a melting-pot society. (A)

265. Damm, John S. The Growth and Decline of Lutheran Parochial Schools in the United States, 1638-1962. Columbia (Teachers College), 1963. 371p. (DA 24:2796)
This project is concerned with the growth and decline of the two major parochial-school movements within the Lutheran Church in the United States. The first movement began in the earliest colonial days and was carried on in the eastern colonies and states by several regional Lutheran synods and reached the high point of development in 1830, after which it declined steadily and ceased altogether by 1890. The second movement began with the arrival of the Saxon Lutherans in Missouri in 1839 and the formation of the Missouri Synod in 1847. The Missouri Synod school system flourished and continues to the present day. This project attempts to ascertain just why the schools of the older Lutheran bodies declined during the very decades of the nineteenth century when the Missouri Synod was active in establishing schools. The factors that contributed to the school's growth and decline are discussed and viewed against the larger background of the doctrinal issues at stake in these two Lutheran groups. (A)

266. Dapp, Charles F. John Henry Miller, German Printer, Journalist and Patriot. Pennsylvania, 1913. 240p.
Published under the same title (Philadelphia: Pennsylvania German Society [Vol. 32], 1924).

267. Dimock, Alice B. Organization Study of Moravian Churches in the New York City Metropolitan Area. Columbia, 1969. 391p. (DA 30:4559-A)
This study attempts to relate the present condition of 12 Moravian congregations in or near New York City to the denomination's history. The Moravian Church in America derives from a colony of refugees from religious persecution at Herrnhut in Saxony. Herrnhut became the first of the Moravian settlement congregations, which integrated church, civic, and economic life. Other social experiments initiated there were organized foreign-mission work and the Moravian "Diaspora" societies (Pietist conventicles within the European state churches). (A)

268. Dobbert, Guido A. The Disintegration of an Immigrant Community: The Cincinnati Germans, 1870-1920. Chicago, 1965. 447p.
Published under the same title (New York: Arno, 1980). The scope of this investigation initially was to have been limited to a study of the German community in Cincinnati during World War I, for it was begun with the assumption that American nativism of the World War I era had destroyed or at least given the coup de grace to German culture in America. As it soon turned out, the German community, at least in Cincinnati, was moribund before the war had even begun in Europe. Therefore, if it died during the war, its death was of its own making; the war served only to heighten its agony. In this sense, nativism, upon reaching its full strength at the war's end, had found only a dead or dying horse to flog. Further, should one think in terms of nativism applying the coup de grace with Prohibition and influenza as its accessories, it should be seriously questioned whether it was not really the other way around. In the case of Cincinnati decay was manifested primarily by two major symptoms: one physical, the other sociopsychological, with, of course, considerable interaction. The community's physical disintegration showed itself not only biologically in the decrease of new blood coming from Germany, but also geographically in its members being spread increasingly thin over an ever-expanding metropolitan area.

269. Dollin, Norman. The Schwenkfelders in Eighteenth Century America. Columbia, 1971. 209p. (DA 32:3182-A)
Part I of this two-part dissertation begins with a sketch of the theology of Caspar Schwenkfeld von Ossig (1489-1561). Schwenkfeld's pietism was elaborated as a result of his disappointment with the Reformation. He felt that Luther had betrayed Protestantism by: (1) retaining unchanged the sacraments of baptism and the Lord's Supper, (2) accepting the coercive power of the State for the maintenance of the Lutheran Reform, and (3) overobjectifying Christian faith, thereby entering into a theology of biblical legalism and literalism contrary to the spirit of Christ. Chapters III-IV deal with the arrival and settlement of the Schwenkfelders in Pennsylvania and the efforts of the leadership to maintain a Christian nucleus without violating Schwenkfeld's theology, especially his warning against erecting an ecclesiastical superstructure. (A)

270. Donnelly, Dale J. The Low German Dialect of Sauk County, Wisconsin: Phonology and Morphology. Wisconsin, 1969. 158p. (DA 31:754-A)
This study is a descriptive analysis of the Low German dialect currently spoken in parts of northern Sauk County, Wisconsin. The dialect originated near Uelzen, Germany, and is therefore basically an Eastphalian dialect with many North Saxon features. (A)

271. Drummond, Robert R. Early German Music in Philadelphia. Pennsylvania, 1909. 88p.

Published under the same title (Philadelphia: University of Pennsylvania [Americana Germanica, No. 9], 1910). This narrative history, based on contemporary sources and relying mainly on information found in newspapers, places the emphasis on secular music. The discussion is divided into three sections. The first chapter deals with church music and secular music before 1750. Chapter Two, entitled "The Period of Progress" (1750-83), discusses concert music, music education, music publishing, and distribution. The third chapter, "Period of Greatest Development," focuses on Alexander Reinagle, Philip Roth, and Philip Phile. The appendix includes programs of concerts in 1791, and a chronological list of the compositions of Alexander Reinagle.

272. Easum, Chester V. The Americanization of Carl Schurz. Wisconsin, 1928. 224p.
Published under the same title (Chicago: University of Chicago Press, 1929). A detailed portrait of the leading figure among German immigrants of the mid-nineteenth century, with particular focus on Schurz's first ten years in the United States.

273. Eller, David B. The Brethren in the Western Ohio Valley, 1790-1850: German Baptist Settlement and Frontier Accommodation. Miami, 1976. 250p. (DA 37:3087)
This study describes the settlement and frontier accommodation of German Baptist Brethren (Dunkers) in three geographic areas of the western Ohio Valley. These areas are the Green River country in western Kentucky, Union County in southern Illinois, and along the White River in Orange and Lawrence counties, Indiana. The congregations formed in these areas may be considered representative of Brethren activity in the western Ohio Valley between 1790 and 1850. The Dunkers were a Pietist and Anabaptist background sect whose trans-Allegheny frontier experience has not been adequately studied, for its impact either on the Brethren in the later nineteenth century or on wider Protestant development. Because the Brethren left few church records, extensive use has been made of various federal, state, and county records to plot migration patterns and congregational activity. (A)

274. Eller, Paul H. Revivalism and the German Churches in Pennsylvania, 1783-1816. Chicago, 1933. 168p.
Published under the same title (Chicago: University of Chicago Press, 1935).

275. Engerrand, George C. M. The So-Called Wends of Germany and Their Colonies in Texas and in Australia. Texas, 1935. 276p.
Published under the same title (San Francisco: R & E Research Associates, 1972). An overview of Slavic colonies from Germany in Texas from 1850 to 1900.

276. Everest, Kate A. German Immigration into Wisconsin. Wisconsin, 1893. 104p.

The dissertation's major text is published as "Geographical Origins of German Immigration to Wisconsin. " State Historical Society of Wisconsin. Collections 14 (1898): 341-393.

277.   Falconer, Joan Ormsby. Bishop Johannes Herbst (1735-1812), an American-Moravian Musician, Collector, and Composer. Columbia, 1969. 564p. (DA 32:6475-A)
One of the primary sources for Moravian music studies is the collection of manuscripts assembled by the German-born Moravian Johannes Herbst, both before and after he emigrated to this country in 1786. The present study provides a guide to this collection and also undertakes an analysis of Herbst's own compositional style. Photographs of 33 of his "geistliche Lieder" are included in the text, while a supplementary volume contains the scores of 21 anthems. (A)

278.   Fogel, Edwin M. Superstitions of the Pennsylvania Germans. Pennsylvania, 1907. 387p.
Published under the title Beliefs and Superstitions of the Pennsylvania Germans (Philadelphia: University of Pennsylvania [Americana Germanica, No. 18], 1915). A compilation of more than 2, 000 sayings reflecting the beliefs and superstitions of Pennsylvania Germans, collected from oral sources. The sayings are given in the vernacular with their English translation and also in their original German version. The grouping of the sayings is by topic; they are applied to such subjects as marriage, dreams, childhood, omens, cooking, trees, the moon, the weather, and others. Pronunciation is indicated.

279.   Fortenbaugh, Robert. The Development of the Synodical Polity of the Lutheran Church in America, to 1829. Pennsylvania, 1926. 141p.

280.   Fox, Harry C. German Presbyterianism in the Upper Mississippi Valley. Iowa, 1941. 137p.
Published under the same title (Ypsilanti, Michigan: University Lithoprinters, 1942).

281.   Frey, John W. The German Dialect of Eastern York County, Pennsylvania. Illinois, 1942. 140p.
Published under the title A Simple Grammar of Pennsylvania Dutch (Clinton, South Carolina: Frey, 1942).

282.   Garner, Joel P. The Vision of a Liturgical Reformer: Hans Ansgar Reinhold, American Catholic Educator. Columbia (Teachers College), 1972. 321p. (DA 33:6195-A)
The son of a prominent Hamburg Catholic, a veteran of over four years as a German soldier in the First World War, a dedicated Seamen's Chaplain, one of the initial organizers of the International Apostolate of the Sea, and a priest forced to flee his homeland under Gestapo pressure in 1935, Hans Ansgar Reinhold came to America to spend the remainder of his life and to play a leadership role in the American Catholic liturgical movement. This

study investigates Reinhold's vision as liturgical educator and popularizer within the American liturgical movement from 1936 until his death in 1968. (A)

283. Gaspar, Steven. Four Nineteenth-Century Hungarian Travelers in America. Southern California, 1967. 540p. (DA 27:3810-A)
The New World, specifically the United States, has had a great and continuous effect on the continent of Europe and its peoples. In the text the visits to and the life in the United States of four Hungarian travelers are discussed. All four made their journeys between 1830 and 1880. (A)

284. Gelzer, David G. Mission to America: Being a History of the Work of the Basel Foreign Missions Society in America. Yale, 1952. 390p. (DA 28:3253-A)
The occasion of the Basel Mission's work in America was provided by religiously destitute German immigrants who appealed for ministers to serve among them. In conformity with its principle the Basel Mission, having accepted this challenge, aimed at extending the Christian Gospel and not at transplanting German traits and mores upon American soil. It differed, therefore, from some German missionary efforts in the New World that were directed toward the preservation of the racial ties with the German nation. (A)

285. Gilbert, Glenn G. The German Dialect Spoken in Kendall and Gillespie Counties, Texas. Harvard, 1963. 163p.

286. Glatfelter, Charles H. The Colonial Pennsylvania German Lutheran and Reformed Clergyman. Johns Hopkins, 1952. 301p.

287. Gleason, John P. The Control-Verein, 1900-1917: A Chapter in the History of the German-American Catholics. Notre Dame, 1960. 422p. (DA 21:1540)
Published under the title The Conservative Reformers: German-American Catholics and the Social Order (Notre Dame: Notre Dame University Press, 1968). The German Roman Catholic Central-Verein was founded in 1855 and still exists at the present time. Its organization began as a national federation of local benevolent societies; at first it confined its activities closely to mutual insurance, but gradually broadened its interest to include education and other matters affecting the German American Catholic population. In the 1880s and 1890s the Central-Verein became involved in controversies with the American Catholic Church and developed attitudes that persisted into the twentieth century. (A)

288. Gollin, Gillian G. Communal Pietism and the Secular Drift: A Comparative Study of Social Change in the Moravian Communities of Bethlehem, Pennsylvania and Herrnhut, Saxony in the Eighteenth and Nineteenth Centuries. Columbia, 1965.

634p. (DA 27:3677-A)
This study of two communities founded by the Moravian Brethren in the eighteenth century seeks to describe the changes in their institutions of religion, the family, the economy and the polity, 1722-1850; to compare strategic differences in the dynamics of these social changes; and to analyze the principal determinants of social change in the two settlements. (A)

289. Good, William A. A History of the General Council of the Evangelical Lutheran Church in North America. Yale, 1967. 326p. (DA 28:4251-A)
The General Council of the Evangelical Lutheran Church in North America, of which this dissertation is a history, existed from 1867 until it merged with two other Lutheran bodies to form the United Lutheran Church in America in 1918. Origins of the General Council are related to a large extent to the confessional issue among some of America's Lutherans, and particularly to the involvement of the Ministerium of Pennsylvania in that issue. Some Lutherans had been advocating an accommodation of the sixteenth-century Lutheran Confessions to the nineteenth-century American scene. Others believed that the only churches justified in using the name "Lutheran" were those that subscribed to the doctrines of the Reformation as they were originally given. (A)

290. Graebner, Alan N. The Acculturation of an Immigration Church: The Lutheran Church--Missouri Synod, 1917-1929. Columbia, 1965. 398p. (DA 26:3263)
The Lutheran Church--Missouri Synod is a conservative Lutheran denomination organized by German immigrants in 1847. It grew to be the largest of the original immigrant Lutheran groups, expanding from the Midwest to both coasts. The Synod retained, however, both a remarkably monolithic structure and a distinctly German character well into the twentieth century. By the First World War German was still the language of most worship services and religious instruction. Such usage indicated the general lack of Americanization within the Synod. The Missouri Synod was not completely Americanized by 1929, but it had changed remarkably since 1917, and gave every indication of having established the base for future growth among American, rather than immigrant, denominations. (A)

291. Grenke, A. The Formation and Early Development of an Urban Ethnic Community: A Case Study of the Germans in Winnipeg, 1872-1919. Manitoba, 1975. 282p.

292. Groen, Henry J. A History of the German-American Newspapers of Cincinnati Before 1860. Ohio State, 1945. 230p.

293. Haney, James L. The Religious Heritage and Education of Samuel Simon Schmucker: A Study in the Rise of "American Lutheranism." Yale, 1968. 519p. (DA 29:666-A)
An introduction to the life and work of Samuel Simon Schmucker (1799-1873) explains the importance of a study of his religious

heritage and education. Schmucker's own knowledge of his heritage provides an outline for an examination of four aspects of its development: German Lutheran Pietism and the men American Lutherans regarded as church "fathers"; the thought of a group of late-seventeenth-century radical Pietists who initially shaped his heritage in America; the religious thought and influence of Henry Melchior Muhlenberg; and the work of three men who led the American church after Muhlenberg's death and who mediated the theological content and character of what had become a tradition to Schmucker. (A)

294. Haug, Hans R. The Predestination Controversy in the Lutheran Church in North America. Temple, 1968. 977p. (DA 29:1282-A)
Through the centuries many a controversy has erupted over the problem of predestination. In the 1870s and especially 1880s a fiercely fought predestination controversy raged in the Lutheran synods in America that lasted into the 1930s. Although it was limited to the Lutheran Church, the controversy spread to Germany, Australia, and New Zealand. In the main it was a conflict between the Missouri Synod under the leadership of C. F. W. Walther on the one hand and Gottfried Fritschel of the Iowa Synod, F. A. Schmidt of the Norwegian Synod, and Matthias Loy and Friedrich W. Stellhorn of the Joint Synod of Ohio on the other. (A)

295. Haussman, Carl F. Kunze's Seminarium and the Society for the Propagation of Christianity and Useful Knowledge Among the Germans in America. Pennsylvania, 1916. 160p.
Published under the same title (Philadelphia: University of Pennsylvania [Americana Germanica, No. 27], 1917).

296. Haussmann, William A. German-American Hymnology, 1683-1800. Johns Hopkins, 1895. 124p.

297. Head, Violet. The 1956 Hungarians: Their Integration into an Urban Community. Chicago, 1963. 241p.

298. Heckman, Samuel B. The Poetry of the Dunker Bishop Alexander Mack. Pennsylvania, 1906. 87p.

299. Helling, Rudolf A. A Comparison of the Acculturation of Immigrants in Toronto, Ontario, and Detroit, Michigan. Wayne State, 1962. 282p. (DA 28:4730-A)
The research investigates the acculturation of German immigrants into two cultural systems, the U.S. American and the Canadian. By using the same ethnic minority under the influence of two environments, it attempts to measure the influences of the host cultures on the immigrant. The methodology of the study is an experimental design using the effect-to-cause ex post facto approach. The control sample consists of 50 German residents of Wilhelmshaven, Germany. The experimental groups are German-immigrant residents in Toronto and Detroit. (A)

300. Hirst, David W. German Propaganda in the United States, 1914-1917. Northwestern, 1962. 281p. (DA 23:3334)
In this study of German propaganda the author has identified the leading propagandists and their associates, has described various operations at propaganda headquarters in New York, and has examined the agencies and organizations utilized by the propagandists in their campaigns. Further, he has selected a number of more important issues and events and has analyzed German propaganda as it appeared in newspapers, periodicals, books, and pamphlets. (A)

301. Huber, Donald L. The Controversy over Pulpit and Altar Fellowship in the General Council of the Evangelical Lutheran Church, 1866-1889. Duke, 1971. 311p. (DA 32:5333-A)
The dissertation seeks to ascertain why the General Council, a federation of confessionally conservative Lutheran synods, argued for more than 20 years over the question of whether to admit non-Lutherans to Lutheran celebrations of the Lord's Supper, or to admit non-Lutheran pastors to preach and administer the sacraments in Lutheran churches. It also seeks to ascertain what the theological and institutional results of the controversy were, both for the General Council and for American Lutheranism as a whole. (A)

302. Iverson, Noel. Germania, U.S.A.: The Dynamics of Change of an Ethnic Community into a Status Community. Minnesota, 1964. 245p. (DA 25:2093)
Published under the title Germania, U.S.A.: Social Change in New Ulm, Minnesota (Minneapolis: University of Minnesota Press, 1966). The social and cultural history of the United States has been made by immigrants. Each wave of immigrants set into motion forces that led to the formation of ethnic communities on American soil. The present study examines the experiences of one group of German-Americans who, in the mid-nineteenth century, founded a semi-utopian trading and agricultural center at the edge of the frontier in south-central Minnesota. (A)

303. Johnson, Niel M. George Sylvester Viereck: Pro-German Publicist in America, 1910-1945. Iowa, 1971. 409p. (DA 32:1443-A)
Published under the title George Sylvester Viereck, German-American Propagandist (Urbana: University of Illinois Press, 1972). George Sylvester Viereck was a many-sided figure who gained considerable public attention, first as a sensuous poet of the progressive period, and then, beginning in 1914, as an eloquent apologist and publicist for the policies of the German government. During the interwar period he became a recognized novelist and peripatetic journalist and historian, but with the rise of the Nazi regime in the 1930s he again took up the propaganda battle and exhibited his dual loyalties. He refused, on the one hand, to join any of the neo-Nazi organizations in America, and, presenting himself as a loyal American devoted to keeping Amer-

ica out of European or Asian entanglements, he helped to research and ghost-write speeches for several anti-interventionist members of Congress. He worked, on the other hand, for two German-based agencies, writing and editing pro-German literature and offering judgments of American public opinion. The federal government finally found the means to muzzle and punish him. In late 1941 it charged him with providing incomplete and misleading information on the forms required by the Foreign-Agent Registration Act of 1938. He went to trial a few weeks after the bombing of Pearl Harbor and was convicted. The Supreme Court a year later reversed the conviction, but he was retried and convicted again. These events effectively ended his career as a pro-German propagandist. This dissertation concentrates upon Viereck's career as America's outstanding spokesman for German nationalism and as an advocate of isolationist policies in the United States. (A)

304. Jordahl, Leigh Donald. The Wauwatosa Theology, John Philip Koehler, and the Theological Tradition of Midwestern American Lutheranism, 1900-1930. Iowa, 1964. 351p. (DA 25:2635)
This dissertation represents an examination within the historical context of the Wauwatosa Theology and concentrates especially upon the work of the most able of the three Wauwatosa men, John Philip Koehler. Special attention has been given to the three significant aspects of Koehler's approach: his biblical hermeneutics, his historical emphasis, and his criticism of the American Lutheran situation. (A)

305. Jordan, Arthur C. On the German Language in Colonial, Secular, Prose Documents from Philadelphia and Germantown. Pennsylvania, 1916. 107p.

306. Jordan, Terry G. A Geographic Appraisal of the Significance of German Settlement in Nineteenth Century Texas Agriculture. Wisconsin, 1965. 356p. (DA 26:5364)
Published under the title German Seed in Texas Soil: Immigrant Farmers in Nineteenth-Century Texas (Austin: University of Texas Press, 1966). The study revealed many striking similarities between the farming systems established by the Germans and the southerners, as well as some clear differences. Certain European practices were successfully transplanted to the new homeland. In the more subtle aspects of farming--intensity, productivity, locational stability, and land tenure--major and persistent differences were detected. The Germans put more into the land in terms of labor and capital, got more out of it in value of production, and were more likely to own their land than the native southerners. In addition, the Germans devoted more attention to small grains, white potatoes, market gardening, tobacco, and wine-making than did the southerners, and they were less likely to own slaves. (A)

307. Juhnke, James C. The Political Acculturation of the Kansas Mennonites, 1870-1940. Indiana, 1968. 299p. (DA 29:1495-A)

The Mennonites who were brought to central Kansas by the railroads in the 1870s inherited a dualistic Anabaptist conception of the church and world that discouraged political involvement and forbade participation in warfare. Statistics of voting, naturalization, and office-holding show that many Mennonites avoided political involvement through 1940, but also that a minority was involved in politics from the beginning in party votes not widely divergent from a non-Mennonite norm. Most of the central Kansas Mennonites emigrated from Russia or Europe in search of isolation and cultural autonomy, but they settled without guarantees of the preconditions of a closed settlement and exemption from national military service. Their trust in America was rewarded through the assistance of the railroads, the growth of prosperous farming communities, and an extended period of national peace, which postponed the potentially disruptive question of military conscription. (A)

308. Kallassay, Louis A. The Educational and Religious History of the Hungarian Reformed Church in the United States. Pittsburgh, 1939. 204p.

309. Kamman, William F. Socialism in German-American Literature. Pennsylvania, 1917. 124p.
Published under the same title (Philadelphia: University of Pennsylvania [Americana Germanica, No. 24], 1917). The study deals with ideas, the literary vehicles through which they were disseminated, authors, and organizations, such as the Freie Gemeinden and the liberal athletic groups. The impact of socialistic ideas on German-American literature is explored in depth and is interpreted as a revolt of rationalistic thought against revealed religion. The material was drawn mainly from German-language works.

310. Keim, Jeannette. Forty Years of German-American Political Relations. Pennsylvania, 1919. 141p.

311. Keller, Phyllis. German-America and the First World War. Pennsylvania, 1969. 489p. (DA 30:4896-A)
This examination of the experience of German-Americans during World War I moves from the most general considerations to the most particular; from a description of the political circumstances and social conditions that shaped their time of crisis, to a study of the ways in which it was perceived within the German-American community, and finally to an exploration of the responses of unusually sensitive individual German-Americans. (A)

312. Kelso, Thomas J. The German-American Vote in the Election of 1860: The Case of Indiana with Supporting Data from Ohio. Ball State, 1967. 213p. (DA 28:4226-A)
This study was conducted to test the traditional thesis that in the states of the former Northwest Territory German-Americans voted overwhelmingly for Abraham Lincoln in 1860. Census data and election returns were employed from Indiana and Ohio, plus a variety of nonempirical data from Indiana. (A)

313. Kent, Donald P. The Refugee Intellectual. Pennsylvania, 1950. 317p.
Published under the title Refugee Intellectual: The Americanization of the Immigrants of 1933-1941 (New York: Columbia University Press, 1953). This study examines the social experiences of the intellectuals who emigrated to the United States from Germany and Austria from 1933-1941. The material is drawn largely from questionnaires and interviews with the refugees themselves.

314. Knauss, James O. Social Conditions Among the Pennsylvania Germans in the Eighteenth Century, as Revealed in German Newspapers Published in America. Cornell, 1918. 217p.
Published under the same title (Lancaster: Pennsylvania German Society, 1922). Includes (1) a descriptive analysis of Pennsylvania German newspapers, and (2) social analysis of their readers. The history and characteristics of the newspapers and their publishers are described; and the religious aspects, charities and humanitarian organizations, education, language, occupational distribution, and political ideas and aspirations are explored. Includes a checklist of German-language newspapers of the eighteenth century, and the U.S. libraries holding them.

315. Knoche, Carl H. The German Immigrant Press in Milwaukee. Ohio State, 1969. 302p. (DA 30:2926-A)
The goal of this dissertation was to present an introductory study of the publications that influenced the German immigrant. An attempt had to be made to give life and meaning to the statistical data already published in newspaper catalogs. Special attention was paid to the function of the publications within the community, and to this end an effort was made to determine why a particular paper came into being and why it eventually failed; whether a paper was related to another publication either by ownership or ideological program, and whether the individual papers were successful in maintaining their original policies or ideals. Wherever possible information on the editors and owners was included. It was also necessary to include a skeletal view of the German community in which these papers played so large a role. (A)

316. Koch, John B. Relations Between the Lutheran Church-- Missouri Synod and the Evangelical Church of Australia, 1846-1965. Concordia Seminary, 1968. 273p.

317. Koenning, Alton R. Henkel Press: A Force for Conservative Lutheran Theology in Pre-Civil War Southeastern America. Duke, 1972. 266p. (DA 33:5818-A)
The present study seeks to examine the role of the printery founded and operated in New Market, Virginia, by Paul Henkel and his descendants, as a theological influence upon the Lutherans in Virginia, North Carolina, South Carolina, and Tennessee of pre-Civil War America. The means of determining the nature of the theological identity that Henkel Press sought to develop among Lutherans in the southeastern states is the examination of

the intent, character, and influence of the publications of the printery in the context of the emerging Lutheran synods of the period. The North Carolina Synod and the Tennessee Synod receive special consideration, because of the close association of the Henkels with these bodies. (A)

318. Komjathy, Aladar. The Hungarian Reformed Church in America: An Effort to Preserve a Denominational Heritage. Princeton Theological Seminary, 1962. 336p. (DA 24:3863)
The Hungarian Reformed Church in America is the only autonomous Hungarian Reformed denomination in the United States, but the majority of Hungarian Reformed congregations in America are affiliated with other denominational bodies. All these churches originated from the Reformed Church of Hungary, one of the oldest and largest church bodies of Calvinistic Reformation in Europe, which preserved its unity since Reformation times without schisms and church divisions. This study attempted to examine the reasons why Hungarian Reformed churches divided in the United States and why only a minority of these churches decided for its own denominational organization. (A)

319. Kraybill, Donald B. Ethnic Socialization in a Mennonite High School. Temple, 1976. 234p. (DA 36:8312-A)
The purpose of the study was to determine the impact of Lancaster, Pennsylvania, Mennonite High School on the attitudes of junior and senior students along the following dimensions: Religious Orthodoxy, Ethnic Identity, Ethnic Ritual, and Avoidance of Normative American behaviors. The sample consisted of three groups varying in their degree of socialization in the ethnic school culture. Ethnics (N = 228) had attended the Mennonite school prior to the study and continued there during the study. Transfers (N = 64) were Mennonite students who transferred from public schools to the ethnic school at the beginning of the school year. Publics (N = 102) were a control group of Mennonite students who attended seven public high schools. (A)

320. Kremling, Helmut J. German Drama on the Cleveland Stage: Performances in German and English from 1850 to the Present. Ohio State, 1976. 213p. (DA 37:2909-A)
Concentrating on the historical periods, the varying audiences, the criticism in the press, and the actors, the first five chapters of this study trace the history of Cleveland's German-language theater from its beginnings in the 1850s to its sudden and unnecessary demise in 1904. The concluding part of the study deals with German drama in translation, as performed in Cleveland since the First World War. Had it not been for the Cleveland Playhouse, one of the first and best-known Little Theaters in the United States, and to a lesser extent for Karamu House, a neighborhood recreational center famous for its interracial theater, only a handful of German plays would have been presented in Cleveland in the past 60 years. Road shows featuring German plays from New York were rare, since much of modern German drama is not popular entertainment. (A)

The Germanies, Austria-Hungary 77

321. Lasby, Clarence G. German Scientists in America: Their Importation, Exploitation and Assimilation, 1945-1952. California (Los Angeles), 1962. 386p.
Published under the title Project Paperclip: German Scientists and the Cold War (New York: Free Press, 1971.)

322. Leuchs, Frederick A. H. The Early German Theatre in New York, 1840-1872. Columbia, 1928. 298p.
Published under the same title (New York: Columbia University Press, 1928). A study in cultural history focusing on the medium of the German theater in New York City. Chapters are devoted to the seasons and productions of the city's main German-language stages, the plays, playwrights, actors, and drama criticism in contemporary periodicals. Includes appendixes that list halls and theaters in New York City used for German-language productions (1840-48), plays produced in German (1840-48), amateur theaters, a roster of the staff of the Altes and Neues Stadttheater, a nearly complete list of plays produced between 1854 and 1872, and a chronological listing of German-American periodicals that regularly carried critical reviews.

323. Lewis, Orlando F. History of German Drama in Philadelphia. Pennsylvania, 1900. 105p.

324. Liemohn, Edwin T. The Lutheran Chorale as a Congregational Hymn. Union Theological Seminary, 1945. 245p.

325. Luebke, Frederick C. The Political Behavior of an Immigrant Group: The Germans of Nebraska, 1880-1900. Nebraska, 1966. 389p. (DA 27:3402-A)
Published under the title Immigrants and Politics: The Germans of Nebraska, 1880-1900 (Lincoln: University of Nebraska Press, 1969). The purpose of this study is to reveal the nature and quality of the political acculturation achieved by the German immigrant group in Nebraska during the last two decades of the nineteenth century. Largely a lower-middle-class people, the Germans formed a significant part of Nebraska's population ever since territorial organization. The majority were farmers, although artisans and shopkeepers were also common among them. Mostly Protestant in religion, they often settled in rural ethno-religious ghettos where the pressures to conform to group standards were strong and where opportunities for interpersonal contacts with native Americans were minimal. (A)

326. MacArthur, Mildred S. The German Element in Colorado. Cornell, 1914. 51p.
Published under the same title (San Francisco: R & E Research Associates, 1972). An introductory work giving an overview of German-Americans in Colorado. It stresses German contributions to the development of the economy of the state with a discussion of their role in religion, education, and politics. It is the author's view that although the German element in Colorado is proportionally smaller than in states like Pennsylvania, Mary-

land, and Wisconsin, their influence was pervasive. The work was based on local archival sources, supplemented by the author's personal observations, correspondences, surveys, and interviews. The work also includes information on local German institutions and organizations. A list enumerates German-American officeholders in local government from 1864 to 1876.

327. Major, Mark I. American Hungarian Relations: 1918-1944. Texas Christian, 1972. 373p. (DA 33:2295-A)
The purpose of this study is to point out how the United States was involved in Hungarian affairs between the world wars. In keeping with this final intention, however, it was necessary, for the sake of better understanding, to give some details of Hungary's foreign policy in general and to elaborate on her internal problems. The key to the understanding of Hungarian history during this period is Hungary's attitude toward the Treaty of Trianon. The chief aspiration of Hungarian foreign policy was the desire for revision of this treaty. The Treaty of Trianon, imposed on Hungary at the close of World War I, effectually destroyed the historic Hungarian state. (A)

328. Marquardt, Carl E. The German Drama on the New York Stage, 1840-72. Pennsylvania, 1915. 201p.

329. Martens, Hedda. Language Attitudes of German Immigrants and Their Families As Observed in Rochester, N.Y. Rochester, 1972. 198p. (DA 32:2356-A)
This is a descriptive study of the linguistic behavior of German immigrants and their families who have settled in Rochester, New York, covering approximately the period from 1850 to 1970. The attitudes of the World War II immigrants are compared with those who settled here in the 1850s as well as in the 1950s, with focus on maintenance of German acquisition of English.

330. Massman, John C. German Immigration to Minnesota, 1850-1890. Minnesota, 1966. 270p. (DA 28:3117-A)
This study reviews the causes of emigration and government attitudes, with emphasis on their interrelationship to fluctuations in German emigration. It deals intensively with the promotional efforts and techniques utilized by settlers, missionaries, colonization groups, Minnesota's government, and railroads to attract German settlers to Minnesota. Attention also is focused on the hazards encountered and the efforts to protect the immigrants on their journey from Europe to Minnesota. The final chapters analyze the growth of German settlement in Minnesota, their ratio to the total population and to other national groups, and distribution patterns. German social, religious, and educational activities are discussed briefly in terms of their influence on the problems of population growth and distribution patterns. (A)

331. Mavelshagen, Carl. The Effect of German Immigration upon the Lutheran Church in America, 1820-1870. Minnesota, 1935. 243p.

332. McCord, Stanley J. A Historical and Linguistic Study of
the German Settlement at Roberts Cove, Louisiana. Louisiana State, 1969. 301p. (DA 30:3017-A)
This study was undertaken to trace the history of the German settlement established at Roberts Cove in Acadia Parish, Louisiana, in 1881 and to investigate the Low German dialect in use there. It has been shown in this study that the continued observance of German customs and the continued use of the German language gave the Roberts Cove community a unique place in the history of German immigration into Louisiana, since no other German community maintained these elements of German culture for so long without the support of continuing immigration. (A)

333. Metraux, Guy S. Social and Cultural Aspects of Swiss Emigration into the United States in the Nineteenth Century. Yale, 1949. 369p. (DA 25:3540)
Swiss emigration in the nineteenth century was one of the consequences of the economic changes that took place in Switzerland as a result of industrial and agricultural crises. It was not provoked by political or religious persecutions. Swiss emigrants came to the United States in larger numbers than to other countries. Availability of land and opportunities for work in industry were the main attractions. It was, however, a relatively small immigration movement. Swiss immigrants were farmers, skilled workers, tradesmen, and, in some cases, members of the liberal professions. Until the late 1870s it was largely a family immigration. The educational level of immigrants was relatively high. (A)

334. Meyer, Luciana R. German-American Migration and the Bancroft Naturalization Treaties, 1868-1910. City University of New York, 1970. 299p. (DA 31:1731-A)
The Bancroft naturalization treaties were a group of related agreements between the United States and the five German states (North German Confederation, Bavaria, Baden, Württemberg, and Hesse) that subsequently united to form the German Reich. No single unifying treaty between the United States and the Reich was ever negotiated, nor was any agreement ever reached that would have formally extended the provisions of the original treaties to Alsace-Lorraine, the territory annexed to the Reich after its formation. The dissertation sketches the historical background of these naturalization treaties in an attempt to demonstrate the peculiar and transitory circumstances that led both the United States and the original German partner states to sign the agreements in the first place. In doing so it attempts to bring out the defects of loose phraseology and lack of consistency in the treaties that resulted from over-eagerness to reach early agreement and that were to be a constant source of difficulty in later treaty administration. (A)

335. Moehlenbrock, Arthur H. The German Drama on the New Orleans Stage. Iowa, 1941. 183p.

336. Moore, Wallace H. The Conflict Concerning the German
Language and Propaganda in the Public Secondary Schools of
the United States, 1917-1919. Stanford, 1937. 187p.

337. Nau, John F. The German People of New Orleans, 1850-
1900. South Carolina, 1954. 154p.
Published under the same title (Leiden, Netherlands: Brill,
1958). This work deals with the social and economic role of
the Germans who emigrated to the South, and with those who settled in New Orleans and its surrounding area. The focus is the
period between 1850 and 1900. The impact of slavery and the
Civil War on New Orleans is examined. The documentation
is drawn from local German-language newspapers, the records
of churches and societies, census reports, some personal interviews, and personal accounts.

338. Neve, Paul E. The Contribution of the Lutheran College
Choirs to Music in America. Union Theological Seminary,
1967. 237p. (DA 28:4201-A)
The Lutheran Church had its origin in America in the seventeenth
century but did not become a denomination of significance until
the eighteenth. The arrival of many German immigrants during
the eighteenth century and the strong leadership of Henry Melchior
Muhlenberg during this period created an organization of Lutheran churches into a synod that gave status to this denomination.
During the last half of the nineteenth century Lutheran colleges
in the Middle West began to include music in the curriculum.
Glee clubs were the earliest type of choral organization that became established at these schools. Oratorio societies were organized at several colleges of Swedish background. Choral unions were popular at colleges founded by Norwegians and Danes.
(A)

339. Nolle, Alfred H. The German Drama on the St. Louis
Stage. Pennsylvania, 1915. 83p.
Published under the same title (Philadelphia: University of Pennsylvania [Americana Germanica, No. 32], 1917). Covers the
period 1842 to 1914.

340. Olson, Audrey L. St. Louis Germans, 1850-1920: The Nature of an Immigrant Community and Its Relation to the Assimilation Process. Kansas, 1970. 355p. (DA 31:2853-A)
Published under the same title (New York: Arno, 1980). Historians of German immigration to the United States have recorded
the deeds and contributions of that ethnic group to American life.
Their study of the German community with relation to its assimilation into the host society has led them to conclude that the German ethnic group was progressing toward assimilation until the
First World War forced them into a self-awareness of their nationality; that the ethnic community was not becoming assimilated
until the First World War broke the hyphen in "German-American"; and that the wealthy German-Americans abandoned the community, resulting in a resurgence of ethnic self-consciousness on

the part of the less economically and socially mobile members of the group. These conclusions were based on the predication of the existence of a close-knit German ethnic community. This study investigates a German community in an urban setting, St. Louis, Missouri, in order to determine the nature of that community and its relation to the process of assimilation. (A)

341. Overmoehle, M. H. The Anti-Clerical Activities of Forty-Eighters in Wisconsin, 1848-1860: A Study in German-American Liberalism. St. Louis, 1941. 260p. (DA 4 no. 2:94)

342. Ozolins, Karlis L. Book Publishing Trends in the American Lutheran Church and Its Antecedent Bodies, 1917-1967. Michigan, 1972. 460p. (DA 33:2402-A)
The study surveys and appraises book production under the auspices of the American Lutheran Church (1960-) and its antecedent synodical bodies; the American Lutheran Church (1930-1960), the Evangelical Lutheran Church (formerly the Norwegian Evangelical Lutheran Church), the United Evangelical Lutheran Church (formerly the United Danish Evangelical Lutheran Church), the Lutheran Free Church, the Evangelical Lutheran Joint Synod of Ohio, the Evangelical Lutheran Synod of Iowa, and the Lutheran Synod of Buffalo. (A)

343. Prewitt, Terry J. German-American Settlement in an Oklahoma Town. Ecologic, Ethnic and Cultural Change. Oklahoma, 1979. 186p. (DA 40:2151-A)
This study is concerned with the social and economic conditions surrounding the establishment and development of the community of Okarche, Oklahoma. Demographic, technologic, and cultural characteristics of different ethnic groups in the area of the town are considered in a historical framework spanning the period from 1889 through World War II. The establishment of a stable, long-term German-American population is examined, especially in the context of a very broadly based initial settler population profile. (A)

344. Reed, Carroll E. The Pennsylvania German Dialect Spoken in the Counties of Lehigh and Berks: Phonology and Morphology. Brown, 1941. 120p.
Published under the same title (Seattle: University of Washington Press, 1949).

345. Robbins, Walter L. The German-American Custom of Wishing In and Shooting In the New Year. North Carolina, 1969. 436p. (DA 31:322-A)
The German-American custom of wishing in and shooting in the New Year is as follows. A group of men ("shooters") make the rounds of homes, where they practice a ceremony for householders, prominent people, and eligible girls, consisting of playing musical and noise-making instruments, wishing, singing, and shooting, and are then served refreshments in return. Filling the need for a comprehensive survey of the custom, this dissert-

ation is a comparative study of it, of the wishes used in connection with it and of the origins of both the custom and the wishes in the German-speaking area of Europe. (A)

346. Rodgers, Harrell R. Community Conflict, Public Opinion, and the Law; The Amish Dispute in Iowa. Iowa, 1967. 161p.
Published under the same title (Columbus, Ohio: Merrill, 1969). The work deals with the confrontation in the 1960s between the Oelwein school district and the six conservative Mennonite groups in the district. Members of these religious communities refused to send their children to public schools beyond the eighth grade, fearing that its "corruptive" influence would turn the children away from their religion. The suit brought against the Mennonite communities by the state of Iowa drew national attention. The study explores legal aspects of the case and sampled public opinion.

347. Roemer, Theodore. The Ludwig-Missionsverein and the Church in the United States (1838-1918). Catholic, 1934. 127p.
Published under the same title (Washington, D.C.: Catholic University of America Press, 1934).

348. Rothan, Emmet H. The German Catholic Immigrant in the United States, 1830-1860. Catholic, 1947. 172p.
Published under the same title (Washington, D.C.: Catholic University of America Press, 1947). A study of German Catholic immigration and the role of the Catholic Church among the immigrants in regions of the United States. The scope extends to: (1) German immigration, 1830-60; (2) German Catholic immigrants in the East; (3) German Catholic immigrants in the Midwest; (4) settlers in the Northwest and the Southwest; (5) apostolic immigrants from Germany; (6) life in the land of adoption; (7) German Catholic schools; and (8) German Catholics and rural communities. The work includes a 160-item classified bibliography.

349. Rothfuss, Hermann E. The German Theatre in Minnesota. Minnesota, 1949. 240p.

350. Rudisill, Alvin S. The Doctrine of the Church in American Lutheranism with a View to Future Ecumenicity. Drew, 1967. 337p. (DA 28:1894-A)
Against the background of a survey of the history of American Lutheranism, the thesis of this study is that the story of Lutheranism in America is the story of a search for self-understanding, leading to a polity and to a theological vitality that gives living expression to the Gospel as witnessed to by the Lutheran Confessions. This search was encouraged by the freedom afforded by the Lutheran Confessions in the area of polity and by the freedom afforded by the American religious scene. The concept of "congregational autonomy" and a suspicion of centralized structures and authority complicated and distorted the search.

351. Saalberg, Harvey. The Westliche Post of St. Louis: A Daily Newspaper for German-Americans, 1857-1938. Missouri (Columbia), 1967. 446p. (DA 28:1779-A)
The Westliche Post was a daily newspaper published in the German language in St. Louis, Missouri, from September 27, 1857, to June 14, 1938. Although primarily serving the German immigrant, whose number was large in St. Louis during the latter half of the nineteenth century, the Westliche Post played an active part in the affairs of St. Louis and Missouri, as it guided the political direction of German-Americans to some extent. (A)

352. Sokoll, Carl A. The German-American Bund as a Model for American Fascism: 1924-1946. Columbia (Teachers College), 1974. 336p. (DA 36:6247-A)
In order to tell the Bund's story the study describes the origin and political concepts of Nazism in general as well as the history of the Bund from its inception, in Chicago, as the Teutonia Society, through its flowering in the 1930s, its wartime suppression, and finally its implied judicial authority to reemerge at the war's end. Careful consideration is given to its doctrinal differences as exemplified by the administrations of "Führers" Heinz Spanknöbel and Fritz Kuhn and the problems generated in the post-Kuhn years in neutral America. The study describes the Bund's cooperation with other like-minded groups and how the Bund became the model for fascist organizations in America and the leader for the political right wing in America during the "New Deal" period. Finally, the study explores the legal and ethical problems inherent in an exotic political ideal. In many ways America's conscience and legal system were challenged by the Bund's existence, and certain perplexing problems still remain as to how a democracy should handle an element in its midst that is dedicated to the destruction of that democracy. (A)

353. Schaefer, Lyle L. An Institutional History of the Colorado District of the Lutheran Church--Missouri Synod from the Earliest Mission Work, 1872-1968. Denver, 1976. 395p. (DA 37:3101)
This study traces Lutheran activity in Colorado; Utah; New Mexico; El Paso County, Texas; and the Navajo Indian Reservations of Arizona up through 1968. It includes tables concerning the Colorado District's pastors and teachers, its statistical growth, the names and locations of mission stations and missionaries, stewardship and financial activities, and District Conventions. This is a topical and institutional study; chapters portray specific aspects of the work of the Church, chronologically developed. Especially stressed are missionary activities, education, work of charitable groups, the organization of the District, and its conventions, conferences, and elections. (A)

354. Schaumann, Herbert F. Fundamental Characteristics of German-American Lyrics: A Study of the German-American's

Attitude Towards Life, with Special Regard to Lyrics of the
Seventeenth and Eighteenth Centuries and the Theme of Homesickness in the Nineteenth Century. Cornell, 1936. 110p.

355. Schelbert, Leo. Swiss Migration to America: The Swiss
Mennonites. Columbia, 1966. 335p. (DA 27:2486-A)
The study is part of an attempt to write a comprehensive history of Swiss migration to preindustrial America from the vantage point of American immigrant history. It tries to understand the cultural background, the dislocating forces, the migratory experience, and the final settling and acculturation of this particular immigrant group. The first part of the essay, written in view of the larger project, deals with the Swiss in general. First a geographic, socioeconomic, and historical interpretation of Switzerland is presented; this leads to a brief characterization of the Swiss immigrant type. Then the traditions of Swiss emigration are briefly outlined as they found expression in military, seasonal, and settlement migration. The second part of the study focuses on the migration of the Swiss Mennonites. The rise of this close-knit group is first described in order to explain the special nature of their emigration; special attention is given to the emergence of the United States as the main goal of Swiss Mennonite emigration. Finally, the founding of settlements and Swiss Mennonite life patterns in eighteenth- and nineteenth-century America are analyzed in some detail. The central role of the religious persuasion emerges as a main characteristic of Swiss Mennonite immigration to America.

356. Schmidt, Wayne E. Wisconsin Synod Parochial Schools: An
Overview of the Years 1850-1890. Wisconsin, 1968. 380p.
(DA 32:804-A)
The Wisconsin Evangelical Lutheran Synod is an independent Lutheran church body with a strikingly vigorous commitment to parochial-school education. This tradition of the parochial school goes back to the very founding of the Synod in 1850. The present dissertation examines some aspects of the religious and cultural milieu within which this Lutheran parochial system appeared. (A)

357. Schneider, Carl E. Origin of the Deutsche Evangelische
Kirchen-Verein des Westens [German Evangelical Church Society of the West]. Chicago, 1935. 579p.
Published under the title The German Church on the American Frontier. A Study of the Rise of Religion Among the Germans of the West Based on the History of the Evangelischer Kirchenverein in Des Westens (St. Louis: Eden, 1939). A comprehensive analysis appraising the reciprocal influence of the frontier on German settlers on the one hand, and the impact of the Germans on the molding of the frontier on the other. A contention is made that the German church played an important role in this process. The time span covered extends from 1800 to 1860, and the frontier comprised Missouri, Iowa, Minnesota, Illinois, Indiana, Ohio, and Wisconsin.

The Germanies, Austria-Hungary 85

358. Schrag, Lester D. Elementary and Secondary Education As
      Practiced by Kansas Mennonites. Wyoming, 1970. 234p.
      (DA 33:1002-A)
      Kansas Mennonites and Amish descended from Western European
      Anabaptists of the Reformation period. Suffering persecutions
      because of their opposition to infant baptism, swearing of oaths,
      participation in war and in government, and a state church, they
      were forced to live inconspicuously and in fear of their lives.
      Whenever governments opened new land for settlement the Mennonites looked with new hope for a place to live in religious freedom. This study was designed to trace the historical development of the principles of the Mennonite faith, to describe the
      educational practices as they emerged within the group both before immigration and immediately thereafter, and to discuss some
      problems caused by strict adherence to their beliefs. (A)

359. Schuchat, Molly G. Hungarian Refugees in America and
      Their Counterparts in Hungary: The Interrelations Between
      Cosmopolitanism and Ethnicity. Catholic, 1971. 200p.
      (DA 32:1975-B)
      Field research among Hungarian refugees in Washington and urban residents in Hungary between December 1968 and January
      1970 provided data on the functions of ethnicity in the contemporary world. The particular focus of research was food practices
      --food-consumption patterns in relation both to migration and to
      radical change in the processing of food. (A)

360. Seifert, Lester W. J. The Pennsylvania German Dialect
      Spoken in the Counties of Lehigh and Berks: Vocabulary.
      Brown, 1941. 130p.
      Published under the same title (Allentown: Pennsylvania German
      Folklore Society [Vol. 9], 1944).

361. Seipt, Allen A. The First Printed Hymn-Book of the
      Schwenkfelders and Its Sources. Pennsylvania, 1906. 112p.
      Published under the same title (Philadelphia: University of Pennsylvania [Americana Germanica, No. 7], 1909). Traces the
      European sources in the sixteenth century and the evolution of
      Schwenkfelder hymnology in American through the late eighteenth
      century. Christopher Sower's 1762 hymnbook is discussed in
      detail, together with the contributions of Caspar and George
      Weiss, Balthasar and Christopher Hoffman, Hans Christian Huebner, and Christopher Schultz. A chapter is devoted to the
      chronological listing from 1545 to 1869 of printed Schwenkfelder
      hymn collections in German with descriptive annotation.

362. Sessler, Jacob John. Communal Pietism Among the Early
      American Moravians. Studies in Religion and Culture.
      Columbia, 1933. 265p.
      Published under the same title (New York: Holt, 1933). Focuses on the history of the Moravian Church in Bethlehem, Pennsylvania, in the seventeenth century. The European background,
      the activities of Count Zinzendorf, and the economic development
      of the Moravian communities are discussed in some detail.

363. Shoemaker, Alfred L. Studies on the Pennsylvania German Dialect of the Amish Community in Arthur, Illinois. Illinois (Urbana), 1940. 141p.

364. Smith, Henry. The Mennonites in Pennsylvania. Chicago, 1907. 140p.

365. Spanheimer, Mary E. Heinrich Armin Rattermann: His Life and Letters, 1832-1923. Catholic, 1938. 148p.
Published under the same title (Washington, D. C.: Catholic University of America Press, 1938).

366. Steininger, Russell F. History of the Female Diaconate in the Lutheran Church in America. Pittsburgh, 1934. 275p.

367. Stine, Clyde S. Problems of Education Among the Pennsylvania Germans. Cornell, 1938. 111p.

368. Svendsbye, Lloyd. The History of a Developing Social Responsibility Among Lutherans in America from 1930 to 1960, with Reference to the American Lutheran Church, the Augustana Lutheran Church, the Evangelical Lutheran Church and the United Lutheran Church in America. Union Theological Seminary, 1966. 533p. (DA 28:290-A)
Lutherans in America have generally been described as a group lacking a vital social consciousness and a sense of corporate social responsibility, except for the area of institutional welfare. They have been depicted as quietistic supporters of the status quo rather than as a group interested in social reform. This portrait has, by and large, been correct. In the last few decades, however, several significant changes have taken place so that the attitudes and actions relating to social issues on the part of many Lutheran individuals and groups can no longer be portrayed by the usual phrases. Gradually a new sense of social responsibility has emerged, new understandings concerning social issues have developed, and new patterns for social action have evolved. Some of these new emphases stand in sharp contrast to the past tradition. The change is reflected most clearly in the reaction of the churches to the issues of war and race. (A)

369. Szamek, Pierre E. The Eastern American Dialect of Hungarian: An Analytical Study. Princeton, 1947. 145p. (DA 15:580)

370. Townsend, Andrew J. The Germans in Chicago. Chicago, 1927. 160p.
Published under the same title (Chicago: University of Chicago Press, 1927). This work examines the roles Germans played in the city's history from 1850 to 1920. The impact of the "Forty-Eighters" is analyzed along with the rise of the various radical movements. The social attitudes during World War I are explored along with other aspects, such as German churches and

press, cultural, and civic organizations. Includes statistical and cartographic material.

371. Tucker, Marlin T. Political Leadership in the Illinois-Missouri German Community, 1836-1872. Illinois (Urbana), 1968. 391p. (DA 30:262-A)
Between 1830 and 1860 German political refugees of the risings of 1830 and the Revolution of 1848 clustered in new settlements around St. Louis and Chicago. In these centers German communities of sufficient population and quality of education to provide significant political leadership arose, and a close-knit constellation of German-American politicians of local, statewide, and national significance evolved. By 1860 German-Americans constituted approximately 10 percent of the electorate in both Illinois and Missouri, and small enclaves of German voters were present in most central and northern Illinois towns, and in communities along the Missouri River between St. Louis and Jefferson City. (A)

372. Uhlendorf, Bernhard A. Charles Sealsfield: Ethnic Elements and National Problems in His Works. Illinois (Urbana), 1920. 240p.
Published under the same title (Urbana: University of Illinois Press, 1922). Uhlendorf was an Austrian immigrant.

373. Ulrich, Robert J. The Bennett Law of 1889: Education and Politics in Wisconsin. Wisconsin, 1965. 580p. (DA 26: 3145)
In 1889 Wisconsin placed upon its statute books the Bennett Law, an apparently innocuous piece of legislation that provided that all the children of the state be taught the common branches of education in the English language. Over this law there arose, in 1890, a bitter and acrimonious social debate that resulted in a political catastrophe for the long-seated Republican Party. Prior to 1890 Wisconsin school law applied mainly to the public institutions only, but the Bennett Law extended state supervision to the parochial schools by requiring them to offer the common branches of English. To the friends of the parochial school, and to the leaders of Deutschtum (Germandom), the law appeared to be an entering wedge of state domination over the church school, the church itself, and over German culture and language. To a lesser degree, nationality groups other than the Germans--such as the Scandinavians--entertained similar fears, but the main burden of the battle fell to the Germans, both Catholic and Lutheran. These parties believed their fundamental rights of freedom of conscience and parental control of their children to be violated by an overweening and paternalistic state. The Bennett Law was but one facet of the general school crisis of the 1890s. The cultural-religious-state conflicts that centered on this particular school controversy only reflected some of the numerous collisions that unsettled American society at that time. Few educational problems, as such, were solved by the Wisconsin battle royal, but the congeries of social forces operating upon the school were dramatically displayed for the benefit of the entire nation.

374. Umbeck, Sharvey G. The Social Adaptations of a Selected Group of the German-Background Protestant Churches in Chicago. Chicago, 1941. 167p.

375. Van De Luyster, Nelson. Emigration to America As Reflected in the German Novel of the Nineteenth Century: Especially in the Fiction of Bitzius, Laube, Gutzkow, Auerbach, Freytag, Storm, Keller, Spielhagen, Hayse, Raabe. North Carolina (Chapel Hill), 1943. 243p.

376. Walker, Mack. Germany and the Emigration, 1815-1855. Harvard, 1959. 284p.
Published under the title Germany and the Emigration, 1816-1885 (Cambridge, Massachusetts: Harvard University Press, 1964). Emigration from Germany in the nineteenth century, from the Napoleonic Wars (1815) to the rise of the German colonial empire in the 1880s, was worldwide in scope and not limited just to the United States. The intent of this work is to examine the causes in Germany that both stimulated and discouraged emigration from its borders. The most useful sections for studying the background of emigration from Germany to America is the time period from 1830 to 1854, when it was at its highest. The emigrants were first the Auswanderers, the lower-class farmers seeking a better lot, and later the political refugees of the 1848 revolution. Includes a sizable bibliography of primary and secondary sources.

377. Wayland, John W. The German Element of the Shenandoah Valley of Virginia. Virginia, 1907. 312p.
Published under the same title (Harrisonburg, Virginia: Carrier, 1978). Covers 300 years up to the early 1900s, with emphasis on the pre-1850 era. All aspects of society are dealt with. Archival materials are brought together in the appendix relating to Augusta, Frederick, Rockingham, and Shenandoah counties. The work offers leads for genealogical research. The participation of local Germans in federal and state politics is illustrated by lists of congressmen of German descent from the area.

378. Weber, Samuel E. The Charity School Movement in Colonial Pennsylvania. Pennsylvania, 1905. 74p.
Published under the same title (Philadelphia: University of Pennsylvania Press, 1905). The term refers to such organizations as the English Society for the Propagation of Christian Knowledge. Their activities in Pennsylvania among the German population from 1683 to the end of the eighteenth century are discussed, together with the role of the press and publishing in the educational process. The author attributes their ultimate failure to the fact that these schools neglected to cultivate the German tongue and culture.

379. Weinstock, S. Alexander. The Acculturation of Hungarian Immigrants: A Social-Psychological Analysis. Columbia, 1962. 130p. (DA 27:3519)

This is a study of some factors that influence the acculturation of post-1956 Hungarian refugees. Fifty-three respondents were interviewed and given a number of personality measures. Two measures of acculturation were used: the Campisi Scale and an Information Scale developed by the author. The two measures were combined to form a single index of acculturation. (A)

380. Weng, Armin G. The Language Problem in the Lutheran Church in Pennsylvania, 1742-1820. Yale, 1928. 143p.

381. Wenger, Marion R. A Swiss-German Dialect Study: Three Linguistic Islands in Midwestern U.S.A. Ohio State, 1969. 263p. (DA 31:749-A)
This Swiss-German dialect study comprises the findings of a journeyman linguistic field investigation. In order to acquire facility in the techniques of conducting dialect study in the field the author undertook to describe the structure of an unwritten dialect. The native speakers of Schwyzerduutsch are bilingual inhabitants of three small communities in Ohio and Indiana, whose first language reflects their ethnoreligious derivation from the Alemannic highlands of the Canton of Berne, Switzerland. (A)

382. Wentz, Abdel R. The Beginnings of the German Element in New York County. George Washington, 1914. 120p.
Published under the same title (Lancaster: Pennsylvania German Society [Vol. 24], 1916).

383. Wilhelm, Hubert G. H. Organized German Settlement and Its Effects on the Frontier of South-Central Texas. Louisiana State, 1968. 252p. (DA 29:3359-B)
In 1845 organized settlement of German immigrants was concentrated in that part of Texas known as the hill country of the Edwards Plateau. Anglo-Americans coming primarily from states of the Old South had begun to settle the same general area. Both ethnic groups provided for initial permanent occupancy of a region that had been thinly populated by roving Indian bands and the almost equally transient Spaniards. The introduction of several thousand German colonists to a new and strange habitat and their subsequent contact with the American frontiersmen poses the principal problem of the study--how did the immigrant react to the new influences and what, if any, is the evidence of a German cultural imprint on the landscape? (A)

384. Williams, Hattie P. A Social Study of the Russian German. Nebraska, 1916. 142p.

385. Winfield, Oscar A. The Control of Lutheran Theological Education in America. Yale, 1930. 167p.
Published under the same title (Rock Island, Illinois: Augustana Historical Society, 1933).

386. Wirth, James B. Career Determinants Within a Denominational Organization: The Missouri Lutheran Minister. Loyola

(Chicago), 1978. 260p. (DA 39:1854)
This dissertation explores the structure of career processes
within the ministry of the Lutheran Church--Missouri Synod
through the interface of occupations-professions and complex organizations. An open-systems perspective links career processes
to the functional imperatives of the LCMS organization. There
is a pervasive effect of ascribed or social origin attributes in
the LCMS. A dominant effect is that of occupational inheritance.
Occupational inheritance is related to a familistic occupational
subculture, elite background factors, and attitudes of professionalism and innovative decision-making. (A)

387. Wolf, Richard C. The Americanization of the German Lutherans, 1683 to 1829. Yale, 1947. 594p. (DA 32:4708-A)
The economic, political, ecclesiastical, physical, and psychological conditions existent in Germany between 1618 and 1776 moved
a large number of German Lutherans to emigrate to America between 1683 and 1776 and conditioned the emigrants toward a
readiness to acclimatize themselves in America. The long, arduous, costly, and dangerous journey to America served both as
a guarantee of the permanent settlement of the German Lutherans
in America and as a deterrent to any return to Germany. The
unorganized condition in which these German Lutherans arrived
in America and the absence of a German colony to which they
could resort made them dependent upon and subject to the prevalent English culture in which they found themselves. The indenture system, the obligatory oaths of allegiance to the British
Crown, and the exigencies of frontier life afforded a condition of
malleability that facilitated their adjustment to the new culture
in which they found themselves. The ecclesiastical disorganization of the German Lutherans, marked by a lack of pastors and
congregational organization, prepared the way for Henry Melchior
Muhlenberg, who by his personal life, organizational policies,
and ecclesiastical and political attitudes led them to a high degree of accommodation to and participation in the life and culture
of the American colonies. (A)

B. ITALY, GREECE, AND THE MEDITERRANEAN BASIN

---

388. Alatis, James E. The American English Pronunciation of
Greek Immigrants: A Study in Language Contact with Pedagogical Implications. Ohio State, 1966. 244p. (DA 27:
3027-A)
The purpose of this study is to compare the sound patterns of
Modern Greek and American English in order to determine the
similarities and differences of their phonological systems, identify and isolate the areas of difficulty in English pronunciation for
Greeks, and provide a sound basis for the preparation of English

pronunciation into lessons for Greeks. A comparison of Greek and English writing systems is also provided. The linguistic part of the dissertation is preceded by a discussion of the sociocultural background of the Greeks in America. This includes a brief history of Greek immigration to the United States and an account of the tribulations of the early Greek immigrants. (A)

389. Alissi, Albert S. Boys in Little Italy: A Comparison of Their Individual Value Orientations, Family Patterns, and Peer Group Associations. Western Reserve, 1967. 209p. (DA 28:2360-A)
Published under the same title (San Francisco: R & E Research Associates, 1978). The major purpose of the research was to examine the degree to which there was social class heterogeneity in a small, Italian-American neighborhood that is usually taken to typify a single ethnic, working-class neighborhood. More specifically, the study sought to determine whether there were corresponding relationships among the three variables as evidenced in differential value orientations, family patterns, and peer-group associations among boys. (A)

390. Anderson, Nels. The Social Antecedents of a Slum: A Development of the East Harlem Area of Manhattan Island, New York City. New York, 1930. 205p.
Largely concerned with the evolution of the Italian-American community in East Harlem, which numbered over 100,000 at the time of the author's study.

391. Baiamonte, John V. Immigrants in Rural America: A Study of the Italians of Tangipahoa Parish, Louisiana. Mississippi State, 1972. 261p. (DA 33:3521-A)
During the late nineteenth and early twentieth centuries there was a great need for additional laborers on Louisiana's sugar plantations. Tapping the large influx of Italians into the United States, the planters hired thousands of immigrants to harvest the cane from the months of December to March. After harvesting they returned to New Orleans and other urban centers to seek other employment. As early as the 1890s the Italians migrated to Tangipahoa Parish to pick strawberries. After laboring as pickers or sharecroppers, nearly 2,000 Italians settled on small berry farms. During the first two decades of the twentieth century they became the best strawberry growers in the parish and dominated the industry by organizing farmers' organizations and auction houses. (A)

392. Bauer, Barbara G. Cautela, D'Angelo, D'Agostino and Di Donato: The Achievement of First and Second Generation Italian-American Writers of the New York Region. St. John's, 1979. 191p. (DA 40:2659-A)
Due to the general lack of critical analysis regarding the achievements of four Italian-American writers of the New York region the representative works of each author are presented and assessed as literature. While all four of these authors took Italian

immigrants as their subjects and set most of their works in the
New York metropolitan area, the results of their efforts encompass almost every literary genre and vary widely in scope and
method of treatment.

393. Bauer, John. Economic and Social Conditions of the Italians in the United States. Yale, 1908. 124p.

394. Bianco, Carla D. The Two Rosetos: The Folklore of an Italian-American Community in Northeastern Pennsylvania. Indiana, 1972. 547p. (DA 33:4280-A)
Published under the title The Two Rosetos (Bloomington: Indiana University Press, 1974). This study is based on field research made in the two villages of Rosetos, one in the United States and one in Italy. Its aim is to identify and discuss traditional values and orientations of American Rosetans today. Additional research made among Italians of New York and Chicago provides a basis for comparison with the Italian-American experience at large. (A)

395. Biondi, Lawrence H. The Linguistic Development and Socialization of Italian-American Children in Boston's North End. Georgetown, 1975. 411p. (DA 36:336-A)
Published under the title The Italian American Child: His Sociolinguistic Acculturation (Washington, D.C.: Georgetown University Press, 1975). This work discusses the investigation of the manner in which monolingual and bilingual children of the Boston North End Italian American community speak English and the manner in which they learn the rules for social interaction in an acculturating community.

396. Bohme, Frederick G. A History of the Italians in New Mexico. New Mexico, 1958. 301p. (DA 19:1376)
Published under the same title (New York: Arno, 1975). Second only to natives of Mexico, Italians comprise the next-largest foreign-born group in New Mexico. "They are significant because Italian churchmen and Italian settlers, more than any others, provided a 'bridge' between the Anglo-Saxon and Hispano cultures found there." Bohme traces the missionary efforts of Jesuits in New Mexico between 1867 and 1919, the founding of religious schools, and the establishment of parishes in Albuquerque and Las Vegas. Of particular importance is his study of Rev. Donato Gasparri and the widely circulated Revista Catolica, and the ill-fated attempt to incorporate territorial institution with broad powers exempt from government control. Italians have moved readily into both "Anglo" and "Hispano" society. While they tended to marry within their own Italian social group, they have had a higher "exogamy" rate than their countrymen in other parts of the country.

397. Briggs, John W. Italians in Italy and America: A Study of Change Within Continuity for Immigrants to Three American Cities, 1890-1930. Minnesota, 1972. 382p. (DA 33:2852-A)

Published under the title An Italian Passage: Immigrants to Three American Cities, 1890-1930 (New Haven: Yale University Press, 1978). This study of Italians in Utica and Rochester, New York, and Kansas City, Missouri, largely eschews the well-studied story of exploitation, discrimination, and rejection in order to take the immigrants on their own terms. It portrays them as active agents, capable of initiative as well as accommodation, and as possessors of a viable culture that shaped the perception of their American experience, in many ways giving a sense of continuity between past and present. (A)

398. Buxbaum, Edwin C. The Greek-American Group of Tarpon Springs, Florida: A Study of Ethnic Identification and Acculturation. Pennsylvania, 1967. 472p. (DA 28:1769-B)
This is the study of the acculturation process of a Greek-American group. More precisely, it is the investigation of those factors affecting Greek ethnic identity. The main objective of the study has been to examine basic aspects of the social structure from the viewpoint of social interaction and cultural equilibrium. A synchronic and diachronic orientation became important in applying a model of "organic" insularity and for the testing of a hypothesis on social stability and cultural continuity. (A)

399. Capponi, Guido. Italy and Italians in Early American Periodicals (1741-1830). Wisconsin, 1958. 467p. (DA 18:2136)
Seeks "to record the nature and extent of early American interest in Italy and its literature," and describes the change in attitude from initial ignorance and lack of concern in the eighteenth century to an expanded interest in the early nineteenth century because of American travel abroad and the emerging nationalism of Italy.

400. Caroli, Betty Boyd. Italian Repatriation from the United States: 1900-1914. New York University, 1972. 160p. (DA 33:689-A)
Published under the same title (New York: Center for Migration Studies, 1974). The peak in Italian repatriation from the United States occurred between 1900 and 1914, when more than 1.5 million Italians left North America. A majority of the reemigrants were male, unskilled laborers who had spent fewer than five years in the United States. Italian government officials deemphasized the magnitude of the return migration in the early years of the twentieth century because of American objections to "birds of passage." United States immigration statistics did not include figures on departing aliens before 1908, but Italian reports available earlier showed that hundreds of thousands of the peninsula's potentially productive workers left their families each year to seek temporary employment in America. (A)

401. Carter, John B. American Reaction to Italian Fascism, 1919-1933. Columbia, 1953. 503p. (DA 14:96)

402. Cassimates, Louis P. Greek-American Relations, 1917-1929. Kent State, 1978. 400p. (DA 40:5662-A)

A widely accepted thesis regarding American involvement in
Greece is that the intervention of the United States in Greek internal affairs after World War II was a sudden, dramatic, and
unprecedented departure from established policy. To be sure,
the dominant influence of the large European powers in Greece
before 1940 is undeniable and should not be underestimated. It
is equally true, however, that during the interwar period the
United States, far from playing the role of a passive bystander,
was an active, viable force in many aspects of Greek life. The
American involvement in Greek affairs had modest beginnings,
but it rapidly evolved into a commitment that reached its full
fruition in the generation following the Second World War. The
evolution of this transitional process is the subject of this dissertation. (A)

403. Castiello, Kathleen R. The Italian Sculptors of the United
States Capitol: 1806-1834. Michigan, 1975. 196p. (DA 36:6346-A)
In 1806 Latrobe, the Chief Architect of the Capitol, commissioned two Italian sculptors, Giuseppe Franzoni and Giovanni
Andrei, to begin the sculptural decoration of the Capitol building
following a program devised by Latrobe and Jefferson. The latter, with his broad classical education, interest in architecture,
and admiration for Roman cultural achievements, worked closely
with the Chief Architect. Latrobe's professional skill and flexibility in adapting classical motifs to his own purposes served as
a valuable counterpoise to the more traditional classicism of
Jefferson. (A)

404. Cerase, Francesco P. From Italy to the United States and
Back: Returned Migrants, Conservative or Innovative?
Columbia, 1971. 389p. (DA 33:832-A)
Published under the title Innovazione o reazione? L'esperienza
dell'emigrazione di ritorno dagli Stati Uniti d'America (Rome:
Carucci, 1971). The study surveys a group of Italians who migrated to the United States in the last 50 years or so and then
returned to their mother country after some time in America.
The study is a contribution to an unwritten chapter in the history
of Italian immigration to the United States. The returnees interviewed are made up of subgroups living in several areas throughout Italy. But this study of the returned migrants is relevant
also to Italian history, and it was designed to test a general
hypothesis connected to the Italian "Southern Question." This
hypothesis relates Italian mass emigration to the United States
to the peculiar way in which a liberal state was established in
Italy in the nineteenth century and in which industrialization was
brought about. It then states that the southern peasants, the
protagonists of that emigration, although unwilling to tolerate any
longer the state of misery to which they had been reduced, remained on the whole unaware of the economic laws that had produced that misery. To the extent that this is true, emigration,
and more specifically the return, represented for them an individual act through which they expected to resolve the problem. (A)

405. Child, Irvin L. A Psychological Study of Second-Generation Italians. Yale, 1939. 208p.
Published under the title Italian or American? The Second Generation in Conflict (New Haven: Yale University Press, 1943). Intended as a study of second-generation Italians in New Haven, Connecticut. Primarily serves as a sociopsychological approach to immigrant groups and their acculturation.

406. Chock, Phyllis P. Greek-American Ethnicity. Chicago, 1970. 241p.

407. Churchill, Charles W. The Italians of Newark: A Community Study. New York, 1942. 173p.
Published under the same title (New York: Arno, 1975). At the time of Churchill's study the Newark Italian subcommunity of all ages numbered 70,000 to 80,000. The fieldwork for this dissertation was based on interviews with some 700 Italians. "As it was, realizing that Italians were a difficult population to interview because of their suspicions of the purpose of the interviewers, only Italian speaking interviewers were used." The early history of the Italian community was constructed from available source materials, and "organizations of all kinds were visited and functions of each group attended." Churchill deals with the history of the emigration; early life in Newark; "adjustment to beginnings of integration"; World War II and its effects; work and occupations; family life; religion; political life; organizations; recreation and social life; education; and Italian public opinion. Churchill's monograph is one of the most extensive studies available of an Italian-American community at the height of its existence in a city in which Italians constituted the largest ethnic group.

408. Cohen, Miriam J. From Workshop to Office: Italian Women and Family Strategies in New York City, 1900-1950. Michigan, 1978. 360p.

409. Collins, Donna M. Ethnic Identification: The Greek Americans of Houston, Texas. Rice, 1976. 412p. (DA 37:2446-A)
This study examines the role of ethnic identification in maintaining the Greek-American community of Houston as a distinctive group. Two aspects of ethnic identification are found to be important: (1) identification by oneself and by others as a member of the Greek ethnic group, and (2) conception of the self as being Greek. These two factors frequently coexist, but they may exist independently. Group membership is the more significant of the two factors for the continued existence of the ethnic group, and, accordingly, it is the major focus of this study. (A)

410. Concistre, Marie J. Adult Education in a Local Area: A Study of a Decade in the Life and Education of the Adult Immigrant in East Harlem, New York City. New York, 1943. 531p.

Describes the full "round-of-life" of the Italian subcommunity in
East Harlem. Provides detailed vignettes of Italian traditions
and heritages, the Italian family, language difficulties of immigrant groups, Italians and politics, economic status and housing,
mobility and social effects, and the multiplicity of religious institutions.

411. Constantakos, Chrysie M. The American-Greek Subculture:
Processes of Continuity. Columbia (Teachers College),
1971. 734p. (DA 33:1969-A)
The present investigation was designed as an exploratory study
of the American Greek subculture, stressing "hypothesis generation" rather than "hypothesis testing." It constituted a study of
old and recent migrants and native-born Greek-Americans of the
second and third generation, using generational status as a dimension of continuity. The areas of subcultural continuity explored included: (1) factors in the current setting, such as ethnic
identification in its various manifestations, ethnic language preservation, church adherence, endogamy, community organizational
involvement, family and kin; (2) origin factors, such as region
of origin in Greece, and urban or rural residence prior to United
States migration. (A)

412. Correa-Zoli, Yole. Lexical and Morphological Aspects of
American Italian in San Francisco. Stanford, 1970. 175p.
(DA 31:2365-A)
The principal aim of this dissertation is to analyze and describe
the linguistic influence of American English on the lexicon of
Italian-born residents of San Francisco. The second objective
is to describe the sociocultural setting of the language and to
characterize the speech community with respect to the original
dialects of the speakers. (A)

413. Covello, Leonard. The Social Background of the Italo-American School Child: A Study of the Southern Italian Family
Mores and Their Effect on the Social Situation in Italy and
America. New York, 1944. 488p.
Published under the same title (Leiden, Netherlands: Brill,
1967). A major study of ethnicity, of the context of poverty, of
a minority's children, and the challenges to the American school.
Part I: Social Background in Italy; Part II: The Family as the
Social World of the Southern Contadino Society; Part III: Italian
Family Mores and Their Educational Implications; Part IV: Summary and Conclusions.

414. Crispino, James. The Assimilation of Ethnic Groups: The
Italian Case. Columbia, 1977. 310p. (DA 40:3540-A)
The present investigation is a study of the assimilation process
as it applies to Italian-Americans. Its purpose is to determine
whether and to what extent the Italian ethnic group has lost its
corporate identity, has become acculturated to the larger society's
cultural and value system, and has assimilated into its social
structure. It is intended to specify the areas of social life and

the degree to which Italians have become less "Italian." The research is basically a study of intra-ethnic cultural and social structure, with emphasis on cultural traditions and social participation in the neighborhood, in friendship groups, and in marriage-partner selection.

415. De Bileo, Francis D. Protestant Mission Work Among Italians in Boston. Boston, 1949. 212p.

416. Dickinson, Joan Y. The Role of the Immigrant Women in the U. S. Labor Force 1890-1910. Pennsylvania, 1975. 239p.
Published under the same title (New York: Arno, 1980). In the decades between 1890 and 1910 immigrant women from Europe and Canada comprised one-fourth of the white female labor force of the United States. Primarily concerned with occupational roles, Dickinson brings forward and interprets neglected data in this important dissertation. Immigrant women, as a whole, were found chiefly in three kinds of "women's work" in these decades: domestic service, textile work, and in the needle trades. Clustering by ethnic (or nativity) groups within these work areas was very marked. Dickinson documents distinctions between the work roles of English, Irish, German, and Scandinavian immigrant women (the "old" immigration), and those of Italian, Russian, Polish, and Slavic immigrant women (the "new" immigration); most of the former were engaged as domestic workers: the latter were in manufacturing. A major conclusion is drawn from this study: "The menial role of the immigrant women workers between 1890 and 1910 served to advance the women of other nativity classes both in the labor force itself, and outside, for it is probable that without the presence of the immigrant women workers in the kitchens, nurseries, textile mills, and clothing factories, the turn-of-the-century leisure class of women volunteers in church, community, and suffrage work might not have been possible."

417. Diggins, John P. Mussolini's Italy: The View from America. Southern California, 1964. 369p. (DA 25:1170)
Published under the title Mussolini and Fascism: The View from America (Princeton: Princeton University Press, 1972). The rise of Italian fascism may well be considered the first major reaction to the idea of democracy in the twentieth century. Dramatized by the blustering Benito Mussolini, the Italian experiment presented to a surprised world a historical antithesis that was as attractive as it was repugnant. As a nation professing a dedication to democracy, America's response to and interpretation of Mussolini's Italy deserves to be carefully examined. The study is interpretive rather than exhaustive. Instead of presenting a quantitative treatment of all the printed and published material on Mussolini's regime, an attempt was made to select and analyze those contemporary accounts that best reflected the main currents of American opinion. (A)

418. Di Pietro, Robert J. The Structural Description of an Alcamese Sicilian Dialect in America. Cornell, 1960. 187p.

419. Duke, Francis J. A Phonetic Study of Italo-American Speech in Richmond, Virginia. Virginia, 1938. 173p.

420. Easterly, Frederick J. The Life of Rt. Rev. Joseph Rosati, C. M., First Bishop of St. Louis, 1789-1843. Catholic, 1942. 203p.
Published under the same title (Washington, D. C.: Catholic University of America, 1942). Largely on the missionary activities of Bishop Rosati.

421. Fairchild, Henry P. Greek Immigration to the United States. Yale, 1909. 278p.
Published under the same title (New Haven: Yale University Press, 1911). An overview of the economic causes of Greek emigration to the United States, with notices of Greek community life in America, but seriously weakened by the author's restrictionist views.

422. Fallon, Joseph. Influence of Role Perception and Opportunity Structure on the Increase of Priestly Vocations Among Italian-Americans. Fordham, 1970. 412p.

423. Femminella, Francis X. Ethnicity and Ego Identity. New York University, 1968. 150p. (DA 29:2432-A)
This study identifies, describes, and analyzes relationships between ethnicity and ego identity in a selected sample of Italian-Americans. Hypotheses concerning the continuance of ethnic affiliation through successive generations and residential mobility are tested. The significance of the relationships between the ethnic ideological themes and identifications of Italian-Americans and a control group of non-Italo-Americans residing in the same suburban city in Long Island, New York, is tested. (A)

424. Fenton, Edwin. Immigrants and Unions: A Case Study: Italians and American Labor, 1870-1920. Harvard, 1957. 630p.
Published under the same title (New York: Arno, 1975). Fenton's study is a comprehensive examination of the evolving experience of Italian immigrants and their relation to the development of American trade unionism in the critical half-century from 1870 to 1920. Although Fenton's greatest concern is with the southern Italian peasant immigrants who became factory workers and construction laborers in an expanding urban and industrial America, he also deals with the ofttimes forgotten yet numerous Italian anarchist, socialist, and syndicalist artisans who emigrated from northern Italy and who became leaders of the peasants in the large American cities. The author also considers the unstable organization of many AF of L unions, policies of socialist groups, and divisions within the ranks of the Italian-American radicals. Particularly graphic are Fenton's descriptions of the

spectacular strikes taking place between 1910 and 1913. These were led by the IWW in industries in which Italian workers predominated, e.g., the great textile-mill strike of 1912 in Lawrence, Massachusetts.

425. Ferroni, Charles D. The Italians in Cleveland: A Study in Assimilation. Kent State, 1969. 292p. (DA 30:5376-A) Published under the same title (New York: Arno, 1980). Four institutions were examined to determine the degree of assimilation the Italians of Cleveland have reached since the late 1920s. These included the churches, both Roman Catholic and Protestant; the organizations, both local and national; the public schools; and the settlement houses. The effects that certain events had on the changes that occurred in these institutions were emphasized. Patterns that developed out of the information collected revealed the four major institutions involved in the assimilation of Cleveland's Italians. Moreover, an examination of the changes that occurred in each institution offered evidence as to how the process of assimilation worked. One conclusion reached was that the assimilation of Cleveland's Italians has involved a reciprocal process whereby the immigrants not only receive from but also contribute to the culture of their adopted land. It was also concluded that such events as the restrictive immigration legislation of the late 1920s, Prohibition, the Depression, and World War II stimulated Italian assimilation. Among these events World War II proved to be a watershed in the history of Cleveland's Italian community as it resulted in increased intermarriages between Italians and non-Italians, improved economic conditions, the decentralization of the solid Italian communities, and, most important, the final settlement of the question of loyalty.

426. Fiore, Alphonse T. History of Italian Immigration in Nebraska. Nebraska, 1938. 79p.
An analysis of Italian communities in Omaha and Lincoln, particularly, with some notices of general Italian emigration patterns to America.

427. Flouris, George. The Self-Concept and Cross-Cultural Awareness of Greek-American Students in the Monolingual and Bilingual Schools. Florida State, 1978. 269p. (DA 39:3240-A)
Like many other minority children, many children of Greek-American background may begin school with limited or no knowledge of the English language and Anglo-American culture. As they are raised in two cultures, some elements of which are in conflict with each other, they may find themselves caught between the culture of their families and the culture of the school. As a result, Greek-American children may experience personality conflict and/or uncertainty. Due to the conflicting values of their homes and school, the development of their self-concept, attitudes toward native and/or Anglo cultures, as well as the overall academic progress may be affected in a negative way. The purpose

of this study is to determine the self-concept and cross-cultural awareness held by Greek-American children enrolled in bilingual and monolingual schools, and to establish if there are any differences between the two selected groups of Greek-Americans. (A)

428. Foerster, Robert F. Emigration from Italy, with Special Reference to the United States. Harvard, 1909. 556p. Published under the title The Italian Emigration of Our Time (Cambridge: Harvard University Press, 1919). A comprehensive study of the Italian migratory movement that analyzes the causes of emigration by considering conditions in Italy, follows the emigrants into the countries of settlement in Europe, Africa, South America, and the United States, and attempts to discover their economic and cultural contributions as well as the nature of their personal fortunes.

429. Francher, Joseph S. Benjamin Nelson's "Directive System" as a Paradigm for Anthropological Taxonomy: The Successful Italo-American Male as an Instance of Cultural Possibility. Syracuse, 1968. 333p. (DA 29:1245-B)
The social scientists who have studied the Italo-American assert that a number of traits are present within the Italo-American's cultural system that impede the individual's attainment of the socioeconomic symbols of success in the United States. This present study is designed to investigate the cultural framework of the Italo-American and its relationship to the type of successful achievement sanctioned in America. (A)

430. Furio, Columba M. Immigrant Women and Industry: A Case Study. The Italian Immigrant Women and the Garment Industry, 1880-1950. New York, 1979. 376p.
This study examines four questions in American immigration and labor history: first, what was the impact of immigration on Italian women? second, what were the factors that determined whether or not Italian women joined and remained members of the garment unions at various time periods? third, how did the union affect Italian immigrant women? and fourth, what contributions did these women, in turn, make to the American labor movement? Immigration was the answer to the economic necessities of the Italian peasants. Although immigrant women experienced social and economic problems in their efforts to adapt to their new environment, the longest, and often most wrenching adjustments had to be made in cultural transplantation and amalgamation; therein the crisis of immigration was truly evident. In southern Italian society sociocultural forces and the personalities of the individual members in that society interacted with each other. Each made demands of the individual. The behavior of Italian women was in many ways an expression of the sanctions that operated within that culture. Preindustrial or peasant values persisted when the family unit emigrated to an industrial society. One of these values was familialism. Values of the dominant American culture entered into the social consciousness of these women, though at a slower rate than for the men. Thus, factors

Italy, Greece, Mediterranean Basin 101

that determined whether or not Italian women joined and remained
union members varied according to time periods. This study
shows that unions were a tripartite force in the assimilation of
Italian women to American society. Evidence has also shown
that Italian women engaged in labor struggles through most of the
twentieth century. "Italian-ness" and "rebel-ness" were not necessarily dichotomous qualities, but often appeared side by side
in women unionists.

431. Gallo, Patrick J. Political Alienation Among the Italians
of the New York Metropolitan Region. New York, 1971.
303p. (DA 33:1205-A)
Published under the title Ethnic Alienation: The Italian American
(Cranbury, New Jersey: Fairleigh Dickinson University Press,
1974). This study has attempted to see if the American political
system tended toward the integration or exclusion of ethnic
groups. By focusing on the Italian-American the study sought to
determine whether the political system of the United States tended
to neutralize or sharpen their sense of exclusion from the dominant values, roles, and institutions of society. (A)

432. Georges, Robert A. Greek-American Folk Beliefs and Narratives: Survivals and Living Tradition. Indiana, 1964.
251p. (DA 26:5360)
This is a study of the folk beliefs and narratives of Greek immigrants and their descendants living in the United States today.
The primary objective of the study is to prove that Greek-Americans have not abandoned their traditional beliefs, practices, and
tales completely since their arrival in the New World, as many
cursory studies of American immigrant folklore suggests must
inevitably be the case for all alien groups. It indicates, rather,
that a distinct dichotomy exists within the entire body of Greek-
American folklore. There are folk beliefs and narratives that
persist in America today because they serve as an important
means of perpetuating Greek culture among the immigrants and
their American-born children. (A)

433. Giannotta, Rosario O. Contributions of Italians to the Development of American Culture During the Eighteenth Century. St. John's, 1942. 267p.

434. Gilkey, George R. The Effects of Emigration on Italy, 1900
to 1923. Northwestern, 1951. 423p.

435. Giordano, Paul. The Italians of Louisiana: Their Cultural
Background and Their Many Contributions in the Fields of
Literature, the Arts, Education, Politics, and Labor. Indiana, 1978. 256p. (DA 39:4445-A)
Although Italians have lived in Louisiana from the days of the
French explorers, they did not immigrate to the state in substantial numbers until after the Civil War. These people chose Louisiana because it offered them some of the basic things they had
left behind in Italy: a climate that closely resembled that of their

native land; an opportunity to work with the land, instead of laboring in factories; and the opportunity to buy land. In the twentieth century, after having overcome much of the prejudice and hostility directed toward them by native Louisianans, Italians began to flourish. Economically they had become a major power in various parts of Louisiana; by 1920 Italians were responsible for the bulk of the lucrative fruit and vegetable trade with Latin America; in Tangipahoa Parish the 1926 strawberry crop yielded well over $6 million. The twenties and thirties also saw the emergence of Italians on the political scene. Riding the popular wave of Longism, many Italians began to be elected to a variety of local and state offices. (A)

436. Green, Rose B. The Evolution of Italian-American Fiction as a Document of the Interaction of Two Cultures. Pennsylvania, 1962. 256p. (DA 23:4343)
Published under the title The Italian American Novel: A Document of the Interaction of Two Cultures (Cranbury, New Jersey: Fairleigh Dickinson University Press, 1974). The prose fiction written by Americans of Italian ancestry is here analyzed and evaluated as a document of the interaction of two cultures. The influence of these writers upon the national literature is explored as a factor that contributes to a more realistic representation of the whole culture of the United States. An analysis is also made of the distinctive quality of the contribution that has been made by Italian-American writers. How this quality developed while the growth of the concepts in Italian-American fiction parallels the established pattern of the national culture is the problem undertaken in this study. (A)

437. Halley, Helen. A Historical Functional Approach to the Study of the Greek Community of Tarpon Springs. Columbia, 1952. 220p. (DA 13:3)
It is a study of the Greek community of Tarpon Springs, Florida, composed primarily of islanders coming from the sponge-fishing islands within the Dodecanesian Island cluster in the southeastern Aegean of the Greek archipelago, who represent a distinct aspect of a cultural segment from the point of view of geographical, historical, economic, and other phases of Hellenic culture. The material reported in this essay has been basically drawn from the sociopolitical, economic, and religious orientation of the Greek islanders of this community. Historical perspective and synchronic data help to bring out those functional aspects of culture that have exerted a distinct influence upon the adaptational patterns of this group in the American environment. (A)

438. Hill, Henry S. The Effects of Bilingualism on the Measured Intelligence of Elementary School Children of Italian Parentage. Rutgers, 1935. 220p.

439. Hutchens, Nancy C. Recent Italian Immigrants in Brooklyn: Their Social Worlds. Rice, 1977. 195p. (DA 38:1501-A)
This study concerns recent immigrants from southern Italy living

in Jamesville, a pseudonym for a section of Brooklyn, New York. The nature of their social relations and the cultural factors that have molded the forms of these relationships are described and discussed. Two distinctive modes of social life are seen to apply among these immigrants that relate to their backgrounds in Italy as being of lower or middle social class. Attention is given to both in-group and out-group relations of the immigrants, including those with Italian-Americans and the general American population. Immigrants of middle class, who are well educated, have white-collar jobs, and speak fluent English and Italian have developed close conjugal relationships and loose-knit social networks. An extreme dependence upon the nuclear family has been fostered among them by the immigration of the family as a unit and their relative cultural and social isolation in Jamesville. Relationships between middle-class and lower-class immigrants and between both of these groups and second-generation Italian-Americans, who dominate Jamesville, are awkward and tense. Middle-class immigrants are not economically or socially dependent upon either of the other groups and view themselves as being far superior socially to lower-class immigrants and slightly superior to Italian-Americans. However, the view of Italian-Americans places all immigrants in a single category socially beneath themselves.

440. Ianni, Francis A. The Acculturation of the Italo-Americans in Norristown, Pennsylvania: 1900-1950. Pennsylvania State, 1953. 260p. (DA 15:568)

441. Iorizzo, Luciano J. Italian Immigration and the Impact of the Padrone System. Syracuse, 1966. 256p. (DA 27:1320-A)
Published under the same title (New York: Arno, 1980). In essence, the padroni had a vital role in stimulating and directing Italian immigration to America. They awakened the Italians to the tremendous opportunities awaiting them in America and established an institutional mechanism that allowed for systematic distribution of industrial workers. In accepting the direction of padroni, Italians were exposed to many areas of the United States and were able to select a community for permanent settlement. The wonder is not that the majority of Italians chose the Northeast, but that so many preferred to make their homes in every sector of the country. (A)

442. Jordan, Laylon W. America's Mussolini: The United States and Italy, 1919-1936. Virginia, 1972. 427p. (DA 33:1648-A)
The present work attempts to answer the questions: What were the communal American attitudes and conceptions of Italian character and destiny in the halcyon days of Mussolini's rise and consolidation of power, and what was the nature of relations between the United States and Italy in the same years, 1919-1936? Although Italy, Mussolini, and Fascism occupy a central position in this study, it is not about these things except as they were objects

443. Juliani, Richard N. The Social Organization of Immigration: The Italians in Philadelphia. Pennsylvania, 1971. 262p. (DA 32:7095-A)
This study examines the social organization of immigration as an alternative to the more usual research upon the demographic aspects of international migration or the social psychology of assimilation. Although the author used all available sources of information (e.g., government documents, church records, newspaper materials, and previously published research), he obtained his basic data through a series of tape-recorded oral histories provided by Italian-born male immigrants, between 66 and 93 years old, who came to the United States from 1894 to 1924. (A)

444. Jursa, Paul E. A Case Study of the Impact of Out-Migration and Return on a Southern Italian Commune (and Province). Texas, 1972. 346p. (DA 33:4624-A)
The purpose of this study is to evaluate the feasibility of utilizing out-migration and return as a strategy for inducing economic development and change. A case study of the impact of out-migration and return on a southern Italian commune (and province) is used to make this evaluation. During the postwar period a variety of push-pull forces have been making out-migration a feasible alternative for many southern Italians. The southern Italians who out-migrate tend to be poor, unskilled, and from the agricultural sector of the South. Many emigrate to northern Europe, where they work as unskilled laborers in the industrial sector for periods of short duration. After accumulating a certain amount of savings, or because of family connections in the sending area, many decide to return. (A)

445. Karlin, Jules A. The Italo-American Incident of 1891. Minnesota, 1940. 421p.
A detailed examination of the mob lynching of 11 Sicilian immigrants on March 15, 1891, the background of the event, and its political consequences.

446. Kelly, Richard J. A History of the Los Angeles Greek Theatre Under the Management of James A. Doolittle and the Los Angeles Greek Theatre Association, 1952-1969: The Professional Theatre Producer as a Lessee of City Government. Southern California, 1970. 432p. (DA 31:4941-A)
Today the professional theater in the United States increasingly seeks the support of federal, state, county, and municipal governments. This growing intimacy between government and theater raises the question: How will political theatrical partnerships affect theatrical endeavors? A study of the outdoor civic Los Angeles Greek Theatre offered a chance to examine an 18-year record of a major theater operating within this context. Since 1953, at the Greek Theatre, a landlord-tenant relationship has existed between the City of Los Angeles and the Los Angeles

Greek Theatre Association--a nonprofit production organization with James A. Doolittle as its executive producer. (A)

447. Kessler, Carolyn. The Acquisition of Italian and English Syntax in Bilingual Children. Georgetown, 1971. 257p. (DA 32:3284-A)
Published under the title The Acquisition of Syntax in Bilingual Children (Washington, D. C.: Georgetown University Press, 1971). This study investigated the sequencing and rate of syntactic acquisitions for children bilingual in Italian and English. Focusing on late acquisitions in children age six to eight, the study asks the basic question of whether structures common to Italian and English develop in the same order and at the same rate in the bilingual child. The hypothesis was drawn that shared structures develop in a parallel manner, since they find their source in a common underlying base structure and are realized by the same set of transformational rules. (A)

448. Kiriazis, James W. A Study of Change in Two Rhodian Immigrant Communities. Pittsburgh, 1967. 296p.
The study attempts to compare the differential changes that have occurred in two Rhodian-immigrant communities in Warren, Ohio, and Canonsburg, Pennsylvania. It is divided into three time periods: the initial period, pre-World War II, and post-World War II. (A)

449. Lopreato, Joseph. Effects of Emigration on the Social Structure of a Calabrian Community. Yale, 1960. 242p. (DA 28:2351-A)
Published under the title Peasants No More: Social Class and Social Change in an Underdeveloped Society (San Francisco: Chandler, 1967). The relation between emigration and social change in the emigrants' community of origin is investigated. The community selected is Stefanaconi, an agricultural village of South Italy, from which there has been a heavy flow of migrants during the last 12 years. The unit of study is the family. (A)

450. Lovell-Troy, Lawrence A. Kinship Structure and Economic Organization Among Ethnic Groups: Greek Immigrants in the Pizza Business. Connecticut, 1979. 322p. (DA 40:1112-A)
At a time of increasing rationalization in the American economy in general, and in the service sector in particular, recent Greek immigrants in Connecticut are occupationally concentrated as self-employed entrepreneurs in the pizza business. Since research has indicated that self-employment is a difficult status for native-born Americans to attain, such occupational concentration by recent immigrants to this country suggests the importance of ethnicity in the explanation of entrepreneurship. From data collected primarily through tape-recorded, unstructured interviews, this thesis analyzes the ways in which the ethnicity of Greek immigrants in Connecticut has facilitated their mobility from the status of rural peasants to that of self-employed proprietors of small businesses. The concept of ethnicity, it is argued, should be

viewed in both its cultural and structural aspects and therefore the analysis of the Greek-immigrant concentration in small, family-run pizza businesses follows this dual approach. (A)

451. Macris, James. An Analysis of English Loan Words in New York City Greek. Columbia, 1955. 178p. (DA 16:335)
This dissertation comprises an analysis, in terms of the two sound systems that are in contact, of a selected number of American English loan words used by speakers of Greek in New York City. The first chapter deals with the environment in which the contact takes place. This is followed by a discussion of the informants and of the methods used in the collection of the data. Of the 20 informants ten have arrived in the United States in recent years. Nine of them were born in Greece, and the tenth was born in Rumania of Greek parents. The other ten informants are children of Greek immigrants who were born in the United States. There were three female and 17 male informants, with ages ranging from 18 to 43. Thirteen of the informants were between 21 and 25 years of age. Many of the informants were students. (A)

452. Maiale, Hugo V. The Italian Vote in Philadelphia Between 1828 and 1946. Pennsylvania, 1950. 227p.

453. Mancuso, Arlene. Women of Old Town. Columbia (Teachers College), 1977. 167p. (DA 38:354-A)
The purpose of this study is to present a description of the family life of a small number of Italian-American women living in an ethnic enclave of a large urban eastern city. The study, using a variety of ethnographic research techniques, is based on day-to-day observation of behavior in the community over a period of 18 months. The community has been disguised for purposes of confidentiality. The major theoretical perspectives that inform this work are ethnicity, social role, and sex-role identity as an aspect of social role. These concepts are examined primarily as they relate to the female, within the framework of a descriptive study of family life. Although mostly gathered from second-generation Italian women, married and raising children, the data were not limited to this group. The researcher also actively sought out and interviewed women in the first, third, and fourth generations as well, and also had access to husbands and male kin of these women across generations. This study shows that the Old Town woman today stands at the center of a family system that stresses family solidarity and pragmatism. She is the core of the family and the nurturer and transmitter of those values. As the manager of internal affairs she handles the purse strings and has a great deal of decision-making power in the family unit. Her role in the emotional, economic, and social functioning of the unit is essential to its continuance.

454. Mariano, John H. The Second Generation of Italians in New York City. New York, 1920. 317p.
Published under the title The Italian Contribution to American

Democracy (Boston: Christopher, 1921). Mariano's dissertation is an elaborate study of the socioeconomic conditions of the Italian-American community (i. e., population and distribution; occupations; health; and standard of living, including notices of child labor and housing) against the background of Italian immigration and unsettled problems relating to its restriction. He includes chapters on literacy, citizenship, and social welfare; an intricate psychological "traits" profile; and a detailed examination of social organizations that developed in the Italian community. In a final section he considers "What the American of Italian Extraction Contributes to American Democracy, " which he places in the framework of what he terms "a socio-ethnic problem. "

455. Mathias, Elizabeth L. From Folklore to Mass Culture: Dynamics of Acculturation in the Games of Italian-American Men. Pennsylvania, 1974. 419p. (DA 36:455-A)
This work explores game-playing as expressive culture among three generations of Italian-American male groups who trace their origin to the contadino of southern Italian villages. Fieldwork for the study was conducted between July 1970 and July 1972 in the Italian community of South Philadelphia. The research objectives were to observe the relationship between degree of acculturation and level of persistence of Italian traditional games, such as bocce, passatella, and morra, and to note the process of change within the games, relating this process to the changing forms of Italian-American male groups. An additional focal point of the study was the changes in social-interaction patterns among the men as related to the types of games played. Games are viewed not only as revelations of past and present realities but as prestructures that may suggest, by their forms and interaction patterns, future changes within the male groups. (A)

456. Matthews, Mary F. The Role of the Public School in the Assimilation of the Italian Immigrant Child in New York City, 1900-1914. Fordham, 1966. 378p. (DA 27:3133-A)
This is a study of the role that the public school in New York City played in the life of the Italian immigrant child between the years 1900 and 1914, the period when immigration from Italy was at its height. The study had two major objectives. The first objective was to interpret the experience of Italian immigrants in New York City early in the twentieth century in terms of the most recent theoretical developments in the area of cultural assimilation. The second objective was to bring together in a single source the relatively inaccessible data that had a bearing on this problem and to integrate and interpret these data. (A)

457. McLaughlin, Virginia Y. Like the Fingers of the Hand: The Family and Community Life of First-Generation Italian-Americans in Buffalo, New York, 1880-1930. State University of New York (Buffalo), 1970. 579p. (DA 31:4683-A)
Published under the title Family and Community: Italian Immigrants in Buffalo, 1880-1930 (Ithaca, New York: Cornell University Press, 1977). The dissertation emphasizes the danger of

employing ideal types to specific conditions among particular immigrant groups, as Handlin does in The Uprooted. The extended-family household, for example, rarely existed in southern Italy. Therefore, the prevalence of the nuclear form among immigrants in the United States cannot be viewed as proof of disruption or instability. Other significant indexes of family disorganization and change, including percentages of matriarchal or female-dominated households, desertion by male family heads, illegitimacy rates, intergeneration conflict, and exogamous marriages remained relatively low. (A)

458. Milano, Fred A. The Generational Divide: A Study of Italian-American Veterans and Non-Veterans of the Vietnam Era. Penn State, 1977. 213p. (DA 38:1036-A)
This is a study of the politicizing effects of military service: specifically, its impact upon socioeconomic, political, and ethnic attitudes and behavior. The research was conducted in a small steel town in southeastern Pennsylvania. The sample consisted of 15 veterans and 15 nonveterans from a homogeneous Italian-American working-class community. All 30 of the respondents had similar background characteristics: age, sex, ethnicity, religion, education, occupation, and area of residence. Only a single major factor differentiated the two groups: their military service or nonservice. The data for the study were obtained by means of in-depth interviews and by the participant observation of the author, who resided in the town for the first 21 years of his life. (A)

459. Mondello, Salvatore A. The Italian Immigrant in Urban America, 1880-1920, As Reported in the Contemporary Periodical Press. New York, 1960. 266p. (DA 21:2260)
Published under the same title (New York: Arno, 1980). The reaction of the American periodical press, from 1880 to 1920, to the Italian immigrants in urban America in this period is the subject of this study. At any given moment the quantity of periodical literature on the Italian newcomers was in direct proportion to the physical dimensions of the influx. Awareness of their coming as reflected in periodicals is largely confined to the years between 1900 and 1920. Magazine opinion of the Italian immigrants was generally unfavorable. This aversion toward the Italian migration found expression in comments on the causes of the migration. The majority of magazine writers argued that the presumed misery in southern Italy was caused primarily by numerous agricultural problems, demographic pressures, and burdensome taxes. Moreover, it was generally believed that the South Italians also emigrated to take advantage of economic opportunities, especially those resulting from the expansion of industry and urban services in America. The motivation of their migration was criticized as being primarily economic rather than political or idealistic. Furthermore, fears were expressed that their alleged backward way of life and poor working standards, which had supposedly impelled the exodus, might be transplanted to the American scene.

Italy, Greece, Mediterranean Basin 109

460. Monos, Dimitrios I. Upward Mobility, Assimilation, and Achievements of the Greeks in the United States with Special Emphasis on Boston and Philadelphia. Pennsylvania, 1976. 299p. (DA 37:2447-A)
This is a study of the socioeconomic mobility, assimilation, and outstanding achievements of the Greeks in the United States, with special emphasis on the Greek communities of Boston and Philadelphia. Specifically, answers were sought to the following questions: (1) To what extent have the Greeks in America achieved social, economic, and professional mobility as compared with native Americans and members of 21 other ethnic groups?; (2) In terms of the same indexes of upward mobility, how do the Greeks of Philadelphia and Boston compare with the natives and other ethnics?; (3) What is the relative presence of the Greeks among outstanding men and women in America?; (4) How do the Greek communities of Boston and Philadelphia compare in terms of rearing outstanding men and women?; (5) What factors explain the upward mobility of Greeks in general and the differential rates of upward mobility of the Greeks in Boston and Philadelphia? (A)

461. Myers, Jerome K. The Differential Time Factor in Assimilation: A Study of Aspects and Processes of Assimilation Among the Italians of New Haven. Yale, 1950. 256p. (DA 33:3798-A)
The New Haven Italians are selected as a representative ethnic group for a study of the time element and the steps or stages in social assimilation. Assimilation is measured operationally by the following indexes: adoption of the total population's pattern in the residential, occupational, and political systems; high school graduation; and intermarriage. (A)

462. Nelli, Humbert S. The Role of the "Colonial Press" in the Italian-American Community of Chicago, 1886-1921. Chicago, 1965. 300p.
Parts of the dissertation are incorporated in the author's Italians in Chicago, 1880-1930: A Study in Ethnic Mobility (New York: Oxford University Press, 1970).

463. Norman, John. Italo-American Opinion in the Ethiopian Crisis: A Study of Fascist Propaganda. Clark, 1942. 363p.

464. O'Brien, Thaddeus J. Attitudes of Suburban Italian-Americans Toward the Roman Catholic Church, Formal Education and the Parochial School. Chicago, 1972. 213p.

465. Onesto, Serene F. The Effects of Special Multi-Media Lessons on Italian History and Culture on the Attitudes of Italian-American School Children. Northern Illinois, 1975. 157p. (DA 36:6407-A)
The purpose of this study was to measure the relationship between a child's exposure to positive ethnic teaching and the amount of positive attitude change that occurred as a result. The study

investigated whether a series of Italian-American ethnic lessons had any effect on the attitudes of seventh-grade Italian-American students toward themselves or other Italian-Americans. The lessons, developed by the researcher, utilized selected commercially prepared film, filmstrips, and audiocassettes. They were presented to an experimental group, while a control group participated in regularly scheduled social studies classes. (A)

466. Palisi, Bartholomew J. Ethnicity, Family Structure, and Participation in Voluntary Associations. Nebraska, 1963. 187p. (DA 24:3453)
In this inquiry the author studied the relationship between ethnicity (limiting himself to first- and second-generation Italian-Americans), family structure, and participation in voluntary associations. Participation of the respondent with both immediate-family and extended-family members was examined and, with regard to voluntary associations, the author took into account both informal associations (number and intimacy of friendships) and membership and time spent in formal voluntary associations. In his consideration of the relationship between formal and informal participation he posed such questions as whether participation in formal and informal voluntary associations varied directly and whether participation in associations was related to family structure. (A)

467. Palmer, Hans C. Italian Immigration and the Development of California Agriculture. California (Berkeley), 1965. 457p. (DA 26:783)
California's unique development has been based on individual resource endowment and response to growth forces in the American economy, among them the flow of immigrants from Europe. Since the Italians were the second-most-numerous group of such immigrants and since they comprise the third-largest foreign-born group in California, their contribution to the growth of California is of interest to analysts of that growth and forms the basis for this study. (A)

468. Papaiovannu, George. Patriarch Athenagoras I and the Greek Orthodox Church of North and South America. Boston, 1976. 452p. (DA 37:3824-A)
The purpose of this dissertation is to describe and evaluate the leadership and the contributions of Athenagoras I to the American Orthodox Churches both as Archbishop of North and South America and as Ecumenical Patriarch of Constantinople. The author's method is historical and critical. The major sources of this study were the archival materials of the Greek Archdiocese, to which the author had free access. (A)

469. Parenti, Michael J. Ethnic and Political Attitudes: A Depth Study of Italian Americans. Yale, 1962. 350p. (DA 25: 3657)
Published under the same title (New York: Arno, 1975). Parenti explores "the ways in which ethnic attitudes and experiences

influence and interact with political opinions and values. " A group of 18 Italo-American males consisting of immigrant fathers, their sons, and grandsons, and representing six New York City families, were interviewed in depth. These interviews covered topics of political, ethnic, and personal significance. Parenti deals with assimilation aspirations, generational status, and marginality feelings and examines past- and present-oriented ethnic militancy. The study shows that participation and loyalty are often functions of assimilation and acculturation needs.

470. Passero, Rosara L. Ethnicity in the Men's Ready-Made Clothing Industry, 1880-1950: The Italian Experience in Philadelphia. Pennsylvania, 1978. 380p. (DA 39:1788)
This study examines the influence of ethnicity on the developments in the men's ready-made clothing industry. Various ethnic groups influenced the industrial development of men's-clothing manufacture in different ways. Consequently men's-clothing centers developed different industrial characteristics according to the ethnic composition of the groups involved in manufacturing men's clothing. A comparative analysis of the ethnic composition and industrial characteristics was made of the men's-clothing industry in New York City, Chicago, Philadelphia, Baltimore, Boston, Rochester, and Cincinnati. The prominent ethnic groups engaged in men's-clothing manufacture were divided into the following categories: (1) Eastern European Jews; (2) Eastern European non-Jews; (3) Northern and Western Europeans, non-Jews; (4) German Jews; (5) Southern Italians. The industrial characteristics that were examined included: structure of the industry, size of firms, grade of garment produced, use of machines and extent of subdivision of labor, and the sexual composition of the work force. (A)

471. Patterson, George J. The Unassimilated Greeks of Denver. Colorado, 1969. 277p. (DA 31:1032-B)
The thesis investigates the history of the Greeks in the United States, Colorado, and Denver and focuses on the habitués of the coffeehouse and the inhabitants of Greek Town and their peripheral relationship to the larger Greek community and church. It looks at their values and behavior, the life histories of selected kafeneion regulars, attitudes of the larger Greek community toward the area and its residents, conflict and factionalism within the group, flowback to the homeland, applicable acculturation and assimilation theory, and the future of the unassimilated Greeks of Denver and of Greek Towns in America. (A)

472. Peebles, Robert W. Leonard Covello: A Study of an Immigrant's Contribution to New York City. New York, 1967. 414p. (DA 28:4463-A)
Published under the same title (New York: Arno, 1978). Leonard Covello spent nearly a half-century in educational service in the New York City schools and was a leading advocate of bilingual-bicultural education. In the East Harlem Italian and Puerto Rican ghetto, as principal of Benjamin Franklin High School,

Covello created the first successful community-oriented school.
Peeble's dissertation is a dimensionally rich biographical study,
drawing on all of Leonard Covello's activities in behalf of the
immigrant child, educational innovations that provided the beginnings of bicultural education, and the struggle for the implementation of pluralistic models in American educational practice, all
of which are singularly relevant to contemporary problems in
American urban education.

473.   Petropoulos, Nicholas P. Social Mobility, Status Inconsistency, Ethnic Marginality, and the Attitudes of Greek-Americans Toward Jews and Blacks. Kentucky, 1973. 355p.
(DA 34:1391-A)
The purpose of this research was to account for Greek-American
attitudes toward Jews and Negroes. It was felt that variations
in three structural factors--social mobility, status inconsistency,
and ethnic marginality--might help account for variations in racial-ethnic attitudes. A common social-psychological theory, the
frustration-aggression (scapegoat) theory was used as the theoretical framework. It was predicted that lack of upward mobility, the presence of status inconsistency, and ethnic marginality
would be associated with negative attitudes toward Jews and
blacks. (A)

474.   Pioppi, Isabelle R. Insights to Italy: Broader Perspectives
in the Teaching of Italian Culture. Florida State, 1975.
277p. (DA 36:3754-A)
Each chapter of this study deals with a specific aspect of Italian
culture that should enable the teacher or reader to interpret lifestyles, mores, and achievements with more acuity. The insights
gained are the prime objective for suggested model lessons that
are included in the first appendix. The methods stressed are
interdisciplinary, since interdisciplinary approaches encourage
what the Romans called "a world view." Interdisciplinary techniques also spark the imagination and creative teaching. (A)

475.   Pozetta, George E. The Italians of New York City, 1890-1914. North Carolina (Chapel Hill), 1971. 433p. (DA 32:5161-A)
This study examines the New York City Italian immigrant community during the period 1890 to 1914, a time span that saw the
bulk of Italian migration flow into both the city and nation. Its
primary objectives are to ascertain the impact of an American
urban environment upon immigrants possessing an alien, rural
culture and to view the changes in New York society occasioned
by the introduction of this foreign mass. These goals necessarily require an examination of the following broad categories:
southern Italian backgrounds; causes of immigration; city settlement patterns; urban crime and Italians; the political, economic,
and religious adjustments of Italians; and the New World ethnic
community. (A)

476.   Ragucci, Antoinette T. Generational Continuity and Change
in Concepts of Health, Curing Practices, and Ritual Expres-

Italy, Greece, Mediterranean Basin 113

sions of the Women of an Italian-American Enclave. Boston, 1971. 303p. (DA 32:1974-B)
This study, utilizing the method of participant-observation, delineates the convergence and divergence of folk concepts of health and healing practices. Continuities and discontinuities along a three-generation dimension are indicated. The women of the first or immigrant generation, i.e., emigrants of Italy five to six decades previously, comprise the baseline for the study. The recurring themes associated with folk or laymen's health and healing practices, and the manner in which these are expressed and reinterpreted within an urban milieu are identified. (A)

477. Reed, Dorothy. Leisure Time of Girls in a "Little Italy": A Comparative Study of the Leisure Interests of Adolescent Girls of Foreign Parentage, Living in a Metropolitan Community, to Determine the Presence or Absence of Interest Differences in Relation to Behavior. Columbia (Teachers College), 1932. 69p.

478. Reimer, Toni T. Genetic Demography of an Urban Greek Community. Ohio State, 1977. 316p. (DA 38:6805)
Considerable attention has been given to the need for including more industrialized urban breeding populations in studies of genetic anthropology. This thesis presents the results of an anthropological study in genetic demography conducted during 1976-1977 on an urban Greek-immigrant community in Columbus, Ohio. The three substantive aims of this study were to describe the historic and extant demographic characteristics of the community; to determine the potential for microevolution within the population; and to examine, by inference, the ways in which cultural factors influenced the potential for change in this population's gene frequencies. The methodological aim of this study was to develop a computer program for the determination of demographic characteristics in small populations. (A)

479. Ribordy, François-Xavier. Conflict de culture et criminalité des Italiens à Montreal. Montreal, 1970. 242p.

480. Roche, John P. Ethnic Attitudes and Ethnic Behavior: Italian Americans in Two Rhode Island Suburban Communities. Connecticut, 1977. 292p. (DA 38:5064)
Studies have come to emphasize pluralism (ethnic persistence) as well as assimilation (ethnic change). Several scholars have even argued that there has been a recent rise in ethnic consciousness. Others suggest that ethnicity continues to decline in a "straight-line" fashion with each succeeding generation. From this debate questions emerge that can be tested empirically. Within this context this research examines the degree to which ethnicity exists among suburban residents of a common nationality. More specifically, this study investigates the ethnic attitudes and ethnic behavior of a sample of Italian-Americans drawn from two suburbs of Providence, Rhode Island. One suburb is ethni-

cally heterogeneous; the other suburb is ethnically homogeneous and may be characterized as an ethnic enclave. (A)

481. Rubin, Vera D. Fifty Years in Rootville: A Study in the Dynamics of Acculturation of an Italian Immigrant Group in an Urban Community. Columbia, 1951. 196p.

482. Russo, Nicholas J. The Religious Acculturation of the Italians in New York City. St. John's, 1968. 349p. (DA 29: 3238-A)
With regard to the religious practices and attitudes of the immigrants and their descendants, it is not certain whether Italian-Americans of the second and third generations neglected the religious practices of their parents or maintained a pattern of increased religious activity associated with increased Americanization. The purpose of this study, therefore, was to reconcile apparently incompatible sociological findings in regard to immigrants and their descendants, by: (1) isolating the religious factor in the assimilation process of the Italian-Americans; (2) evaluating the role of the Catholic Church in their acculturation to American life; and (3) delineating a before-and-after situation of the religious practices and attitudes of the Italian-Americans, who were contrasted with the Irish, as the dominant Catholic group in New York City. (A)

483. Scarpaci, Jean A. Italian Immigrants in Louisiana's Sugar Parishes: Recruitment, Labor Conditions, and Community Relations, 1880-1910. Rutgers, 1972. 362p. (DA 33:4320-A)
Published under the same title (New York: Arno, 1980). In the late nineteenth century a chronic labor shortage in the Louisiana sugar plantations led the State of Louisiana and prominent planters to initiate a movement to import foreign workers. After attempts to use Chinese and Scandinavian laborers failed, attention focused on Italian workers. Evolving patterns of immigration from Sicily to the southern United States created a large Italian community in Louisiana (the largest ethnic group in the state), but official census figures did not reflect the impact of immigrant workers in the sugar parishes. Each year at harvest time thousands of Italians traveled from Sicily, Chicago, New York, St. Louis, and New Orleans to the sugar plantations, remaining in the cane fields from October through March, when they retraced their steps (estimates of this migration range from a conservative 16,000 to an unlikely 80,000). In this important study Scarpaci deals with the phenomena of immigration from Sicily to Louisiana, Italian immigrants in agriculture, Italian relations with American black workers (and the attempts to replace blacks with Italian immigrants), and the continuing efforts to recruit Italian laborers. In a larger sense, the dissertation is a sociohistorical study of the Louisiana immigrant community and its evolving relationships with the native dominant white American community.

484. Scherini, Rose D. The Italian American Community of San Francisco: A Descriptive Study. California (Berkeley),

1976. 256p.
This study of the Italian-American population of an urban center is a description and analysis of the institutions and organizations of this ethnic community. The purpose is to document the changes in this community over its 100-year history and to identify the ways in which its ethnic cohesion is maintained. The community is described in terms of its demographic characteristics, residential patterns, social institutions, media arts, voluntary associations, and relations with the Italian government. The description developed through interviews with 38 community leaders, observation of association meetings and public events, and monitoring of the ethnic media. Census data, recorded historical accounts, and oral-history recollections provide the historical background. The problems of ethnic population estimates are discussed in an appendix, and a change in operational terminology is proposed. The study's major findings are that the Italian-American population in the San Francisco area is declining rapidly; that the formerly dense Italian neighborhoods have all but disappeared; that ethnic political influence is insignificant. Moreover, it was also found that activity in the ethnic associations remains high and that new organizations are being formed. The character of the community's activities suggests that it is the Italian-American experience, rather than the Italian heritage, that is most cherished by the group. This broad-ranging study provides a data base for more extensive examinations of the process of ethnicity among Italian-Americans.

485. Scourby, Alice. Third Generation Greek Americans: A Study of Religious Attitudes. New School for Social Research, 1967. 106p. (DA 28:2354-A)
This study is an attempt to explore the extent to which third-generation Greek-Americans identify themselves with the religious community. The study is focused on Will Herberg's thesis that religious institutions are becoming a very important feature of American life as ethnicity becomes a less potent force. The persistent need for some kind of communal identity persists (so runs his thesis), causing each group to turn to one of the major religions: Protestantism, Catholicism, Judaism. This excludes Greek Orthodox, who disclaim membership in any of these categories. According to Herberg, the third generation in America is experiencing a religious revival, thus making membership in the religious community an alternative way of being an American. We sought to discover what relevance, if any, this thesis had for third-generation Greek-Americans. (A)

486. Seaman, Paul David. Modern Greek and American English in Contact: A Socio-Linguistic Investigation of Greek-American Bilingualism in Chicago. Indiana, 1965. 451p. (DA 26:6033)
Published under the same title (The Hague: Mouton, 1972).
This dissertation is an attempt to describe some of the essential tendencies of Modern Greek in contact with American English. It is primarily a study of the spoken vernacular based upon tape-recorded interviews with 41 bilingual Americans of Greek descent

of various generations. The linguistic part of the dissertation is preceded by the analysis of 444 responses to a bilingual questionnaire designed to gain data on the sociocultural background of Americans of Greek descent regardless of generation and linguistic status, and to reveal the functional role of Greek as a shifting language in the United States. (A)

487. Serino, Gustave R. Italians in the Political Life of Boston: A Study of the Role of an Immigrant and Ethnic Group in the Political Life of an Urban Community. Harvard, 1949. 227p.

488. Sidlofsky, Samuel. Post-War Immigrants in the Changing Metropolis, with Special Reference to Toronto's Italian Population. Toronto, 1969. 240p. (DA 32:1651-A)
This is a study of immigrants in a large city. It examines how a particular industry affects the finding of work, securing of residences, and participating in voluntary associations that enable migrants to find their place in a new environment. It centers upon Italian immigrants who came to Toronto between 1951 and 1956 and entered the residential construction industry. Although the Italians had become a large, highly visible component of Toronto's population, the role played in their migration and settlement by the institutions of their own receiving groups was largely unknown. The examination of Toronto's postwar Italian immigrant population in the context of their involvement in the residential construction industry provided the means of understanding the heterogeneity of an ethnic community and the process of settlement they experienced. Further analyses of the characteristically predominant industrial-occupational networks of other ethnic groups would enhance the understanding of the essential differences and similarities of their social structures within an urban society. (A)

489. Stellos, Marie H. The Greek Community in St. Louis (1900-1967): Its Agencies for Value Transmissions. St. Louis, 1968. 81p. (DA 29:2454-A)
The ideas and values of the Greek in the old country have been described as a mingling of idealism tempered by centuries of practical experience, nationalism, and religion. Aware that certain of their traditional values through which they achieved both national and personal identity would almost inevitably be lost simply through contact with the new environment they encountered in America, Greek immigrants to St. Louis attempted to reproduce their old-country atmosphere as nearly as possible through establishing in their new surroundings institutions that they had known at home to serve as agencies to preserve and transmit their values. (A)

490. Stephanides, Marios C. Educational Background, Personality Characteristics and Value Attitudes Towards Education and Other Ethnic Groups Among the Greeks in Detroit. Wayne State, 1972. 224p. (DA 33:2524-A)

This dissertation studied some of the political, social, and educational attitudes of the first-generation Greeks in Detroit. The theory was built on cultural and historical conditions; that is, it assumed that the existence of those variables was due to cultural rather than psychological reasons. Thus, although the theory depended largely on the original "Authoritarian Personality" studies for support and insights, it rejected its basic premise of explaining the existence of the authoritarian personality syndrome in terms of psychological insecurities and Freudian latent explanations. (A)

491. Stibili, Edward C. The St. Raphael Society for the Protection of Italian Immigrants, 1887-1923. Notre Dame, 1977. 350p. (DA 38:1588-A)
Italian mass migration to the Americas, which increased dramatically after 1887, confronted Italy and the host nations with both opportunities and problems. The latter included the rise of exploitative activities by immigrant recruiters in Italy and the usual resettlement problems. Two additional factors complicated the migration process, especially in the United States. The first was the emergence of the padroni, who provided the immigrants with services and jobs, but in exchange exploited them. The second involved the cultural identity of the immigrants, who brought with them a religious style that was repugnant to both the Protestant majority and the Catholic minority in America. These problems prompted Bishop Giovanni Battista Scalabrini of Piacenza, Italy, to establish in 1887 a missionary institute to recruit, train, and send missionaries to the Italian settlements in the Americas. At the same time he established an auxiliary lay emigrant society, with the Marchese Giovanni Battista Volpe Landi as president. Its aim was to protect and assist the emigrants at ports of embarkation, on board ship, at the ports of arrival, and in the places of settlement.

492. Swidersky, Richard M. General and Particular in Anthropological Theory: A Study of an Italian-American Fisherman's Festival. Princeton, 1973. 222p. (DA 34:1354-B)
A number of hypotheses are tested by a study of St. Peter's Festival celebrated annually by the Italian-American community of Gloucester, Massachusetts.

493. Tait, Joseph W. Some Aspects of the Effect of the Dominant American Culture upon Children of Italian-born Parents. Columbia, 1943. 72p.
Published under the same title (New York: Teachers College Press, Columbia University, 1943). This study explores the character traits of Italian children and undertakes to determine in what direction and to what extent children of Italian-born parents were affected by different degrees of contact with the dominant American culture.

494. Tavuchis, Nicholas. An Exploratory Study of Kinship and Mobility Among Second Generation Greek-Americans.

Columbia, 1968. 340p. (DA 32:558-A)
This study focused on the kinship and mobility patterns of a purposive sample of 50 upper-middle-class Greek-American families residing in the New York metropolitan area. Because of the dual emphasis on kinship and mobility found in this ethnic group, there was a unique opportunity for examining some of the putative relationships between family and mobility variables. Interviews based on open-ended and structured questions were conducted with the male heads of households. Specific areas of kinship that were examined were intergenerational and intragenerational patterns of interaction, mutual assistance, normative and affective orientations, and conflict between marital couples and their parents, siblings, and siblings-in-law. Data were also gathered on differential mobility between the respondents and their parents, parents-in-law, siblings, and siblings-in-law. (A)

495. Thompson, Bryan. Settlement Ties as Determinants of Immigrant Settlement in Urban Areas: A Case Study of the Growth of an Italian Neighborhood in Worcester, Massachusetts, 1875-1922. Clark, 1971. 202p. (DA 32:4005-B)
Published under the same title (New York: Arno, 1980). Much of the history of urban America has been the story of immigrant adjustment to an urban way of life. This study examines the growth of the Italian community in Worcester, Massachusetts from the time of first settlement, around 1875, to the time that in-migration virtually was cut off, following the immigration laws of the early 1920s. The study is divided into three parts. Part I is a general review of the literature dealing with ethnic settlement in urban areas. Chapter I considers factors that determine the initial and subsequent settlement patterns of new immigrants. Chapter II looks at the more general question of urban growth and its relation to the study of ethnic community expansion. Part II, the empirical section, is divided into two chapters. Chapter III analyzes the form of settlement up to 1900, a period during which the Italian community grew slowly. Chapter IV examines the changes in the Italian community during the first 23 years of this century, when growth was rapid. Part III relates characteristics of Italian settlement and Italian-community growth in Worcester to more general models of urban structure.

496. Tomasi, Silvano M. Assimilation and Religion: The Role of the Italian Ethnic Church in the New York Metropolitan Area, 1880-1930. Fordham, 1972. 445p. (DA 33:4550-A)
Published under the title Piety and Power: The Role of Italian Parishes in the New York Metropolitan Area, 1880-1930 (New York: Center for Migration Studies, 1975). This dissertation is an examination of the process of assimilation of Italian immigrants in the New York metropolitan area from the viewpoint of their religious experience. The study of the religious experience of the Italian immigrants, however, is limited to its institutional aspect. The Italian ethnic parish was identified as a religious and social institution that emerged in the immigrant community as a quasi-sect and that played a relevant role in the process of linkage between the national and the ethnic social systems. (A)

Italy, Greece, Mediterranean Basin 119

497. Ulin, Richard O. The Italo-American Student in the American Public School: A Description and Analysis of Differential Behavior. Harvard, 1958. 200p.
Published under the same title (New York: Arno, 1975). Ulin studied the academic and school-related performance of a selected group of Italian-American second- and third-generation boys in a Massachusetts high school. He determined "in what ways the in-school and circa school performance of the Italo-American boy paralleled and in what ways it differed from the performance of other high school students." This is a significant sociological study, which delves directly into current concerns on intergroup and interethnic relations. Ulin's major conclusion: "... that Italians have taken on so many of the surface aspects of American culture only tends to obscure the fact that in several respects they are still not middle class Yankee Americans, that they do not yet think and feel as middle class Yankee Americans do. Their traditional family patterns have changed, but as yet these patterns are not the family patterns of American suburbia. Old World attitudes still affect not only their approach to family, to jobs, to government, and to religion but also to education."

498. Valletta, Clement L. A Study of Americanization in Carneta: Italian-American Identity Through Three Generations. Pennsylvania, 1968. 502p. (DA 29:2164-A)
Published under the same title (New York: Arno, 1975). This study deals with the cultural adaptation and identity formation of three generations of an Italian-American group. This group, mainly of peasant origin, settled in a rural and industrial area in eastern Pennsylvania and established the borough of Carneta (a pseudonym). The study, covering the years 1890-1965, offered an opportunity to evaluate the Americanization of "new" immigrants in an environment that was both rural and industrialized. The approach used was cultural/anthropological, with participant-observer techniques, and with the use of oral histories and archival records. The author's conclusions suggest that the experience in Carneta, unlike that of Italian-Americans studied in urban environments, was one that allowed the Carnetans to "unify their individual, family, communal, and ethnic images as they went about becoming American."

499. Varbero, Richard A. Urbanization and Acculturation: Philadelphia's South Italians, 1918-1932. Temple, 1975. 414p. (DA 36:3971-A)
This dissertation analyzes the experiences of South Italian immigrants in Philadelphia, the industrial city, between 1918 and 1932. The basic approach consisted of viewing immigrant life against the backdrop of the city's major institutions, especially those designed to acculturate immigrants and their children. Thus, Philadelphia's public schools, Catholic churches, political organizations, and occupational networks were analyzed to determine the rate and form of immigrant adaptation to American social values. Since Philadelphia's Italians were primarily from the South of Italy--the Mezzogiorno--and were predominantly peasant in back-

ground, their Old World culture was an important element in adjustment to a complex urban society. Their values concerning family life, child-rearing, marriage, associational links, religion, education, and social innovations were often tenaciously held and only gradually surrendered. (A)

500. Vecoli, Rudolph J. Chicago's Italians Prior to World War I: A Study of Their Social and Economic Adjustment. Wisconsin, 1963. 495p. (DA 23:4339)
By 1900 Chicago had become a major center of the Italian immigration, rivaling Philadelphia for second rank among American cities in number of Italian residents. This study seeks to analyze the process of emigration from Italy to Chicago and the social and economic adjustments of the immigrants within the urban environment. In this study Vecoli shows that the traditional character of the Italian peasants was poorly suited for life in the urban jungle of Chicago. With time the immigrants gradually adapted to the city's harshly competitive society. Yet the stereotypes of the Italians as organ-grinders, banana-vendors, or--worse yet--as criminals and Black Handers, persisted and aroused much prejudice against them. Divided by regional animosities, the Italians were unable to present a unified front and to defend themselves from their detractors. The Italians met with little sympathy or understanding in Chicago; rather, it was their fate to be among the most despised and exploited of immigrants.

501. Vlachos, Evangelos C. The Assimilation of Greeks in the United States: With Special Reference to the Greek Community of Anderson, Indiana. Indiana, 1964. 287p. (DA 25:4857)
The purpose of the study was to investigate the relationship between exposure, as resulting from migration, and assimilation. It was generally assumed that the pattern of immigration and the various generations of an ethnic group set not only the limits and conditions of assimilation, but they also determine the rate of the assimilation process. Thus, the main objective of the study was basically the exploration of differential exposure of three generations of Greek-Americans to the U.S. culture. (A)

502. Von Raffler, Walburga. Studies in Italian-English Bilingualism. Indiana, 1953. 129p. (DA 14:142)
This dissertation addresses the controversial issue of bilinguals making use of one, two, or one and a half phonemic systems. The comparison of the American English and Italian-American speech of the same bilingual informant leads to the conclusion that bilinguals on the phonological level operate with two separate systems, although the division is not so clean-cut in lexicon, morphology, and syntax.

503. Webster, Jesse A. The Discovery of Enrico Leboffe, Immigrant American-Italian Composer. Oklahoma, 1978. 144p. (DA 39:5797-A)

It was necessary to reconstruct, as much as possible, the story of Leboffe's life, his music, and his immigration to America. An extensive search of various sources, such as public records, telephone directories, former places of employment, obituaries, and the use of Silva Mind Control made it possible to locate Leboffe's widow and son, now living in California. Subsequently most of Leboffe's compositions, numbering approximately 100 (with about half being solo songs), and a great quantity of biographical information were made available to the writer. With this information a biographical sketch of the composer was constructed.

504. Whyte, William F. Street Corner Society: The Social Structure of an Italian Slum. Chicago, 1943. 284p.
Published under the same title (Chicago: University of Chicago Press, 1943; 2nd ed., 1955).

505. Winsey, Valentine R. A Study of the Effect of Transplantation upon Attitudes Toward the United States of Southern Italians in New York City as Revealed by Survivors of the Mass Migration, 1887-1915. New York, 1966. 373p. (DA 27: 3962-A)
The problem of this study was to investigate the effect of transplantation upon attitudes of Italian immigrants toward the United States, as revealed by interviews of eye-witnesses who arrived during the period of mass migration, 1887 to 1915. These eye-witness accounts constitute a primary historical source, hitherto untapped, from representatives of the second-largest foreign group in the United States. Insights into their attitudes, therefore, contribute to a better understanding of some of the attitudes of present-day immigrants undergoing similar experiences. (A)

506. Ziegler, Suzanne G. The Adaptation of Italian Immigrants to Toronto: An Analysis. Colorado, 1971. 170p. (DA 32: 3758-B)
A questionnaire was distributed to Italian-born immigrants in Toronto. The questionnaire was designed to collect information on background and on postmigratory behavior, in order to discover meaningful relationships between them. Of particular interest in this respect was the influence of premigratory environmental poverty, as reflected by Italian regional differences in income, and by subjects' own rating of the relative poverty of their birthplaces. Also of interest is the relationship between various forms of postmigratory adaptation, called integration, acculturation, and assimilation. (A)

C. POLAND, RUSSIA, THE BALKANS, AND SLAVIC EUROPE

507. Babics, Walter V. Assimilation of Yugoslavs in Franklin County, Ohio. Ohio State, 1964. 144p. (DA 25:7416)

Published under the title Yugoslav Assimilation in Franklin County, Ohio (San Francisco: R & E Research Associates, 1972). The basic problem of this study was the assimilation of Yugoslavs in Franklin County, Ohio, a primary concern being the question of differential assimilation of the several Yugoslav ethnic categories in the County. Specific areas of interest included an examination of the relationship between assimilation and urbanity, mutual aid, discrimination, reasons for emigration, ties with country of origin, and neighborhood location among the Franklin County Yugoslavs. (A)

508. Baden, John A. The Management of Social Stability: A Political Ethnography of the Hutterites of North America. Indiana, 1967. 205p. (DA 30:5035-A)
The communally organized Hutterites of North America consist of three endogamous groups. This division has derived from their initial settlement pattern in the Dakota territories during the 1870s. Their 200 settlements are predominantly located in South Dakota, Montana, and the prairie provinces of Canada. Although communally organized societies have tended to be short-lived, the Hutterites have survived for four centuries in Europe and North America and are currently experiencing their second "Golden Age." This paper is focused upon features of their organization which have contributed to their survival as a distinct group while in North America. (A)

509. Barendse, Michael A. Slavic Immigrants in the Pennsylvania Anthracite Fields, 1880-1902: A Study of the Contrast Between Social Expectations and Immigrant Behavior. Ball State, 1976. 165p.
The study analyzes the apparent contrast between community expectations concerning Slavic immigrants in the anthracite region of northeastern Pennsylvania in the late nineteenth century and the actual behavior of the immigrants. While established groups in the anthracite fields, and American society at large, expected that the immigrants would threaten wage scales in the anthracite industry, primary evidence indicates that the Slavs did not do so. However, the community expectations proved to be so strong that almost all accounts of the immigration of Slavic labor assert that the many union failures and the traditionally depressed wages in the anthracite region, were the results of the Eastern European influx. This contrast between historical fact and social perception is explained by using the hypothesis proposed by social psychologist Erving Goffman and modified by sociologists Peter Berger and Thomas Luchmann. That thesis asserts that social reality is based on perceptions of events, rather than the events themselves. Since those perceptions are based on social expectations, it can be said that, in the case of the Slavic anthracite workers, the negative expectations of American society concerning the eastern Europeans produced negative conclusions concerning their behavior, despite much evidence to the contrary. Those negative conclusions remained in the literature of the anthracite industry until the publication of a study by historian Victor

Greene, The Slavic Community on Strike, in 1968, which finally revised the record concerning the Slavic mine workers. Of interest to all Slavic groups: Ukrainians, Byelorussians, Slovaks.

510. Baretski, Charles A. A Content Analysis of the "Polish American Journal" Newspaper in Reflecting the Political Attitudes, Issues and Perspectives of the Polish-American Group During the Period, 1950-1966. New York, 1969. 840p. (DA 30:3511-A)
The Polish ethnic group in the United States, with the help of its ethnic press, has maintained in a pluralist society its identity as a separate group. To ascertain the political behavior, attitudes, values, and perspectives of this group a content analysis of the national, biweekly newspaper the Polish American Journal, published in Scranton, Pennsylvania, under the editorship of Henry J. Dende, was undertaken for the period 1950 through 1966. (A)

511. Baskauskas, Liucija. An Urban Enclave: Lithuanian Refugees in Los Angeles. California (Los Angeles), 1971. 181p. (DA 32:3752-B)
This is a study of an ethnic group that has no visibility, is demographically dispersed and fully incorporated both economically and politically in the larger society, and yet maintains a "sense of peoplehood" based on national origin and culture. The study population is a Lithuanian group of refugees residing in greater Los Angeles who came to the United States as a result of the Displaced Persons Act after World War II. These refugees were selected according to specific criteria that were to facilitate their rapid adjustment and ultimate assimilation as well as their acceptance by the host population. (A)

512. Bennett, Linda A. Patterns of Ethnic Identity Among Serbs, Croats, and Slovenes in Washington, D.C. American, 1976. 385p.
This study explores patterns of ethnic-identity maintenance among a group of individuals for whom maintenance or abandonment of ethnic identity is primarily a matter of personal choice, with relatively minimal pressure generated by the sociocultural climate in which they live. Washington, D.C., provides such a climate; the study group is composed of individuals of Serbian, Croatian, and Slovenian descent--the largest ethnic groups in contemporary Yugoslavia. This study takes a different approach from most ethnic-group research in the United States in concentrating on some of the less-vivid aspects of ethnic identity as found among less-visible concentrations of ethnic-group members. In Washington such individuals are relatively few in number, recent in settlement, and dispersed over all parts of the metropolitan area with no one geographical locus of ethnicity. Approximately 3,400 first- through third-generation Serbs, Croats, and Slovenes live in the Washington area; Serbs constitute more than half, with the remaining population roughly evenly divided between Croats and Slovenes. Primarily a suburban population,

first- and second- generation members are younger, more geographically mobile, more highly educated, and more often employed in professional, technical, or clerical occupations than comparable ethnic communities elsewhere in the United States. By combining a summary of the historical background of the South Slavs in southeastern Europe and their migration and settlement in the United States, a demographic overview of the ethnic groups in Washington, and an extensive discussion of ethnographic material on the study group, patterns of ethnic-identity maintenance among these three groups in Washington may be scrutinized and placed in perspective.

513. Berger, Marshall D. The American English Pronunciation of Russian Immigrants. Columbia, 1951. 202p. (DA 12: 417)
The main aim of this study is to compare the sound patterns of Great Russian and of American English as manifested in the everyday speech of Russian immigrants residing mostly in New York City, and thereby to describe and explain the nature of the Russian "accent" in American English. The main assumption on which the investigation is based is that the phonemic pattern of Russian speakers is the starting point for their approach to English as a foreign language, regardless of their greater or lesser ability to speak it. (A)

514. Bogusas, Joseph. The Lithuanian Family in the United States. Fordham, 1942. 176p.

515. Cable, John N. The United States and the Polish Question, 1939-1948. Vanderbilt, 1972. 569p. (DA 33:1621-A)
This study documents, largely with published primary sources and unpublished manuscript collections, the onset of the Cold War between Russia and the United States over the Polish issue. Secondly, this study emphasizes the relationship between American foreign policy concerning Poland and domestic American politics from 1939-1948. The diplomacy of the two Democratic administrations concerning the Polish question was neither so threatening to Stalin as some revisionist historians suggest, nor so weak and unprincipled as many Republicans and Polish-American pressure groups have alleged. (A)

516. Cink, Kenneth. Czech-American Radicalism in the United States, 1849-1924. Chicago, 1970. 241p.

517. Colakovic, Branko M. Yugoslav Migrations to America. Minnesota, 1970. 305p. (E8da 32:367-B)
This dissertation is an examination of the Yugoslav experience of emigration to the United States in the late nineteenth and twentieth centuries. A major conclusion regarding the Yugoslav-emigration experience is that it was unusual in the degree to which emigrants went to the United States intending to stay a short time, to earn money, and to return to Yugoslavia. The actual return-emigration rates are distinctively high among European

emigrant groups. Among Serbians and Montenegrins the rate was 89 returning emigrants for every 100 emigrants to the United States. Among Croats and Slovenes 51 persons returned for every 100 emigrants to the United States. (A)

518. Davis, Jerome D. The Russian Immigrant. Columbia, 1922. 219p.
Published under the same title (New York: Columbia University Press, 1922). Describes the patterns of Russian emigration, settlements, and life experiences in receiving nations. Includes some notices of conditions in Russia in the period 1918-1922.

519. De Marr, Mary J. In a Strange Land: Contributions to American Literature by Russian and Russian-Jewish Immigrants. Illinois (Urbana), 1963. 343p. (DA 25:1907)
Despite the existence of Russian colonies in Alaska and Fort Ross, California, very little immigration of literary significance took place from Russia to the United States before 1881. A few members of the radical intelligentsia did come, some as immigrants and some on extended visits: for example, Agapy Goncharenko, G. A. Machtet, and A. S. Kurbsky. From 1881 to 1914 large numbers of Russian Jews immigrated, a few of whom had been assimilated into the radical Russian-speaking intelligentsia. They produced literature of two major sorts: autobiographies (Elizabeth Hasanovitz and Mary Antin) and fiction, frequently autobiographical, about the Jew in the New World (Anzia Yezierska, Abraham Cahan, Elias Tobenkin, John Cournos, and Charles Angoff). This Jewish immigration was stopped after World War I by the refusal of Soviet Russia to permit emigration and the restrictive quota legislation of the United States. (A)

520. Emmons, Charles F. Economic and Political Leadership in Chicago's Polonia: Some Sources of Ethnic Persistence and Mobility. Illinois (Chicago Circle), 1971. 287p. (DA 32: 4122-A)
The purpose of this study is to examine the roles mainly of economic, and, to a lesser extent, of political leaders in Chicago's Polish community, or "Polonia." Two classes of phenomena are considered in relationship to these roles: (1) the persistence of ethnic community activity, and (2) the social mobility of Poles in Chicago, especially that of the leaders themselves. (A)

521. Galitzi, Christine A. A Study of Assimilation Among Roumanians in the United States. Columbia, 1929. 282p.
Published under the same title (New York: Columbia University Press, 1929). Does not cover all phases of Rumanian immigration but endeavors "to present the chief facts" and "particularly to show the processes of assimilation at work among these immigrants under the pressure of the American environment." Chief groups studied are: Rumanians from the Old Kingdom; the Transylvanians from prewar Austria-Hungary, who make up the large majority; and Rumanian Macedonians. The author believes that the major problem in assimilation is the adjustment of the

transported Rumanian peasant culture to industrial American culture.

522. Galush, William J. Forming Polonia: A Study of Four Polish-American Communities, 1890-1940. Minnesota, 1975. 339p.
A comprehensive study of the Polish community in Cleveland, Minneapolis, and Utica (New York), with special attention to the churches, fraternal lodges, ethnic press, and local societies.

523. Gerber, Stanford N. Russkoya Celo: The Ethnography of a Russian-American Community. Missouri (Kansas City), 1967. 136p. (DA 28:773-B)
This dissertation is based upon 11 months of ethnographic research on a Russian-American ethnic community in the midwestern United States. The community described was established in 1911 and is presently a small enclave of approximately 120 persons. The community under consideration has maintained a relatively high degree of cohesion since its establishment, and the members of the community have attempted to avoid the establishment of primary, and in most cases, secondary relationships outside the community boundaries itself. The ethnographic data were collected primarily through the usual anthropological techniques of participant observation and intensive interviews with selected informants within the community. (A)

524. Gobetz, Giles E. Adjustment and Assimilation of Slovenian Refugees. Ohio State, 1962. 214p. (DA 23:744)
Published under the same title (New York: Arno, 1980). The Slovenes, the smallest, westernmost Slavic people, with a population of only a million and a half, have successfully resisted Germanization, Italianization, and Hungarianization. Since they had neither legal nor military resources, forced assimilation was resisted on moral grounds alone. This successful millennial resistance makes the study of the adjustment and assimilation processes of Slovenian immigrants in America of special interest. The dissertation consists of three parts: (1) conceptual analysis of adjustment and assimilation; (2) a sample of refugee correspondence (1945-1955); and (3) analysis of 115 questionnaires completed by Slovenian refugees who have settled in the United States and Canada since 1947. After an extensive examination of various definitions of and assumptions about assimilation, the conclusion is reached that its final test is the development of reciprocal identifications between minority- and majority-group members. An immigrant is assimilated when he or she habitually and unreservedly identifies with the majority group and when members of the majority group reciprocate by identifying him or her with themselves. Commonly used indicators of assimilation are critically examined and some oversimplifications exposed.

525. Golab, Caroline A. The Polish Communities of Philadelphia, 1870-1920: Immigrant Distribution and Adaptation in Urban

America. Pennsylvania, 1971. 480p. (DA 32:2012-A)
This work views immigrant adaptation as a function of spatial distribution. It presents a model for analyzing the distribution of immigrant groups throughout America as well as within specific urban areas. Immigrant distribution is also used to analyze the city as it functioned before 1920. Attempts are made to explain why Philadelphia supported the smallest percentage of immigrants of all large northern cities; why her Polish population, when compared with that of other cities, was very small, both proportionately and absolutely; why Italians in Philadelphia outnumbered Poles four to one and Eastern European Jews outnumbered Italians two to one; and why Pennsylvania was receiving more Poles than any other state. (A)

526. Goldenweiser, Emanuel A. Russian Immigration to the United States. Cornell, 1907. 160p.

527. Gould, Ketayun H. Social-Role Expectations of Polonians by Social-Class, Ethnic Identification and Generational Positioning. Pittsburgh, 1966. 178p. (DA 27:3140-A)
In the present stage of the ethnic-island development ethnicity seemed to be taking on different forms rather than disappearing. The disappearing impact of the foreign culture was seen in the third generation in the nonexistent use of the ethnic language, the lesser significance of ethnic food, the lack of attendance at an ethnic church, and the lack of membership in ethnic organizations. The folk-religiosity components of ethnicity, and particularly the rituals that stressed generational solidarity, were the best indicators of ethnicity. (A)

528. Govorchin, Gerald G. The Grey Falcon in the United States: A Short History of Yugoslav-Americans. Northwestern, 1946. 307p.
Published under the title Americans from Yugoslavia (Gainesville: University of Florida Press, 1961).

529. Greene, Victor R. The Attitude of Slavic Communities to the Unionization of the Anthracite Industry Before 1903. Pennsylvania, 1963. 604p. (DA 24:1995)
Published under the title The Slavic Community on Strike: Immigrant Labor in Pennsylvania Anthracite (Notre Dame, Indiana: Notre Dame University Press, 1968). Concerned with the relation of immigration to the American labor movement, the study examines the attitude of Polish, Slovak, Lithuanian, and Ukrainian immigrant mineworkers toward labor difficulties in the Pennsylvania anthracite districts before 1903. Through an attempt to learn the sociological and group sentiment of the Slavic communities the aim is to assess the Slavic immigrants' role in the establishment of unionism in the industry. (A)

530. Halich, Wasyl. Economic Aspects of Ukrainian Activity in the United States. Iowa, 1935. 174p.
Published under the title Ukrainians in the United States (Chicago:

University of Chicago Press, 1937). Includes a brief description of Ukrainian-immigrant backgrounds, movement to the United States, adjustment in the economic sphere, organization, churches, press, and social activities. Sources include official immigration records, newspapers, other publications of Ukrainian organizations, personal documents of Ukrainian leaders, and interviews.

531. Hall, Robert L. B. Population Biology of the Russian Old Believers of Marion County, Oregon. Oregon, 1970. 196p. (DA 31:3817-B)
Presented here is a historical résumé, a brief description of cultural variables, and a biological study of the founding population of Old Believers in Northern Marion County, Oregon. The population was formed in the mid-1960s by three separate groups of the same religion. These came from Turkey, Sinkiang Province in China, and Manchuria in approximate proportions of 1:3:6 respectively, and numbered roughly 2,000 persons in 1969. (A)

532. Herman, Harry V. Ethnicity and Occupation: Comparative Analysis of the Occupational Choices of Croatian and Macedonian Immigrants to Ontario. Toronto, 1978. 183p. (DA 40:938-A)
One of the very prominent features of complex industrial and multiethnic societies, such as Canada, is the coincidence of ethnic and occupational categories. The study of this phenomenon in Canada has been undertaken for the most part by students of social structure using census data. As a result we have acquired the knowledge of how the "tiles" within the "Vertical Mosaic" were distributed. The why of the phenomenon, however, was open for speculation. In order to contribute to the understanding of the reasons for the concentration of some ethnic collectivities within some occupations or occupational classes this study deals with the members of two such collectivities, Croatians and Macedonians. This comparison is restricted to the study of Croatian and Macedonian immigrants to Canada in the period up to the Second World War. The actions of individual immigrants upon their arrival in Canada are analyzed. (A)

533. Hewitt, William P. The Czechs in Texas: A Study of the Immigration and the Development of Czech Ethnicity, 1850-1920. Texas, 1978. 431p. (DA 40:6914-A)
This history is based on an analysis of the connections between the social, economic, and geographic origins of the immigration and the settlements and settlement patterns of Czech Texans. These determinants shaped the structure and development of Czech ethnicity in Texas. The ethnicity in turn is viewed not in the constructs of the melting pot, cultural pluralism, or Americanization theories. Instead it is interpreted as the loci of Gemeinschaft through which the Czech immigrants expressed their response to their Texas environment. Thus, it is a study of immigration as social history. (A)

534. Hill, Robert F. Exploring the Dimensions of Ethnicity: A Study of Status, Culture and Identity Among Polish-Americans. Pittsburgh, 1975. 350p.
Through participant observation, focused interviews, library research, survey questionnaire, and an analysis of historical documents this study explores the dimensions of status, culture, and identity among Polish-Americans in Pittsburgh, Pennsylvania. Focusing on these three dimensions and the dynamic interrelation between them at different units of analysis--the group, the community, the school, and the individual--the author concludes that observed intraethnic variation can be explained by three adaptive strategies: enclave security, passing, and militancy. Approaches that assume a homogeneity of human response to ethnicity, whether pluralist or assimilationist, are seen as more ideological than factual. The study includes ethnohistorical profiles of the Polish-American group in time and space, a working-class Polish-American community, a Roman Catholic high school where the students are of predominantly Polish-American background, and the life histories of two Polish-American individuals.

535. Horak, Jakub. Assimilation of Czechs in Chicago. Chicago, 1920. 112p.

536. Johannes, M. Eloise. A Study of the Russian-German Settlements in Ellis County, Kansas. Catholic, 1945. 153p.
Published under the same title (Washington, D. C.: Catholic University of America Press, 1945).

537. Johnston, Barrance V. Social Mobility and the Russian-American: The Case of the Achievement Syndrome. Notre Dame, 1974. 214p.
The research presented here deals with the social-psychological dimension of the social mobility of the Russian-American, characterized as America's most successful ethnic group. A historical, structural, and social-psychological orientation is presented as a preliminary analysis of Russian-American mobility. Within this context attention is focused on the social-psychological element and specifically the achievement syndrome as manifested by Russian Orthodox Catholics, Russian Jews, and Russian Eastern Rite Roman Catholics. The findings are suggestive of differential manifestations of the achievement syndrome when the sample is analyzed in terms of religious identity, social class, and maternal mobility. Although such patterns were detected, the expected relationship between the achievement syndrome and actual level of performance is found in only one case, that of the Russian Orthodox Catholic. Therefore, at the theoretical level the research is supportive of the literature that suggests that the role played by social-psychological variables in social mobility is indirect and passive. The term "Russian-American" is very broadly used; thus, the thesis is of interest to Russian, Ukrainian, and Byelorussian ethnic groups.

538. Jonitis, Peter P. The Acculturation of the Lithuanians of Chester, Pennsylvania. Pennsylvania, 1951. 544p. (DA

13:267)
This is a study of the acculturation of Lithuanian immigrants. As a consequence of the continuous and persistent process of acculturation and adjustment during the past half-century, the structure and functions of the Lithuanian peasant family have undergone a marked change from what they were in Lithuania. These changes have been analyzed in terms of a continuum. The continuum ranges from an unacculturated Old World Type to a highly acculturated and urbanized American type of family. (A)

539. Juroczak, Chester A. Ethnicity, Status and Generational Positioning: A Study of Health Practices Among Polonians in Five Ethnic Islands. Pittsburgh, 1964. 255p. (DA 26: 528)
The research problem was concerned with the methodological problem of determining the components of ethnicity operationally and of assessing how ethnicity varies with generational and cohort positioning. The differences lay in socialization, differences of entry (birth order) into the family cycle, differences in the family organization, and the differences of entry (born at a different phase of development) into the ethnic island. (A)

540. Jutronic, Dunja. Serbo-Croatian and American English in Contact: A Sociolinguistic Study of the Serbo-Croatian Community in Steelton, Pennsylvania. Pennsylvania State, 1971. 249p. (DA 33:297-A)
The primary aim of this study was to discover the essential tendencies and changes of Serbo-Croatian produced by contact with American English through three generations of Serbo-Croatian-speaking Americans. Secondly, this study attempted to determine the degree of language maintenance and language shift of Serbo-Croatian (SCr.) under the impact of American English (AE). The answers to the following three questions were sought: (1) To what degree has the interference from AE affected the basic structure of SCr.? (2) What is the most significant differentiating factor in the speech of different generations? (3) Is there any correlation between the process of language interference and language shift? The main hypothesis was: if language interference increases through generations, the habitual use of language undergoing interference should decrease. (A)

541. Kemesis, Fabian S. Cooperation Among the Lithuanians in the United States of America. Catholic, 1924. 178p.
Published under the same title (Washington, D.C.: Catholic University of America Press, 1924).

542. Kernaklian, Paul. The Armenian-American Personality Structure and Its Relationship to Various States of Ethnicity. Syracuse, 1967. 405p. (DA 28:1525-A)
This dissertation analyzes the Armenian-American adolescent in terms of two basic variables--personality and ethnicity. Neither of these two variables, nor their relationship, has ever been investigated for the Armenian-Americans from an objective-empiri-

cal perspective. Specifically, no interdisciplinary study of Armenian-American youth as members of an ethnic minority in the United States exists today. Consequently, this research not only adds to our general knowledge of ethnic minorities but also provides a contemporary picture of ethnic affiliation and its affect upon the personality structure as well as an empirical study of a previously unspecified segment of the ethnic population in the United States. (A)

543. Kolasa, Blair J. The Relationship Between Bilingualism and Performance on a Linguistic Type Intelligence Test. Pittsburgh, 1954. 100p. (DA 14:2396)
A study of high school and college students in which the second language of each bilingual was Polish. Major finding: neither aspect of bilingualism seems to be of influence in performance on a linguistic type of intelligence test.

544. Kovacs, Sandor B. Czechoslovaks in Virginia. Virginia, 1939. 161p.

545. Krzywkowski, Leo V. The Origin of the Polish National Catholic Church of St. Joseph County, Indiana. Ball State, 1972. 272p. (DA 33:3544-A)
The purpose of this study was to determine the causes for the origin of the Polish National Catholic Church in St. Joseph County, Indiana. The first three chapters consider the socioeconomic phenomena that help explain this schism from Roman Catholicism; the fourth traces the actual organization of the new church. Chapter V concludes the study by offering probable causes for this schism, and, for the sake of simplicity, dividing these into the proximate and the remote, that is, the causes that appear at the surface, directly explaining it (the proximate); and the factors that, although separated from the event by greater intervals, give it true meaning (the remote). (A)

546. Kutak, Robert I. The Story of a Bohemian-American Village: A Study of Social Persistence and Change. Columbia, 1934. 156p.
Published under the same title (Louisville, Kentucky: Standard Printing, 1934). The purpose of this study of Czech immigrants is twofold: (1) to discover which modes of behavior had persisted in the New World and which had changed, and to discover the causes of these persistences and changes; and (2) to find out whether the adjustment of the Bohemian immigrants to a rural environment (Nebraska community) differed from that to a city environment.

547. Kuznicki, Ellen M. An Ethnic School in American Education: A Study of the Origin, Development, and Merits of the Educational System of the Felician Sisters in the Polish American Catholic Schools of Western New York. Kansas State, 1973. 288p. (DA 33:6845-A)
Polish-American Sisterhoods have played an important role in the

American parochial-school system. They staffed the Catholic schools the Polish immigrants founded to maintain Old World linguocultural values. By adapting their curriculum to the needs of the children and to the requirements of the local and state departments of education, the Sisters served as agents of cultural transition. The subject of this dissertation is the study of the role of the Felician Sisters in the acculturation of the Polish people of western New York by means of the Polish parochial school. It is an attempt to show how the Sisters provided for a gradual linguocultural transition whereby the Polish children were Americanized without the complete loss of ethnic identity. (A)

548. La Piere, Richard T. The Armenian Colony in Fresno County, California: A Study in Social Psychology. Stanford, 1930. 173p.

549. Leuca, Mary. Development in Ethnic Heritage Curriculum: A Case Study of Romanian Americans in Lake County, Indiana. Purdue, 1979. 226p. (DA 40:3087-A)
The major concern of this dissertation was the development of curriculum resources for use by teachers in the elementary and secondary schools relating to history, social life, economics, literature, music, language, traditions, and customs of Rumanian Americans in northwest Indiana. This study was confined to this group and their descendants residing in that area and relates the Rumanian-American experience in Lake County, Indiana, from its settlement in the early 1900s to the present, thereby adding a Rumanian dimension to the long list of other ethnic groups that have contributed to contemporary American society. (A)

550. Lopata, Helena Z. The Functions of Voluntary Associations in an Ethnic Community: "Polonia." Chicago, 1954. 198p.

551. Lovrich, Frank M. The Social System of a Rural Yugoslav-American Community: Oysterville. South Dakota State, 1963. 370p. (DA 26:6222)
Published under the same title (San Francisco: R & E Research Associates, 1971). The social life in a Yugoslavian-American settlement described in this thesis is based on data collected in "Oysterville," a predominantly oyster-farming community located in Plaquemines Parish, Louisiana. Additional information was collected from Yugoslavs living in New Orleans, Louisiana, and in Biloxi, Mississippi. The interval of time covered by the study is roughly from 1820 to the present. Special emphasis is placed on the years from 1954 to 1961, when the survey data were collected. The basic problem of the study is to ascertain how the Yugoslavs in lower Louisiana have been able to retain their unique ethnic identity in this period of rapid acculturation and change. (A)

552. Mackun, Stanley. The Changing Patterns of Polish Settlements in the Greater Detroit Area: Geographic Study of the Assimilation of an Ethnic Group. Michigan, 1964. 203p.

Poland, Russia, Balkans, Slavic Europe 133

(DA 25:4644)
The objective of this study has been to recreate the original patterns of distribution of people of Polish ancestry within the initial framework of the Greater Detroit Area and to follow the territorial changes of these patterns to the present. This has called for a consideration of such aspects of a growing community as the nature of its expansion, the movements of its residents, and the effects of these on the process of assimilation of the ethnic group. (A)

553. Mamchur, Stephen W. Nationalism, Religion, and the Problem of Assimilation Among Ukrainians in the United States. Yale, 1942. 340p.

554. Markus, Daria. Education in Ethnic Leadership: A Case Study of the Ukrainian Ethnic Group in the United States. Loyola (Chicago), 1977. 336p.
The dissertation deals with the process of "ethnization" in American society. The Ukrainian community was selected, for in the past 25 years it has had no new immigrants to reinforce its ethnicity and has now reached a point where, in order to survive, it must pass the leadership of the organizations to a younger, American-born or American-educated generation, a generation whose ethnic consciousness was produced in the American environment. There are three parts to the study: (1) a historical overview of the development of the Ukrainian community in the United States, its organizational structure, and the issues, conflicts, and dominant ideologies; (2) an analytical description of the community-organized educational efforts conducted by the Church, the school, and youth organizations; and (3) a survey of the young leadership in the community dealing with their educational background, involvement in community activism, and their own assessment of the influence of ethnic education provided by the community on their commitment to ethnic activism.

555. Meyerstein, Ruth G. Selected Problems of Bilingualism Among Immigrant Slovaks. Michigan, 1959. 208p.
The author applies principles of modern linguistic science and bilingualism to the description of some speech features characteristic of Slovak immigrants in the United States. Areas studied include Chicago and Binghamton, New York.

556. Mirak, Robert. The Armenians in the United States, 1890-1915. Harvard, 1965. 351p.
This study examines the origins and development of the Armenian community in the United States in the years 1890-1915. It seeks to describe the background and the forms of adjustment of that community in the quarter-century before World War I. Some attempt is made also to place the Armenians in the perspective of the "newer" immigrant groups. Emigration to the New World for Armenians began in the 1880s. Before that date handfuls of missionary-educated students, teachers, and clergymen had made their way to the United States. Thereafter, spurred by the poli-

tical upheaval of the 1890s and chronic economic backwardness
and political insecurity, thousands of Armenians fled their Old
World homes for the New. The threat of conscription into the
backward Turkish armies and the call of "American letters" increased
the flow. Proportionately, the migration came from the
lower-middle and poorer classes, though not the peasantry rooted
by its poverty. In all, over 60,000 emigrated to America. The
adjustment of the Armenians varied conspicuously in two respects
from others. Generally, despite their hard beginnings, the Armenians
succeeded in their economic adjustment more rapidly
than others. There were a few great success stories, primarily
in the Armenians' control of the Oriental-goods business. The
great majority led humble lives of hard work, savings, and optimism.
However, their backgrounds as an Old World minority,
the fact that they were not the peasantry of eastern and southern
Europe, and a high literacy rate permitted many to adapt to the
American economy. Secondly, the immigrants' communal life
was exceptionally turbulent. The struggle for an independent
Armenia was passionate. The cause divided the community,
bringing forth violence and continual discord. Few immigrant
groups felt the impress of Old World issues so intensely.

557. Morawska, E. Teresa. The Maintenance of Ethnicity: A
Case Study of the Polish American Community in Greater
Boston. Boston, 1976. 178p. (DA 37:1816-A)
This project, a case study of the Polish-American community in
Greater Boston, combines historical, ethnographic, and sociological
survey methods of investigation. In its historical part the
study investigates settlement patterns, socioeconomic position,
and community life of early Polish immigrants in Boston. The
occupational mobility of Polish settlers during the first decades
of our century is analyzed in reference to their subcultural values
and aspirations. The investigation then focuses on the further
development of the Polish-American community in Boston in the
years between the two world wars. It discusses the inward socioeconomic
movement of Poles as well as their outside political
activization. The part dealing with the contemporary life of the
Polish-Americans in Boston outlines the group's structural location,
residential patterns, and the institutional profile of the
community. (A)

558. Mostwin, Danuta. The Transplanted Family, a Study of Social
Adjustment of the Polish Immigrant Family to the United
States After the Second World War. Columbia, 1971. 378p.
(DA 32:5345-A)
The study of the transplanted family examines the patterns of social
adjustment of the immigrant family to its new geographical,
cultural, and national environment. Research is based on findings
derived from the responses of 2,049 Polish post-World War
II immigrants to the United States to the fixed-alternative, mailed
questionnaire. The study is structured around three main research
questions inquiring into selective aspects of adjustment of
the adults (heads of the family), socialization of children, and the
restructuring of ethnic identity. (A)

559. Nelson, Harold. The Armenian Family: Changing Patterns of Family Life in a California Community. California (Berkeley), 1954. 203p.

560. Obidinski, Eugene E. Ethnic to Status Group: A Study of Polish Americans in Buffalo. State University of New York at Buffalo, 1968. 216p. (DA 29:686-A)
Published under the same title (New York: Arno, 1980). A distinct Polish-American subcommunity has existed in Buffalo for almost a century despite continual assimilation of immigrants and their descendants. This study examined variables relevant to (1) the continued existence of the subcommunity, and (2) the transformation or change in subcommunity patterns. The study consisted of a brief history of the subcommunity; an analysis of differences in attitudes and activities of second- and third-generation Polish-Americans; an examination of familial, religious, political, and economic practices; and characteristics of upper-, middle-, and working-class respondents. (A)

561. O'Connell, Lucille. Public and Philanthropic Facilities for the Adjustment of Immigrants in New York City, 1900-1920, As Illustrated in the Polish Experience. New York, 1973. 452p. (DA 34:1196)
Public and philantrhopic agencies active in New York between 1900 and 1920 contributed to the adjustment of the foreign-born to American society. The federal government did little to provide protection and assistance for immigrants from the time of their arrival at Ellis Island until they became settled in an American community. Only the federal Division of Information worked to find jobs for immigrants and distributed informative pamphlets about government and life in America. Its goal was to serve the American economy and relieve urban congestion by distributing the labor force. The agencies promoting adjustment emphasized shaping the behavior of immigrants to the existing patterns of American life. The publications of the agencies stressed patriotism, conformity, and Americanization, as well as hard work and thrift as the path to economic success. (A)

562. Ostafin, Peter A. The Polish Peasant in Transition: A Study of Group Integration as a Function of Symbiosis and Common Definition. Michigan, 1949. 240p. (DA 9 no. 1: 179)
The purpose of this study is to observe the relationship between symbiosis and common definitions to see what the consequences are when these factors either reinforce each other or when they clash with each other. Observations to test relationships were made by referring them to a field situation complex enough to be divisible into a rural and an urban segment. (A)

563. Parot, Joseph J. The American Faith and the Persistence of Chicago Polonia, 1870-1920. Northern Illinois, 1971. 380p. (DA 32:3930-A)
This study approaches the problem of ethnic persistence by examining the institutional forces in Chicago Polonia, primarily

during the height of the 'new immigration" period. The author's main contention is that the process of assimilation and acculturation was a pulsating process, a continuous waxing and waning largely determined by Chicago Polonia's self-interests and aspirations. From a religious standpoint, the Resurrectionist clergy, for instance, worked within the outlines of the Chancery-Polonia pact agreed to by Bishop Thomas Foley and Superior General Jerome Kajsiewicz, C. R., in 1871. In effect, the agreement not only gave the Resurrectionist Congregation exclusive control over Polish parishes in Chicago, but in addition pointed toward increased Irish-Polish cooperation on the parish level. Yet, Resurrectionists like Father Vincent Barzynski, dynamic and aggressive proponent of the community-parish system, designed to maintain Old World religious customs in the New World urban environment, could simultaneously push for ethnic exclusiveness within the Polish Roman Catholic Union and the Association of Polish Priests. However, clerical ambitions were challenged within Chicago Polonia by rival groups, such as Ladislaus Dyniewicz's Gmina Polska, in the 1870s and the Polish National Alliance in the 1880s. These organizations, staunch adherents to the gospel of Poland's nineteenth-century Messianic Romanticism, also maintained ambivalent positions toward assimilation. On the one hand, the Gmina and the Polish National Alliance encouraged their membership to become actively involved in the American political process. However, once Polonia became a viable political force, strength was to be exercised for liberating partitioned Poland.

564. Prpic, George. The Croats in America. Georgetown, 1959. 240p.
Published under the title Croatian Immigrants in America (New York: Philosophical Library, 1971).

565. Renkiewicz, Frank A. The Polish Settlement of St. Joseph County, Indiana: 1855-1935. Notre Dame, 1967. 361p. (DA 28:4102-A)
This study of Polish-Americans in South Bend and in three small farming colonies west of that city assumes two perspectives on its subjects. One chronicles the birth, evolution, and survival of their ethnic community for three generations. The second analyzes the relationship between them and the major events and institutions of American life from 1855 to 1935. (A)

566. Renoff, Richard M. Celibacy and Schism: The Loss of Community Among the American Carpatho-Ruthenians. New York, 1971. 217p. (DA 33:5306-A)
A Vatican decree of 1929, Cum Data Fuerit, stated that clerical celibacy was hereafter mandatory for newly ordained and émigré priests of the Roman Catholic Eastern Rite (Uniat) church in America. This edict stimulated widespread dissatisfaction among the Sub-Carpathian Ruthenians, resulting in a schism in the 1930s. Using Redfield's folk-urban continuum as a theoretical orientation, the author hypothesized that the faction that opposed Rome would

possess characteristics indicative of a "traditional" background while the faction that supported the Vatican was expected to possess characteristics indicative of a "modern" background. This hypothesis was tested upon a nationwide universe of 40 priests who opposed celibacy and 96 priests who did not voice opposition to the discipline, and upon a sample of 526 Bridgeport, Connecticut, laypeople who were members of the newly formed "Carpatho-Russian" Orthodox diocese and 121 Bridgeport laypeople who remained in union with Rome. (A)

567. Sabey, Ralph H. Staroveri and School: A Case Study of the Education of Russian Immigrant Children in a Rural Oregon Community. Oregon, 1969. 185p. (DA 30:3255-A)
The purpose of this inquiry was to examine cross-cultural education in a rural American community. The community selected-- Gervais, Oregon--was one in which the children, from 27 recent immigrant families attend school. These families were of the Staroveri religion and were Russian-speaking peasants, who migrated from northern China to Brazil in 1960 and to Oregon during the period from 1964 to the present. (A)

568. Sandberg, Neil C. Design and Testing of a Group Cohesiveness Scale to Measure the Salience of Ethnic Identity Among Polish-Americans in the Los Angeles Metropolitan Area. Southern California, 1972. 181p. (DA 33:841-A)
Published under the title Ethnic Identity and Assimilation: The Polish American Community (New York: Praeger, 1974). In order to assess current and predicted ethnic identity the author selected Polish-Americans in the Los Angeles metropolitan area as a test population. Changing patterns of assimilation and acculturation were examined through the construction and utilization of a new group-cohesiveness scale, which focused on religious, cultural, and national subconstructs. The model emphasized the interrelatedness of these variables, which together constituted a total measure of ethnicity. Undergirding the use of the scale was the assumption that ethnic identity could be measured empirically. (A)

569. Servaitis, Casmir P. Religious Folkways in Lithuania and Their Conservation Among Lithuanian Immigrants in the United States. Catholic, 1952. 276p.
Published under the same title (Washington, D. C.: Catholic University of America Press, 1952).

570. Shea, William S. The Polish Independent Church Movement in the United States. Boston College, 1934. 187p.

571. Simirenko, Alex. Pilgrims, Colonists, and Frontiersmen: An Ethnic Community in Transition. Minnesota, 1961. 302p. (DA 22:3767)
Published under the same title (New York: n.p., 1964). Following the ideas of four major theorists (Weber, Gerth, Mills, and Martindale) the ethnic community is theorized to be a special kind

of minority or subcommunity produced by the majority community exclusion (prejudice) on the one hand and minority community closure on the other. In order to trace the dynamics of social change by which the Russian community of Minneapolis first took shape and later began to change and eventually to decay under the influence of the wider social environment, various subgroups of the community were divided into generational units following the criteria of Karl Mannheim. (A)

572. Skrabanek, Robert N. Social Organization and Change in a Czech-American Rural Community: A Sociological Study of Snook, Texas. Louisiana State, 1950. 240p.

573. Stein, Howard F. An Ethno-Historic Study of Slovak-American Identity. Pittsburgh, 1972. 536p. (DA 33:2911-B) Ethnohistoric and psychoanalytic frames of reference are used to analyze the Slovak-American experience and explore the relation between personal and group identity process both in traditional feudal Slovakia and for the period 1880 to the present in the urban-industrial region of northeastern, middle Atlantic, and midwestern United States. The dynamics of Americanization are explored along the dimensions of status denigration; cultural role continuity and discontinuity; and of rebellion against dependency and authority--this latter utilized the American ideology of freedom, self-reliance, achievement, and independence as a means of resolving conflicts inherent in traditional Slovak culture. The study explores traditional Slovak society and the Slovak-American experience at several levels, and attempts to integrate these levels into an ethnohistoric and psychohistoric whole: base-line feudal Slovakia; post-serfdom Slovak peasantry (1848 through the great migration of 1880-1914); changes in the economy, kinship structure, and family dynamics, the process of migration, centers of immigration in the United States focusing on the three-rivers area of western Pennsylvania, and finally narrowing down to a study of a Monongahela River mill town, McKeesport.

574. Stipanovich, Joseph P. "In Unity Is Strength": Immigrant Workers and Immigrant Intellectuals in Progressive America: A History of the South Slav Social Democratic Movement, 1900-1918. Minnesota, 1978. 207p. (DA 39:3783-A) This work is a study of the organization and development of social democratic political movements among Slovene, Croat, and Serb immigrants in the United States between 1900 and 1918. In the development of the analysis of these movements special attention is given to the physical characteristics of each migratory group, including motivation for emigration, rates of settlement and repatriation, male/female ratios, occupations acquired by industry, areas of settlement, and information flows within the groups. The effect of indigenous socialist movements upon the immigrant movements, the effect of immigrant movements upon each other, the stimulus provided by working conditions in the U. S. for socialist organization, and the role of immigrant socialists in the formation of immigrant communities are also analyzed. (A)

575. Stolarik, Marian M. Immigration and Urbanization: The Slovak Experience, 1870-1918. Minnesota, 1974. 280p. (DA 35:4407-A)
The Slovak odyssey, which began with landless serfs moving to southern Hungary in the eighteenth century, quickened as peasants in the next 100 years moved to towns in search of work. It reached a climax in the early twentieth century, when one-quarter of the nation found a new home in America. Settling chiefly in cities of the industrial northeast, working mainly as unskilled laborers, and living frugally in boarding houses, Slovak immigrants to America quickly established their own neighborhoods of residence, set up fraternal-benefit societies, initiated parishes, and founded a vigorous newspaper press. (A)

576. Sturm, Rudolf. Sojourn of the Czech Poet Josef Vaclav Sladek in the United States and the American Influences in His Writings. Harvard, 1956. 276p.

577. Sypek, Stanislaus T. The Displaced Polish Persons in the Greater Boston Community. Fordham, 1955. 212p.

578. Taggart, Glen L. Czechs of Wisconsin As a Culture Type. Wisconsin, 1948. 246p.

579. Trutza, Peter G. The Religious Factor in Acculturation: A Study of the Assimilation and Acculturation of the Roumanian Group in Chicago. Chicago, 1956. 268p.

580. Urbanski, Adam. Americanism and the Polish-American Press, 1916-1925. Rochester, 1974. 188p.
The thesis examines the Polish-language immigrant press in America during the 1916-1925 period. The decade selected for emphasis permits an analysis of responses by the Polish-American press to such important issues as World War I, the rebirth of Poland, the Americanization campaign, and the legislation restricting immigration. It was also a period of considerable growth and intense activity for the ethnic press in general and the Polish-American press in particular. The concluding chapter offers a summary of findings and a discussion of the Polish-American press as a source for historical research. It includes also a comparison and contrast with data found in secondary literature, statistical works, interviews with contemporary readers and editors of the Polish-language press, and other sources. The thesis does not attempt to provide final answers but rather constitutes an effort to raise some important questions. It suggests that the Polish-language press in America is a neglected but most valuable and useful source of historical data for the study of Polish immigrant experiences in the United States during one vital period of America's history. Admittedly a pioneer study, it offers also a comment on the direction needed for future historical research in this area of scholarship.

581. Veidemanis, Juris. Social Change: Major Value-Systems of Latvians at Home, As Refugees, and As Immigrants. Wiscon-

sin, 1961. 769p. (DA 22:2099)
Latvian society provides an excellent opportunity for sociological study of social change. This study compared the major kinds of social values in Latvian society during (1) the period of independence (1918-1940), (2) refugee life in western Germany and Austria (1945-1950), and (3) life in resettlement in the United States--specifically in Milwaukee, Wisconsin (1949-1959). The question was: What patterns of change in kinds of values can be discerned over these three phases? Becker's method of constructive typology and his sacred-secular conceptual framework were utilized in the research and analysis. Culture case studies were made, describing in detail the normative realms of Latvian society for each of the three periods. The descriptions are subdivided into chapters according to religion, organizations, communications, integration, stratification, and deviation. All available sources were utilized, with preference given to primary sources (records, documents, publications, interviews). Each culture case study concluded with an idiographic delineation of value uniformities for which consensuses were found in the material. To enable comparison of the three sets of value uniformities and the formulation of a nomothetic hypothesis, the idiographic uniformities were transformed to a nomothetic level represented by the sacred-secular typological schema.

582. Vrga, Djuro J. A Study of Ethnic Factionalism--The Schism in the Serbian Orthodox Church in America. Notre Dame, 1968. 329p. (DA 29:3243-A)
This empirical study of factionalism in the Serbian ethnic minority group represents an attempt to assess the relative importance of sociopsychological factors affecting the adjustment of successive immigrations and their descendants to one another and to the larger society. Findings of this study, based on interview data of a randomly stratified sample of 84 members of a parish in Chicago, demonstrates that intragroup conflicts, especially the latent ones, may arise as a consequence of differential adjustment of various segments of the group to the conditions in the larger society. (A)

583. Warzeski, Walter C. Religion and the National Consciousness in the History of the Rusins of Carpatho-Ruthenia and the Byzantine Rite Pittsburgh Exarchate. Pittsburgh, 1964. 395p. (DA 26:1623)
Published under the title Byzantine Rite. Rusins in Carpatho-Ruthenia and America (Pittsburgh: Byzantine Seminary Press, 1971). This dissertation is a case study of the mutual interaction of religion and nationality as revealed by the history of the Pittsburgh Exarchate of the Byzantine Rite. In order to place the people into their proper perspective the Old World background has been investigated. This includes the historical origins of the Rusins both ethnic and political, together with the part they had in the history of Central Europe. (A)

584. Waschek, Brownlee. Czech and Slovak Folk Music in Masaryktown and Slovenská Záhrada, Florida: Arrangements of

Representative Examples of Folk Songs Illustrating Their Adaptability to School Use. Florida State, 1969. 335p., 370p. (DA 33:780-A)
The purpose of this study was (1) to investigate and collect folk music transplanted from Czechoslovakia to the communities of Masaryktown and Slovenská Záhrada, Florida; (2) to reduce this music to conventional notation; (3) to translate the words of the songs into English; (4) to investigate the ethnology of the Czechoslovak peasant to provide an understanding of the people from whom the music was collected; and (5) to illustrate the adaptability of the songs for school use. (A)

585. White, John P. Lithuanians and the Democratic Party: A Case Study of Nationality Politics in Chicago and Cook County. Chicago, 1953. 204p.

586. Wolniewicz, Richard. Northeast Minneapolis: Location and Movement in an Ethnic Community. Minnesota, 1979. 250p. (DA 40:3535-A)
This study investigated six hypotheses concerning the development of an ethnic area and intra-urban migration in Minneapolis from 1905 to 1945: (1) The clustering of Poles from the three parts of partitioned Poland within Minneapolis was fairly definite although these areas were not exclusively Polish. Provincial clustering was not sharply defined within the Polish community itself. (2) The ethnic core area, typically defined as an area of transient housing populated by single, young males, had less than half of the most recent Polish arrivals in 1905. The "port of entry" was not tied to the old core, but had expanded as the community grew. (3) The length of first-generation move during the 40 years was more closely related to the expansion of Minneapolis than to the length of time since arrival. (4) It cannot categorically be asserted that second-generation individuals are more mobile than first-generation individuals. (5) More Polish moves were explained by the within-group information flow notion than the idea of wedge-shaped mental map movement. Poles moved to areas that already had Poles. (6) Other Slavic groups near the Poles in 1905 had movement patterns similar to them, but non-Slavs had patterns quite different.

587. Yeretzian, Aram S. A History of Armenian Immigration to America with Special Reference to Conditions in Los Angeles. Southern California, 1923. 78p.
Published under the same title (San Francisco: R & E Research Associates, 1974). A cultural profile of the Armenian community in Los Angeles, with a brief history of Armenian emigration to the United States.

588. Zivich, Edward A. From Zadruga to Oil Refinery: Croatian Immigrants and Croatian Americans in Whiting, Indiana, 1890 to 1950. State University of New York (Binghamton), 1977. 124p. (DA 38:5671)
This dissertation describes the historical experiences of Croatian immigrants and their Croatian-American children in the oil-re-

fining city of Whiting, Indiana. It utilizes both traditional and quantitative sources. The Whiting Croatians came from a single emigration district along the Croatian Military Border. Changes from communal to individual ownership of the land in the 1880s, coupled with a rising population, left the peasants in the area land-short. There was no alternative employment in Croatia, forcing the peasants to emigrate to America. (A)

D. EUROPEAN JEWRY

---

589. Alper, Michael. Reconstruction and Jewish Education--The Implications of Reconstructionism for Jewish Education in the United States. Columbia (Teachers College), 1954. 449p. (DA 14:1186)
Reconstructionism is the name of a movement in American Jewish life initiated by Dr. Mordecai M. Kaplan and developed by him and many colleagues and disciples. It is critical of all the existing major theories of Jewish life because of their failure to come to grips, philosophically and educationally, with the twofold challenge of modern democratic nationalism and modern naturalism. Reconstructionism aims to effect a creative adjustment of Jewish life to these new conditions of the modern world. Reconstructionism is a Jewish religious movement that seeks to integrate the patterns of democracy, the naturalistic outlook, the organismic point of view in psychology, and the method and intellectual mood of pragmatism. (A)

590. Antonovsky, Aaron. The Ideologies of American Jews. Yale, 1954. 211p.

591. Atzman, Ezri. The Impact of Educational Programs on the Acculturation of Adult Jewish Immigrants in Metropolitan Detroit (1949-1955). Michigan, 1958. 264p. (DA 19:477)
This is a study of the effect of the educational programs offered to adult Jewish immigrants in Detroit on their acculturation in the following five areas: command of the English language, citizenship, economic status, social relations, and consumption and acceptance of American culture. It is an investigation of the relationship between the acculturation of immigrants and such variables as years of residence in the United States, cultural background, sex, age-level, marital status, educational background, parental economic background, type of immigrant, and length of exposure to the educational programs. (A)

592. Avruch, K. A. American Immigrants in Israel. Social Identities and Changes. California (San Diego), 1978. 413p.
This dissertation examines American Jews who have immigrated to Israel and the problems encountered and strategies utilized in

European Jewry 143

integrating themselves into Israeli society. It is a study whose central concerns include problems of migration, acculturation, and role-set transformation.

593. Bachelis, Faith G. Regional Origin, Personality, and Mothers' Attitudes of Jewish Day School Students. Yeshiva, 1966. 266p. (DA 28:1154-B)
The present research investigated the influence of the subcultural factor of familial regional origin within a single religious group upon children's intellectual and emotional functioning and maternal attitudes. The study also explored the relationship between maternal attitudes and children's intellectual and emotional functioning. The results of the study offered some support to the theoretical formulation that cultural groups are associated with typical patterns of personal functioning of group members. It was suggested that the theory of typical personality may be generalized to smaller divisions within a culture and subculture. It was further suggested that projected research that considers a religious group, such as the Jews, as homogeneous should take into account the heterogeneity of this subculture due to varied familial regional origins. (A)

594. Bennett, Emanuel. An Evaluation of the Life of Isaac Leeser. Yeshiva, 1955. 245p.

595. Berger, Sidney L. The Theme of Persecution in Selected Dramas of the Yiddish Art Theatre. Kansas, 1964. 260p. (DA 25:5901)
For its basic premise this study presumes that a work of art placed in its historical perspective permits a valid glimpse of the interpretation that a cultural or racial group gives to the recorded event. This work attempts to gain some understanding of the way in which persecution was treated on the Yiddish stage in America. (A)

596. Berkson, Isaac B. Theories of Americanization: A Critical Study with Special Reference to the Jewish Group. Columbia (Teachers College), 1919. 240p.
Published under the same title (New York: Teachers College Press, Columbia University, 1920). This study is an early, now classic, statement of the case for cultural pluralism, especially Jewish, in American education.

597. Berman, Barbara A. P. Environmental Impact on the Ideology of a Social Movement Organization: The Jewish Daily Forward, 1897-1966. Michigan, 1972. 220p. (DA 33:6456)
The Jewish Daily Forward, a Yiddish newspaper that was part of the Jewish socialist labor movement, was examined to explore the capacity for and direction of change in ideology and the impact of different environmental factors on ideology. The history of the newspaper since its founding in 1897 indicates a long-run assimilation of the Jewish socialist labor movement and the immigrant Jewish community into American society. This evidence

also indicates periods in which the paper's environment was negative--in which it experienced significant internal movement conflict and societal hostility in the form of anti-Semitic and antiforeign sentiment and activities. This study examined the impact of negative pressures, both internal and external, on the Forward's ideology. (A)

598. Berman, Myron. The Attitude of American Jewry Towards East European Jewish Immigration, 1881-1914. Columbia, 1963. 585p. (DA 24:3306)
The study shows that American Jewry, consisting largely of German Jewish immigrants and their children, in the eighties and nineties feared and tried to discourage East European Jewish immigration. By 1914 the American Jewish community considered their coreligionists welcome additions to the population. Despite the increase of nativism and of anti-Semitism between 1881 and 1914, the overwhelming majority of Jews seeking these shores were granted admission. American Jewry by 1914 not only expended significant sums of money for domestic charities but also collected funds for overseas relief. Section I of the thesis deals chronologically with the reactions of the American Jewish community toward East European immigration as well as with the measures taken by the American Jews to afford the immigrants immediate relief. Section II reviews the reaction of American Jewry toward nativism and immigration restriction. The period of mass Jewish immigration to the United States coincided with an increase of nativism, which was aimed at curtailing all immigration from eastern and southern Europe.

599. Bilik, Dorothy S. The Immigrant-Survivor: Post-Holocaust Consciousness in Recent Jewish American Fiction. Maryland, 1977. 295p. (DA 39:880)
This study analyzes and evaluates selected novels in which an immigrant-survivor of the Holocaust is a central figure and shows that while the earlier fictional immigrant was eager to give up the Jewish past in exchange for a place in the American present, the post-Holocaust immigrant is a rhetorically economical embodiment of Jewish history and tradition, biblical myth, and moral power committed to the preservation and transmission of the Jewish past in the American Diaspora. (A)

600. Bin-Nun, Dave. Religious and Other Cultural Factors in Social Control Affecting the Assimilation of Jews in Los Angeles. Southern California, 1953. 237p.

601. Biskar, Herbert M. A History of the Jewish Centers Association of Los Angeles with Special Reference to Jewish Identity. Southern California, 1972. 177p. (DA 33:1840-A)
This study is concerned with the Jewish identity problem in America. Jews in America experience a problem of identity formation based on their marginal position. The marginal person is one who is initiated into two or more historic traditions, languages, moral codes, or religions in America. Jews in Amer-

ica experience a problem of identity formation based on their marginal position. The identity crisis arises because of inner conflict in making an adjustment to a dual status. (A)

602. Bloore, J. Stephen. The Jew in American Dramatic Literature, 1794-1930. New York, 1950. 256p.

603. Boxerman, Burton A. Reaction of the St. Louis Jewish Community to Anti-Semitism: 1933-1945. St. Louis, 1967. 318p. (DA 28:3092-A)
Evidence of additional groups with anti-Semitic leanings appeared on the scene in the thirties and forties, among them William Dudley Pelley's Silver Shirts, Father Coughlin's Christian Front, and the Reverend Gerald L. K. Smith's America First and Christian Nationalist Crusades. In St. Louis these groups functioned after 1933 and generally followed the same pattern as their national counterparts. The Bundist group was quite active until 1939; Father Coughlin's local group, the Missouri Friends of Social Justice, held many meetings at which anti-Semitism was an integral part of their program; likewise, Smith's Christian Nationalist Party was, for a brief time, in full operation in St. Louis. (A)

604. Bressler, Marvin. Jewish Behavior Patterns As Exemplified in W. I. Thomas' Unfinished Study of the Bintl Brief. Pennsylvania, 1952. 246p.

605. Brickner, Barnett R. The Cincinnati Jewish Community: An Historical and Descriptive Study. Cincinnati, 1935. 256p.

606. Bridger, David. The Consistency of Primary Hebrew Textbooks with the Curricula of the Hebrew Schools in the United States. Southern California, 1953. 243p.

607. Buch, Arthur T. The Jewish Community of Scranton. New School for Social Research, 1949. 197p.

608. Carr, Harriet G. A Study of Discriminatory Practices in Semi-Public Institutions Relative to Jewish People in Washington. Catholic, 1949. 144p.

609. Chammou, E. Migration and Adjustment: The Case of Sephardic Jews in Los Angeles. California (Los Angeles), 1976. 270p.
Data for this study were obtained mostly through scheduled interviews involving 130 households. The object of the study was to examine motives for migration and the problems associated with the adjustment of minority immigrants to their new environments.

610. Chyet, Stanley F. A Merchant of Eminence: The Story of Aaron Lopez. Hebrew Union College, 1960. 307p.
Published under the title <u>Lopez of Newport: Colonial American Merchant Prince</u> (Detroit: Wayne State University Press, 1970).

611. Cohen, Benjamin L. Constancy and Change in the Jewish
Family Agency of Los Angeles: 1854-1970. Southern California, 1972. 178p. (DA 33:7023-A)
This study analyzed the Jewish family agency of Los Angeles
from its incorporation as the original Hebrew Benevolent Society
in 1854 to the year 1970, when it was known as the Jewish Family Service of Los Angeles. The main sources of material were
board minutes, annual reports, committee reports, agency research reports, and agency manuals. The primary data were
considered in the light of the historical context within which the
agency grew. Comparisons and contrasts were made with the
developing public-welfare system. (A)

612. Cohen, Bernard. Social and Cultural Changes in American
Jewish Life As Reflected in Selected Jewish Literature.
Southern California, 1957. 278p.
Published under the title Sociocultural Changes in American Jewish Life As Reflected in Selected Jewish Literature (Cranbury,
New Jersey: Associated University Presses, 1972).

613. Cohen, Naomi W. The Public Career of Oscar S. Straus.
Columbia, 1955. 557p. (DA 15:1226)
This study deals with the secular and Jewish activities of Oscar
S. Straus. One of its major purposes is to show the complete
integration of those two strands in Straus's career. Born in
Bavaria in 1850, Straus spent his childhood in Georgia and removed with his family to New York after the Civil War. He attended Columbia College and Columbia Law School, and after
serving in the legal profession for eight years joined his father's
business firm. Afforded financial security through business, he
was able to enter politics and government service at an early
age. He was known first as a Cleveland Democrat, but "Bryanism" drove him to the Republican fold, where he remained officially except for the short-lived Progressive episode. His major
official appointments were as American envoy to Turkey (under
Cleveland, McKinley, and Taft) and as Secretary of Commerce
and Labor under Theodore Roosevelt. (A)

614. Cohen, Samuel I. History of Adult Jewish Education in Four
National Jewish Organizations. Yeshiva, 1967. 426p. (DA
28:1671-A)
The purpose of the study was to investigate, reconstruct, and
analyze the historical development of adult Jewish education programs in four select national Jewish mass-membership organizations: the American Jewish Committee, American Jewish Congress, B'nai B'rith, and the National Council of Jewish Women.
These four organizations were selected because they possess
common characteristics that distinguish them from other organizations. Secondly, in each case the organization's developing
involvement in the field of adult Jewish education represents a
departure from earlier concerns and activities. Collectively, the
four organizational adult Jewish education programs constitute a
new dimension in adult Jewish education. (A)

615. Crowder, David L. Moses Alexander, Idaho's Jewish Governor, 1914-1918. Utah, 1972. 209p. (DA 33:1104-A)
Moses Alexander, Idaho's governor, 1914-1918, was born in Obrigheim, Bavaria, in 1853. He emigrated to America in 1867. After a short stay in New York City he moved to Chillicothe, Missouri, where he became involved in the merchandizing business, was elected to the city council, and was elected mayor of the city for two terms. Alexander was Idaho's war governor, and he demonstrated his patriotism in all his actions. In response to a call from President Wilson, he sent Idaho National Guardsmen to the Mexican border in 1916 and again mobilized the National Guard for service in the regular army during the world conflict. He directed Idaho's participation in the shipbuilding program, the raising of foodstuffs, and the funding of the war. (A)

616. Dinin, Samuel. Judaism in a Changing Civilization. Columbia (Teachers College), 1933. 204p.

617. Dinnerstein, Leonard. The Leo Frank Case. Columbia, 1966. 350p. (DA 27:2474-A)
Published under the same title (New York: Columbia University Press, 1968). The Leo Frank case highlights the problems of a society in transition. At the beginning of the twentieth century rural Georgians migrated to Atlanta to enjoy the heralded advantages of industrialization. To their chagrin they found harsh working conditions and squalid living quarters. Southern traditions, which glorified the Anglo-Saxon Protestant heritage, and the bitter memories of the Lost Cause, complicated the newcomers' reactions to urban life. Unable to retaliate against the industrialists whose colossal indifference caused them many hardships, the new urbanites vented their pent-up aggressions upon Negroes and other vulnerable ethnic groups. It is against this background that the Frank case has been explored. (A)

618. Dinsky, Samuel H. Secondary Jewish Education in the United States. Dropsie College, 1962. 273p.

619. Dobkowski, Michael N. Ideological Anti-Semitism in America, 1877-1927. New York, 1976. 598p. (DA 37:1717)
Historians looking at the problem of American anti-Semitism have had to deal with the perplexing question of causation. Unlike the Europeanists, who have chronicled and analyzed centuries of Jewish oppression on the Continent as a chapter in the long and intricate story of European religious, political, and economic development, which has often been anti-libertarian, American historians have had the unenviable task of reconciling anti-Jewish prejudice with what is generally interpreted to be a basically democratic society. They have been able to do so by deflating the scope and intensity of anti-Jewish manifestations in America and by emphasizing the social and economic roots of prejudice, which are essentially transient, rather than the ideological and religious factors that may indeed be permanent. This study

seeks, through analysis of literature, popular culture, unpublished letters, sermons, and other writings, to provide a reinterpretation of the origins of American anti-Semitism. (A)

620. Doroshkin, Milton. Yiddish Language and Culture in the American Jewish Community. New School for Social Research, 1968. 278p.
Published under the title Yiddish in America: Social and Cultural Foundations (Rutherford, New Jersey: Fairleigh Dickinson University Press, 1970).

621. Douglas, Martin I. Chronological Summary of Annotated Cards Toward the History of the Jewish Agricultural Communities in South Jersey. Jewish Theological Seminary, 1960. 211p.

622. Dushkin, Alexander M. Jewish Education in New York City. Columbia, 1918. 596p.
Published under the same title (New York: Bureau of Jewish Education, 1918). Extensively treats the educational activities of Jews of New York City both historically and statistically in the light of their relation to American national aspirations as a community attempting to preserve its own special group identity. Covers the whole field of educational activities undertaken by Jews.

623. Engleman, Uriah Z. Jewish Population Trends Since the Industrial Revolution. Buffalo, 1953. 212p.

624. Fauman, Samuel J. The Factors in Occupational Selection Among Detroit Jews. Michigan, 1948. 211p.

625. Feibelman, Julian B. A Social and Economic Study of the New Orleans Jewish Community. Pennsylvania, 1938. 147p.

626. Feierstein, Milton. Isaac Leeser (1806-1868): Founder of Jewish Education in the United States. State University of New York (Buffalo), 1971. 198p. (DA 32:2499-A)
There is a need to establish the foundations and origins of Jewish education in the United States. This study deals with the efforts and contributions of Isaac Leeser in the mid-nineteenth century in establishing institutions of Jewish learning in the United States. Leeser was the leading Jew of his time. He had the responsibility of guiding and informing the Jewish community of Philadelphia and indeed the nation as to what direction they should take. He was a strong traditionalist and a firm adherent of the Orthodox position, and urged American Jews to pursue a traditionalist path. The institutions he created were intended to foster Judaism in America and to guarantee a future for the Jewish people as a thriving religious and cultural group. (A)

627. Feinstein, Marnin. The First Twenty-Five Years of Zionism in the United States, 1882-1906. Columbia, 1963. 342p.

(DA 24:4647)
Zionism commenced in the United States with the establishment of a Hovevei Zion society in New York in 1882. The group was organized by Jews from Eastern Europe who followed the lead of the mother organization in Russia, advocating the establishment and support of agricultural colonies in Palestine for oppressed Jews. Despite enthusiastic efforts by a few zealous workers and the literary support of Emma Lazarus, progress was negligible. (A)

628. Fernberg, Babeth G. Treatment of Jewish Character in the Twentieth Century Novel (1900-1940) in France, Germany, England, and United States. Stanford, 1944. 270p.

629. Fierman, Floyd S. Efforts Toward Reform in American Jewish Education Prior to 1881. Pittsburgh, 1949. 287p.

630. Fleishaker, Oscar. The Illinois-Iowa Jewish Community on the Banks of the Mississippi River. Yeshiva, 1957. 450p. (DA 24:715)
This study has traced the origin and development of the Jewish communities along the Mississippi River boundary between the states of Illinois and Iowa. The area is about 200 miles long and was settled by whites after the Blackhawk War of 1832. The material uncovered in this work is evidence of Jewish participation in the growth of America's frontier from the very beginning. If Jews were found on the eastern seaboard in the twentieth century, they were also on the western frontier in the eighteenth and nineteenth centuries and with their neighbors helped build the beautiful fabric of the American heritage. (A)

631. Frank, Blanche B. The American Orthodox Jewish Housewife: A Generational Study in Ethnic Survival. City University of New York, 1975. 319p. (DA 36:5579-A)
The purpose of this research is to investigate a subgroup of the American Jewish population that has received little sociological attention--the observant American Orthodox. From indicators on the American scene, it appears that the American Orthodox through several generations of living in American culture have managed to sustain a traditional religious commitment and have not turned away from the cultural patterns of the larger American community. This cultural resolution becomes interesting in view of the acculturated patterns identified for most American Jews who appear to have discarded traditional Judaism in the process of Americanizing. (A)

632. Franzblau, Abraham N. Religious Beliefs and Character Among Jewish Adolescents. Columbia (Teachers College), 1934. 144p.
Published under the same title (New York: Teachers College Press, Columbia University, 1934).

633. Freedman, Seymour. The American-Jewish Novel. Cornell, 1968. 208p. (DA 29:259-A)

The principal aim of the thesis was to trace the pattern of Jewish behavior exhibited in American-Jewish novels, using as a model of Jewishness the religious and social patterns of behavior practiced in Eastern European shtetl society. Taking this model as an ideotype, the author attempted to trace survival patterns in the American-Jewish novel. Among the patterns discussed were the Jew's relationship to violence, conception of family and community, economic behavior, and self-perception as victim, scapegoat, sacred sufferer. (A)

634. Freeman, Samuel D. Adult Education in the Jewish Community Center. Columbia (Teachers College), 1953. 207p.

635. Freund, Miriam K. Jewish Merchants in Colonial America: Their Achievements and Their Contributions to the Development of America. New York, 1936. 127p.
Published under the same title (New York: Behrman's Jewish Book House, 1939).

636. Fuchs, Lawrence H. The Political Behavior of American Jews. Harvard, 1954. 264p.
Published under the same title (Glencoe, Illinois: Free Press, 1956).

637. Garfinkle, Harry G. Ideological Elements in the Development of the American Yiddish School Movement. Columbia (Teachers College), 1953. 249p. (DA 14:1348)
In the last half of the nineteenth century the Russians and the Austro-Hungarian empires began to be industrialized, and the social ferment among their peoples also increased. New ideas--democracy, socialism, nationalism--long since current in Western Europe, began to command a following. These new ideas also found adherents in the Jewish communities of Eastern Europe. By 1897, distinct Jewish political movements had emerged; Zionism was the most prominent and largely displaced the others. After the Kishinev pogroms of 1903 many of the supporters of these movements came to America. Here they discovered that values other than their own prevailed in both the American and the Jewish community. They tried, however, with every means possible, to intensify the national-cultural and the socialist consciousness of the Jewish people. (A)

638. Gerstein, Arnold A. The American Reform Rabbi and the East European Jewish Immigrant, 1890-1922. Minnesota, 1971. 488p. (DA 33:251-A)
The author investigated the urban ethnic conflict between a Jewish haute bourgeois class, the Reform Clergy, and the East European immigrant elite. The latter was made up of Conservative, Orthodox, Socialist, and Yiddish-speaking Jews, as well as a dissident group of Reform rabbis. This elite never struck the assimilation bargain in Russia and Poland and was not prepared to do it in America at this time. The Reform benefactors and their Americanized clergy had grave doubts that they ever would act in time

to prevent "American Judaism" from anti-Semitic harm. The social, economic, and ideological determinants of this essentially class conflict intensified the struggle between the two groups and made any lasting cooperation impossible. This was especially true during periods of heavy influx, marked as they were by anti-Semitism in Europe and nativism in America. (A)

639. Giese, James R. Tuberculosis and the Growth of Denver's Eastern European Jewish Community: The Accommodation of an Immigrant Group to a Medium-Sized Western City, 1900-1920. Colorado (Boulder), 1979. 456p. (DA 40:2223-A)
This study fills one void in the historical scholarship of immigrant groups in urban America. It discusses the adjustment of Eastern European Jews to the economy and environment of a medium-sized western city--Denver, Colorado--from 1900 to 1920. The Jewish community that evolved there resulted from the interaction of Jewish immigrants who possessed unique characteristics with the various environments comprising Denver. The final chapter discusses some of the political ramifications endemic to Denver's Jewish community because of its special health-resort function in an evolving national system of Jewish communities. Aspects of this problem include the drain on local resources resulting from the influx of Jewish consumptives, the assertion by local Jewish leaders of Denver's rights in relation to Jewish communities sending consumptives to Denver, the increasing alienation of Denver from other communities, and the rifts created within the local community because of these problems. (A)

640. Ginsburgh, Stanley A. Organized Jewish Youth Groups in America: A Study of Nationally Organized Jewish Youth Groups in America As Educational Agencies for the Preservation of the Jewish Cultural Heritage. Massachusetts, 1940. 270p.

641. Gitin, Louis. The Development of a Reform Jewish Religious School, Buffalo, N.Y., 1864-1953. Buffalo, 1954. 260p.

642. Gittlen, Arthur J. Political and Social Thought Contained in the Jewish-American Novel (1867-1927). Michigan State, 1969. 211p. (DA 30:2527-A)
This dissertation is concerned with the Jewish-American novel written in English between the years 1867 and 1927 by Jewish authors about Jewish subjects and characters. While in the broadest sense this dissertation is concerned with both the esthetic and social characteristics of the Jewish novel during this period, its fundamental consideration is the several social and political attitudes that are apparent in the novels of this time period. Finally, this dissertation argues that esthetically poor literature-- and certainly nearly all of the Jewish novels of this period regrettably fall into this category--serves, in this instance, the

highly valuable purpose of providing an accurate and insightful record of an important American minority group as it moved from the virtually closed society of the Jewish ghettos of the larger American cities into the pluralistic society of the American mainstream. (A)

643. Goldberg, Gordon J. Meyer London: A Political Biography. Lehigh, 1971. 664p. (DA 32:356-A)
Meyer London's life spanned the period from 1871 to 1926. Born in the Russian-Polish province of Suwalki, he moved with his family to New York in 1891. London studied law at night and was admitted to the New York bar in 1898. His practice never became lucrative, but he found fulfillment in the trade-union movement and in the Socialist Party. London played an important role in the formative years of the International Ladies' Garment Workers' Union and the International Fur Workers' Union. He served these unions as legal counsel, adviser, and spokesman in negotiation. In 1910 he led the ILGWU during its great organizational strike and played a similar role two years later with the IFWU. Deploring violence, London believed that political activity and educational propaganda were the best means for advancing the cause of the labor movement. (A)

644. Goldberg, Mark F. The Representation of Love and Romance in American Fiction About East European Jews in New York City: 1894-1917. New York, 1970. 251p. (DA 31:6055-A)
The representation of the American Jew in prose fiction published earlier than 1918 has never been carefully explored. The present investigation examined all of the substantial depictions of New York City East European Jews in American prose fiction from 1894 to 1917. The East European Jews were selected because they constituted the majority of the Jews in America during the period; New York City was chosen because it was the locus of Jewish life in America. The theme of love was isolated as the center of the investigation because it was common to virtually every work in the study and it related to virtually every other important concern of the particular work in which it appeared. (A)

645. Goldman, Henry. School Careers and Subsequent Careers: An Analytical and Comparative Study of the School Records and Subsequent Careers of Those Men Who Graduated from the Hebrew Technical Institute of New York from 1886 to 1907, Inclusive. New York, 1918. 212p.

646. Goldstein, Judith. The Politics of Ethnic Pressure: The American Jewish Committee As Lobbyist, 1906-1917. Columbia, 1972. 358p. (DA 33:2284-A)
The purpose of this doctoral study is to examine and evaluate the lobbying activities of the AJC from 1906 to 1917 with respect to the related issues of the restrictive literacy test and American-Russian relations. The AJC was the most active and important anti-restrictionist lobbying group in each of the four major liter-

acy test battles, beginning in 1906 and ending in 1917, when Congress finally passed the test over President Wilson's veto. The organization sought to delay consideration of the test bills and to block their passage; as a last resort the AJC sought to soften the effect of the test on the Russian-Jewish immigrants by sponsoring a special exemption for them. (A)

647. Goldstein, Philip R. Social Aspects of the Jewish Colonies of South Jersey. Pennsylvania, 1921. 74p.

648. Golovensky, David I. Ingroup and Outgroup Attitudes of Young Pupils in a Jewish Day School Compared with an Equivalent Sample of Pupils in Public (Mixed) Schools. New York, 1954. 321p. (DA 18:2245)
This research is an empirical investigation of the ingroup-outgroup attitudes of pupils in Westchester Day School (a Jewish denominational school) compared with a matched sample of pupils attending public schools. The principal aim of the study is to ascertain whether the fact of "mixing" or isolation per se, provides sufficient basis for positive or negative outgroup perceptions and feelings. (A)

649. Golub, Jacob S. Jewish Youth and Traditions. New York, 1928. 156p.

650. Goodside, Samuel. A Social Studies Syllabus for Secular Teachers in Jewish All-Day Schools. A Companion Bulletin to the Social Studies Curriculum Bulletins of the Board of Education of the City of New York. New York, 1952. 304p. (DA 12:267)
The present study provides teachers of secular subjects in Jewish all-day schools, in particular, and those in general education, in general, with a teaching aid that demonstrates the nature of the Jewish group and its contributions to our American heritage. It offers a study of Jewish culture that may balance a social studies program of study. It also implements the recommendations of the American Council on Education. It may at the same time suggest to students of other minority groups a significant way in which they, too, may demonstrate the role of their group in the American way of life. Eventually such a syllabus as this may be prepared for each group, which should be of great value to some future course of study for New York City, which has so many minority groups. (A)

651. Gordon, Albert I. The Jews of Minneapolis: A Study in Acculturation. Minnesota, 1949. 331p.
Published under the title Jews in Transition (Minneapolis: University of Minnesota Press, 1949). This study's objective is to depict the changes in the life of the Jewish community in Minneapolis. It finds that the Jews of the community have become indistinguishable from the non-Jewish residents of the city. However, the author believes that the Jews will perpetuate themselves as a distinct cultural and religious group. Jewish life would have

little chance of survival if prejudice and discrimination were to disappear, in the author's view; and (he contends) the perpetuation of Jewish life in America appears to be more dependent upon external than internal forces.

652. Gordon, Nicholas Karl. Jewish and American: A Critical Study of the Fiction of Abraham Cahan, Anzia Yezierska, Waldo Frank and Ludwig Lewisohn. Stanford, 1968. 277p. (DA 92:600-A)
This study attempts to define a common theme in the fiction of four of the more important Jewish-American writers of the early twentieth century. The theme is too complex to be contained in a strict definition; it is a core of meaning that can best be elucidated through a careful study of the work of each writer. The major portion of the study is therefore devoted to critical analyses of individual works that demonstrate the theme common to them all. (A)

653. Gorelick, Sherry. Social Control, Social Mobility, and the Eastern European Jews: An Analysis of Public Education in New York City, 1880-1924. Columbia, 1975. 374p. (DA 36:8333)
The sociological literature on ethnicity generally asserts that the Jews have experienced "remarkable upward mobility" by virtue of their "passion for education." Jewish cultural values are said to have made the Eastern Jews particularly suited to take advantage of the trend in the United States occupational structure toward a growth in the proportion of nonmanual occupations. Theoretically, the economic experience of an ethnic group is said to be a result of the character of the group and of the occupational structure at the time of the group's arrival. This thesis uses historical materials in a theoretical and methodological reconceptualization of that literature. Focusing on the period between 1880 and 1924, the period of the first migrations of substantial numbers of Jewish workers and a period of profound social change in the United States' socioeconomic structure, it concentrates on cultural and political implications of Jewish mobility through higher education, particularly at the City College of New York. (A)

654. Goren, Arthur A. The New York Kehillah. 1908-1922. Columbia, 1966. 495p. (DA 27:2476-A)
Published under the title New York Jews and the Quest for Community: The Kehillah Experiment, 1908-1922 (New York: Columbia University Press, 1970). A detailed study of the attempt to maintain the wellsprings of ethnic community, the problems of assimilation, integration, and the decline of the Kehillah (community) effort. The heterogeneity of the Jewish population, the economic and social problems of a new immigrant community, the sheer size of it, a mobile American society that gave no recognition to ethnic organization--these were some of the factors that militated against the Kehillah's success. World War I strengthened these trends and created new stresses. Attention

was diverted to overseas problems. The Kehillah, because of its all-inclusive and democratic character, became the scene of a power struggle between the AJC and the movement for an American Jewish Congress. Finally, the pacifism of Judah Magnes, chairman of the Kehillah, canceled his effectiveness as a leader. Efforts to reorganize the Kehillah from 1918 to 1912 failed. (A)

655. Gottlieb, Moshe. The Anti-Nazi Boycott Movement in the American Jewish Community, 1933-1941. Brandeis, 1967. 547p. (DA 28:2621-A)
This work is a historical study of the anti-Nazi boycott movement within the American Jewish community. Special attention is paid to the ideological issues involved in the boycott movement, the divisions and alignments it produced in the American Jewish community, and the pressure tactics that it employed against recalcitrant offenders. (A)

656. Grand, Samuel. A History of Zionist Youth Organizations in the United States from Their Inception to 1940. Columbia, 1958. 393p. (DA 18:1777)
For the most part the Zionist youth organizations in the United States have been sponsored by adult groups seeking "to hold the youth to them" and thereby to ensure continuity in their efforts on behalf of the Zionist ideal. The ideological orientation of these youth groups was largely determined by the adult sponsors and mentors. The largest number of these organizations was included in the centrist group, known as the general Zionists, and consisted of Young Judaea, Masada, Junior Hadassah, and the Zionist societies on the college campus. (A)

657. Greenberg, Abraham H. The Ethnocentric Attitudes of Some Jewish American Writers: Educational Implications. Yeshiva, 1956. 195p. (DA 19:2088)
This study has considered the ethnocentric attitudes of some Jewish-American writers by examining their writings and, where feasible, by personal interviews. Mary Antin's autobiography, The Promised Land, was examined as an example of complete assimilation. Anzia Yezierska's writings, especially Hungry Hearts and Red Ribbon on a White Horse, described the Americanization of the immigrant in the melting pot. Meyer Levin's autobiography, In Search, expounded the belief that cultural pluralism is possible and desirable in America. Ludwig Lewisohn's writings since 1925, especially The Island Within, The Answer, and The American Jew, espoused "voluntary segregation" to ghettos where positive Jewish values could be encouraged. (A)

658. Greenberg, Donald W. Effect of Ethnicity on Political Attitudes and Behavior: A Study of Jews in Fairfield, Connecticut. City University of New York, 1978. 210p. (DA 38: 7529-A)
The study's major hypotheses are (1) American Jews, regardless

of socioeconomic position, identify the political world by ethnic
criteria, and (2) American Jews believe that their personal self-
interest is inextricably linked to the success or failure of the
ethnic group. The data indicate strong support for both hypotheses. The major general findings of the study are (1) the general importance of ethnicity to American Jews, and (2) the
identification by Jews of their religious and ethnic group to be
the same. The data further indicate that, despite having achieved
a great deal of socioeconomic success, American Jews consider
anti-Semitism to be a serious problem in the United States. (A)

659. Greenberg, Meyer. Changing Observance of Traditional
      Jewish Religious Practices: A Study of Generations. Mary-
      land, 1956. 252p. (DA 16:2545)
Changes in the observance of traditional religious practices among
Jewish families during the course of three generations are the
subject of this paper. The religious practices studied are those
related to the cycle of the year--the Sabbath and holy days--and
kashruth (the dietary laws). The population is a group of 180
families, chiefly from Baltimore and Washington, D.C., with
children in the freshman class at the University of Maryland in
the spring of 1949. (A)

660. Grinstein, Hyman B. The Rise of the Jewish Community of
      New York, 1654-1860. Columbia, 1944. 261p.
Published under the same title (Philadelphia: Jewish Publications
Society, 1945).

661. Gross, Morris B. Exploration of the Differences in Pre-
      School Learning Readiness and Concomitant Differences in
      Certain Cultural Attitudes Between Two Subcultural Jewish
      Groups. Columbia (Teachers College), 1966. 149p. (DA
      27:3721-A)
This study contains two distinct parts, the first dealing with a
hypothesis concerning preschool children and their learning pre-
paredness and the second part an exploratory question seeking
possible parental attitude concomitants. The hypothesis stated:
In this sample the Ashkenazi preschool children will score higher
than the Sephardi children on school-related tests. The desire
was to demonstrate learning-readiness differences in the absence
of variables commonly associated with academic achievement.
Since all of the subjects shared race, color, ethnicity, religion,
and middle-class status, the only discernible variable was subcultural membership. (A)

662. Grossberg, Sidney H. Factors in Historical and Participa-
      tion Identification of Detroit Area Jews. Wayne State, 1971.
      216p. (DA 32:2807-A)
A concern about the controversies of recent years with regard to
"integration," "assimilation," and "pride in group identity" motivated this study. The study of Jews within American society
may be helpful in understanding the process by means of which
large numbers of ethnic minorities have been incorporated within

it, yet retain a strong sense of ethnic identification. We found that in spite of the high degree of cultural assimilation attained by Jews in the United States, our Detroit metropolitan area sample of Jews continues to maintain a high degree of historical and participational identification and a low degree of structural assimilation. (A)

663. Grossfield, Avery J. Some Jewish Juvenile Delinquents: A Study of Three Hundred Cases. Hebrew Union College, 1950. 206p.

664. Guysenir, Maurice G. Jewish Voting Behavior in Chicago's Fiftieth Ward. Northwestern, 1957. 293p. (DA 17:3076) The general objective of this study is to test the hypothesis that Jews do not divide their vote along socioeconomic status (SES) lines. Specifically, this hypothesis is tested with special reference to the 1952 Presidential election and with incidental reference to the Presidential elections of 1940, 1944, and 1948 and the senatorial election of 1954 in Illinois. Chicago's 50th Ward, one of the "Jewish districts" within the city, was chosen as the locale of this investigation, primarily to ensure responses from enough Jews to make any study of this kind meaningful. (A)

665. Hakimian, Leah E. Extent and Nature of Changes in Selected American High School Students as a Result of Participation in Israel Summer Programs. Saint Louis, 1978. 146p. (DA 40:5818-A) The purpose of this study was to examine the extent and nature of changes in selected American high school students as a result of participating in a summer study/travel program in Israel. The specific question that this study attempted to answer was, "What is the effect of an Israel summer program on American high school students' knowledge of Hebrew, knowledge of Israel, attitudes toward Israel, and Jewish behavior?" The sample in the study included 20 American Jewish high school students from the St. Louis area who participated in an Israel study/travel program in the summer of 1977. (A)

666. Hall, Richard M. R. Yiddish Syntax: Phrase Structure, Rules and Optional Singulary Transformations of the Modern Standard Language. New York, 1967. 207p. (DA 28:1064-A) This study is an initial step in the investigation of the syntax of Modern Standard Yiddish. It has been undertaken with two goals in mind: the first was the descriptive formalization of the grammatical regularities of the language as an end in itself; the second was to provide, in a description of the Modern Standard Language, a point of departure for further investigations of dialect differences, the historical development of Yiddish and comparison with other closely related languages, particularly German. (A)

667. Halperin, Samuel. American Zionism: The Building of a Political Interest Group. University of Washington, 1956.

535p. (DA 17:665)
Published under the title The Political World of American Zionism (Detroit: Wayne State University Press, 1964). The general objective of this study is the formulation and testing of new or prevailing hypotheses concerned with the relations between an interest group and its potential supporters, or "public, " and with the expansion of the interest group's influence among that "public. " Specifically, the inquiry traces and analyzes the development of the American Zionist movement between 1930 and 1946 as an extensive case study, from which an attempt is made to derive hypotheses that may be relevant to the pattern of development of interest groups in general. (A)

668. Halpert, Max. The Jews of Brownsville, 1880-1925: A Demographic, Economic, and Socio-Cultural Study. Yeshiva, 1958. 348p. (DA 19:590)
It is important to observe at this time that conclusions, deductions, and shrewd guesses regarding the occupational mobility and occupational choice of all the strata of the Jewish community have often been made on an a priori basis. No such data on this subject are available for the Jewish community nationwide; nor within the different individual community surveys made by individual surveyors or Jewish agencies. (A)

669. Handelman, Sholom. Progressive Education and Its Influence on Jewish Education in the United States, 1900-1965. Dropsie College, 1969. 213p.

670. Harris, Alice K. The Lower Class As a Factor in Reform: New York, The Jews, and the 1890's. Rutgers, 1968. 363p. (DA 29:3948-A)
The thesis examines the role of the lower classes in the promulgation of reform legislation in the United States in the 1890s. It assumes that most legislation was sponsored by the business and professional middle classes, who have been recognized as an important factor in progressive-era reform. Using New York City as a focal point, the thesis attempts to assess the ways in which the lower classes influenced the legislative process. It evaluates the relationships between the lower classes and intermediary groups that directly influenced legislation, and considers the impact of lower-class agitation on middle-class attitudes toward social reform. Throughout the thesis Jews are used as a prototype immigrant group. The rest of the lower class is broadly defined in apposition to the middle class. (A)

671. Hendel-Sebestyen, Giselle. The Sephardic Home: Ethnic Homogeneity and Cultural Traditions in a Total Institution. Columbia, 1969. 439p. (DA 30:4474-B)
This study analyzes the effect of ethnic homogeneity, cultural traditions, kin, and communal ties on the structure and functioning of a formal organization, the Sephardic Home for the Aged. It presents a contrast to studies that maintain that behavior in institutions can be adequately explained in terms of

roles assigned to individuals within the institution itself and that the social structure and relationships are an outgrowth of the functional roles related to the goals of the institution as a formal organization. (A)

672. Hertz, Richard C. Religious Education Among American Reform Jewish Congregations. Northwestern, 1948. 263p.

673. Himmelfarb, Harold S. The Impact of Religious Schooling: The Effects of Jewish Education upon Adult Religious Involvement. Chicago, 1974. 340p. (DA 36:551-A)
This study evaluates the relative effectiveness of different types of Jewish schooling in producing adult religiosity and compares the effects of schools with the effects of other agents of socialization. It is based on a sample of 1,009 Jewish adults currently living in the Chicago, Illinois, metropolitan area. The sample was drawn from persons listed in the Chicago and North Suburban phone directories who had "Distinctive Jewish Names" and from alumni lists of two post-elementary-level Chicago Jewish schools. The study presents a critical review of the literature on multidimensional schemes for measuring religious involvement and attempts to synthesize current approaches by presenting a new typology. (A)

674. Huff, Earl D. Zionist Influence upon U.S. Foreign Policy: A Study of American Policy Toward the Middle East from the Time of the Struggle for Israel to the Sinai Conflict. Idaho, 1971. 303p. (DA 32:3400-A)
This dissertation is a study of the extent to which the American Zionist movement has been successful in influencing the United States foreign policy toward the Middle East over the decade that began with the events surrounding the establishment of Israel and extended through the events related to the Sinai conflict of 1956. For purposes of this study the Zionist movement is viewed as an interest group. The shared attitude that the group sought to promote was the establishment, consolidation, and perpetuation of a Jewish state in Palestine. (A)

675. Isaacman, Daniel. Jewish Summer Camps in the United States and Canada, 1900-1969. Dropsie College, 1970. 243p.

676. Jick, Leon A. Jews in the Synagogue--Americans Everywhere: The German-Jewish Immigration and the Emergence of the American-Jewish Pattern, 1820-1870. Columbia, 1973. 230p. (DA 35:4385-A)
Between 1830 and 1860, 1.5 million immigrants from the provinces which were to become part of the German Empire settled in the United States. A significant proportion of them--perhaps as many as 200,000--were Jews, for whom the contrast between the society they entered and the one they left behind was even greater than for Protestant or Catholic Germans. The experience of these German-Jewish immigrants as they sought to re-

orient themselves and to reconstruct their religious and communal life in the American environment, is the subject of this thesis. (A)

677. Jonas, Franklin L. The Early Life and Career of B. Charney Vladeck, 1886-1921: The Emergence of an Immigrant Spokesman. New York, 1972. 246p. (DA 33:698-A)
The early life and career of B. Charney Vladeck, newspaperman, socialist activist, and civic leader, constitutes a case history in the development of immigrant leadership. Born in 1886 in Dukor, Lithuania, a tiny, predominantly Jewish town, he migrated in 1908 to the United States, where after World War I he emerged as a spokesman for the Jewish labor movement of New York City. (A)

678. Joseph, Samuel. Jewish Immigration to the United States from 1881 to 1910. Columbia, 1914. 209p.
Investigates the "causes of Jewish immigration from Eastern Europe, the course of Jewish immigration in the United States, and the most important social qualities of the Jewish immigrants."

679. Kabakoff, Jacob. The History of Hebrew Literature in America. Jewish Theological Seminary, 1958. 163p.

680. Kachuck, Rhoda S. The Portrayal of the Jew in American Drama Since 1920. Southern California, 1970. 387p. (DA 31:4774-A)
The examination of 65 well-known plays yielded a definite pattern for the portrayal of Jews, a pattern along chronological lines-- not by decades, but by the critical economic, social, and political events of the last 50 years: the great waves of immigration up to 1921, the Depression in 1929, the rise of Hitler in 1933, the end of World War II in 1946, and the rise of black nationalism in the fifties and sixties. The portrayal of the Jew is seen to develop along three major lines: the Jew as representative of the immigrant population and its descendants, as paradigm of the middle-class and its fluctuations of fortune and character, and as symbol of Everyman and his struggles, crises, and destiny. The emphasis on ethnic qualities, social stratum, historical heritage, or common humanity has varied according to the era in which the play was written. (A)

681. Kaganoff, Nathan M. The Traditional Jewish Sermon in the United States from Its Beginning to the First World War. American, 1961. 224p. (DA 22:1141)
Existing scholarship on the history of the American Jewish community is limited almost entirely to the Colonial and Civil War periods and to select aspects of Jewish life in the late nineteenth and twentieth centuries. The impact of the American environment on Jewish religious life and thought have been largely ignored. As a contribution to this somewhat neglected field, this study attempts to trace the development of the traditional Jewish sermon in the United States from its beginnings to the outbreak of the First World War. (A)

682. Kahn, Robert I. Liberalism As Reflected in Jewish Preaching in the English Language in the Mid-Nineteenth Century: An Examination of Jewish Life and Faith (Particularly in the United States) Between 1830 to 1870, As Revealed in the Sermons of the Period. Hebrew Union College, 1950. 203p.

683. Kaplan, Benjamin. Selected Jewish Communities in Louisiana. Louisiana State, 1952. 275p.
Published under the title The Eternal Stranger: A Study of Jewish Life in the Small Community (New York: Bookman Associates, 1957).

684. Katz, Susan G. Jewish Socio-Political Problems in the American Drama: 1920-1962. New York, 1969. 568p. (DA 30:63-A)
The purpose of this research paper is to identify and analyze the sociopolitical issues confronting American Jews during the years 1920-1962, as this phenomenon is depicted by the literature of the American drama. This investigation determined that there exists a correlation between the sociopolitical problems confronting the Jewish people as depicted in the American drama between 1920 and 1962 and those actually experienced by the Jewish group. (A)

685. Kitay, Phillip M. Radicalism and Conservatism Toward Conventional Religion: A Psychological Study Based on a Group of Jewish College Students. Columbia (Teachers College), 1944. 183p.
Published under the same title (New York: Teachers College Press, Columbia University, 1947).

686. Klaperman, Gilbert. The Beginnings of Yeshiva University, the First Jewish University in America. Yeshiva, 1955. 397p. (DA 18:1774)
Published under the title The Story of Yeshiva University: The First Jewish University in America (New York: Yeshiva University Press, 1969). This is a detailed account of the first score of years from the founding of the Rabbi Isaac Elchanan Theological Seminary through its development under the leadership of Dr. Bernard Revel, its first President of the Faculty, into a complete system of Jewish education from elementary school through ordination. The Seminary, which was incorporated early in 1897 by East European immigrants, later absorbed the Yeshiva Etz Chaim, an elementary school founded in 1885, and was the mother institution from which have sprung the 15 schools that make up the University today. (A)

687. Korn, Bertram W. American Jewry and the Civil War. Hebrew Union College, 1948. 276p.
Published under the same title (Philadelphia: Jewish Publication Society, 1951).

688. Koslowe, Irving. The Jewish Community of Mamaroneck. Yeshiva, 1962. 372p. (DA 24:716)

The problem of the thesis is to present a sociological and social history of the Jewish community of Mamaroneck, New York, including some general conclusions regarding the social behavior of suburban Jews. It is necessary to collect the background material by deduction from secondary sources. It is also necessary to determine which historical facts actually refer to those Jews who are residents of the Village of Mamaroneck. (A)

689. Kovacs, Malcolm L. The Dynamics of Commitment: The Process of Resocialization of Baalei Teshuvah Jewish Students in Pursuit of Their Jewish Identity at the Rabbinical College of America (Lubavitch). Union Graduate School, 1977. 318p. (DA 38:5725)
Although it is widely assumed that assimilation of American Jews is an inevitable process, this comprehensive study challenges that assumption by reporting and analyzing a new phenomenon. The research explores and analyzes the process of commitment of 40 young Jewish men who "returned" to traditional Judaism and were studying at the Lubavitch Chassidic Yeshiva, the Rabbinical College of America, when they were first studied in 1974 and periodically thereafter during a three-year period. (A)

690. Kranzler, George C. The Jewish Community of Williamsburg, Brooklyn, N.Y.: A Study of the Factors and Patterns of Change in the Organization and Structure of a Community in Transition. Columbia, 1954. 583p. (DA 14:1833)
Published under the title Williamsburg: A Jewish Community in Transition: A Study of the Factors and Patterns of Change in the Organization and Structure of a Community in Transition (New York: Feldheim, 1961). This study of the Jewish community of Williamsburg is an investigation of the factors and patterns of the major changes that took place in this predominantly Jewish neighborhood of Brooklyn, New York, particularly in the last 20 years. This study attempts to show that the increasing influence of the religiocultural values halted the ecological and economic decline of the neighborhood that was anticipated by official observers during the late thirties. Instead of becoming a gradually disintegrating slum area, Jewish Williamsburg developed into one of the most influential and flourishing centers of orthodox Judaism in the United States. (A)

691. Kuntz, Leonard I. The Changing Pattern of the Distribution of the Jewish Population of Pittsburgh from Earliest Settlement to 1963. Louisiana State, 1970. 314p. (DA 31:5419-B)
The purpose of this study is to ascertain, record, map, and examine the changing pattern of the distribution of the Jewish population in Pittsburgh from earliest settlement to 1963, emphasizing the period between 1938 and 1963. Of the various methods that can be utilized to delineate the distribution of Jewish population, the master-list method was selected for this study. The master list represents an unduplicated register of Jewish families and their addresses compiled from the records of local Jewish or-

ganizations, congregations, philanthropic agencies, and other likely sources within the Jewish community. (A)

692. Kutzik, Alfred J. The Social Basis of American Jewish Philanthropy. Brandeis, 1967. 1067p. (DA 28:4288-A)
This study provides an historical perspective and theoretical framework for clarifying problems of American Jewish philanthropy. It addresses itself to such questions as: What is the rationale for Jewish social services when similar nonsectarian ones are available to Jews? What is the rationale for Jewish agencies serving large numbers of non-Jews? and, What is Jewish about Jewish health and welfare agencies providing professional services with no identifiable "Jewish content"? (A)

693. Larralde, Carlos M. Chicano Jews in South Texas. California (Los Angeles), 1978. 315p. (DA 39:5747)
The purpose of this study is to trace the history of the Chicano Jews in South Texas and to analyze their present social status in contemporary Anglo-American society. In tracing their history, the author first describes popular and racist myths about their origins and shows how these have affected their social evolution. In addition, he deals with their reasons for migrating to South Texas and with their struggle to survive economically and culturally. They had to defend their ethnic identity not only against the internal threat of total Mexicanization, but also against the later external threat of Anglo-Americanization. Then they had to deal with the double weight of both the Mexican and the Anglo cultures that pressed down upon them and crushed their Jewish heritage. (A)

694. Lazar, Robert J. From Ethnic Minority to Socio-Economic Elite: A Study of the Jewish Community of Fargo, North Dakota. Minnesota, 1968. 329p. (DA 29:2812-A)
The Jewish community of Fargo arose in an emerging town at the edge of the Great Plains. Its Jews were isolated from Jewish communities elsewhere. The first arrivals were middle- and upper-class German Jews with better educations and more sophisticated orientations than the majority of their non-Jewish fellow townsmen. The Germans thus became professionals and businessmen with strong assimilative tendencies. The Eastern Europeans who came to the Fargo-Moorhead area were initially drawn by a wayward Jewish social movement of the late nineteenth century that attributed much of the historical persecution of the Jews to urbanism and the curse of trade. Members of this offbeat utopian movement proposed to get back to the land and shake off the curse of trade. Those arriving in Fargo sought above all else to preserve their cultural heritage of Orthodox Judaism and to form a ghetto community centering on an Orthodox synagogue. (A)

695. Leaf, Hayim. The Literary and Ideological Activities of Dr. Pinkhos Churgin. Yeshiva, 1968. 271p. (DA 29:2268-A)
The life of Pinkhos Churgin was devoted to Hebrew education,

community and public service, literary activity, and scholarship. Born in a small town, Pohost, near Pinsk in White Russia, he received a thorough Jewish education in Jerusalem, where his parents had settled when the boy was 11 years of age. When World War I broke out he left for America. Struggling to sustain himself, he accepted Hebrew teaching positions, first in New Jersey and later in New Haven. (A)

696. Lehrman, Irving. History of the Jews in Southern Florida. Jewish Theological Seminary, 1957. 283p.

697. Levinger, Lee J. The Causes of Anti-Semitism in the United States: A Study in Group and Sub-Group. Pennsylvania, 1925. 204p.

698. Levinson, Robert E. The Jews in the California Gold Rush. Oregon, 1968. 288p. (DA 29:3559-A)
The subject of this dissertation was suggested to the writer by a committee whose members had read his Master's thesis, "The Jews of Jacksonville, Oregon," and suggested the same type of study in a larger geographical area. That separate Jewish cemeteries existed in six cities of the Mother Lode and Northern Mines regions of California was sufficient evidence that Jewish communities were active during and after the gold rush a century ago. The problem was to gather documentary evidence relating to these communities, since no organizational records could be located. (A)

699. Levy, Beryl H. Reform Judaism in America: A Study in Religious Adaptation. Columbia, 1933. 186p.
Published under the same title (New York: Bloch, 1933).

700. Lewin, Rhoda G. Some New Perspectives on the Jewish Immigrant Experience in Minneapolis: An Experiment in Oral History. Minnesota, 1978. 307p. (DA 39:3778)
This experimental qualitative study uses 17 taped interviews with East European Jewish immigrants (United States arrivals 1900-1924) to reexamine stereotypes created by historians, social scientists, novelists, and filmmakers who use New York's Lower East Side as a metaphor for the immigrant experience; to discover new aspects of that experience; and to begin a projected social history of Minneapolis Jewry. Immigrant historians tend to emphasize structural regularities; this study emphasizes social process, individual behavior, and probable reasons for such behavior and suggests that some social research is flawed by previous misconceptions or by inadequate historical backgrounding. (A)

701. Lindenthal, Jacob J. Early History of the Jews of Middletown, Connecticut. Yeshiva, 1973. 525p. (DA 34:2520)
A significant proportion of the work done in American Jewish history since the end of the Second World War has concentrated on community studies. These works have dealt with the compara-

tively large urban centers. Many Jews, however, who came to the United States during the great migration at the turn of the century settled in small cities. One such small community was Middletown, Connecticut, the subject of this investigation. One of the major impediments to the writing of the history of the Jews in small communities is the paucity of records they left for posterity. The Jews of Middletown proved to be no exception. Intrigued by both the challenge and the possibility of developing a model for the future writing of the history of the Jews in small communities, the author turned to vital statistics and city directories as a source of historical data. Thus, this study is largely based on birth, marriage, and death certificates and city directories. (A)

702. Maas, Elaine H. The Jews of Houston: An Ethnographic Study. Rice, 1973. 285p. (DA 34:1375)
This research is a pioneer ethnographic study of the Jews of Houston. Although numerous studies of Jewish populations of large American cities have been published, no such study had previously been made of Houston, the sixth-largest city, and one of the fastest growing cities in the nation. The focus of the study is on the Jews of Houston "as a whole." The goal is to provide a general view of their life rather than an intensive account of a portion of it. Within the limits of time and resources imposed upon the study it aims to give as rounded a picture as possible. An effort is also made to compare, insofar as possible, the Jews of Houston with the Jews in cities elsewhere in the United States. (A)

703. Margolis, Isidor. A History of Teacher-Training Schools for Teachers in Jewish Schools in the United States in the First Half of the Twentieth Century. New York, 1960. 535p. (DA 21:3369)
Published under the title Jewish Teacher Training Schools in the United States (New York: National Council for Torah Education, 1964). This study was undertaken to ascertain the development of Jewish teacher-training schools, to evaluate their influence on Jewish education, and thereby to indicate to these schools how they could improve their courses of study.

704. Markovitz, Eugene. Henry Pereira Mendes: Builder of Traditional Judaism in America. Yeshiva, 1961. 317p. (DA 23:1170)
Henry P. Mendes functioned as minister of Shearith Israel in New York City during the turn of the nineteenth century. He was involved in many of the events that transformed the American Jewish community into the most powerful Jewish community in the Diaspora. He helped found some of the most important institutions in American Jewish life and was one of the prime movers in the various ideologies that developed in the Jewish community. (A)

705. Mazur, Allan C. Resocialized Ethnicity: A Study of Jewish Social Scientists. Johns Hopkins, 1969. 240p. (DA 30:830-A)

This is a study of the ethnic attitudes, behaviors, and self-concept notions of 63 Jewish social scientists from the Boston academic community. As a group these men are found to be relatively uncommitted to the Jewish religion. However, their lack of religious commitment does not justify the common stereotype of the Jewish intellectual as being totally detached from ethnic-group concerns. Rather, the ethnicity of this group is an eclectic one, conforming to the general values of the academic community. For example, most academics disdain restricted, parochial behavior, and so the Jewish academic disdains, and dissociates himself from, Jewish clannishness. On the other hand, most academics value intellectuality, and so the Jewish academic is proud of the Jewish intellectual tradition. Ethnicity, viewed in this eclectic manner, is a very strong characteristic of many of the present subjects. (A)

706. Meade, Robert D. Judah P. Benjamin and the American Civil War. Chicago, 1935. 276p.
Published under the title Judah P. Benjamin: Confederate Statesman (New York: Oxford University Press, 1943).

707. Messinger, Jonathan S. The Jewish Community in Syracuse, 1850-1880: The Growth and Structure of an Urban Ethnic Region. Syracuse, 1977. 290p. (DA 39:1106-A)
This study examines the growth of an ethnic community, the Jews in Syracuse, from their initial immigration around 1840 until 1880, by which time they were firmly established in a fully developed ethnic region. The morphology of the ethnic region centered in an ethnic core that was a composite of business, residential, and institutional concentrations. As an area of interaction between German and East European Jews, the core was an appropriate stage for the development of a new ethnicity. Surrounding the ethnic core were peripheral zones whose character reflected both the relative position of the group on the continuum of residential invasion and succession, and the location of certain peripheral areas within the evolving internal spatial structure of the ethnic region. (A)

708. Meyer, Henry J. The Structure of the Jewish Community in the City of Detroit. Michigan, 1940. 241p.

709. Miller, James A. The Resident Yiddish Theater in Detroit from 1920 to 1937. Wayne State, 1965. 207p. (DA 28: 3292-A)
Published under the title The Detroit Yiddish Theater, 1920 to 1937 (Detroit: Wayne State University Press, 1967). This study deals with the development of the Detroit Yiddish Theater from 1920 to 1937. The focus of attention is centered on the resident Yiddish troupe of Abraham Littman that performed continuously from 1924 to 1937. Research consisted chiefly of personal interviews and extensive reading of the Yiddish and Anglo-Jewish press for the years covered and published literature on the Yiddish theater. (A)

710. Minshall, Charles W. A Model of Residential Site Selection: The Jewish Population of Columbus, Ohio. Ohio State, 1971. 350p. (DA 32:4004-B)
When examined from the perspective of the geographer, perhaps the most unique spatial characteristic of the Jewish population in American cities is its concentration in specific urban areas, increasingly a middle- to upper-middle-class suburb. This pattern of spatial cohesion is neither a static nor a recent phenomenon, and has been characteristic of Jewish communities in American cities since the eighteenth century. The purpose of this thesis is to examine the current geographic distribution of Jewish residences in Columbus, Ohio, and to explain how this pattern is related to attempts by individual Jewish households to maximize residential satisfaction. (A)

711. Mitchell, William E. Cognatic Descent Groups in an Urban-Industrial Society: The Jewish Kinship Clubs of New York City. Columbia, 1969. 298p. (DA 32:6177-B)
When the research for this monograph began in 1959 a basic assumption among social scientists was that descent groups were structurally and functionally incompatible with the occupational requirements of an urban-industrial society. It was further assumed that the existence of descent groups was incompatible with the social and geographic mobility required of a population in a highly urbanized and industrialized society. There were no ethnographic examples to contradict these assumptions, and they appeared to be valid. The existence of the Jewish "family circle" and "cousins' club" of New York City, however, provides new data that modify these earlier assumptions. (A)

712. Mizner, John S. Israel Zangwill: Between Orthodoxy and Assimilation. Pennsylvania, 1966. 185p. (DA 27:4227-A)
This dissertation makes no attempt to discuss Zangwill's work in its entirety. It is a critical study of those "Jewish" works for which Zangwill is, with justice, best remembered: Children of the Ghetto, The King of Schnorrers, and The Melting Pot. The King of Schnorrers, obviously much less ambitious than the other two, is included because it is probably Zangwill's greatest "artistic" success. It succeeds, I conclude, largely because its subject is ideally suited to Zangwill's archaic, rhetorical, insistently facetious style. The King of Schnorrers, unlike Zangwill's other works, achieves an admirable conjunction of form and manner. In addition to a detailed discussion of these three works, the dissertation includes a brief biographical sketch, a survey of Zangwill criticism, and a chapter about Zangwill as a critic of literature. (A)

713. Moore, Deborah D. The Emergence of Ethnicity: New York's Jews, 1920-1940. Columbia, 1975. 349p. (DA 36:8255-A)
The second generation, the children of the immigrants, raised dramatically the question of the nature of group assimilation into American society. Acculturation accompanied by ethnic group

persistence was the answer given by second-generation middle-
class Jews to the question of assimilation. In New York City
during the two decades from 1920 to 1940 second-generation
Jews accommodated themselves to American life while they
simultaneously fashioned institutions to promote Jewish ethnic
group separateness. (A)

714. Mowshowitz, Israel. The Study of the Perception of Jewish
and Non-Jewish Faces As It Is Related to Prejudice. Duke,
1953. 141p.

715. Natelson, Herman. The Talmud Torahs: A Study of the
School, the Pupil and His Home. Fordham, 1937. 141p.

716. Nathan, Marvin. The Attitudes of the Jewish Student in the
Colleges and Universities Towards His Religion: A Social
Study of Religious Changes. Pennsylvania, 1932. 187p.

717. Neubauer, Ruth. Differential Adjustment of Adult Immigrants
and Their Children to American Groups (The Americanization
of a Selected Group of Jewish Immigrants of 1933-1942).
Columbia, 1966. 433p. (DA 27:1129-A)
Various studies have been concerned with the adjustment problems
of immigrants. There have been several important studies of the
particular group selected for this study, mostly involving the
early years after resettlement. The emphasis here was focused
on the situation of the immigrants 25 to 30 years after their arrival in the United States, with particular attention to the difference in degree of Americanization of parents and children. The
possibility of altered relationships resulting from such differences
was brought into focus and the effect of religious commitment on
this relationship was studied. (A)

718. Neuringer, Sheldon M. American Jewry and United States
Immigration Policy, 1881-1953. Wisconsin, 1969. 491p.
(DA 32:892-A)
During the period between 1881 and 1953 no public issue inspired
greater concern on the part of American Jews than did the formation of United States immigration policy. The work examines
American Jewish reactions to immigration policy from the onset
of the vast East European Jewish migration to the United States
through the time of the reaffirmation of the national-origins system nearly four decades after it was first adopted. Arranged in
chronological order, the study contains a description and analysis
of Jewish activity during a number of major episodes. These
are as follows: (1) the early reaction to the arrival of the East
European Jews and the attempts to curb their entry, (2) the response to the literacy test, (3) the response to the quota legislation, (4) the effort to admit refugees from Nazism, (5) the reaction to the displaced-persons question, and (6) an effort to modify
the quota system during the early 1950s. A separate chapter is
devoted also to Jewish labor and the immigration issue from 1885
to 1925. (A)

719. Nussenbaum, Max S. Champion of Orthodox Judaism: A Biography of the Reverend Sabato Morais. Yeshiva, 1964. 267p. (DA 25:1879)
The years between 1851 and 1897 were eventful and momentous in the history of the American Jewish community. During that period the Reverend Sabato Morais, L. L. D., presided over the ministry of the influential Orthodox bastion in the United States, Congregation Mickve Israel of Philadelphia. This era witnessed American Jewry's greatest period of growth and development. From an estimated 100,000 in 1850, the Jewish population leaped to one million at the turn of the century. (A)

720. O'Dea, Janet K. Religion and Ethnicity: Situational Factors and Value Conflict in Modern Jewish History: An Essay in Interpretation. Columbia, 1970. 181p. (DA 32:529-A)
Both religion and ethnicity are important elements in the formation of individual and group identities. In a variety of historical circumstances they may be found as mutually supportive of each other or in a condition of tension and conflict. The issues deriving from this dialectal relationship between the two have been worked out again and again in the history of Judaism. This dissertation explores the significance of that relationship as it has evolved in response to the challenges of secularization in modern Jewish experience. (A)

721. Phillips, Bruce A. Acculturation, Group Survival, and the Ethnic Community: A Social History of the Jewish Community of Brookline, Massachusetts, 1915-1940. California (Los Angeles), 1975. 240p. (DA 36:1834)
The dissertation is addressed to the problem of understanding the Jewish ethnic community. The position prevalent in sociology sees the minority community as a reaction to, and determined by, dominant-group discrimination. This stance, represented by Milton Gordon, Tamotsu Shibutani, and Judith Kramer, is described as "externalist" because it understands the ethnic group as the result of forces external to it. This position is found to be overly one-sided, and an alternative model is introduced (as suggested by Marshall Sklare) that takes into account aspirations originating from within the Jewish community. This model posits a synthesis of external and internal factors involved in the creation and maintenance of the Jewish ethnic community. Although criticism of the "externalist" model is justified on a general basis, its implications are examined here with regard to one ethnic community. (A)

722. Pinsker, Sanford S. The "Schlemiel" As Metaphor: Studies in the Yiddish and American Jewish Novel. University of Washington, 1967. 278p. (DA 28:3679-A)
Published under the same title (Carbondale: Southern Illinois University, 1971). The study considers Jewish humor in its relationship to the collective notion of Israel (as developed in Job and Isaiah) as well as in the light of modern psychology. However, it is primarily as literary metaphor that the schlemiel

emerges as a key figure in the Yiddish literature of the East European ghettos (c. 1864). The authors considered in detail are Mendele Mocher Seforim, Sholom Aleichem, Isaac Bashevis Singer, Bernard Malamud, and Saul Bellow. (A)

723. Polish, David. The Development of the Concept of Nationalism in Nineteenth Century Hebrew Literature. Hebrew Union College, 1942. 186p.

724. Pollock, Theodore M. The Solitary Clarinetist: A Critical Biography of Abraham Cahan, 1860-1917. Columbia, 1959. 433p. (DA 1367)
There were, in reality, four Abraham Cahans. As American author, he is a minor but interesting figure--a pioneer realist who wrote our best Jewish-American novel. As Yiddish editor and journalist, he introduced to Yiddish journalism the sure-fire --if not always creditable--circulation-building techniques of American journalism. A natural outcome of his dual role as American author and Yiddish journalist was his contribution to understanding between the two worlds he straddled, explaining the Jewish immigrant to his American audience and Americanizing his Jewish audience. As a socialist, he helped shape the Socialist Party in America through founding, with others, the Social Democratic Party and his repeated support of Eugene Debs. To the extent that many socialist principles were eventually adopted by the major American political parties, Abraham Cahan's legacy forms a portion of the climate of our own time. (A)

725. Polsky, Howard W. The Great Defense: A Study of Jewish Orthodoxy in Milwaukee. Wisconsin, 1957. 458p. (DA 17: 909)
The objective of the study was to analyze the interaction between a sacred religious system and the pattern of an American secular society. Jewish Orthodoxy was separated into three component elements: its organization, with the synagogue as the primary institutional structure, its membership, and its role in the Jewish community. Jewish Orthodoxy, having at its source the rich sacred accumulated heritage of 2,000 years, balanced to some extent the secularizing tendencies of the American social system. The American Jewish community will continue its unique development without a significant traditional Jewish Orthodox movement in its midst; this will result in an acceleration of the process of secularization of Jewish religious traditions and raise new problems and challenges for the survival of Judaism in America. (A)

726. Pomerantz, Israel C. Moshiach Motivn in der Amerikanish Yiddisher Poezye: Messianic Motifs in American Yiddish Poetry. Yeshiva, 1954. 210p.

727. Raphael, Marc L. Intra-Jewish Conflict in the United States, 1869-1915. California (Los Angeles), 1972. 146p. (DA

33:4317-A)
An attempt is made not only to describe the phenomenon of intra-Jewish discord but to suggest the factors, such as the internalization of anti-Jewish stereotypy, minority status, a general "status-panic," and strong feelings of cultural superiority, that explains why, as one Jew put it, "Jews in this country exhibit that same proneness to prejudice toward the Russian Jews which other people exhibit toward the Jews in general." (A)

728. Rappaport, Joseph. Jewish Immigrants and World War I: A Study of American Yiddish Press Reactions. Columbia, 1951. 455p. (DA 12:48)
This is a study of the war reactions of East European Jewish immigrants in the United States. Having arrived in this country with the "new" immigration, this Yiddish-speaking element remained closely attached to Jewish communities in Russia, Poland, Galicia, Hungary, and Rumania. Jewish-immigrant war reactions must be measured in the light of the rejection of the conditions of their former life (which was the basis of the migration), and the desire to see the political, economic, and social emancipation of the East European Jewish community. The origins of Jewish nationalist and socialist strivings, which played an important role in immigrant war attitudes, stemmed from this drive for emancipation, political or otherwise. (A)

729. Rischin, Moses. Jewish Life and Labor in New York City, 1870-1914. Harvard, 1957. 342p.
Published under the title The Promised City: New York's Jews, 1870-1914 (Cambridge, Massachusetts: Harvard University Press, 1962). An elaborate profile of the New York City Jewish community with special attention to the Russian Jews, the growth of Reform Judaism, and the community's growing participation in labor organizations and politics.

730. Rockaway, Robert A. From Americanization to Jewish Americanism: The Jews of Detroit, 1850-1914. Michigan, 1970. 258p. (DA 31:2287-A)
The history of Detroit's Jews from 1850 to 1914 is in a large measure the story of an ethnic group that sought to become fully American in every sense of the word. At the same time, however, most members of the Jewish community desired to perpetuate some of their ancient traditions and maintain their Jewish identity. The tensions and ambivalence created by these contrasting impulses were never resolved and played a continuing role in determining the Jewish community's behavior throughout this period. (A)

731. Rogoff, Abraham Meyer. Formative Years of the Jewish Labor Movement in the United States (1890-1900). Columbia, 1945. 197p.

732. Rosenberg, Stuart E. The Jewish Community in Rochester, 1843-1925. Columbia, 1955. 246p.

Published under the same title (New York: Columbia University Press, 1955).

733. Rosenblum, Herbert. The Founding of the United Synagogue of America, 1913. Brandeis, 1970. 304p. (DA 31:2856-A)
The United Synagogue of America was the last of the three major Jewish congregational federations to be founded in the United States, yet in its half-century of existence it has already become by far the largest among them. This study explores the circumstances that led to its founding in 1913 and the personalities, events and issues that were involved in this process. (A)

734. Rosenstock, Morton. Louis Marshall and the Defense of Jewish Rights in the United States. Columbia, 1963. 517p. (DA 24:4165)
Published under the title Louis Marshall, Defender of Human Rights (Detroit: Wayne State University Press, 1965). Anti-Semitism in the form of social discrimination and part of a broader nativism affected the American Jewish community during the early decades of the twentieth century. The initiative in defending Jewish rights was taken by the American Jewish Committee, whose President from 1912 to 1929 was Louis Marshall (1856-1929). A distinguished lawyer, Marshall functioned primarily as spokesman for the wealthy, confident, German Jewish elite. His ideology consisted of an amalgam of Americanism, reverence for the law, and firm loyalty to Judaism. Usually conservative on economic issues, he was a consistent advocate of civil liberties for all. He did not regard American anti-Semitism as a fundamental problem but was determined to prevent its expression in overt form. Marshall's tactics generally emphasized the traditional methods of rational argument, quiet intercession, and dignified application of pressure, but his effectiveness was strengthened by his political influence and by the implied power of Jewish voters. His leadership was increasingly questioned by the rising East European immigrants, but most Jews and non-Jews acknowledged him as the champion of Jewish rights. (A)

735. Rosenthal, Erich. The Jewish Population of Chicago, Illinois: Size and Distribution As Derived from Voters' Lists. Chicago, 1948. 128p.
Published under the title The Jewish Population of Chicago (Chicago: College of Jewish Studies, 1952). An effort to devise indirect measures of the number and distribution of Jews in large communities. Primarily methodological, the method consisting of a selection of Jewish names from precinct voter-lists, which are part of a permanent registration system.

736. Ross, Jacob M. [also known as Jacob M. Rosenberg]. An Historical Study of the Elimination of the Religious, Civil and Political Disabilities of the Jews in the Thirteen Original States from Their Earliest Days to the Present. New York, 1914. 112p.

737. Rothkoff, Arnold. Vision and Realization: Bernard Revel and His Era. Yeshiva, 1967. 411p. (DA 28:605-A)
Bernard Revel may rightfully be called the father of Torah of the United States. An accomplished European Talmudic scholar, he also understood the challenges of America to the perpetuation of authentic Judaism in the United States. He developed the young Rabbi Isaac Elchanan Theological Seminary into an internationally famous institution and made it capable of influencing contemporary American Judaism. He brought the first leading Roshei Yeshiva to America to teach the Yeshiva. He organized Talmudical Academy High School, Yeshiva College, and the Graduate Department for Semitic Studies because he felt that these institutions would aid authentic Judaism in successfully communicating in the language of contemporary American civilization.

738. Rubinger, Naphtali J. The History of the Albany Jewish Community 1660-1900: Historic Roots and Communal Evolution. Yeshiva, 1970. 600p. (DA 31:4690-A)
This thesis presents the history of the Albany Jewish community from 1660 to 1900. The major area of concern, however, involves the communal development of the German Jewish settlement beginning with the mid 1830s and the subsequent arrival of the East European Jews during the latter part of the nineteenth century. (A)

739. Rudavsky, David. Jewish Education in New York City Since 1918. New York, 1945. 215p.

740. Rutman, Herbert S. Defense and Development: A History of Minneapolis Jewry, 1930-1950. Minnesota, 1970. 163p. (DA 31:3484-A)
During the decades of the 1930s and 1940s the Jewish community of Minneapolis, threatened by Jewish religious and cultural ignorance, by the possible assimilation of its children into the larger non-Jewish culture, by the awareness of its minority status--which engendered feelings of isolation and insecurity--by increasing secularism, by serious and demanding charity and welfare problems, and by severe and pervasive anti-Semitism, instituted various defenses against these threats. These defenses were developed, consolidated, and refined, and the community was transformed into a more complex and efficient entity. (A)

741. Sable, Jacob M. Some American Jewish Organizational Efforts to Combat Anti-Semitism, 1906-30. Yeshiva, 1964. 329p. (DA 26:2716)
This study describes the communal reaction of American Jews to anti-Semitism, as viewed against the background of American history, economy, immigration, wars, and the adjustment to American society. Jews had to overcome social, political, economic, and cultural prejudice, based on religious background, xenophobia, and anti-alienism. Prejudice has been manifested through defamation, social ostracism, economic and educational discrimination, political agitation, and occasionally even violence. As background

a summary of such trends and manifestations between 1654 and 1930 is presented. (A)

742. Schanin, Norman. Young Judaea: A Survey of a National Jewish Youth Movement in 1951-1952. New York, 1959. 317p. (DA 20:789)
This study presents a nationwide survey of Young Judaea during its 43rd operational year, extending from September 1951 to September 1952. Young Judaea is the oldest and largest of the national Zionist youth movements in the United States. This investigation considered data bearing upon the status of Young Judaea in order to determine the nature of its program and the processes through which the national goals are implemented. (A)

743. Schoenfeld, Eugen. Small-Town Jews: A Study in Identity and Integration. Southern Illinois, 1967. 243p. (DA 28: 3791-A)
The purpose of this research is to examine the relationship between Jewish identity and community integration, to discover what aspects or aspects of Jewish identity hinder integration. The study was conducted in 12 small towns in southern Illinois, and a total of 83 Jews were interviewed. Jewish identity in this research was dichotomized into orientations toward "Judaism" and "Jewishness." The first refers to an identity that is centered primarily in the Jewish religion, and the second to one centered in Jewish culture and ethnicity. (A)

744. Scholnick, Myron I. The New Deal and Anti-Semitism in America. Maryland, 1971. 237p. (DA 32:2043-A)
Political anti-Semitism was a comparatively negligible phenomenon in the United States prior to the New Deal era. But the advent of Franklin Roosevelt's reformist Administration, and the concurrent rise to power of Adolf Hitler in Germany, produced a startling change. As a master of ethnic politics and a defender of America's open society, Roosevelt from the start captured overwhelming Jewish loyalty. Thus, enemies of the New Deal had an opportunity to attack it in anti-Semitic terms. Most chose not to, but some did. And a fantastic assortment of professional bigots, viewing events in Nazi Germany as an inspiration, joined in the assault. (A)

745. Schreiber, Emma S. The Jewish Transient. New York University, 1932. 110p.

746. Scott, Graham S. Under Gentile Eyes: Images of the Jew in the Nineteenth-Century Novel of England and America. Brigham Young, 1978. 164p. (DA 40:4289-A)
The traditional critical assumption that the image of the Jew found in the nineteenth-century novel of England and America is necessarily derived from anti-Semitism is refuted on several grounds. Chapter One shows that anti-Semitism was not prevalent in the nineteenth century and points to literary convention as the primary shaper of prose fiction. Chapter Two discusses the

novel's treatment of Jewish religiosity and shows that the negative image of Judaism that is to be found usually results not from anti-Jewish feeling but from a borrowing of the conventions of Gothic fiction. Chapter Three notes that "Jewish looks" are usually not derived from racist feelings but are the consequences of novelists following physiognomic theory. Chapter Four treats the stereotypes of Jewish capitalism and establishes that authorial attitudes to capital rather than Jewishness were what primarily determined the characterization that we find. (A)

747. Seiger, Marvin L. A History of the Yiddish Theatre in New York City to 1892. Indiana, 1960. 616p. (DA 21:3560)
The present study is the first detailed examination of a phase of American theater history long neglected by the scholars. Although the activities of the Yiddish stage come under the heading of a foreign-language theater, the productions and talents were an integral part of the New York theater scene. This volume serves as an introduction to the New York Yiddish stage and attempts to clarify the origins of its efforts, particularly its Eastern European heritage. (A)

748. Seller, Maxine S. Isaac Leeser, Architect of the American Jewish Community. Pennsylvania, 1965. 205p. (DA 27: 1022-A)
How can a minority group maintain its identity while integrating itself into American society as a whole? This paper is a study of how Isaac Leeser, Jewish immigrant from Westphalia, tried to solve this problem for American Jews from his arrival in the United States in 1824 until his death in 1868. (A)

749. Selvan, Ida C. The Columbian Council of Pittsburgh, 1894-1909: A Case Study of Immigrant Education. Pittsburgh, 1976. 161p. (DA 37:1354)
Around the turn of the century Pittsburgh had one of the highest concentrations of adult immigrants in the United States, but few attempts were made by government agencies to educate them. This dissertation deals with the work of a Jewish women's organization, Columbian Council (the Pittsburgh Section of the National Council of Jewish Women) in informal adult education of immigrants between 1894 and 1909.

750. Shapira, Rina N. Patterns of Attitudes Towards Israel Among Jewish Adolescents in New York Jewish Schools. Columbia, 1965. 224p. (DA 27:541-A)
The purpose of this research is to study the attitudes of Jewish adolescents in an American metropolis toward the State of Israel. The study is primarily concerned with the role played by Israel within the specific social context of American-Jewish adolescents; that is, children being educated in systems that accentuate both Jewish and American norms. (A)

751. Shapiro, Max A. An Historical Analysis and Evaluation of Jewish Religious Textbooks Published in the United States,

1817-1903. Cincinnati, 1960. 282p. (DA 21:3708)
The purpose of this study was: (1) to analyze the influence of
the American environment on the first Jewish religious-school
textbooks, (2) to discover the subject matter taught in the Jewish
religious school during the nineteenth century, (3) to evaluate the
religious content and approach of the Jewish texts, and (4) to
analyze the influences of the developing educational psychology
and methodology of the nineteenth century on the texts used by
the Jewish religious school during this period. (A)

752. Shapiro, Ynoathan. Leadership of the American Zionist
Organization, 1897-1930. Columbia, 1964. 621p. (DA 25:
1393)
Published under the same title (Urbana: University of Illinois
Press, 1971). This study deals with the changes Zionist ideology
underwent during the first three decades of the twentieth century.
Starting in Eastern Europe as a nationalist ideology that asserted
that the Jews were and should remain a separate political and
cultural entity, Zionism was transformed in the United States into
Palestinianism, a belief that all Jews should help in the building
up of Palestine as a national Jewish home. (A)

753. Sharfman, Israel H. American Response As a Source for
the History of the Jews of America to 1850. Yeshiva, 1954.
265p.

754. Shlonsky, Hagith R. Growth and Decline of Voluntary Associations: A Comparative Study of Zionist Organizations in
New Haven. Yale, 1960. 290p. (DA 31:3061-A)
The voluntary associations under examination in this study are 11
local Zionist organizations. The major problem studied here
was that of growth or decline of these organizations in the period
between 1948-49 and 1958-59. Growing, stable, and declining
organizations were compared with respect to two main aspects:
(1) their social composition, and (2) their purposes and functions
(manifest and latent). (A)

755. Silver, Arthur M. Jews in the Political Life of New York
City, 1865-1897. Yeshiva, 1954. 241p. (DA 20:1007)
From 1865 to 1885, with few exceptions, the role of the Jews in
politics was tied up closely with the German political movements.
About 1886 the "Jewish" element in politics emerged. Immigration to the city's East Side made the Jews a major factor of the
population. In general, most Jews voted Democratic, as Tammany was more understanding and friendlier to all immigrants,
including, naturally, the Jews. Therefore, in many elections,
particularly Presidential, the Republicans nominated a greater
number of Jews, hoping thereby to draw more Jewish votes for
their ticket and thus win the state. (A)

756. Silverman, Simon S. The Psychological Adjustment of AllDay School (Yeshiva) Students: A Psychological Study of 7th
and 8th Year All-Day School Students Compared with 7th and

8th Year Students Attending Public Schools. Yeshiva, 1954. 195p. (DA 15:231)
Research was carried on to determine the comparability of All-Day and Public School seventh- and eighth-year students. Samples were equated for age, sex, IQ, grade placement, ethnic origin, and socioeconomic status. This study sought to determine if there were any significant differences between both samples in terms of their (1) educational attainments; (2) response to disguised, forced-choice questions involving apperception of Jewish concepts and values; (3) response to a test measuring a moral trait--honesty; (4) adjustment as determined by response to an emotional stability inventory; and (5) response to a background-interest inventory covering such facets of living as family life, interests, and activities; religious practices; and group affiliations. Finally, the study sought to probe the implications of this study for the improvement and growth of the All-Day Schools. (A)

757. Singer, David F. The Acculturation of Ludwig Lewisohn: An Intellectual Portrait. Brown, 1968. 268p.

758. Sklare, Marshall. Conservative Judaism. A Sociological Analysis. Columbia, 1953. 418p. (DA 14:194)
Published under the title Conservative Judaism: An American Religious Movement (Glencoe, Illinois: Free Press, 1955; rev. ed., 1972). The ethnic church category constitutes a suitable frame of reference with which to analyze the development of Conservative Judaism, one of the three divisions in American Jewish religious life. Due to certain factors special to the Jewish tradition, and aggravated by a very high rate of social mobility among the group, certain needs were so accentuated in the Jewish community as to require a greater degree of adjustment on the part of the Orthodox synagogue than this institution was able to make. Distinguished by a pervasive interest in group survival, Jews who shared a similar class position, degree of acculturation, and common background in the Judaism of Eastern Europe, established "Conservative" synagogues--chiefly during the second and third decades of the twentieth century--which brought into harmony newly achieved status with patterns of Jewish worship. (A)

759. Snow, Charles E. Comparative Growth of Jewish and Non-Jewish Pupils in a Greater Boston Public School. Harvard, 1937. 245p.

760. Soltes, Mordecai. The Yiddish Press: An Americanizing Agency. Columbia (Teachers College), 1924. 242p.
Published under the same title (New York: Teachers College Press, Columbia University, 1924).

761. Soviv, Aaron. Attitudes Towards Jewish Life and Education As Reflected in Yiddish and Hebrew Literature in America, 1870-1914. Dropsie College, 1957. 146p.

762. Steigelfest, Annette. The Political Socialization of an American Ethnic Group: The Orthodox Jewish Community of Halacha Institute. Bryn Mawr, 1978. 231p. (DA 39:5705)
This study examined an Orthodox Jewish community in a large metropolitan area, an ethnic group that has practiced bilingual/ bicultural separatism for generations. The subjects were children attending a private elementary day school, Halacha Institute. A case-study method was used to investigate the concepts of diffuse support, power and legitimacy, sense of community, and sex-role learning.

763. Steinberg, Abraham H. Jewish Characters in the American Novel to 1900. New York, 1955. 308p. (DA 16:1142)
This dissertation undertakes, in the absence of any other preliminary account, to provide a panoramic view of the treatment of the Jew in the American novel up to and including the year 1900. Jewish characters appeared as early as the eighteenth century, when the novel form was just taking root in our soil, and in works by such nineteenth-century authors as Cooper, Simms, Hawthorne, James, and hosts of others. An attempt is made to convey something of the flavor of the approximately 250 novels surveyed, as background for a brief scrutiny of their handling of Jews.

764. Stern, Herman D. Jewish Social Work in the United States, 1654-1954. Columbia, 1958. 268p.

765. Stern, Malcolm H. Two Studies in the Assimilation of Early American Jewry. Hebrew Union College, 1957. 167p.

766. Stevens, Richard P. The Political and Diplomatic Role of American Zionists As a Factor in the Creation of the State of Israel. Georgetown, 1960. 270p.
Published under the title American Zionism and United States Foreign Policy, 1942-1947 (New York: Pageant, 1962).

767. Strong, Donald S. Anti-Revolutionary, Anti-Semitic Organizations in the United States Since 1930. Chicago, 1939. 210p.
Published under the title Organized Anti-Semitism in America: The Rise of Group Prejudice During the Decade 1930-1940 (Washington, D.C.: American Council on Public Affairs, 1941).

768. Sutker, Solomon. The Jews of Atlanta: Their Social Structure and Leadership Patterns. North Carolina (Chapel Hill), 1950. 260p.

769. Tarshish, Allan. The Rise of American Judaism: A History of American Jewish Life from 1848-1881. Hebrew Union College, 1937. 243p.

770. Teitelbaum, Samuel. Patterns of Adjustment Among Jewish Students in Midwestern Universities. Northwestern, 1953.

267p. (DA 14:195)
The purpose of this study is to explore the attitudes and patterns of adjustment among Jewish students in several midwestern institutions of higher learning, particularly Northwestern University. The problem of special concern is to discover those patterns of adjustment that the members of the Jewish minority establish or tend to establish on university campuses, both within their own group and in their relationship to the members of the non-Jewish majority.

771. Temkin, Sefton D. Isaac Mayer Wise, 1819-1875. Hebrew Union College, 1965. 246p.

772. Todes, David U. History of Jewish Education in Philadelphia, 1782-1873. Dropsie College, 1953. 267p.

773. Wechman, Robert J. Emanuel Gamoran: Pioneer in Jewish Religious Education. Syracuse, 1970. 329p. (DA 31:5583-A)
Emanuel Gamoran (1895-1962) served as Director of Education of the Union of American Hebrew Congregation (UAHC) from 1923-1958. The creation of rich Jewish experiences for the Jewish child was the major objective of Emanuel Gamoran's philosophy of education. He believed that this could only be achieved in the Jewish school. In the context of the American situation Gamoran viewed the Jewish school as the primary means of helping the immigrant Jew adjust from the ghetto environment of Eastern Europe to the modern industrial society of the United States, without the loss of Jewish heritage. (A)

774. Weinberger, Abe L. Judaism in America: The Influence of America As a New World Frontier upon Judaism of Tradition. Texas (Austin), 1953. 247p.

775. Werb, Morris R. Jewish Suburbia--An Historical and Comparative Study of Jewish Communities in Three New Jersey Suburbs. New York, 1959. 284p. (DA 20:3423)
The purpose of this study was to investigate the results of suburbanization upon the Jewish inhabitants of three New Jersey suburban communities, to determine the history and growth of Jewish institutional and communal life in these communities, and to compare their social characteristics with other suburban Jewish communities. The intent of this investigation was to examine to what extent the Jewish institutional life of these suburbs was being modified and to discover trends and patterns of Jewish communal activity in order to aid us in securing some knowledge of the impact of suburbia upon Jews and Jewish life. (A)

776. Winograd, Leonard. The Horse Died at Windberg: A History of Johnstown Jewry. Hebrew Union College, 1967. 211p.

777. Wirth, Louis. The Ghetto: A Study in Isolation. Chicago, 1926. 238p.

Published under the same title (University of Chicago Press, 1928). Jews in Chicago, and Wirth's classic analysis of the development of the ghetto as an evolving process.

778. Wisse, Ruth R. The Schlemihl As Hero in Yiddish and American Fiction. McGill, 1969. 250p. (DA 30:2983-A)
Published under the same title (Chicago: University of Chicago Press, 1971). The schlemihl is a Yiddish subspecies of the universal fool figure. Victim of endless misfortune, the schlemihl of Yiddish folk humor converts losses to verbal advantage and defeats into psychological victories. Yiddish storytellers, including Rabbi Nachman of Bratzlav, Mendele Mocher Sforim, Sholom Aleichem, and Isaac Bashevis Singer, created versions of the schlemihl-hero to explore the irony of a faith that could coexist with doubt. Though originally alien to America, Yiddish humor penetrated the general culture, particularly after World War II. American Jewish writers, like Saul Bellow and Bernard Malamud, used the schlemihl to explore the paradox of failure as success within a secular humanist culture. The schlemihl-stance coincided with the national mood for over a decade; it may not survive the sixties. (A)

779. Yapko, Benjamin L. Jewish Elementary Education in the United States from the Colonial Period to 1900. American, 1958. 197p. (DA 19-1996)
This study, in the form of a general survey, traces the historical development of Jewish elementary education in the United States from its earliest beginnings to the start of the twentieth century. Inquiry is made into the general background of Jewish settlement in the United States and the effects of subsequent Jewish migrations. One of the primary concerns of this study is with Jewish communal and religious life and the institutions that evolved, since all of these aspects are vitally connected in Jewish education. (A)

780. Yodfat, Aryeh Y. The Jewish Question in American-Russian Relations (1875-1917). American, 1963. 287p. (DA 24:2006)
Jews in Tsarist Russia were discriminated against because of their national minority status and because of their religion. That discrimination was applied also to American Jews who visited Russia and led to protests in the United States and by its representatives in Russia. According to the Russian interpretation of the U.S.-Russian Treaty of Commerce and Navigation of 1832, American Jews were supposed to be treated in Russia in the same way as Russian Jews were treated. The United States did not accept these views and the differences of opinion brought about the termination of that treaty by the United States in December 1911. (A)

781. York, Lawrence F. The Image of the Jew in Modern American Fiction. Connecticut, 1966. 153p. (DA 27:3475-A)
This study is concerned with the image of the Jew in American

fiction during the last 50 years. As the condition of Jews in society has changed during this period, so has their reflected image in the fiction of American authors, both Jewish and non-Jewish. As old stereotypes and caricatures of Jews vanished, and as Jews assimilated into American society, it has become progressively more difficult to identify Jews in fiction as being unique or different from any other character. If Jews become Americans, in what ways do they remain Jews? Because the term "Jew" is ambiguous and refers to both an adherent of the religion of Judaism and to a member of the Jewish people, the author has attempted to classify Jews in fiction in three different ways: traditionally, culturally, and existentially. (A)

782. Youngerman, Louis M. The Jew in His American Environment, 1933-1955: As Evidenced in the Proceedings of the Central Conference of American Rabbis, the Rabbinical Assembly of America and the Rabbinical Council of America: A Psychological Study. Temple, 1958. 279p.

783. Zeitlin, Joseph. Disciples of the Wise: The Religious and Social Opinions of American Rabbis. Columbia (Teachers College), 1943. 187p.
Published under the same title (New York: Teachers College Press, Columbia University, 1943).

784. Zerin, Edward. Selected Theological and Educational Factors in the Personality Development of Jewish Youth. Southern California, 1953. 257p.

III. MULTI-GROUP, INTERETHNIC, AND RELATED STUDIES

785. Abraham, Sameer Y. Contextual Homogeneity/Hetereogeneity and Class Consciousness: The Effects of Class, Racial and Ethnic Milieux on Affluent Workers. Wayne State, 1979. 285p. (DA 40:2276-A)
This study examines the validity of the general assumption that ascribes a lack of class consciousness to white affluent workers. The Marxist and mainstream sociological literature is first reviewed with the object of extracting the common components of class consciousness. The problem is then specifically formulated from the standpoint of the social milieux of which the workers are an integral part. The varied homogeneous/heterogeneous effects of class, race, and ethnicity are hypothesized as the direct sources and correlates of class-conscious attitudes and behaviors among a probability sample of 678 white "middle mass" respondents residing in the Detroit metropolitan area. (A)

786. Abrahamson, Harold J. The Ethnic Factor in American Catholicism: An Analysis of Inter-Ethnic Marriage and Religious Involvement. Chicago, 1969. 207p.
Published under the title Ethnic Diversity in Catholic America (New York: Wiley, 1973). Contends that, contrary to the idea of America as a religious melting pot, ethnically based marriage patterns still exist among American Catholics.

787. Agocs, Carol. Ethnic Neighborhoods in City and Suburbs: Metropolitan Detroit, 1940-1970. Wayne State, 1977. 275p. (DA 38:6962)
Ethnic pluralism continues to be a significant dimension of American urban life, but its nature and range are still to be explored. This census-based examination of the urban ecology of 11 of the largest ethnic populations in the Detroit standard metropolitan statistical area from 1940 to 1970 focused on group and generational variations in degree of residential clustering, dispersion and segregation, and amount and timing of participation in suburbanization trends. Statistical analyses and mapping procedures, using country of origin, mother tongue, and racial data, were used to study changes in ethnic presence in six metropolitan zones, corresponding to phases in Detroit's development--the inner city, the middle zone, the urban periphery, older suburbs, postwar suburbs, and new suburbs. (A)

788. Arsenian, Seth. Bilingualism and Mental Development: A Study of the Intelligence and the Social Background of Bilingual Children in New York City. Columbia (Teachers College), 1937. 164p.
Published under the same title (New York: Teachers College, Columbia University, 1937). Largely concerned with Jewish and Italian children.

789. Axelrod, Herman C. Bilingual Background and Its Relation to Certain Aspects of Character and Personality of Elementary School Children. Yeshiva, 1951. 192p. (DA 13:1245)
Published under the same title (New York: Arno, 1978). More than 1,200 elementary school children (with varying degrees of bilingual background) attending public schools and representing three groups (Italian, Jewish, and Polish) were selected for this study. All were born in the United States and lived in predominantly bilingual neighborhoods in New York City. Axelrod's major aim in this investigation was "to study by means of objective measures certain aspects of school conduct and adjustment among bilingual children." The conclusions indicate that the "problem of bilingualism in the United States involves much more than the use of two languages. Bilingual background, viewed more broadly, implies a bicultural background which may produce social and emotional conflicts." It is not the inherent use of two languages by the native-born child of immigrant parents that leads to maladjustment. In Axelrod's view, "where a conscious and intelligent effort is made by the parents and the school to harmonize and reconcile divergent elements in both cultures, the conflict may be reduced or eliminated, and a major cause of maladjustment removed."

790. Bailey, David T. Stratification and Ethnic Differentiation in Santa Fe, 1860 and 1870. Texas (Austin), 1975. 158p. (DA 36:6986-A)
This dissertation is an analysis of differences between Hispanos and Anglos in Santa Fe, New Mexico, in the mid-nineteenth century. The primary differences examined are those concerning social stratification: occupation, wealth, and authority. In addition, differences in marital status, family size, migration patterns, and other variables are examined. The major data sources are the manuscript federal censuses of 1860 and 1870. Where comparable data are available the 1970 census is used to indicate long-term change. (A)

791. Baker, Gwendolyn C. The Effects of Training in Multi-Ethnic Education on Preservice Teachers' Perceptions. Michigan, 1972. 152p. (DA 33:4994-A)
This study focused on the effects of training in multi-ethnic education on preservice teachers' perceptions of ethnic groups. The purpose of the study was to determine whether a change could be made in the perception of ethnic groups held by students enrolled in a course in elementary school methods that emphasized a multi-ethnic approach to teaching. The design of the methods

course provided the students with incentive, knowledge, and skills that were requisite to the utilization of a multi-ethnic approach to teaching in the elementary school. The "multi-ethnic approach," as it relates to this study, is a way of organizing learning experiences for children that reflects the influences and contributions of black, Indian, Japanese, Jewish, and Mexican-American cultures to the total culture of America. (A)

792. Bales, Robert F. The "Fixation Factor" in Alcohol Addiction: An Hypothesis Secured from a Comparative Study of Irish and Jewish Social Norms. Harvard, 1945. 209p.

793. Barton, Josef J. Immigration and Social Mobility in an American City: Studies of Three Ethnic Groups in Cleveland, 1890-1950. Michigan, 1971. 217p. (DA 32:1429-A) Published under the title Peasants and Strangers: Italians, Rumanians, and Slovaks in an American City (Cambridge, Massachusetts: Harvard University Press, 1975). Immigration was a process that separated those who bore the marks of foreign origin from those who did not. Immigration has been a source of social and cultural distinctions and divisions--of social differentiations, in short, with their origins in the entrance of particular groups of people into the receiving society. This study approaches three aspects of the impact of immigration in this limited sense. First, what was the importance of different patterns of migration in the social adjustment of newcomers? Second, how did an ethnic leadership, conscious of its own status outside the host society, emerge in the process of migration and settlement? And third, what meaning did ethnic origins have for the process of occupational adjustment in an American city? (A)

794. Bayer, Alan E. The Assimilation of American Family Patterns by European Immigrants and Their Children. Florida State, 1965. 160p. (DA 26:4860)
This study attempts to (1) establish the degree of assimilation of American family life by second-generation European immigrants, and (2) specify some conditions and factors that affect the degree of assimilation. Data from the U. S. Bureau of the Census 1 in 1,000 sample of the 1960 population of the United States is used to compare four family variables (marital status, nuclear-extended family membership, age at first marriage, and number of children) of white native Americans with native parents to those of second-generation European immigrants and those of foreign-born European immigrants. Age, sex, rural-urban residence, socioeconomic score, and region of European origin are controlled in all analyses. (A)

795. Bayor, Ronald H. Ethnic Conflict in New York City, 1929-1941. Pennsylvania, 1970. 287p. (DA 31:2830-A)
Published under the title Neighbors in Conflict: The Irish, Germans, Jews, and Italians of New York City, 1929-1941 (Baltimore: Johns Hopkins University Press, 1978). Social scientists have spent much time studying the interrelationships between eth-

nic groups in order to understand ethnic conflict. Their theories will serve as the starting point for this study, which attempts to determine the causes of ethnic conflict in a particular area. The author limits the study to New York City during the ethnically turbulent period of 1929-1941. The groups chosen for study-- the Germans, Irish, Jews, and Italians--were the leading ethnic groups in New York at that time. The author sees the conflict as between the old (Germans and Irish) and the new (Jews and Italians) ethnic groups in New York. There was no trouble between the Germans and Irish. There were some difficulties between the Jews and Italians, which, however, never reached the actual conflict stage. (A)

796. Bellemarre, Marcel. Social Networks in an Inner-City Neighborhood: Woonsocket, Rhode Island. Catholic, 1975. 204p.

797. Bere, Mary. A Comparative Study of the Mental Capacity of Children of Foreign Parentage. Columbia (Teachers College), 1924. 105p.
Published under the same title (New York: Teachers College Press, Columbia University, 1924). Deals with immigrant Italian, Bohemian, and Russian-Jewish children.

798. Berger, Morris I. The Settlement, the Immigrant and the Public School: A Study of the Influence of the Settlement Movement and the New Migration upon Public Education, 1890-1924. Columbia (Teachers College), 1956. 196p. (DA 16:1230)
Published under the same title (New York: Arno, 1980). Historians of education have long been aware that the turn of the present century marked a transformation of the American public schools. In attempting to explain this transformation they have given extensive attention to such obvious factors as industrialism, Progressivism, Pragmatism, and the findings of educational research. Little if any attention, on the other hand, has been accorded the specific and direct influence of the social settlement and the immigrant. The result has been an unfortunate omission and a consequent imbalance in most interpretations of recent educational history. The social settlement arose as a reaction to the evils of industrialism. It was born of an effort by socially conscious reformers to combat the ugliness, poverty, and social disintegration of the urban slum. Its goal was nothing less than a total regeneration of the slum neighborhood--a regeneration whose character was first and foremost educational. The settlement was to be the center of a new self-conscious community; and from this center the people were to draw their strength. This study describes the transformation. It begins by briefly describing the beginnings of the settlement movement, its activities, and its aspirations. An analysis is then made of the impact of the new migration upon American society and the close connection of the settlement movement with this migration. The history of the Educational Alliance, an institution that combined

settlement work with immigrant education, follows as a case study. The impact of the settlement movement and the new migration upon public education is subsequently considered. Finally, the study shows how settlement work and the activities of immigrant institutions coalesced with other forces to support the movement to make the public school the center of community life.

799. Berrol, Selma C. Immigrants at School: New York City, 1898-1914. City University of New York, 1967. 438p. (DA 28:1365-A)
Published under the same title (New York: Arno, 1978). In this study of immigrant Jewish and Italian children in New York City schools Berrol provides historical backgrounds on the responses of American schools to the culturally different and language-minority child. The objectives of the study were to find out what changes were made in the educational structure of the city under the pressure of the Italian and Jewish immigrant groups, and to determine "if there were any clues to the viability of the New York City schools of today ascertainable in the developments of sixty years ago." Among the many new educational programs initiated during the period (intended largely to assimilate the immigrant child), Berrol discusses the "Grade C" classes, rudimentary beginnings of bilingual education, intended for the non-English-speaking child.

800. Bleda, Sharon E. Socioeconomic, Demographic, and Cultural Bases of Ethnic Residential Location in Selected Metropolitan Areas of the United States. Ohio State, 1975. 132p. (DA 36:5555-A)
The results of an analysis using indirect standardization provided more support for an ethnic-status explanation of residential dissimilarity than for one emphasizing social class. In particular, mother tongue accounted for a much greater proportion of ethnic residential dissimilarity than did age structure or three common measures of socioeconomic status. The only exceptions to this trend involved comparisons between predominantly English-speaking groups. Consequently, socioeconomic differences and the ability to compete for desired locations in the housing market appeared to be less important in perpetuating ethnic residential separation in major American metropolitan areas than did cultural differentiation and the attendant quest for community. (A)

801. Bodnar, John E. Steelton's Immigrants: Social Relationships in a Pennsylvania Mill Town, 1870-1940. Connecticut, 1975. 246p. (DA 36:4705-A)
This dissertation on Steelton, Pennsylvania, is a case study of the social relationships of immigrants in an industrial community between 1870 and 1940. The mill town was dominated by steel-company officials, professionals, and merchants. Ranking just below this community elite were the skilled workers who together with them shared a white, Anglo-Saxon, Protestant heritage. The mass of Steelton's lower class, however, consisted of unskilled and semiskilled steelworkers who were largely Slavic, Italian, and

black. Interaction between these social strata is the central problem examined in this study. Also the effort of the dominant groups to retain social control is treated. Besides exploring the role of ethnic consciousness, the dissertation furthermore examines the withdrawal of working-class groups into ethnic communities. (A)

802. Boody, Bertha M. A Psychological Study of Immigrant Children at Ellis Island. Johns Hopkins, 1924. 163p.
Published under the same title (Baltimore: Williams & Wilkins, 1926). This dissertation describes the results of a psychological survey of immigrant children, testing the charge of innate inferiority of recent nationalities. The author, a professional psychologist, stationed herself at Ellis Island in the years of heaviest migration, 1922 and 1923, to examine incoming children.

803. Born, David O. Value Orientation and Immigrant Assimilation in a Southern Illinois Community. Southern Illinois, 1970. 148p. (DA 31:5517-A)
Research conducted during the 1950s and 1960s revealed that certain sociocultural differences still existed between the native and immigrant/immigrant-descendant populations of a southern Illinois coal-mining community. The present study focused upon value orientations of the two groups and, using seventh- and eighth-grade students, sought to determine the extent to which the immigrant group could be distinguished from the natives. The Kluckhohn-Strodtbeck Value Orientation Schedule, a semantic differential, and an Inner-Other Social Preference Scale, based upon the work of Riesman, were used as testing instruments. (A)

804. Breton, Raymond J. Ethnic Communities and the Personal Relations of Immigrants. Johns Hopkins, 1961. 240p.

805. Brown, John A. Voluntary Associations Among Ethnic Minority Groups in Detroit, Michigan: A Comparative Study. California (Berkeley), 1975. 238p. (DA 37:606-A)
The purpose of this historical, comparative study was to explore the relationships between the blacks' slow progress in assimilation in the United States and their propensity to form voluntary associations. The blacks' associational behavior with reference to social welfare and mutual aid was compared with the Irish, the Poles, and the Chinese in Detroit, Michigan, in the years 1900-1925. Black associational behavior was also analyzed in the 1960s and early 1970s to determine if the findings of the earlier study would hold constant. These two periods of time were selected due to the great social stress that occurred and affected the blacks during these significant periods of American history. (A)

806. Brown, Laurence G. Immigration: Cultural Conflicts and Social Adjustments. Ohio State, 1932. 338p.
Published under the same title (New York: Longmans, Green, 1933). Deals with cultural conflict in contexts of urban industrial society.

807. Buell, Charles C. The Workers of Worcester: Social Mobility and Ethnicity in a New England City, 1850-1880. New York, 1974. 204p. (DA 35:996-A)
The city of Worcester lends itself to the study of mid-nineteenth century workers. Its dynamic and diversified economy provided employment for the laborers, shoeworkers, and machinists under study. Irish and Yankee workers in these groups had similar patterns of horizontal mobility but differed in vertical mobility. Worcester patterns compare with those found by Stephen Thernstrom in Poverty and Progress, Clyde Griffin in his "Workers Divided" article, and Richard J. Hopkins's "Occupational and Geographical Mobility in Atlanta." Especially noticeable was the eventual lower horizontal mobility of the Irish work force everywhere, and their increase in real-estate ownership. These similarities overshadowed differences in rates of growth and in variations in persistence found in the four cities. (A)

808. Burstein, Alan N. Residential Distribution and Mobility of Irish and German Immigrants in Philadelphia, 1850-1880. Pennsylvania, 1975. 379p. (DA 36:5572-A)
The data base of the Philadelphia Social History Project was employed for the study of the residential patterns assumed by Irish and German immigrants in Philadelphia between 1850 and 1880, the change in those patterns during the 30 years, and the role of residential mobility in bringing about such change. Although the two immigrant groups comprised a substantial proportion of Philadelphia's population, their residential patterns were viewed not in a vacuum, but rather within the context of change in the city's general residential pattern. Thus, the research was directed toward the two substantive areas of ethnic residential settlement and overall urban spatial structure in a major nineteenth-century American city. (A)

809. Campisi, Paul J. A Scale for the Measurement of Acculturation. Chicago, 1947. 242p.
Largely concerned with French Canadians, Portuguese, and Italians. Intended as a review of existing instrumentalities, with recommendations for modifications of existing scales and typologies.

810. Carlin, Marianne B. Education and Occupational Decisions of the Children of Italian and Polish Immigrants to Rome, New York, 1900 to 1950. Cornell, 1978. 104p. (DA 39: 4088-A)
This dissertation studies the means that the first-generation American-born children of Italian and Polish immigrants employed to attain status levels and occupational distributions approaching those of the general population. The educational experiences and the entire careers of a sample of men from Rome, New York, were examined. The results were used to study three separate concerns: (1) the influences on the eventual status levels of the sample; (2) the degree of assimilation of the two ethnic groups in Rome, New York; and (3) the representativeness

of the models of personal occupational development that form the bases of the new career-education programs.

811. Castagnera, James O. Patterns of Ethnic Group Assimilation and Conflict in Carbon County, Pennsylvania. Case Western Reserve, 1979. 337p. (DA 40:838-A)
This study is focused upon the interaction of the several racial and ethnic groups that have inhabited Carbon County in the anthracite-coal region of central eastern Pennsylvania. Beginning with the Lenni Lenape, or Delaware Indians, and their relations with the Anglo-Saxon colonists arriving in Pennsylvania during the eighteenth century, the study examines the sociocultural matrices of five major groups of peoples that have inhabited the county: Lenni Lenape, Anglo-Saxons (English, Scotch-Irish, Welsh), Germans (Pennsylvania Dutch and later German immigrants), Irish, and the so-called "Slavs" (Italians, Polish, Hungarians, etc.), representing the last great wave of immigration.

812. Chudacoff, Howard P. Men in Motion: Residential Mobility in Omaha, Nebraska, 1880-1920. Chicago, 1969. 239p.
Published under the title Mobile Americans: Residential and Social Mobility in Omaha, 1880-1920 (New York: New York University Press, 1972).

813. Clinchy, Everett R. Some Educational Aspects of Protestant, Catholic, Jewish Relationships in American Community Life. Drew, 1934. 207p.

814. Cohen, Jessica L. A Comparison of Norms and Behaviors of Child-Rearing in Jewish and Italian American Mothers. Syracuse, 1977. 276p. (DA 39:1134)
The maintenance of ethnic boundaries can be examined through an investigation of patterns of kinship and socialization in ethnic families. Studied in this research were the norms and behaviors of child-rearing and kinship solidarity of Italian-American and Jewish women in Syracuse, New York. While both groups are noted for their similar values of family solidarity, nurturance of the mother, and similar dates of immigration, differences have been noted in their divergent patterns of achievement and social mobility. Selected randomly from marriage records were 40 middle-class Jewish and 40 middle-class Italian-American women married between the years of 1952 and 1964. A semistructured interview was utilized to gather data along with the Parental Attitude Research Instruction (PARI) and a scale designed to measure attitudes toward familism. (A)

815. Cohen, Steven M. Patterns of Interethnic Marriage and Friendship in the United States. Columbia, 1974. 323p. (DA 35:6813-A)
By analyzing the patterns, determinants, and consequences of interethnic marriage and friendship in two surveys of American and New York adults this dissertation examines three theories of ethnic assimilation in the United States. The Melting Pot model

predicts eventual complete assimilation of American ethnic groups. The assimilation is ostensibly associated with increasing nativity in this country and social-status attainment. The Cultural Pluralist model predicts a leveling off of assimilation rates by the second or third generation. Assimilation is not seen as necessarily correlated with social class. The Triple Melting Pot differs from the Melting Pot in that it predicts ethnic assimilation within the religious boundaries of the three major American religions. (A)

816. Coleman, Marietta R. Educational Goal Development: Sex, Age, Ethnicity, and Relationships Among Student Characteristics, Parental and Teacher Expectations and Student Goals and Attainments. California (Riverside), 1975. 234p. (DA 36:6084-A)
Problems addressed include assumptions and generality of the Status Attainment Processes model, which links student characteristics with educational orientations and attainments through academic performance and referent expectations. Questions include: relative direct effects of student characteristics on referent educational expectations and of characteristics and referents on student perceptions of parental aspirations and student orientations; effects among categories of respondents; validity of student reports on parents; influences between student academic performance and parental expectations; and relationships of early characteristics and respondent expectations with student early educational attainments. (A)

817. Cressey, Paul F. The Succession of Cultural Groups in the City of Chicago. Chicago, 1930. 183p.
Largely a history of Bohemians, Irish, Polish, and Swedish immigrants with emphasis on interethnic relations, and, in a larger frame, immigrant relationships with the greater Chicago community.

818. Danesino, Angelo. Contrasting Personality Patterns of High and Low Achievers Among College Students of Italian and Irish Descent. Case Western Reserve, 1961. 266p.

819. Dann, Martin E. Little Citizens: Working Class and Immigrant Childhood in New York City, 1890-1915. City University of New York, 1978. 486p.
This study is an examination of ideological, experiential, and institutional aspects of immigrant and working-class childhood in urban America--with specific emphasis on New York City--in the period from 1890 to 1915. This includes the ways in which children were perceived, their changing role and function in the labor force and the family, and their social organization, particularly in schools and in settlement houses. A fundamental concern is to understand the ways in which childhood was transformed and how this transformation affected the processes of assimilation and social change. Industrialization and immigration fostered new conceptions of childhood and the family. The status of children was

enhanced, if not idealized; there were major cultural conflicts
between parents and children over issues of assimilation; and the
content and context of experiences that constituted childhood
changed substantially. Childhood was transformed from the private province and responsibility of the family to a symbolic representation of national destiny, protected by the state and its
public agencies. The new "rights" of children--which became an
essential aspect of the reform movement--did not involve choices
on the part of children as much as they allowed professionals
and reformers to intervene in socialization within the family and
in public space, like schools and settlements. This involved an
extension of childhood through restrictions on child labor and
promotion of compulsory education. Children who did not work
were required to attend school and encouraged to participate in
new social organizations where expectations different from those
at home or at work prevailed. As Progressive Reformers grappled with the problem of assimilation and the changes taking
place in society they turned to children as vehicles for this
transformation, conceptualizing them as "little citizens" in whose
hands the destiny of America rested.

820. Darcy, Natalie. The Effect of Bilingualism upon the Measurement of the Intelligence of Children of Preschool Age.
Fordham, 1945. 260p.

821. Davidson, Harry C. The Immigrant Autobiography as a
Document of Cultural Assimilation. Chicago, 1930. 263p.

822. De'ath, Colin E. Patterns of Participation and Exclusion:
A Poor Italian and Black Urban Community and Its Response
to a Federal Poverty Program. Pittsburgh, 1970. 285p.
(DA 31:5528-A)
International development personnel, such as the researcher,
have an interest in how various governments, including those in
so-called developed or postindustrial nations, deal with the problems of poverty, race, and the treatment of minority groups.
In this study the results of a year's fieldwork by a foreign participant observer in a black and Italian poor urban community in
Pittsburgh are presented in such a way that the importance of
these factors can be examined at the local or community level.
(A)

823. De Groot, Dudley E. The Assimilation of Postwar Immigrants in Atlanta, Georgia. Ohio State, 1957. 117p. (DA
18:2243)
The purposes of the study were to investigate factors related to
the degree of assimilation of post-World War II immigrants to
the United States and to compare the assimilation of samples of
immigrants who had settled in Columbus, Ohio, and in Atlanta,
Georgia. A major focus of the study was upon the relationship
between motives for immigration and degree of assimilation.
Three major categories of motivations for migration were developed and employed in the study. Those immigrants who mi-

grated because it was physically impossible for them to maintain themselves in their original environment were placed in a "survival" category. Immigrants whose motivation was primarily a desire to improve their social status or economic position were placed in a "socioeconomic" category. Finally, those immigrants who migrated because of problems of ideological or political compatibility in their native lands were placed in a "political" category. (A)

824. Dell, Robert M. The Representation of the Immigrant on the New York Stage--1881 to 1910. New York, 1960. 300p. (DA 21:1287)
The purpose of this study was to investigate possible relationships between the arrival in America of three immigrant groups and the emergence of each group in American plays professionally produced in New York City between 1881 and 1910. The principal aim was to determine how German, Irish, and Italian immigrants were represented by playwrights whose works were produced during this same period and to indicate whether such characterizations coincided with the social and economic status of those immigrants as reported by standard authorities. (A)

825. Dempsey, Arthur D. Culture and the Conservation of Time: A Comparison of Selected Ethnic Groups in Arizona. University of Arizona, 1971. 77p. (DA 32:5660-A)
The purpose of this study was an attempt to determine if children of non-Western cultures perceive time in a similar manner as children of Western culture and whether or not these children conform to the stages postulated by Piaget. The study also attempted to determine if the ages of the achievement of these stages approximated the ages of the transitions as postulated by Piaget. The samples were drawn from seven cultures, Anglo and Mexican American, and Hopi, Pima, Papago, Apache, and Navajo Indians. Fifteen children from each of the ages seven, nine, and 11 were tested from each group for a total of 315 subjects.

826. Dolan, Jay P. Urban Catholicism: New York City, 1815-1865. Chicago, 1971. 221p.
Published under the title The Immigrant Church: New York's Irish and German Catholics, 1815-1865 (Baltimore: Johns Hopkins University Press, 1975). Concerned with the impact of the mass migration of Irish and German Catholics on the Catholic Church, its hierarchy, and its policies in New York City before the Civil War.

827. Drachsler, Julius. Intermarriage in New York City: A Statistical Study of the Amalgamation of European Peoples. Columbia, 1921. 204p.
Published under the same title (New York: The Author, 1921). A statistical analysis of intermarriage of first- and second-generation immigrants. Fusion of nationality groups is most rapid where barriers of religion and color are not marked. The lower

the ratio of intermarriage in the first generation, the greater the
ratio in the second, and therefore, the greater the relative increase. The ratio of intermarriage for women is slightly lower
than for men. The largest proportion of intermarriage takes
place among persons of the middle culture plane rather than on
the high or low cultural level.

828.   Edson, C. H. Immigrant Perspectives on Work and School-
       ing: Eastern European Jews and Southern Italians, 1880-
       1920. Stanford, 1979. 287p. (DA 40:3826-A)
Traditional Eastern European Jewish and southern Italian attitudes
toward work and schooling were varied and complex, stemming
from strongly held beliefs, social experiences, and cultural traditions. Through a reanalysis of sources published in English, this
study explores the ways in which ethnicity related to the formulation of attitudes toward work and schooling. Juxtaposed with
educators' perceptions in the final chapter, this analysis of traditional Eastern European Jewish and southern Italian attitudes illuminates the class- and culture-bound notions educators held
about the relationships between work and schooling. (A)

829.   Efron, David. Gesture and Environment: A Tentative Study
       of Some of the Spatio-Temporal and "Linguistic" Aspects of
       the Gestural Behavior of Eastern Jews and Southern Italians
       in New York City. Columbia, 1942. 184p.
Published under the same title (New York: King's Crown, 1942);
and in Italian translation as Gesto, razza, e cultura (Milan:
Bompiani, 1974).

830.   Ernst, Robert. Immigrant Life in New York City, 1825-
       1863. Columbia, 1949. 331p.
Published under the same title (New York: King's Crown, 1949).
A detailed description of the German- and Irish-immigrant com-
munities.

831.   Esslinger, Dean R. The Urbanization of South Bend's Immi-
       grants, 1850-1880. Notre Dame, 1972. 227p. (DA 32:
       6337-A)
The social and economic impact that immigration, urbanization,
and industrialization made on American life in the nineteenth century has been studied in a variety of ways. Historians, utilizing
methods drawn from the other social sciences, have examined the
effects these forces had on the masses of population living in
major American cities, particularly those along the eastern seaboard. Few studies, however, have attempted to analyze the
interaction between immigration and urban growth that took place
in the smaller industrial cities of the Middle West. This dissertation attempts to fill that gap by examining the immigrant
population of South Bend, Indiana, during the years between 1850
and 1880. (A)

832.   Fandetti, Donald V. Sources of Assistance in a White, Work-
       ing Class, Ethnic Neighborhood. Columbia, 1974. 180p.

(DA 35:6809-A)
This study examines attitudes toward sources of assistance among residents in a working-class, ethnic neighborhood. An attempt is made to identify perceived sources of assistance in four areas of family need: child care, care of the aged, financial assistance, and personal problems. The study aims at determining the degree to which working-class ethnics are oriented to informal and traditional sources of assistance in the local community. The study is based on a random sample of 100 neighborhood residents in east Baltimore. The sample includes 50 Polish-Americans and 50 Italian-Americans between the ages of 21 and 50. (A)

833. Farrar, Ronald D. The Non-Visa Foreign Student at Los Angeles City College: A Study of the Relation of Various Administrative and Academic Factors to the Immigrant Student. California (Los Angeles), 1968. 241p. (DA 30:487-A)
The dissertation recommends that research be undertaken to determine the number and distribution of the immigrant students in the junior colleges and to investigate the various factors affecting these students; that this program of research incorporate dissemination of the resultant findings to the junior colleges; that current junior-college entrance, probation, disqualification, and similar procedures be examined critically and that admissions procedures be redesigned to allow for more effective study of such segments of the student population; that certain specific categories both within the foreign-student group and outside of it be investigated in depth; and that counseling services, curriculum offerings, and instructional approaches be augmented and improved.

834. Farrell, John J. The Immigrant and the School in New York City: A Program for Citizenship. Stanford, 1967. 196p. (DA 28:4458-A)
Published under the same title (New York: Arno, 1980). New York City, during the years 1895-1915 provides the focal point for the investigation into the nature of immigrant education and its impact upon American education. The meaning of the term "Americanization" was debated heavily during the years 1895-1915. To one group the term meant the acquisition of essential elements of a "true" American, i.e., intense loyalty to the United States and a rapid assimilation of the foreign-born into the American social fabric. The other group felt Americanization meant a gradual transition of the immigrant into the American value system with a conscious effort made to secure the best features of the old traditions while instilling the new. In 1910 the American public school began to devise new curricula to establish a more realistic and progressive program for a gradual assimilation into the democratic value system. The search for the meaning of Americanization caused the schools to re-examine its programs and to discover the most meaningful approach to educate without alienating the foreign-born student. Two main divisions of citizenship education constituted the general school curriculum.

Dry legalism, taught through naturalization, constituted the first; the other stressed democratic values and the responsibilities of citizenship. From a narrowly conceived course in 1900 citizenship education became a total conception of public education by 1915. The approach of World War I and the education of the immigrant provided two major impulses for the development of citizenship-education programs. The desire for national unity and the need for self-understanding caused fundamental changes in the school program.

835. Feldon, Victoria B. Symbols of Ethnicity in Three Los Angeles Churches: A Comparative Study. California (Riverside), 1976. 289p.
The reactions of immigrants and ethnics to acculturation are often symbolically expressed. The objective was to use qualitative material systematically to document and examine the experience and emotions of these people. The data are artifacts and activities from three Los Angeles churches. A primary source is interviews on tape with volunteers from a Lithuanian Roman Catholic church, a conservative synagogue of Eastern European Jewish origin, and a Lutheran parish of German-Scandinavian descent. The author photographed the objects under discussion as corroborative evidence, attended events, analyzed newsletters, visited homes and churches, and examined the historical and cultural background of each church. The study juxtaposes verbatim statements with the artifacts and activities in church, homes, and community.

836. Finestone, Harold. A Comparative Study of Reformation and Recidivism Among Italian and Polish Adult Male Criminal Offenders. Chicago, 1964. 193p.

837. Fishman, Joshua A. Negative Stereotypes Concerning Americans Among American-Born Children Receiving Various Types of Minority-Group Education. Columbia (Teachers College), 1953. 123p. (DA 13:895)
Published under the same title (Genetic Psychological Monographs [Vol. 51:107-182], 1955). This study examines the readiness with which American-born Jewish children accept negative stereotypes concerning the majority American group and culture in the midst of which they live. In addition, the content of the negative stereotypes most widely accepted by the children of this minority group is examined. The Jewish children studied were pupils of various types of Jewish schools that differed widely in ideological and structural respects. The central issue investigated by this study was whether the children receiving such widely different indoctrinations for minority-group membership would also differ significantly either in their degree of acceptance of negative stereotypes concerning the majority of Americans or in the content pattern of their most frequently accepted negative stereotypes. (A)

838. Ford, Margaret L. The Development of an Instrument for Assessing Levels of Ethnicity in Public School Teachers.

Houston, 1979. 110p. (DA 40:1426-A)
The purpose of this study was to test James Banks's hypothesis that teachers distribute themselves differently among the stages of ethnicity. This study was pursued because of its perceived significance and potential contributions to the field of education. In an effort to test the major hypothesis, this study constituted developing, validating and establishing the reliability of an instrument. After the instrument was developed the study tested the following hypotheses: (1) secondary teachers distribute themselves differently among the stages of ethnicity; (2) there is a significant relationship between the gender of the secondary teacher and the level of ethnicity; (3) there is a positive relationship between years of teaching experience and the secondary teacher's level of ethnicity; (4) there is a significant relationship between the region of the country where the secondary teacher has lived longest and the level of ethnicity; (5) there is a positive relationship between the age of the secondary teacher and the level of ethnicity; and (6) there is a significant relationship between the ethnic group of the secondary teacher and the level of ethnicity. (A)

839. Ford, Raymond W. Germans and Other Foreign Stock: Their Part in the Evolution of Reading, Pennsylvania. Pennsylvania, 1963. 224p. (DA 24:1738)
This study has sought to trace the development of a town largely in terms of its human ingredients. Reading was chosen because it was remarkably free of elements that would tend to distort the picture. Essentially homogeneous in population, it has been unvisited by natural or human-caused disaster, economic boom and bust cycles, or population upheavals. In addition, and more positively, the city was born in, and for much of its life has been the largest community in, what is probably the largest enclave in the United States--the German land of southeast Pennsylvania. (A)

840. Forrester, James R. Correlates of Ethnic Identification and the Potential for Political Violence. West Virginia, 1979. 260p. (DA 40:1664-A)
Until recently the prevailing explanation of ethnic political violence has been relative deprivation (Gurr, 1970). However, Edward N. Muller, in a comparative test of two models at the microlevel of analysis, found that his data did not support the relative-deprivation explanation of political violence. Instead, Muller found evidence in testing attitudes of blacks and whites in Waterloo, Iowa, for the hypotheses of his diffuse-support explanation (Muller, 1972). Diffuse support is based on the notion that legitimacy sentiments (trust in political authorities) acts as the pivotal factor in determining the potential for political violence among individuals. It is the purpose of this dissertation to determine whether Muller's diffuse-support explanation of the potential for political violence can be utilized outside of his conspicuously violent context of black-white relations. The major research question is to what extent are (nonblack) ethnic respondents who are self-identified with their ethnic groups more

prone to sentiments favoring political violence than respondents not so identified? (A)

841. Fowler, Mary E. Literature for International Understanding: A Study of the Presentation of Foreign Peoples and Cultures in Secondary School Literature Anthologies. New York, 1954. 521p. (DA 14:1708)

842. Franzblau, Rose N. Race Differences in Mental and Physical Traits: Studied in Different Environments. Columbia, 1935. 44p.
Published under the same title (New York: Teachers College Press, Columbia University, 1935). Studies Italian children in Italy, Danish children in Denmark, and Italian-American and Danish-American children in the United States.

843. Gabriel, Richard A. Ethnic Attitudes and Political Behavior in City and Suburb: The Irish and Italians of Rhode Island. Massachusetts, 1969. 317p. (DA 30:2580-A)
Published under the same title (New York: Arno, 1980). This study concerns itself with an examination of ethnic attitudes and political behavior on the part of Irish and Italian ethnic group respondents in a selected city and suburb of Rhode Island. The purpose of this examination is twofold; first, to attempt to explicate more thoroughly the findings and propositions of the two most widely accepted theories of ethnic political behavior; and second, to relate the findings of this study concerning the role of ethnic attitudes in ethnic political behavior to the actual governing of a polity in which such attitudes and behavior are found to exist. (A)

844. Galford, Justin B. The Foreign Born and Urban Growth in the Great Lakes, 1850-1950: A Study of Chicago, Cleveland, Detroit, and Milwaukee. New York, 1957. 388p. (DA 18:214)
Studies Germans in Milwaukee, Canadians in Detroit, Poles in Chicago, and Poles and Slovaks in Cleveland. Settlement and growth of immigrant communities in these cities is explained by availability of work, patterns of industrial recruitment, and a complex set of social and cultural factors. The principal object of this study has been to bring together and analyze the population statistics for the foreign-born, and for separate nationality elements, in the Great Lakes cities of Chicago, Cleveland, Detroit, and Milwaukee. The discussion is based primarily upon census reports from 1850 through 1950. Such conclusions as emerge may point the way to further generalizations concerning immigrant distribution to the nation's larger cities, and perhaps to the historical importance of immigrant dispersal in general.

845. Garrido, Armando R. The Relationship Between Disruptive Behavior and Socio-Economic Status, Ethnicity, and Sex of the Student; The Size, Location, and Ethnicity of the School, in Selected Tri-Ethnic Junior High Schools. Florida, 1978.

166p. (DA 40:5818-A)
The purpose of this study was to ascertain whether there existed significant relationships between disruptive behavior and the socioeconomic status, ethnicity, and sex of the student; and the location and size of the school. A secondary purpose was to determine whether there was a relationship between the ethnicity of the school principal and the kinds of students who exhibited disruptive behavior. The sample consisted of 1,080 students drawn from 12 junior high schools in Dade County with a total population of 14,281 students. (A)

846. Gartner, Carol B. A New Mirror for America: The Fiction of the Immigrant of the Ghetto, 1890-1930. New York, 1970. 238p. (DA 31:1797-A)
While many immigrants expressed their feelings about America in essays and autobiographies, few had either the desire or the ability to write fiction. When they did attempt it their motivation was not exclusively artistic. They combined powerful desires to speak out for the immigrant as effectively as possible with hopes both of contributing to American literature and of succeeding as writers, as fellow immigrants were succeeding in other fields. The most important of the immigrant writers who adopted English as their language were those from city ghettos. Most significant among their writings were novels and stories that transmuted into fiction their own experiences in America. This group of writers included Italians, a few Irish and English (for whom language was no problem), and many Russian and Polish Jews. (A)

847. Garvey, William P. The Ethnic Factor in Erie Politics, 1900-1970. Pittsburgh, 1973. 250p. (DA 34:2512)
The ethnic factor in the twentieth century of Erie politics has been--and continues to be--a significant one. As the century began Erie's political fortunes were largely under the control of a native Yankee-German, upper-middle-class, Protestant and business-oriented group. Opposition to them came from Catholic Polish and Italian immigrant workers who between 1900 and 1930 changed the political balance of power in the city. Under stimulus of such issues as the popular election of water commissioners, a Molders strike, and a vice crusade, the "native" and "new" elements of the city battled for control of City Hall. (A)

848. Gersman, Elinor M. Education in St. Louis, 1880-1900: A Case Study of Schools in Society. Washington University, 1969. 399p. (DA 30:5260-A)
The purpose of the paper is to study aspects of education in St. Louis between 1880 and 1900 and to investigate the social measures that influenced the schools. Historical research media were used to investigate four main areas: (1) the city of St. Louis and its schools; (2) the organization and administration of its schools; (3) schooling in St. Louis, including programs of study and teachers; and (4) the population using the schools with special emphasis on Negroes and immigrants. (A)

849. Glad, Donald D. Attitudes and Experiences of American-Jewish and American-Irish Male Youths As Related to Differences in Inebriety Rates. Stanford, 1945. 260p.

850. Glasco, Laurence A. Ethnicity and Social Structure: Irish, Germans, and Native-Born of Buffalo, New York, 1850-1860. State University of New York (Buffalo), 1973. 381p. Published under the same title (New York: Arno, 1980). This study of the ethnic structure of Buffalo, New York, is based primarily on an analysis of the 71,850 residents listed in the manuscript schedules of the 1855 New York State census. It focuses on the Irish, Germans, and native-born whites--who together comprised four-fifths of the city's population; compares their demographic, economic, and family structures; and concludes that the dynamics underlying those structures pointed less in the direction of social pathology and conflict than in the direction of accommodation and stability. Demographic and family patterns probably aided ethnic adjustment and accommodation. Foreign-born family heads were not younger than their native-born counterparts, nor did they have a preponderance of either men or women. Moreover, they were newcomers to the city in a limited sense. Native-born residents were recent arrivals also and had been present on the average only five years longer than the immigrants. Finally, most residents lived in a family situation. Large boarding houses were rare and the city's boarders generally lived with a family. The family structure itself showed signs of stability. The nuclear family predominated, and "broken" or female-headed families were exceptional. Foreign-born immigrants had a much higher birth rate than the native-born, but no group was overly burdened with children. Particularly for the immigrants, domestic service for their adolescent daughters functioned both to regulate their family size and also to introduce a sizable part of their population to native-born households, and presumably, to native-born values and language.

851. Golden, Loretta. The Treatment of Minority Groups in Primary Social Studies in Textbooks. Stanford, 1964. 352p. (DA 25:3912)
The main procedure used in analyzing the books was qualitative content analysis. The qualitative approach was selected because of the infrequent occurrence of minority-group persons in the books and the significance attached to the nonoccurrence of certain content features. The treatment of the following minority groups was studied: American Indians, Orientals, European immigrants, Jews. (A)

852. Good, Patricia K. Ethnicity in America: A Unit in a Senior High School American History Course. Carnegie-Mellon, 1975. 445p. (DA 36:4389-A)
Focuses on the concepts of the functions, formation, and adaptation of ethnic groups. Students utilize these concepts to analyze the experiences of seven ethnic groups in American history. These ethnic groups include the Puerto Ricans, Cherokee Indians,

Irish, blacks, Scotch-Irish, Italians, and Jews. Students learn a four-step method of inquiry to investigate the experiences of each ethnic group. (A)

853. Grabowski, John J. A Social Settlement in a Neighborhood in Transition: Hiram House, Cleveland, Ohio, 1896-1926. Case Western Reserve, 1977. 283p.

854. Graves, Nancy B. City, Country and Child Rearing: A Triculture Study of Mother-Child Relationships in Varying Environments. Colorado, 1971. 303p.

855. Gregg, Catherine E. Ethnic Membership in Community Organizations of an Ohio Steel Town: A Study of the Rate of Social Assimilation. Columbia, 1954. 339p. (DA 14:1475)
The secondary, or community-participation, phase of the process of social assimilation of external immigrants into American communities was studied in a laboratory community that had experienced continuous waves of foreign immigration for many years. Sixty organizations or bodies were selected as representative of the ongoing community life and the extent of participation in them by members of various ethnic groups found. The rates of social assimilation, using such participation as a criterion, proved the same for all ethnic groups regardless of country of origin, a function of the American culture rather than of the extent of difference between the original and the American culture. (A)

856. Guignard, Michael. Ethnic Survival in a New England Mill Town. The Franco-Americans of Biddeford, Maine. Syracuse, 1977. 281p.

857. Haas, Joyce H. Ethnic Polarization and School Library Materials: A Content Analysis of 1,939 Fiction Books from 30 New Jersey School Libraries. Rutgers, 1971. 211p. (DA 32:3339-A)
The investigation sought answers to two questions: (1) Do the fiction books provided by school libraries present an overall picture that supports our polarized ("ethnic majority" and "ethnic minority") society, or do they present an overall picture which might prepare children for changes in that society? and (2) Does the ethnic view of society presented in school-library fiction collections vary significantly in schools of varying ethnic enrollment?

858. Haebler, Peter. Habitants in Holyoke: The Development of the French Canadian Community in a Massachusetts City, 1865-1910. New Hampshire, 1976. 306p.

859. Handlin, Oscar. Boston's Immigrants, 1790-1865: A Study in Acculturation. Harvard, 1940. 230p.
Published under the same title (Cambridge, Massachusetts: Harvard University Press, 1941; rev. ed., New York: Atheneum, 1970; rev. ed., Cambridge, Massachusetts: Harvard University

Press, 1980). A classic study of Irish immigrants in Boston, their evolving history and fortunes.

860. Hannon, Joan U. The Immigrant Worker in the Promised Land: Human Capital and Ethnic Discrimination in the Michigan Labor Market, 1888-1890. Wisconsin (Madison), 1978. 417p. (DA 38:7474)
A large historical literature maintains that ethnic discrimination played a role in determining the initial position of immigrants in late-nineteenth-century America and in blocking their efforts to scale the economic ladder. This view has been challenged by a revisionist literature that not only contends that skill differentials can explain the immigrants' initial handicap but also holds that the foreign-born had ample opportunity to learn new skills and thereby catch up quickly with their native-born counterparts. The purpose of the thesis is to test these competing hypotheses. (A)

861. Hannon, Thomas J. The Process of Ethnic Assimilation in Selected Rural Christian Congregations, 1800-1976: A Western Pennsylvania Case Study. Pittsburgh, 1977. 394p. (DA 38:7557-A)
The dissertation is confined to an examination of ethnic groups who represented the earliest migrations to the United States. Therefore, the focus is upon the Scottish, Scots-Irish, English, Welsh, Germans, and Irish who settled at the turn of the nineteenth century in a four-county area lying midway between Pittsburgh and Lake Erie. The investigation is largely confined to the rural landscape and to the process of assimilation in selected Christian congregations organized during the nineteenth century by representatives of the aggregations identified above. (A)

862. Harlow, Justin E. An Analysis of Psychological and Sociological Factors in Crime in the Foreign Born. Florida, 1952. 112p. (DA 14:866)
Cross-comparisons were made of foreign-born, native-born of native parents, and native-born of foreign parents in terms of proportional commitments of 12,423 white males taken serially to investigate comparative rates of commitment, types of crime committed, differences in type and amount of crime committed by various ethnic groups, and resemblance of natives of foreign parents to both foreign and natives of native parents. (A)

863. Harper, Richard C. The Course of the Melting Pot Idea to 1910. Columbia (Teachers College), 1967. 420p. (DA 28: 3093-A)
Historical attention paid to the melting-pot idea has never been systematic. Usual references to it mention Crèvecoeur and Zangwill and indicate that America seemed to be a melting pot of nationalities. The purpose of this study was to fill the historical gap by defining the melting-pot idea and identifying the major elements of American thought that fostered the idea and the thinking about the melting pot that modified and clarified its

meaning. Since no treatment of this subject is likely to be definitive, sources become important. Secondary literature dealing with immigration, nationalism, nationality, race, assimilation, and education was an important reliance, and from it the most noteworthy controversies or events bearing upon the issues relevant to American nationality were identified. In addition, outstanding advocates or spokesmen for the melting-pot viewpoint, as well as their major opponents, produced books and pamphlets that were valuable, full developments of basic lines of argument. Other sources included debates in the Congressional Record, Congressional reports, and National Education Association discussions in the Proceedings from 1865-1900.

864. Hartwell, Elizabeth A. Cultural Assimilation, Social Mobility, and Persistence of Cognitive Style. Brandeis, 1968. 207p. (DA 29:333-A)
By focusing mainly on the Irish and using the Italians as a comparison group the author differentiated seven orientations that showed up frequently among the Irish but rarely among the Italians; then, by dividing the Irish into middle and working class groups, she checked for the presence or absence of the orientation in each of the two classes. In every case the orientation was present as strongly among the middle-class subjects as among the working-class ones, showing the persistence of each orientation and thus of the Irish cognitive style in general, whether there had been upward mobility or not. (A)

865. Heinrich, Desdemona L. Dietary Habits of Elementary School Children: An Evaluation of the Quantitative and Qualitative Adequacy of the Daily Food Intake of 463 Elementary School Children of American, Jewish, and Italian Parents Living in Urban and Suburban New York City. New York, 1932. 144p.

866. Helling, Rudolf A. A Comparison of the Acculturation of Immigrants in Toronto, Ontario, and Detroit, Michigan. Wayne State, 1962. 282p. (DA 28:4730-A)
The research investigates the acculturation of German immigrants into two cultural systems, the U. S. American and the Canadian. By using the same ethnic minority under the influence of two environments, it attempts to measure the influences of the host cultures on the immigrant. The methodology of the study is an experimental design using the effect-to-cause ex post facto approach. The control sample consists of 50 German residents of Wilhelmshaven, Germany. The experimental groups are German immigrant residents in Toronto and Detroit. (A)

867. Henderson, Thomas M. Tammany Hall and the New Immigrants, 1910-1921. Virginia, 1973. 302p. (DA 34:5869-A)
Published under the same title (New York: Arno, 1976). In this quantitative analysis of Tammany Hall politics, 1910-1921, Henderson discusses the challenge of new Italian and Jewish immigrants to Irish political power in New York City. This chal-

lenge forced New York Irish politicians to be more concerned
with social-welfare politics, culminating in the figure of Al Smith,
who pioneered the New Deal as Governor of New York State in
the 1920s. In general, the new social consciousness of Tammany
was directed at the Jewish vote, ignoring the Italian. This Irish
policy of political appeasement captured the Jewish vote for the
Democratic machine but antagonized the Italians into a volatile
political ethnicity, which led to LaGuardia's mayoralty in the
1930s. The rise of Italian political power meant the decline of
Irish influence in Tammany.

868. Hoffman, Moses N. H. The Measurement of Bilingual Background. Columbia (Teachers College), 1934. 75p.
Published under the same title (Teachers College Press, Columbia University, 1934). Deals with the American-born children of Italian and Jewish immigrants.

869. Holland, John B. Attitudes Toward Minority Groups in Relation to Rural Social Structure. Michigan State, 1950. 339p. (DA 11:192)
An inquiry was made into the attitudes prevalent in the rural Midwest toward three minority groups (Jews, Negroes, and Mexicans) and the relationship of these attitudes to rural social structure. A representative sample of 429 adult residents of a county selected as typical of certain midwestern Corn Belt areas, was obtained. Each respondent was interviewed by means of a formal schedule, and information was secured regarding organizational activities, general social characteristics, and attitudes (as measured by a series of attitude questions). (A)

870. Holte, James C. The Newcomer in America: A Study of Italian and Puerto Rican American Personal Narratives. Cincinnati, 1978. 192p. (DA 39:5513-A)
This study examines the autobiographies of nine Italian-Americans and three Puerto Rican-Americans within the context of the American autobiographical tradition defined by such works as Franklin's Autobiography and Adams's Education. The autobiography has been a neglected genre in American literature, and the autobiographies of ethnic Americans have been even more neglected. Those critics who have examined American autobiographies note that American literature, from its very beginnings, has always been autobiographical to a large degree and that Franklin and Adams provide models for other American autobiographers: Franklin's Autobiography is the perfect promotional personal narrative, and Adams's Education is the quintessential critical narrative. Both of these works, growing out of the Puritan habit of introspection and self-analysis, establish ways of ordering personal experience in America. (A)

871. Hopkins, Thomas W. Educational Standardization and the "Foreign Child." New York, 1933. 276p.
Primarily concerned with Polish children, but with many references to Italian and Slavic children.

872. Hornberger, Mark A. The Spatial Distribution of Ethnic
 Groups in Selected Counties in Pennsylvania 1800-1880: A
 Geographic Interpretation. Pennsylvania State, 1974. 309p.
 (DA 34:3603-A)

873. Hosay, Philip M. The Challenge of Urban Poverty: Charity
 Reformers in New York City, 1835-1890. Michigan, 1969.
 280p. (DA 31:2285-A)
 Published under the same title (New York: Arno, 1980). By the
 1830s the growth of New York's poor population already challenged the sympathies of contemporary observers and their belief in a democratic society where all had equal opportunity. A
 group of social reformers, old-stock Americans with roots in
 New England, attempted to meet this challenge through charity
 work. Their ideological goal was to make the urban poor selfreliant members of a cohesive community, united by a common
 commitment to social values. The manner in which they sought
 to achieve this goal and their willingness to strive for it depended on their diagnosis of the causes of poverty. These
 causes fell into three broad categories: moral, environmental,
 and hereditarian. During the Civil War charity workers gradually turned against the poor. Although still intent on making New
 York into a cohesive community, reformers began to believe that
 dependent persons suffered from hereditary diseases that made
 them incapable of becoming an integral and productive part of
 this community. This hostile attitude was rooted in the antiIrish nativism of charity workers. As the Irish made rapid social advances and assumed political control of the city, reformers, filled with resentment, stereotyped them as a people incapable of self-support. They considered them a permanent class
 of hereditary paupers. Their pessimistic view of the Irish
 widened to include all of the poor when the economic depression
 of 1873 and a large influx of poor immigrants created a tremendous burden of poverty that strained to their utmost limits the
 capabilities of private charity. By the end of the 1880s the
 charity movement declined in importance as a vehicle for molding New York into a cohesive community. Another economic
 depression and more impoverished immigrants sustained a hereditarian diagnosis of poverty.

874. Houtman, Loren H. Response of Detroit Public Schools to
 Immigrant Groups. Michigan State, 1965. 229p. (DA 26:
 4421)
 Detroit, founded in 1701 by Antoine de la Mothe Cadillac, has
 been settled by peoples from nearly every region of the world.
 As this myriad of nationalities arrived they founded schools and
 vastly affected the schools in existence. This thesis suggests
 that they had a huge and lasting influence on the public schools
 of the city.

875. Irvine, William B. A Study of Relative Participation of the
 Children of Foreign-Born, Native, and Mixed Parentage in
 Eight Recreational and Religious Agencies in Sharon, Pennsylvania. Pittsburgh, 1938. 203p.

876. Javetz, Shai. The Ethnic Factor in Fall River, Massachusetts. Boston, 1972. 197p. (DA 33:7039)
The main purpose of this study was to examine the degree of inclusion of ethnic groups in a community and to study their role within this social structure. The theoretical framework was based on the paradigm of social change developed by Talcott Parsons, which suggests four major components of social change processes: (1) differentiation was explored along ethnic lines; consideration was also given to religion, class, and spatial distribution; (2) adaptive upgrading of ethnic groups was examined mainly by comparing their socioeconomic positions in the class structure; this analysis was made controlling for the number of generations in the United States; (3) value generalization was assessed by using the Work Ethic, a value pattern generally accepted as dominant in American society; and (4) inclusion in the societal community, as seen by ethnic groups, was inferred from the groups' changing position along the above components, as well as by their manifested degree of alienation. (A)

877. Jebsen, Harry A. A. Blue Island, Illinois: The History of a Working Class Suburb. Cincinnati, 1971. 335p. (DA 32:3208-A)
This study shows that suburbs are not static institutions, but rather, that they, like other definable urban subareas, are constantly evolving entities. It also shows that the term "suburbia" is a stereotype and that the American suburban experience has been very complex. Blue Island, as one example of the complexity, was not created as a residential site for Chicago's middle class; it had a long history of its own prior to becoming a suburb. As a result Blue Island tended to be quite parochial, and leaders frequently failed to take cognizance of the changing metropolitan patterns. The dissertation also shows that some immigrants moved into the suburbs soon after their arrival in America. Responding to job opportunities and a low unemployment rate in this community, Poles, Slovaks, and Italians came to Blue Island soon after 1900. These people found that Blue Island offered superior living conditions compared with Chicago. (A)

878. Jirak, Ivan Lloyd. "The Farmer" and "Immigration": Two Curriculum Units for Slow Learners. Carnegie-Mellon, 1970. 208p. (DA 32:860-A)
In cooperation with the Pittsburgh Public Schools, the Slow Learner Project of Carnegie-Mellon University's Social Studies Curriculum Center constructed a course in American history for junior high school. Project personnel examined all available material for slow learners and then wrote and tested an initial version of a new course. The author's contribution to the slow-learner junior high school course in American history includes the text, workbook, audiovisual kit, test, and teacher's manual for Chapter Ten, "The Farmer," and Chapter Twelve, "Immigration." Both of these chapters are discussed in this dissertation and appear in their original form as "Appendix A" and "Appendix

B." Chapter Three of this dissertation describes the evaluation and revision of these chapters, which became part of the version of the course published in April 1970. (A)

879. Johnston, William M. On the Outside Looking In: Irish, Italian, and Black Ethnic Politics in an American City. Yale, 1977. 330p. (DA 39:1806-A)
There is a need for a new framework for analysis of ethnic politics, one that studies ethnicity in political terms but does not overemphasize such outcomes as ethnic voting. We need, instead, to understand the more fundamental processes that make ethnicity politically significant. This inquiry into Irish, Italian, and black ethnic politics in New Haven, Connecticut, is a first step toward that goal. The inquiry is guided by two sets of questions: (1): Substantive. What is ethnicity and how does it become politically significant? What processes are involved in the development and change of ethnic politics? How much change within, and variation among, ethnic political experiences will we find in a common political system? (2): Methodological. How can we analyze political change in subnational units, over time and in varying situations, in political terms? (A)

880. Jordan, Riverda H. Nationality and School Progress: A Study in Americanization. Minnesota, 1921. 105p.

881. Keller, Kenneth W. Diversity and Democracy: Ethnic Politics in Southeastern Pennsylvania, 1788-1799. Yale, 1971. 282p. (DA 32:6868-A)
This dissertation is a study of how politicians used ethnic and religious antagonisms in southeastern Pennsylvania to win elections in early national times. Elections in Philadelphia City and County and Lancaster, York, Berks, and Northampton counties are examined in detail. The author used English- and German-language newspapers from both the city and backcountry. Election-district returns were collected and examined for the contests of 1796 and 1799. (A)

882. Kenneson, Susan R. Through the Looking-Glass: A History of Anglo-American Attitudes Towards the Spanish-Americans and Indians of New Mexico. Yale, 1978. 334p. (DA 39: 2484)
An interdisciplinary study of the personal level of cross-cultural contact, this dissertation is based on a wide variety of Anglo sources (including official reports, journals, letters, autobiographies, ethnographic studies, travel literature, and fiction) and deals in detail with the years from 1807 to 1865, as well as summarizes developments from 1865 to 1940. The emphasis is on Anglo attitudes toward the peoples of New Mexico and on how these attitudes were related to Anglo culture and to the broad outlines of the contact situation. Thus, it is a study both of American social history and of the dynamics of cross-cultural contact. (A)

883. Kerstan, Reinhold J. Historical Factors in the Formation
of the Ethnically Oriented North American Baptist General
Conference. Northwestern, 1971. 296p. (DA 32:3412-A)
This dissertation is a critical study of the origin of the North
American Baptist General Conference. It begins with an analysis
of the historical background of German migrations during the
eighteenth and nineteenth centuries in general, and then more
specifically lists several motives for the emigrations of Germans
to America and the Eastern European countries. (A)

884. Kessner, Thomas. The Golden Door: Immigrant Mobility
in New York City, 1880-1915. Columbia, 1975. 345p.
(DA 36:3071-A)
Published under the title The Golden Door: Italian and Jewish
Immigrant Mobility in New York City, 1880-1915 (New York:
Oxford University Press, 1977). Between 1880 and 1915 New
York attracted a very large number of immigrants. Many of
these newcomers came from countries in Europe that until this
time had not been major sources of American immigration.
These "New Immigrants" stood out from most of the others who
preceded them because of their non-Protestant religion and their
strange, often peasant-based folkways. Yet, despite their backgrounds in the small towns and peasant villages of Europe, these
newcomers were drawn to America's metropolitan centers, especially the hustling city of New York. Impoverished immigrants
from south Italy and East Europe formed the majority of this
immigration. These groups, which settled New York's downtown
neighborhoods, caused much concern among nativists who feared
that they were too poorly prepared for life in America, and particularly in the great cities. Precisely for these reasons the
New Immigrant Italians and Jews provide a good focus on the issue of social mobility in America. (A)

885. Kirk, Gordon W. The Promise of American Life: Social
Mobility in a Nineteenth Century Immigrant Community.
Holland, Michigan, 1847-1894. Michigan State, 1970. 299p.
(DA 31:5968-A)
The purpose of this study was to examine social and geographic
mobility from 1847 to 1894 in a small Michigan community composed of the towns of Holland, Zeeland, and Holland Township.
Differing from the previous communities studied, Trempealeau
County, Newburyport, and Philadelphia, Holland typified a fourth
type, an ethnically homogeneous community experiencing rapid
economic and population growth. The small community at this
time still remained the residence of the vast majority of Americans as well as being an important social institution; if mobility
and attitudes toward it are to be examined, the small town must
be studied extensively. (A)

886. Kirkpatrick, Clifford. Intelligence and Immigration, with
Special Reference to Certain New England Groups. Pennsylvania, 1925. 127p.
Published under the same title (Baltimore: Williams & Wilkens,
1926). Attention to Finns, Italians, and French Canadians.

Multi-Group Studies

887. Knights, Peter R. The Plain People of Boston, 1830-1860: A Demographic and Social Study. Wisconsin, 1970. 222p. (DA 31:710-A)
Published under the title The Plain People of Boston, 1830-1860: A Study in City Growth (New York: Oxford University Press, 1973). To investigate the process of urbanization (the concentration of people in cities) as related to a single nineteenth-century city, this study focused on Boston, Massachusetts, 1830-1860. A sample of 1,540 heads of household, drawn equally and randomly from the federal censuses of 1830, 1840, 1850, and 1860, was traced through city directories, assessment records, and vital-statistics records and state vital-statistics records.

888. Koepplin, Leslie W. A Relationship of Reform: Immigrants and Progressives in the Far West. California (Los Angeles), 1971. 239p. (DA 32:887-A)
A study of immigrants in California, Washington, Idaho, Montana, and Nevada, which finds that the ethnic press generally supported Progressive reforms.

889. Kogut, Alvin B. The Charity and Organization Societies, the Settlements and National Minorities in the Progressive Era. Columbia, 1970. 455p. (DA 33:5830-A)
The formative period of modern social work--the Progressive Era--was rich in experience with minority groups. The newly formed Charity Organization Societies and settlements, whose bases of operation were the large urban areas, came into contact with the immigrants streaming in from southeastern Europe (and to a lesser extent with the Negro migrating to the North). Sharply divergent views have been expressed by historians as to the role of social work vis-à-vis minorities in that period. However, social work as such was not the central concern of those studies. This essay identifies, and to some extent evaluates, the policies and programs of the Charity Organization Societies and settlements in the field of intergroup relations in the Progressive Era. (A)

890. Kolivosky, Michael E. Intermarriage Between Divergent Ethnic Groups as an Index of Assimilation. Michigan State, 1953. 108p. (DA 14:565)
This is a case study of interethnic assimilation, with primary focus on intermarriage, between Slovaks and Swedes in Grassflat, a rural nonfarm community in central Pennsylvania. The particular value of this study, in terms of its purpose, lies in the discovery of unique ways by which two divergent ethnic groups participated in an assimilative process in which they had been engaged for more than six decades. (A)

891. Kolm, Richard. The Change of Cultural Identity: An Analysis of Factors Conditioning the Cultural Integration of Immigrants. Wayne State, 1966. 265p. (DA 27:2627-A)
Published under the same title (New York: Arno, 1980). Integration is suggested as being the most suitable term for the immigrant's adjustment and change of identity and is defined as

a continuous process including economic, social, and cultural aspects. Accommodation, adjustment, and identification are identified as the three main phases of the integration process. The concepts of bicultural personality and bicultural community are suggested as reflecting best the nature of the immigrant's integration process and as most appropriate from the point of view of desirable ends.

892. Kovacik, Charles F. A Geographical Analysis of the Foreign-Born in Huron, Sanilac, and St. Clair Counties of Michigan with Particular Reference to Canadians: 1850-1880. Michigan State, 1971. 230p. (DA 32:369-B)
It is the purpose of this dissertation to analyze the demographic characteristics, interrelationships, and significance of the Canadian-born and other significant foreign-born groups and their impact in the settlement of Huron, Sanilac, and St. Clair counties of eastern Michigan from 1850 to 1880. Such demographic attributes as nativity, age, and sex are examined with respect to distribution, interrelationships, change, and significance of change on both a spatial and temporal basis. Economic and political activities of the Canadian and other major foreign-born groups, such as occupation, voting behavior, and participation in local government, are also considered.

893. Krall, Dorothy N. The Second Generation Immigrant in America with Special Reference to Problems of Adjustment. Yale, 1937. 205p.

894. Krassowski, Witold. Naturalization and Assimilation--Proneness of California Immigrant Population: A Statistical Study. California (Los Angeles), 1963. 183p. (DA 24:1740)
The variations in the speed of naturalization of American immigrant groups were analyzed in terms of membership in the racial and cultural groups as well as in terms of the immigrant occupational level, degree of coethnicity of ethnic milieu in the United States, and in terms of the variable of the recency of immigrant arrival. The hypotheses so developed were based on the study of assimilation conducted by Warner and Srole. The racial and cultural typologies employed in this study of the immigrant populations are based on the typologies developed by Warner and Srole. (A)

895. Kraus, Harry P. The Settlement House Movement in New York City, 1886-1914. New York, 1970. 295p. (DA 31: 1727-A)
Published under the same title (New York: Arno, 1980). The settlement-house movement began in London, England, with the establishment of Toynbee Hall in 1884. Its founder, Canon Samuel A. Barnett, believed that the complex industrial, urban world of his time was contributing to the widening gap between rich and poor and that existing institutions were not interested in meeting this problem of an alienated, slum society. Barnett proposed to connect "the centres of learning with the centres of

industry. " University men, "settling" or residing in the slums, would provide "education by permeation" and stimulate the underprivileged to aspire to higher goals. In this process the university men would fulfill an ethical and religious obligation to serve their fellow human beings. This concept of a university settlement was adopted by Stanton Coit when he founded the Neighborhood Guild in 1886 as the first settlement in New York as well as in the United States. Profile sketches of New York City settlement workers reveal a predominantly Protestant, college-educated group of men and women, motivated by a need to fulfill religious and ethical obligations by serving the less fortunate members of the urban community. These settlement workers, of small-town or rural background, were the first representatives of the middle class voluntarily to enter and live in the ghetto. Their purpose was to help improve the way of life of the slum residents whose condition, in this instance, was aggravated by their immigrant status. Settlement houses were the first to welcome the European immigrants without rejecting their Old World culture.

896. Kristufek, Richard. The Immigrant and the Pittsburgh Public Schools, 1870-1940. Pittsburgh, 1975. 177p. (DA 36: 5887)
The purpose of this study was to identify and to examine the ways in which the public schools of Pittsburgh responded to the challenge of providing educational opportunities for those immigrants of all ages who settled in the city during the seven decades between the Civil War and World War II. The city of Pittsburgh and the areas immediately surrounding it encompass one of the most diversified concentrations of ethnic groups to be found in the entire United States. Although present-day Pittsburgh offers parallels in many ways to the social and educational characteristics of similar large cities across the nation, the history of its public schools is unique to the city itself. (A)

897. Krueger, Nancy M. Assimilation and Adjustment of Postwar Immigrants in Franklin County, Ohio. Ohio State, 1955. 138p. (DA 16:1811)
The purpose of the study was to ascertain the rapidity and the degree of assimilation and adjustment achieved by the post-World War II immigrant to the United States. The factors related to the degree and rapidity of adjustment and assimilation were sought. The Latvian, Estonian, Lithuanian group had a mean assimilation index of .308, while the Yugoslavian, Austrian, Rumanian, Hungarian group had a .144 assimilation index. The German assimilation index was .074; the Italian was -.601. The highest adjustment index was that of the Germans, .375. The Latvian, Lithuanian, Estonian group was next with .362. The Yugoslavian, Austrian, Hungarian, Rumanian group had an adjustment index of .114, and the Italians rated -.250. Sixteen nationalities were represented in the study. (A)

898. Kuznicki, Ellen M. An Ethnic School in American Education: A Study of the Origin, Development, and Merits of the Edu-

cational System of the Felician Sisters in the Polish American Catholic Schools of Western New York. Kansas State, 1973. 288p. (DA 33:6845-A)
The subject of this dissertation is the study of the role of the Felician Sisters in the acculturation of the Polish people of western New York by means of the Polish parochial school. It is an attempt to show how the Sisters provided for a gradual linguocultural transition whereby the Polish children were Americanized without the complete loss of ethnic identity. The study traces the origin of the Felician Congregation in Poland and the early involvement of the Sisters in educating children of low-status factory workers and peasants. It notes the sociopolitical conditions of the Polish nation responsible for the linguocultural adherence of Polish immigrants and for the ideology of "cultural pluralism" the Felician Sisters supported in America.

899. Labovitz, Sherman. Attitudes Toward Blacks Among Jews: Historical Antecedents and Current Concerns. Pennsylvania, 1972. 165p. (DA 33:6453-A)
The major focus of the dissertation is upon the Jewish community and upon Jewish attitudes towards blacks. It grew out of and was influenced by the more than 300 years of collective injustices heaped upon black Americans. It is concerned with identifying the bases for tensions between blacks and Jews in order to find ways for intervening to minimize them. The study found that the intensity of anti-black attitudes among the respondents varied according to the area of concern and that significant differences existed between the two samples. It also found considerable confusion and ambivalence regarding the concepts of integration and separation. The overwhelming majority of respondents maintained an ideological commitment to integration that had been eroded or compromised during the past decade. (A)

900. Lane, Francis E. American Charities and the Child of the Immigrant: A Study of Typical Child Caring Institutions in New York and Massachusetts Between the Years 1845 and 1880. Catholic, 1932. 217p.
Published under the same title (Washington, D.C.: Catholic University of America Press, 1932).

901. Langley, Sarah. An Exploratory Study of the Effects of Age, Ethnicity, Religion, Education, Sex and Health on the Formation of Death-Related Behaviors. New York, 1979. 269p. (DA 40:2771-A)
The hypothesis upon which this descriptive study is based states that one or more identifiable variables affect the responses of people to a questionnaire on death-related behaviors. These variables are: age, ethnicity, religion, education, sex, and health. The test sample was drawn from three communities in the state of Connecticut, and was limited to Christian denominations. Of these, Roman Catholics, Lutherans, and Unitarians comprise the major groups used in the analysis. The major ethnic groups used are French, Italian, Hispanic, and Latvian. (A)

902. Laurie, Bruce G. The Working People of Philadelphia, 1827-1853. Pittsburgh, 1971. 293p. (DA 32:6897-A)
Historians have advanced numerous explanations for the apparent lack of class consciousness among American wage-earners. Some of them have stressed that workers were more wage-conscious than class-conscious, while others have argued that most workingpeople, rather than opposing middle-class values, aspired to join the middle class. These historians view workers too narrowly, treating them as economic beings whose lives are confined to earning a living. This dissertation postulates that the antebellum working class of Philadelphia is best understood as consisting of ethnic and occupational groups differing in status, lifestyles, and values. Workers were normally more aware of their differences than of their common condition as a class. They identified as a class rarely, doing so only when ideology, economic change, and leaders encouraged them to submerge their differences. (A)

903. Lazerson, Marvin. The Burden of Urban Education: Public Schools in Massachusetts, 1870-1915. Harvard, 1970. 278p. Published under the title Origins of the Urban School: Public Education in Massachusetts, 1870-1915 (Cambridge, Massachusetts: Harvard University Press, 1971). Drawing extensively upon the experience of ten cities, Lazerson focuses on the kindergarten, manual training, vocational education, evening schools, and citizenship education. In the process he studies the responses of American schoolmen to the immigrant child.

904. Leifer, Anna. Ethnic Patterns in Cognitive Tasks. Yeshiva, 1972. 143p. (DA 33:1270-B)
The present study examined four cognitive abilities in disadvantaged four-year-olds from four different cultural backgrounds. Four tests considered to be valid instruments for the measurement of four cognitive abilities were administered to 80 participants in Head Start centers in New York City and Long Island, New York. The experimental population consisted of 20 Chinese, 20 Italian, 20 Negro, and 20 Puerto Rican preschoolers, with ten boys and ten girls in each cultural group. (A)

905. Leonard, Stephen J. Denver's Foreign-Born Immigrants, 1859-1900. Claremont Graduate School, 1971. 271p. (DA 32:2609-A)
Between 1860 and 1900 Denver grew from a town of less than 5,000 population to a regional center with over 130,000 residents. Although principally populated by native Americans, the city also had a sizable foreign-born contingent, comprising nearly 25 percent of the total population from 1870 to 1890. Germans, Irish, British, Scandinavians, and Canadians accounted for over one-half of the foreigners; there were also numerous Chinese and Italians. Small coteries of investors and mining experts, most of them British-born, located in Denver, where they formed a distinctive subculture. Most of the city's foreign-born, however, were engaged in more mundane pursuits. (A)

906. Lewis, Charles A. Communication Patterns of Recent Immigrants: A Study of Three Nationality Groups in Metropolitan Detroit. Illinois (Urbana), 1955. 242p. (DA 15: 2196)
This study is concerned with what happens to the communication patterns of peoples when they come to the United States as immigrants. Emphasis was upon mass-communication patterns, although personal communication was also considered. Fieldwork was directed to post-World War II immigrants of three nationality groups representing widely differing conditions in the homeland and in Detroit: Latvians and Poles, both of whom came under the Displaced Persons Act of 1948, and Italians, who came under long-established immigration regulations. (A)

907. Lewis, Charles S. The Treatment of Foreign Peoples and Cultures in American High School Literature Books. Michigan, 1956. 195p. (DA 17:1255)
The purpose of this investigation has been to determine the extent of material and the nature of such material dealing with foreign peoples and cultures to be found in American high school literature books. It was hoped that such a study might result in the improvement of high school literature books toward better international understanding. (A)

908. Lewis, Ronald G. An Analysis of Alcohol Drinking Patterns Among Four Ethnic Groups. Denver, 1974. 130p. (DA 35:3119-A)
This research study was designed to help fill the knowledge gap that has existed between the areas of alcoholism and ethnicity. Although programs established by the federal government have focused on new ways of dealing with the alcoholic, in order to be effective these new policies ought to take into account the unique cultural milieu and social response patterns of the consumer. Therefore, this comparative study was undertaken to expand existing knowledge with respect to alcoholism and ethnicity. Of special concern was the American Indian, both in the urban setting and on the reservation.

909. Lichtenstein, Jules H. White Ethnic and Black Economic Assimilation and Mobility: A Study of Employment Patterns and Determinants in Selected SMSA's. Cornell, 1975. 480p. (DA 36:4809-A)
The processes by which ethnic and racial newcomers become integrated into the urban economy and improve their well-being have important planning and policy implications, yet they are not clearly understood. This study attempts to describe and explain ethnic and racial economic assimilation and mobility in American labor markets. Two facets are specifically dealt with. First, historical patterns are analyzed. After constructing an intergenerational model of occupational and industrial employment, the hypothesis--that blacks are following the same pattern of assimilation and mobility within the local labor markets as white ethnic groups, is examined. Second, the determinants of ethnic and

racial economic performance, measured in terms of labor-force participation and occupational standing, are probed. It is hypothesized that conditions related to the demand for labor are more important determinants of the economic performance of rural-urban migrants, the first generation, while supply factors are more significant factors influencing the economic well-being of their descendants, the second generation.

910. Licon, Lena L. The Influence of Students' Socioeconomic Status and Ethnic Identity on Preservice Teachers' Decision Making and Curriculum Assignments. Washington State, 1979. 76p. (DA 40:1938-A)
The purpose of the study was to investigate the influence of students' socioeconomic status and ethnic identity on preservice teachers' decision-making and curriculum assignments (tracking). The study was based upon the responses of 190 students enrolled in teacher-training classes at Washington State University, Pullman, Washington. Subjects responded to three experimental tasks that employed a simulated school situation and simulated student cumulative records (representing Anglo and Chicano students). Information on the cumulative records was limited to socioeconomic status indicators and ethnic identity.

911. Lieberson, Stanley. Comparative Segregation and Assimilation of Ethnic Groups. Chicago, 1960. 257p.
Published under the title Ethnic Patterns in American Cities (Glencoe, Illinois: Free Press, 1963).

912. Linkh, Richard M. Catholicism and the European Immigrant, 1900-1924: A Chapter in American Catholic Social Thought. Columbia, 1973. 200p. (DA 34:3934-A)
Published under the title American Catholicism and the European Immigrant, 1900-1924 (New York: Center for Migration Studies, 1975). The author argues that the Church leaders during these years rejected the idea of hasty "Americanization" of the immigrant and opted instead for gradual assimilation into a "melting pot with an extremely low flame," a theory similar in many respects to cultural pluralism. Church leaders, considering the newcomers' language and culture essential for the preservation of their faith, were reluctant to encourage rapid "Americanization" lest the immigrants be lost to the Church.

913. Lovrich, Nicholas P. Political Culture and Civic Involvement: A Comparative Analysis of Immigrant Ethnic Communities in San Pedro, California. California (Los Angeles), 1971. 273p. (DA 32:3388-A)
The study focuses upon the analysis of differences in patterns of civic involvement and formal voluntary-association effectiveness across ethnic groups. It entails an empirical testing of a number of hypotheses suggested in comparative political literature, including theories of "amoral familism," social trust/misanthropy, ethnic assimilation, etc. Comparative analysis is based upon the study of data taken from Yugoslav-Americans, Italian-Americans, and native Americans in San Pedro, California.

914. Loxley, William A. The Household Production and the Distribution of Cognitive Skills Within Six Racial-Ethnic Cultures. Chicago, 1979. 267p. (DA 40:3555-A)
When some minority cultures do poorly in school while others seem to thrive on the scholastic-competition process, we may wish to blame the results on poor school-entry skills and or poor achievement motivation produced in the home. This would be so because the level of cognitive achievement demanded by parents varies with the constraints they face. Here, too, it is believed that cultural traits can affect preferences for cognitive-skill acquisition just as they affect tastes and demands for other consumption items, such as food, music, or clothes. In this thesis the author assumes that such initial school-entry skills as verbal, abstract, memory, quantitative, and spatial reasoning are produced and distributed within racial-ethnic family networks based upon the manner in which certain household resources are nonrandomly allocated across the sibling structure (sibling rank and brood size being two commonplace stratifiers). On the basis of NLS data collected in 1972, a linear structural equation model was applied separately to Mexican, Oriental, black, white, Jewish, and native American sample data.

915. Luke, Oral S. Differences in Musical Aptitude in School Children of Different National and Racial Origin. California (Berkeley), 1939. 149p.

916. Mamone, John R. Italian and Puerto Rican Male Social Bonds in Schools, Factory, and Community. Rutgers, 1978. 491p. (DA 39:3015)
The central problem of this study is the relationship between the mechanisms of male social bonding and acculturation among Italians and Puerto Ricans in the industrial center of Paterson, New Jersey. The focus of the research was upon the nature of male social bonds among males in a high school and their near peers in textile factories. Attention was given to generational, ecological, and historical circumstances as well as to primordial attributes in order to develop systemic sets of bonding patterns.
Male bonding patterns define and govern ethnic social encounters that affect the ways ethnic groups are perceived by agents of the dominant society and their rate of mode of acculturation into the dominant society.

917. Marcuson, Lewis R. The Irish, the Italians, and the Jews: A Study of Three Nationality Groups As Portrayed in American Drama Between 1920 and 1960. Denver, 1966. (DA 27:1141-A)
During the four decades between 1920 and 1960 the portrayal of Irish, Italian, and Jewish immigrants and their descendants in plays produced on the New York stage underwent a variety of changes--although many themes and characteristics continued throughout this period. During the 1920s and 1930s a number of comedies achieved popular success through their humorous treatment of ethnic traits; in other plays the personalities of immi-

grants and their children were explored in a more serious, penetrating manner. In dramas of social protest Jewish and Italian characters appeared as victims of exploitation and as critics of the American political and economic system. Other plays objectively explored the milieu of the urban "melting pot" in which Italian, Jewish, and Irish characters lived in close proximity, expressing varying degrees of friendship and hostility toward each other. (A)

918. Marjoribanks, Keven M. Ethnic and Environmental Influences on Levels and Profiles of Mental Abilities. Toronto, 1970. 231p. (DA 32:6052-A)
Studies that have examined the relationship between the environment and ethnic-group differences in intellectual performance have largely concentrated on using global measures of both the environment and intellectual performance. The use of these global measures, however, has obscured important differences among ethnic groups. Therefore, in the present study an examination was made of the relationship between a refined measure of the learning environment of the home and ethnic-group differences in the levels and profiles of a set of mental-ability test scores. Fifth-grade boys and their parents from five ethnic groups formed the sample for the study. The groups were Canadian Indian (Iroquoian), French Canadian (Franco Ontarian), Jewish, southern Italian, and white Anglo Saxon Protestant. The final sample within each group included 18 middle-class and 19 low-class families. The social-class classification was based on an index consisting of two equally weighted components: the occupation of the main support of the family, and a rating of the parents' educational level. (A)

919. Marsh, May C. The Life and Work of the Churches in an Interstitial Area. New York, 1932. 146p.
A detailed portrait of the East Harlem (New York City) Italian-immigrant community and the social work of Protestant and evangelical churches.

920. Marty, Myron A. Missouri Synod Lutherans and Roman Catholicism: Opposition and Reappraisal, 1917-1963. St. Louis, 1967. 305p. (DA 28:3116-A)
Published under the title Lutherans and Roman Catholicism: The Changing Conflict, 1917-1963 (Notre Dame, Indiana: Notre Dame University Press, 1969). This is a case history of the opposition to Catholicism offered by Missouri Synod Lutherans. It records and characterizes this opposition and identifies its significance for the future relations between the two denominations. The period treated marks the 400th anniversary of the span of years between the beginning of the Lutheran Reformation in 1517 and the closing of the Council of Trent in 1563.

921. Matulich, Loretta K. A Cross-Disciplinary Study of the European Immigrants of 1870 to 1925. New Mexico, 1971. 267p. (DA 32:5236-A)

Both native-born and foreign-born Americans throughout the twentieth century have written about the European immigrants who came to American shores between 1870 and 1925. Many of the social-science accounts and fiction works about these newcomers centered on one implicit question: How could these immigrants become Americans? Two views of assimilation into American society are presented in this study: Henry Pratt Fairchild's static definition of the goal of Americanization and Jane Addams's dynamic definition of American cultural growth. Rejecting Fairchild's view that immigrants must lose all traces of their foreign origin in order to become real Americans, this study adopts Addams's belief that the majority of immigrants could only become Americans if one sees both the native- and foreign-born growing toward each other into one culture. (A)

922. Mayer, John E. Jewish-Gentile Courtships: An Exploratory Study of a Social Process. Columbia, 1959. 340p. (DA 20:789)
What are the postcontact influences that lead individuals to marry those whom they had formerly looked upon as being maritally unsuitable? Or, putting the question more generally, how does it happen that individuals become intimately associated with persons who were regarded, at an earlier point, as being unfit or unqualified? By interviewing Jews and Christians who had been intent upon contracting an ingroup marriage but who subsequently married out, it was hoped to throw some light upon this problem. More specifically, the author hoped to be able to identify some of the factors accounting for the marriage and to develop hypotheses in explanation of the outcome. (A)

923. Mayer, Jonathan D. The Journey-to-Work, Ethnicity, and Occupation in Milwaukee, 1860-1900. Michigan, 1977. 275p. (DA 38:6937-A)
Little is known about the evolution of journey-to-work patterns in nineteenth-century cities. This study analyzes the dual influences of occupation and ethnicity on the journey-to-work in Milwaukee between 1860 and 1900. During this period Milwaukee was experiencing its greatest growth. Relying on city-directory data for the three sample years of 1860, 1880, and 1900, the author analyzes statistically and cartographically journey-to-work patterns. The average journey-to-work increased between 1860 and 1880 and decreased more rapidly between 1880 and 1900. This was because of the physical growth of the city and because of the construction of transportation routes. The increases differed for the various ethnic groups that were present in Milwaukee; the Americans, Germans, Scandinavians, East Europeans, and Irish all demonstrated considerable diversity of commuting patterns. (A)

924. McAvoy, Thomas T. The Catholic Church in Indiana, 1789-1834. Columbia, 1940. 263p.
Published under the same title (New York: Columbia University Press, 1940). Focuses on the period of transition from the

French Church foundations to the American transformation. Based on letters and documents, many of them primary sources.

925. McBride, Paul W. The Cultural Cold War: Immigrants and the Quest for Cultural Monism, 1890-1917. Georgia, 1972. 224p.
Published under the title Cultural Clash: Immigrants and Reformers, 1890-1920 (San Francisco: R & E Research Associates, 1975). The prize contended for in the cultural cold war was the self-image and loyalty of ethnic America. The war pitted settlement worker against political boss, public school against parochial, charity worker against the preindustrial unemployed "paupers," and YMCA operatives against labor unions and demon rum. The underlying theme of all of this infighting was cultural monism versus cultural pluralism. This study examines the motives, techniques, and hysteria generated by cultural conflict. (A)

926. McKay, Ralph Y. A Comparative Study of the Character Representation of California's Dominant Minority Groups in the Officially Adopted California Reading Textbooks of the 1950s, 1960s and 1970s. University of the Pacific, 1971. 272p.

927. McLeod, Joseph A. Baptists and Racial and Ethnic Minorities in Texas. North Texas State, 1972. 385p. (DA 33: 6281-A)
This study examines the relations of white Baptists with racial and ethnic minorities in Texas from the beginning of organized Baptist work in Texas in the mid-nineteenth century through the United States Supreme Court decision in the Brown v. Topeka case in 1954. Emphasizing the role of attitudes in forming actions, it examines the ideas of various leaders of the chief Baptist bodies in Texas: the Baptist General Convention of Texas, the Baptist Missionary Association of Texas, and the American Baptist Convention. The minorities included in the work are the Negroes, the Mexican-Americans, non-Anglo-Saxon Europeans, American Indians, Orientals, and Jews.

928. Meister, Richard J. A History of Gary, Indiana: 1930-1940. Notre Dame, 1967. 369p. (DA 28:1770-A)
This dissertation is a general history of Gary, Indiana, during the decade of the thirties. It begins by tracing the history of Gary from its founding in 1906, when northwest Indiana was little more than sand dunes and sloughs, up to the eve of the Depression. Gary, a creation of the United States Steel Corporation, remained for its first quarter-century a one-industry town, but only the Northside of the city was under the direct influence of the mill. On the Northside lived the skilled and the semiskilled workers, the management of the mills, and the business leaders of the community. Thousands of eastern and southern European immigrants settled on the Southside. During and after the war years the Negroes from the Deep South followed the immigrant into this same area.

929. Millard, William E.   The "Sale of Culture. "   Minnesota, 1969.   280p.   (DA 30:4658-B)
The central themes of the study are: the identification of the "Sale of Culture, " its morphology and operation, an interpretation of its role in each community, and an analysis of the salable cultural items, cultural relicts, economic stagnation, site and situation, and leadership.   For this initial probe into the "Sale of Culture" three communities in the Midwest were selected. They represent three salable themes: New Glarus, Wisconsin-- ethnic (Swiss); Nauvoo, Illinois--historical-religious (Mormon- Icarian); and Galena, Illinois--historical (Yankee).

930. Miller, Abraham H.   Ethnicity and Political Behavior: An Investigation of Partisanship and Efficacy.   Michigan, 1968. 227p.   (DA 30:372-A)
Scholarly concern with ethnicity tends to restrict itself generally to the incipient processes of assimilation.   When the immigrants first arrive everyone is aware of them.   The residual implica- tions of ethnicity across generations have received very little attention.   This is, in many ways, more true of political science than any other relevant discipline.   The purpose of this project is twofold: to assess the importance of the distinct racial and ethnic composition of America for two long-term components of the electoral decision-making process--partisanship and efficacy-- and to make some attempt toward opening a neglected aspect of the American political process.   (A)

931. Miller, Max D.   Patterns of Relationships of Fluid and Cry- stallized Mental Abilities to Achievement in Different Ethnic Groups.   Houston, 1972.   214p.

932. Minard, Ralph D.   Race Attitudes of Iowa Children.   Iowa, 1930.   138p.

933. Mol, Johannis J.   Theology and Americanization: The Ef- fects of Pietism and Orthodoxy on Adjustment to a New Cul- ture.   Columbia, 1960.   248p.   (DA 21:3545)
Using representatives of two ethnic denominations (the Dutch Re- formed and the German Lutheran), the author attempts to ascer- tain whether an evangelical-pietistic theology and a conservative- orthodox theology have different effects on adjustment in a new country.   The author studies the sermons and personal papers of the clergy as well as minutes of church meetings from both denominations in the first half of the eighteenth century in New York, New Jersey, and Pennsylvania.

934. Mormino, Gary R.   The Hill upon the City: An Italo-Amer- ican Neighborhood in St. Louis, Missouri, 1880-1955.   North Carolina (Chapel Hill), 1977.   505p.   (DA 38:3683-A)
The history of the Hill has not been an uprooting or alienating experience, but rather an uplifting story of how several thousand immigrants purposefully came to St. Louis to build a coherent and cohesive settlement.   The colony was first settled in the late

nineteenth century by Lombard emigrants who came to the Gateway City to labor in the city's brickyards and clay mines. Sicilians soon followed, prompting the enclave to be dubbed "Dago Hill" by disgruntled natives. Italians developed their associational life, such as the mutual-aid societies, on the basis of the old-country village attachments. New World conditions, such as economic patterns, soon altered Italo-American behavior. (A)

935. Morrison, Kenneth M. The People of the Dawn: The Abnaki and Their Relations with New England and New France, 1600-1727. Maine, 1975. 493p. (DA 36:6854-A)
"The People of the Dawn" outlines a narrative history of Abnaki relations with French and English peoples to 1727. Particular emphasis is given to the developing political connections between the three peoples and, consequently, to the extraordinary effect the imperial conflict between the English and the French had in shaping those relationships. It also estimates Abnaki recognition of, and response to, the issues of the postcontact world. Finally the study re-evaluates the mutual impact of the Abnaki, French, and English on each other and those factors that relegated northeastern Algonkian peoples to an increasingly marginal existence in a white-dominated world. (A)

936. Mulhern, James. A History of Secondary Education in Pennsylvania. Philadelphia, 1932. 714p.
Published under the same title (Philadelphia: Science Press, 1933). A comprehensive history with considerable attention to German-immigrant communities, and the education of immigrant children.

937. Mulligan, Jane S. The Madonna and Child in American Culture, 1830-1916. California (Los Angeles), 1975. 673p. (DA 36:4679-A)
This dissertation is a study of the cultural concept of motherhood in America from 1830 to 1916. Commencing in the early nineteenth century, a new genre of literature appeared that focused on the mother in the family. The figure as created by ministers, doctors, and women writers was depicted as a redeemer, with the character traits of Mary and Christ. The main function of this madonna-like person was identified as providing ethics for the new democratic, egalitarian society through child nurture. The literature that glorified domestic material responsibility drew on European child-rearing experts, such as Locke, Rousseau, and Froebel, who designated the child and its nurture as the means for modern salvation for individuals and society. American religious and secular writers sought out new means to provide morals and stability in the context of a secularizing, urbanizing, and mobile society. An internalization of the Protestant conscience was to be used by the mother redeemer to prevent a fall into sin for mobile, self-seeking individuals.

938. Murphy, John C. An Analysis of the Attitudes of American Catholics Toward the Immigrant and the Negro, 1825-1925.

Catholic, 1940. 158p.
Published under the same title (Washington, D. C.: Catholic University of America Press, 1940). Records the development of Catholic thought on two questions: immigration and race relations between 1825 and 1925, and on the larger issue that these two questions involve, the relations between dominant and minority groups in American social history. The author concludes that the Catholic Church and Catholic observers usually consider social questions (i.e., the race question and immigrants) only in respect to the Catholic Church and not their general effects upon society.

939. Nair, Murali D. New Immigrants' Use of Four Social Service Agencies in a Canadian Metropolis. Columbia, 1978. 225p. (DA 39:5150)
Relatively little is known about immigrants' use of social-service agencies that are set up to help them. The purpose of this study is to examine the new immigrant's use of social service agencies in a metropolitan city in Canada. Five hypotheses have been developed in relation to the two basic subsystems under study. The dependent variable is the new immigrant's use of social agencies; and the antecedent variables are derived from the characteristics of immigrants. The hypotheses, which this study tests, were derived from a review of the relevant literature in the field of immigration, the history of social services to new immigrants in Canada, and the present structure of social services to new immigrants to Canada. (A)

940. Nam, Charles B. Nationality Groups and Social Stratification: A Study of the Socioeconomic Status and Mobility of Selected European Nationality Groups in America. North Carolina (Chapel Hill), 1959. 232p. (DA 20:2947)
The present research was undertaken in order to answer the following questions: (1) What variations in socioeconomic status exist among specific nationality groups in America? (2) Are nationality groups with a dominant language and culture like that of the natives most closely assimilated to native status patterns? (3) Has the second generation of each nationality group bettered the position of the foreign-born generation? (4) To what extent are differences in educational level related to the socioeconomic status and mobility of the groups? (5) Are status patterns for nationality groups similar for different areas of the country?

941. Neidle, Cecyle S. The Foreign-Born View America: A Study of Autobiographies Written by Immigrants to the United States. New York, 1962. 410p. (DA 24:4178)
The purpose of this study is to examine the autobiographical records of immigrants. Since the days of Captain John Smith, William Bradford, and John Winthrop, who were the first settlers as well as the first autobiographers, a steady current of subjective writings has issued from the pens of newcomers to this continent. These autobiographical statements offer evidence of the difficulties and triumphs immigrants experienced and contain au-

thoritative comments on the American environment. In the course of this study close to 100 autobiographies of the foreign-born were examined. More than 60 are discussed in detail.

942. Newander, Mary C. The Cultural Heritage of the Metropolitan St. Louis Area As Reflected in the Songs and Folk Songs of Its European Ethnic Groups: A Collection of Songs and Folk Songs Appropriate for Use in Elementary and Junior High Schools. Washington University, 1976. 442p. (DA 37:2046-A)
There has been great interest in the ethnic heritage of St. Louis, as demonstrated by the large crowds who attend the many ethnic festivals in the area. Music is an important part of these events. Many of the songs of the ethnic groups are unavailable in printed sources, or, if printed, are not accessible to the general public. This dissertation is a collection of the songs sung by the members of 15 European ethnic groups in Metropolitan St. Louis, suitable for use in elementary and junior high schools by musically educated teachers. (A)

943. Newman, Dorothy R. K. The Second-Generation Immigrant in America: With Special Reference to Problems of Adjustment. Yale, 1937. 592p. (DA 27:3529-A)
Members of the second generation make various types of responses in reaction to their unique cultural position, some becoming aggressive in their efforts to gain acceptance by American society, others withdrawing within the intimacy of their own group. A number of agencies are active in attempting to help the children of immigrants to make adjustments. Most noteworthy among these are immigrant national organizations and the societies and English-language publications established by the second generation themselves. Complete adjustment of the second generation of immigrants, however, will come only with their assimilation. (A)

944. Nicolson, M. The Irish Catholics in Toronto, 1840-1900. Guelph, 1976. 311p.

945. Okazaki, George-Doyen K. Increasing Social Work Relationship Skills of Ethnic Minority Students. Utah, 1977. 154p. (DA 38:7565)
In recent years an area that has received special attention is that of teaching communication skills to convey empathy, respect, and authenticity (warmth, empathy, and genuineness) through the competency-based laboratory method. Various studies substantiate the efficacy of this method. However, results of a previous study conducted at the University of Utah indicated that the ethnic-minority students scored significantly lower than the nonminority students in the pretest and posttest of the Index of Therapeutic Communication. Because increasingly more ethnic minority students are entering the professional schools, it is urgent that educators seek ways to develop the ethnic-minority students who may not be as well prepared academically as the nonminority students.

The main purposes of this study were to ascertain if ethnic-minority students do score lower on the pretest and posttest of the Index than nonminority students, and to see if special conditions can increase the ethnic-minority students' posttest score of the Index to be equivalent to those of the nonminority students. (A)

946. O'Reilly, Charles T. Race Prejudice Among Catholic College Students in the United States and Italy: A Comparative Study of the Role of Religion and Personality in Inter-Group Relations. Notre Dame, 1954. 236p. (DA 16:1008)
This study of anti-Jewish and anti-Negro attitudes tested several hypotheses about the relationship between prejudice and personality and prejudice and religion. Questionnaires were distributed to 120 Catholic Italian men and women university students, and to 559 Catholic men and women attending Catholic colleges in the midwestern, northeastern, and south central United States. Stress was placed upon the comparability of data obtained in the United States and Italy, and that obtained by the present study and by prior studies of prejudice. The study thus presents material from the point of view of replication and also serves as a source of cross-cultural data. (A)

947. Osborne, William A. The Race Problem in the Catholic Church in the U.S.: Between the Time of the Second Plenary Council (1866) and the Founding of the Catholic Interracial Council of New York (1934). Columbia, 1954. 248p. (DA 14:2432)
Published under the title The Segregated Covenant: Race Relations and American Catholics (New York: Herder & Herder, 1967). The emancipation by the Civil War of some 4 million Negro slaves, over half of whom had no religious affiliation, presented a unique opportunity for expansion of the Christian churches of the United States. Shortly after the end of the war the American Catholic bishops assembled in Baltimore for their Second Plenary Council. Among other items on the agenda was the problem of how to meet the rare opportunity presented by emancipation. This dissertation is concerned with the ways in which the Catholic Church faced the challenge. What did it do, for example, to bring these people into the Church? How did it treat those Negroes who were already members? Was the pattern of conduct within the Church different from that of American society at large? These are the general questions around which the study revolves. (A)

948. Paul, Daniel L. The Effect of Integrated Grouping and of Studying Minority Culture in Reducing Cultural Cleavage in Elementary Classrooms. Western Michigan, 1973. 175p.
The question examined was whether prejudice could be significantly reduced by studying the minority culture and integrating ethnic groups. The samples were in Holland, Michigan, schools. Among the findings that existed in both groups were that studying the minority culture did not significantly reduce prejudice and that ethnic contact in class did not significantly reduce prejudice.

949. Pedersen, Harold A. Acculturation Among Danish and Polish Ethnic Groups in Wisconsin. Wisconsin, 1949. 268p.

950. Pogue, Frank G. A Study of Ethnic Background and Role Strain Among Policemen. Pittsburgh, 1973. 261p. (DA 34:6763)
This study examines role strain among policemen that emanates from simultaneous organizational or occupational membership and ethnic membership. The hypothesis of the research is that the overlapping role sets (occupational and ethnic background) will result in strain for police officers. The ultimate goals of the study were: (1) to provide insight into the problem of adjusting to constant cross-pressures emanating from two discordant yet omnipresent life spaces; (2) to show that the black policeman operates in a different professional and personal context from that of other policemen, regardless of the latter's ethnicity; (3) to explore the practical consequences of having black policemen and nonblack policemen in different life spaces; and (4) to explore the extent to which ethnic-group membership interferes with inter-ethnic relationships and affects attitudes toward various kinds of people. (A)

951. Portis, Bernard. Education as a Factor in Ethnic Attitudes. Harvard, 1962. 263p.

952. Powell, James H. The Concept of Cultural Pluralism in American Social Thought, 1915-1965. Notre Dame, 1971. 340p. (DA 32:4536-A)
The present essay describes the major forms of the concept represented by the term "cultural pluralism" as they have emerged --with or without the term itself--in the discussion of American minority groups from 1915 to 1965. It also attempts to indicate the amount of interest in cultural pluralism during particular periods, and to suggest the contemporary issues and events, as well as those factors in the backgrounds of the men who dealt with the concept, which may explain that interest.

953. Punch, T. The Irish Community of Halifax, 1815-1867. Dalhousie, 1975. 275p.

954. Purcell, Roderick N. The Writing Vocabularies of Children of Native-Born and Foreign-Born Parents. George Peabody, 1952. 142p.

955. Reader, William A. Yankees, Immigrants, and Social Climbers: A Study of Social Mobility in Greenfield, Massachusetts, 1850-1970. Massachusetts, 1973. 394p. (DA 34:1837-A)
The idea of America as a land of opportunity in which merit was the sole determinant of social position has long been a central belief in a culture that praised "success" and idealized the "self-made man" who rose from "rags to riches." Until recently, however, few historians have discussed the validity of these ideas,

described their social consequences, or related them to the social and economic changes transforming American society in the nineteenth and twentieth centuries. These ideas formed the basis of the ideology of mobility. In order to compare them with social reality the author studied social mobility in the town of Greenfield, Massachusetts, from the years 1850 to 1970. To avoid the limitations of earlier studies a new methodology was devised. Cohorts of resident males married in Greenfield in the years 1850-57, 1880-86, 1910-12, and 1940-41 were traced through census records, town directories, and tax-assessment records to determine whether these persons remained in the community, achieved occupational mobility, or acquired property. Since marriage records listed place of birth and name of the officiating individual, it was possible to determine the ethnic origins and religious affiliations of cohort members, and to assess the impact of ethnicity and religion on social mobility. (A)

956. Reese, John L. A Comparative Study of Jewish and Italian Intergenerational Occupational Mobility in Syracuse, New York. Syracuse, 1975. 102p. (DA 36:6980-A)
Two themes are generally advanced to explain the phenomenon of rapid Jewish intergenerational mobility in America. The first of these asserts that it can largely be explained in cultural terms. The second theme maintains that the comparatively large number of first-generation American Jews in "petty proprietorship" positions greatly expanded mobility possibilities for their sons. The hypothesis in the study is that the relatively rapid upward Jewish intergenerational occupational mobility was due to first-generation Jews being in "petty proprietorship" occupations as compared with first-generation Italians, who, because they were laborers, were less likely to have sons who were upwardly mobile. (A)

957. Reynolds, Collis J. The Treatment of the Immigrant in American Textbooks. Harvard, 1951. 268p.

958. Rosen, Philip. The Neglected Dimension: Ethnic Groups in the City. Carnegie-Mellon, 1972. 537p. (DA 33:2534-A)
"The point about the melting pot is that it did not happen," say Nathan Glazer and Daniel Patrick Moynihan in their trailblazing book, Beyond the Melting Pot. However, public school American history and sociology textbooks present a bland, homogenized picture of American society broken only by the glaring exception of a large unassimilated black group. The diversity of the American people is not faithfully portrayed in existing secondary texts. This unit was created to eliminate this weakness in the education of our youth and to devote some attention to the realities of ethnicity in America as suggested by recent scholarship. This dissertation contains a rationale for the unit, a bibliographic-historiographic essay that examines ethnicity in two time periods, 1890-1925 and 1960-1971; student materials and a teacher's guide for a seven-week curriculum unit entitled "The Neglected Dimension: Ethnic Groups in the City"; and a report of classroom tryouts of the unit in the schools. (A)

959. Schoem, David L. Ethnic Survival in America: An Ethnography of a Jewish Afternoon School. California (Berkeley), 1979. 297p. (DA 40:3941-A)
The Jewish school closely reflected the conditions of the Jewish community. Many Jews in the school community had little or no behavioral Jewish identity and had an empty and confused attitudinal Jewish identity. Nevertheless, these Jews felt strongly about being a part of the Jewish group regardless of the fact that many neither acted nor thought in any particular or unique manner because they were Jewish. Major changes were occurring in the school's Jewish community that were not being confronted. These changes were present in the family, the neighborhood, the workplace, the public school, and within the internal Jewish organizational network. Just as these people had to "step out" of their daily lives to be Jewish, so it was that for them the Jewish community had come to exist "outside" of themselves. (A)

960. Schuler, Paul J. The Reaction of American Catholics to the Foundations and Early Practices of Progressive Education in the United States. Notre Dame, 1970. 437p. (DA 32:214-A)
The purpose of this study has been to present the record of the reaction of American Catholics to the foundations and early practices of progressive education in the United States from 1892 to 1917. No attempt has been made to determine the American Catholic attitude toward general educational theory or practice during this period. Nor has any comparison been made of the Catholic position on progressive education during this period with a later position taken by American Catholics on progressive education, based either on writings or on educational practice. (A)

961. Schultz, Stanley K. The Education of Urban Americans: Boston, 1789-1860. Chicago, 1970. 283p.
Published under the title The Culture Factory: Boston Public Schools, 1789-1860 (New York: Oxford University Press, 1973). Traces the history of the bureaucratization of urban public schooling, and its provisions for social control over the poor and the immigrants.

962. Scott, Woodrow W. Interpersonal Relations in Ethnically Mixed Small Work Groups. Southern California, 1959. 290p. (DA 20:3880)
This study was undertaken to investigate the interpersonal relations of individuals from different ethnic backgrounds in work groups of a factory. Four research hypotheses were developed for this study: (1) antagonistic conflict attitudes toward fellow workers from different ethnic backgrounds working together under production-efficiency procedures will tend to be lessened; (2) cooperative attitudes of individuals from different ethnic backgrounds working together under production-efficiency procedures will tend to be developed; (3) under these conditions active friendships tend to develop; and (4) the development of "balanced work groups" in which no one ethnic group has numerical advantage over the other groups tends to stimulate cooperative and friendship attitudes among the members of the work group. (A)

963. Seder, Doris L. The Influence of Cultural Identification on Family Behavior. Brandeis, 1966. 249p. (DA 28:1906-A)
This study considered the influence of cultural identification on family behavior with the aim of contributing to concepts for family diagnosis. The hypotheses were: (1) a strong tie to the ethnic culture is associated with a high degree of segregation in the spouse relationship; a weak tie is associated with a low degree of segregation; (2) a strong tie to the ethnic culture is associated with a high degree of intimacy in the spouse relationship with kin; a weak tie is associated with a low degree of intimacy; and (3) a strong tie to the ethnic culture is associated with defining emotional difficulties in self-help terms; a weak tie is associated with defining emotional problems in mental-health terms. (A)

964. Sengstock, Mary C. Maintenance of Social Integration Patterns in an Ethnic Group. Washington, 1967. 423p. (DA 28:808)
Recent sociological investigations have indicated that assimilation of ethnic minorities into the dominant society proceeds at a slow rate and that many ethnic groups retain their distinctiveness as social entities after they have lost many of the distinctively foreign characteristics of the early immigrants. This paper is an attempt to determine the degree to which the American-reared descendants of a single ethnic group have retained the social patterns of their immigrant parents, in spite of having dropped such ethnic characteristics as foreign-language use, ethnic food patterns, and old-country religious customs. (A)

965. Shanabruch, Charles H. The Catholic Church's Role in the Americanization of Chicago's Immigrants: 1833-1928. Chicago, 1975. 2 vols. (DA 36:4718-A)
Between 1880 and 1921 the Catholic Church in the United States grew rapidly due to unrestricted immigration. The impact of the influx of a polyglot membership upon the Church and its influence on the immigrants have not received deserved attention. Intellectual histories as well as studies of particular nationalities have given only a partial picture of the growth and development of the Catholic Church. This dissertation examines that institution's work among immigrants in Chicago, the nation's most cosmopolitan city, and shows how the Church responded to the immigrants, joined together more than 25 nationalities, and fostered a new identity that was more American than foreign. (A)

966. Shasteen, Amos E. Value Orientations of Anglo and Spanish American High School Sophomores. New Mexico, 1967. 165p.

967. Sirota, David. Some Functions of the Nationalistic Ideologies of Minority Ethnic Groups. Michigan, 1959. 254p. (DA 20:1887)
This is a study of the nationalistic ideologies of the American-born and the immigrant sectors of two American ethnic groups:

the Irish and the Jews. These groups are used to test a general theory of the functions of immigrant and nonimmigrant ideologies. It is hypothesized that the nonimmigrant ideology serves to relieve the status-deprivation resulting from the inability of members of disvalued ethnic groups to affiliate with higher-status reference groups. The ideology serves this function by providing a more acceptable image of the ethnic group for its members. According to the initial hypothesis of this study, the nonimmigrant ideology stresses an ancient prestigeful condition of the group (biblical Israel, medieval Ireland).

968. Slocum, Walter L. Ethnic Stocks as Culture Types in Rural Wisconsin. Wisconsin, 1940. 237p.

969. Spengler, Paul A. Yankee, Swedish and Italian Acculturation and Economic Mobility in Jamestown, New York, from 1860 to 1920. Delaware, 1977. 389p. (DA 38:2311-A)
This dissertation is a study of three ethnic groups in a northeastern industrial city during the Gilded Age and the Progressive Era. The study discusses the development of Jamestown and the economic and cultural backgrounds of the Yankees, Swedes, and Italians and analyzes neighborhood and family patterns, ethnic clubs, schools, churches, and economic mobility. Between 1860 and 1920 Jamestown grew from a town of 1,155 people to a city of 38,917, which manufactured photographic paper, worsted cloth, and, most importantly, wooden and metallic furniture. Most factories were small or medium-sized, and nearly all were locally owned. Until after the Civil War the city's population was mainly of Yankee origin. By 1920, 40 percent of Jamestown's population was of Swedish stock, 10 percent was of Italian origin, and other immigrant groups accounted for 15 percent. Immigrants in Jamestown adapted successfully to conditions in America while maintaining their ethnic traditions. Neighborhoods reflected rational economic adaptation, as immigrants settled near their work. Ethnic neighborhoods were rigidly segregated. There was considerable overlapping, and as their occupational patterns diversified and they bought property Swedes and Italians settled throughout the city. Immigrants maintained ethnic unity through institutions that did not require an isolated geographic base. Both Swedes and Italians maintained strong family ties. The Italian Catholic parish church unified the Italians. Religion was less of a unifying force among the Swedes, who were divided among several denominations. Still, the Swedish churches upheld traditions and provided associational ties. Ethnic clubs also preserved immigrant traditions and associations, but they did not involve the rejection of values leading to upward mobility.

970. Spiegel, Joseph A. Test Score Performance of Irish and Italian College Freshmen. Rutgers, 1969. 62p. (DA 31: 3802-A)
The present investigations involved a comparison of scholastic aptitude, academic achievement, personality characteristics, and occupational preferences of Irish and Italian college freshmen.

Based upon past analyses of the cultural patterns in families of Irish and Italian origin, certain hypotheses concerning differences in aptitude, achievement, personality, and interest characteristics were developed. The Irish were expected to present a more inhibited pattern of emotional response than the Italian college students. On the basis of this expectation Irish and Italian students were further expected to prefer occupations that permit the satisfaction of these needs.

971. Srole, Leo. Ethnic Groups and American Society: The Ethnic Communal System. Chicago, 1940. 318p.
Much of the dissertation's data is found in William L. Warner and Leo Srole, The Social Systems of American Ethnic Groups (New Haven, Connecticut: Yale University Press, 1945) [No. 3, Yankee City Series]. Groups considered are Irish, French Canadians, Jews, Italians, Armenians, Greeks, Poles, and Russians.

972. Stack, John F. The City as a Symbol of International Conflict. Boston's Irish, Italians, and Jews, 1935-1944. Denver, 1977. 371p. (DA 38:5698-A)
This study evaluates the role of the international system on the outbreak of urban ethnic conflict in Boston between 1935 and 1944. Consequently, the dissertation is divided into roughly two sections. The first examines the theoretical dynamics of ethnicity and its relationship to international politics. The concept of ethnicity lacks precise meaning. The interdisciplinary basis of ethnicity helps to explain much of its lack of precision. Chapter II examines a wide range of approaches to ethnicity, concluding that a macro orientation, e.g., group perspective, must be integrated with a micro orientation, e.g., individual perspective, in order to fully appreciate the dynamics of ethnicity. Chapter III ties the concept of ethnicity to the role of the international system via three models of urban ethnic conflict. Thus, the remainder of this study is an attempt to ascertain the way in which the international system of the 1930s exacerbated ethnic conflict in Boston. (A)

973. Stein, Rita F. An Exploration of Ethnic Group Differences in Problems of Adolescent Adjustment. State University of New York (Buffalo), 1966. 662p. (DA 27:836-A)
Published under the title Disturbed Youth and Ethnic Family Patterns (Albany: State University of New York, 1971). This study was primarily concerned with the differential effects that ethnic groups have upon adolescent adjustments. It was proposed that adolescents socialized with the familial framework of one-ethnic group would show different patterns of values, adjustment processes, and disturbance modality from those adolescents socialized within the framework of the other ethnic group. The groups of disturbed adolescents would differ from the control groups by a greater intensification of ethnic-reaction patterns; their disturbance modality being a function of ethnic characteristics. (A)

974. Stofflet, Elliot H. A Study of National and Cultural Differences in Criminal Tendency. Columbia, 1935. 60p.

Published under the same title (New York: Columbia University Press, 1935). In this study the criminal tendencies as indicated by the type of crime committed by immigrants of various national groups (e.g., Poles, Italians) are compared with the tendencies exhibited by American-born descendants of the same nationality in order to determine whether the criminal tendencies are natural or cultural in nature.

975. Stuart, Irving R. A Study of Factors Associated with Inter-Group Conflict in the Ladies' Garment Industry in New York City. New York, 1952. 226p. (DA 12:226)
This study investigates the relationship between economic competition and racial and nationality prejudice by examining the reported industrial experiences of different ethnic groups from 1890 to 1947. The ladies' garment industry, considered a traditionally "immigrant" field, was selected for intensive study of the processes by which newcomers are integrated into crafts that required varying levels of skill and experience. For purposes of bringing the study up to date, the Business Agents of the Dressmakers' Union, Local 22 of the International Ladies' Garment Workers' Union, who are concerned with adjusting grievances, were interviewed concerning the nature of the relations among the ethnic groups that make up the 27,000 members of the union. It was understood that their reports represented value judgments. (A)

976. Sullivan, Margaret J. Hyphenism in St. Louis, 1900-1921: The View from Outside. St. Louis, 1968. 335p. (DA 29: 2658-A)
"Hyphenism in St. Louis" investigated the devotion of immigrants and their descendants to some country or concept in addition to their loyalty to the United States in the period from the turn of the century to immigration restriction in 1921. Hyphenates fell into two groups. Old immigrants, their children, and their grandchildren made up the mature hyphenisms. No longer strangers in America dependent upon one another for aid, protection, and companionship, the German-Americans, Irish-Americans, and German-Jewish-Americans had become an integral part of St. Louis's social, economic, and political life. New immigration supplied the city with nascent hyphenates. Still more foreign than American, they were in the process of building the ghettos that would give them the needed security and experience to eventually enter fully into American life. (A)

977. Supervielle, Alfredo F. The Bilingual Bicultural Communities and the Teaching of Foreign Languages and Cultures in the United States. Florida State, 1973. 135p.

978. Swain, Bruce M. Majority and Minority Americans: A Content Analysis of Magazine Fiction in 1962 and 1968. Columbia (Teachers College), 1970. 92p. (DA 31:3185-A)
White Protestant characters enjoyed as favored a position in American magazine fiction of 1962 and 1968 as they had 25 years earlier. The lot of minority-group characters in such fiction,

however, gradually improved through the years. That is one of
the major findings of this study, a content analysis of short fiction published in Saturday Evening Post, Cosmopolitan, Ladies'
Home Journal, True Story, and True Confession during 1962 and
1968. The purpose of the study was to investigate the differential
treatment provided characters who were portrayed as members
of various ethnic groups. (A)

979. Syrjamaki, John. Mesabi Communities: A Study of Their
Development. Yale, 1940. 216p.
Includes many notices of Slovenes, Italians, Finns, and other
immigrant groups.

980. Terwilliger, Marlene P. Jews and Italians and the Socialist
Party, New York City, 1901-1917: A Study of Class, Ethnicity, and Class Consciousness. Union Graduate School,
1977. 123p. (DA 39:506)
The purpose of this study was to explain the relationship between
class, ethnicity, and revolutionary class consciousness. The
author chose to do this by focusing on the Italian and East European Jewish immigrants in New York City between 1901 and 1917
and by attempting to explain the different relationships of these
two ethnic groups to the Socialist Party. Both the Italian and
Jewish immigration to the U.S. reached great proportions just
prior to the turn of the century. Both groups settled in New
York in similar residential areas, worked at similar occupations,
and experienced similar forms of discrimination. They did not,
however, have a similar orientation toward the Socialist Party.
Italians were but a small minority of the New York SP, while
the Jews constituted a major proportion of the Party. To explain this difference the author examined: (1) the cultural and
historical experience of the two groups; (2) their experience in
New York; and (3) the nature of the New York Socialist Party
itself. (A)

981. Thacker, Charlene M. Ethnic Change in the Urban Subarea:
A Study of the Dynamics of Residential Mobility. Fordham,
1973. 247p. (DA 34:5345-A)
The focus of the present study was the rapidly changing racial
and ethnic character of the population of the Tremont section of
the Bronx in New York City. The study area was delineated in
terms of census-tract boundaries and corresponded in large
measure to one of the city's community-planning districts, District 6. Census data were used to document the changing racial
and ethnic character as well as the changing age structure of the
area from 1950 through 1970. In addition to ethnic and age comparisons, educational, occupational, and income levels in Tremont were compared with respective levels in the city and the
borough for the years 1950 and 1960. Since residential mobility
was seen as the key factor in the rapidly changing racial and
ethnic composition of the study-area population, it was proposed
that empirical findings from the study of differential mobility and
of intraurban mobility patterns would provide insight into the
dynamics of racial and ethnic change in the urban subarea. (A)

982. Thatcher, Mary A. Immigrants and the 1930s: Ethnicity and Alienage in Depression and On-Coming War. California (Los Angeles), 1973. 342p. (DA 34:7172-A)
During the 1920s the United States adopted a policy of immigration restriction that reduced considerably the annual inflow of newcomers. Nearly a third of all Americans in 1930, nevertheless, were either foreign-born or the children of immigrants. In view of the public debate attendant on the quota legislation of the 1920s, strangely neither general histories nor specialized immigration accounts pay adequate attention to the status of immigrants during the ensuing decade. This dissertation attempts to determine in what ways the Depression experience of newer Americans was unique. The study focuses on immigrants from Europe and on the federal government's attitude toward them. Only occasional references are made to immigrants from other areas and to the particular problems of the Jewish refugees from Nazi Germany. Chief emphasis is placed on the Hoover and Roosevelt administrations and on their contemporary Congresses, with only slight treatment of developments at lower government levels. (A)

983. Thernstrom, Stephan A. Class and Mobility in a Nineteenth Century City: A Study of Unskilled Laborers in Newburyport, Massachusetts. Harvard, 1962. 285p.
Published under the title Poverty and Progress: Social Mobility in a Nineteenth Century City (Cambridge, Massachusetts: Harvard University Press, 1964). Includes detailed notices of Irish immigrant workers.

984. Tregoe, Benjamin B. Assimilation and the Parent-Child Relationship: A Study of Ethnic Conformity and the Socialization of Agression and Dependency in Four Ethnic Groups. Harvard, 1956. 163p.
Groups studied are Irish, Italian, Portuguese, and French Canadian.

985. Tsushima, William T. A Comparative Study of the Attitudes of Irish and Italian Patients of Two Social Levels Under Pre-Operative Stress. Fordham, 1967. 101p. (DA 28:1216-B)
The aim of this study was to investigate some of the attitudinal and emotional differences that persons stemming from different ethnic and socioeconomic backgrounds in the United States manifest in their reactions to surgery. The results of a number of research projects indicate that there is a relationship between patterns of behavior and subcultural groupings. These findings imply that cultural differences in family structure and practices play a critical role in personality development. If indeed there are distinct patterns of behavior among American ethnic groups and social classes, then differences should be observable when comparing the reactions of persons from different subcultural backgrounds in a stressful situation, such as surgery. (A)

986. Wall, Muriel F. A Content Analysis of the Treatment of Ethnic Minorities in Current Education Newsletters. New

York, 1979. 197p. (DA 40:1344-A)
This study involved an analysis of the content of selected education newsletters published in the United States for the period of one year, 1976-1977, to determine the extent to which the multiethnic diversity of American life is reflected in these publications. Specifically, answers to these questions were sought: Which group of people are most evident in this medium based on the amount of space allocated to each, in terms of their racial, religious, and national backgrounds? What proportion of space is allocated to each group in relation to their population in the United States? Do federally funded education newsletters reflect the multi-ethnic diversity of American life more than those published by institutions which are not federally funded? (A)

987. Weisz, Howard R. Irish-American and Italian-American Educational Views and Activities, 1870-1900: A Comparison. Columbia, 1968. 477p. (DA 31:2861-A)
Published under the same title (New York: Arno, 1976). Irish-Americans established the Catholic parochial-school system in the 1840s because they were convinced that public schools were agents of Protestant proselytism. They continued to found and support their own schools after King James-version Bible-reading disappeared from the public school curriculum because they believed that a religious education was necessary to counter the secular influences in American life. Although Irish-Americans supported Catholic schools with a large portion of their financial resources, they have continually, and without success, demanded state aid to Catholic education as a contribution to the public welfare. Although Catholic schools have been Irish institutions, dominated by predominantly Irish faculties and administrative staffs, presenting an Irish expression of Catholicism, they have undermined Irish identity by culturally Anglicizing and Romanizing their students.
In this study of American Catholic parochial education Weisz indicates that Italian-Americans have been far less committed than the Irish to Catholic schools and are more inclined to use public school facilities. He suggests that reason for this difference is that the Irish more than the Italians connect their ethnic and religious identities. Perhaps if the Italians in the old country had been victims of the imperialism of a Protestant power and like the Irish confronted early nineteenth-century Anglo-American Protestant nativism, they might have shared the Irish commitment to Catholicism as an expression of ethnic identity.

988. Weitz, Marvin. Black Attitudes to Jews in the United States from World War II to 1976. Yeshiva, 1977. 432p. (DA 38:5646)
This thesis attempts to document the development of black attitudes to Jews since World War II through study and analysis of statements and events among black intellectual, political, religious, factional, and organizational leaders, as seen in their writings, speeches, conferences, journals, newspapers, and other mass media. Focusing on urban America, where large populations of blacks and Jews facilitate contacts, examination suggests

that although blacks and Jews have much in common and were allied in some ways through the Civil Rights movement, there was latent hostility to Jews in the black community even before World War II. With the growth of black militancy in the 50s and 60s this hostility expanded and was openly expressed in many quarters. Militant identification with Arab and Third World nations as fellow "oppressed peoples" excluded Israel, seeing it as an oppressive power. There was militant anti-Zionism in the rhetoric of many black spokespeople, often involving personal condemnation of Jews supporting Israel. (A)

989. Wessel, Bessie B. An Ethnic Survey of Woonsocket, Rhode Island. Columbia, 1931. 290p.
Published under the same title (Chicago: University of Chicago Press, 1931). A statistical study describing the public school population in terms of geographic origin, ethnic ancestry, ethnic fusion, and the degree of "Americanism." The data were obtained from reports on 4,978 schoolchildren, with information concerning parents and grandparents.

990. White, George C. Immigration and Assimilation: A Survey of Social Thought and Public Opinion, 1882-1914. Pennsylvania, 1952. 163p.

991. Willie, Charles V. Socio-Economic and Ethnic Areas of Syracuse, New York. Syracuse, 1958. 327p. (DA 18:326)
This analysis tests three major theories of urban organization. The ecological organization of Syracuse in 1950 is analyzed according to the concentric circle, the sector, and the multiple-nuclei theories of urban structure. Also an analysis is made of the distribution of occupational, educational, and age characteristics throughout the city. Census tabulations are the chief source of data, and census tracts are the basic units of analysis. Socioeconomic and ethnic areas are delineated. (A)

992. Woodland, L. A. Ottawa Irish, 1825-1870: A Study in Acculturation. British Columbia, 1973. 245p.

993. Wozniak, Paul R. Assimilation into Pan-Catholicism: A Sociological Study of Structural Assimilation Among Catholic National Origins Groups. Massachusetts, 1967. 181p. (DA 28:1542-A)
The primary objective of the study has been to examine the extent to which and the lines across which structural assimilation among the descendants of Catholic immigrants has occurred, and thereby to estimate the degrees to which various types of subsocieties are developing. It has been hypothesized that a white pan-Catholic subsociety is emerging as the dominant communal form among the Catholic population. However, the literature also indicated that nationality-background communalism has not yet completely disappeared and that communalism that transcends both religious and nationality (but not social-class) boundaries may be occurring.

994. Wu, Charles L. Attitudes Toward Negroes, Jews, and Orientals in the United States. Ohio State, 1927. 77p.
Published under the same title (Columbus, Ohio: Hendrick, 1930).

995. Young, Kimball. Mental Differences in Certain Immigrant Groups: Psychological Tests of South Europeans in Typical California Schools with Bearings on the Educational Policy and on the Problems of Racial Contacts in This Country. Stanford, 1921. 103p.
Published under the same title (Eugene: University of Oregon Publications, Vol. 1, No. 11, July 1922).

996. Young, William L. A Study of the Attitudes of High School Students Towards Groups That Are Different in Race, Religion, and Nationality. Pittsburgh, 1946. 263p.

IV. EMIGRATION/IMMIGRATION:
HISTORY, POLITICS, ECONOMICS, AND POLICY

997. Adams, Russell B. Migration Geography: A Methodological Inquiry and United States Case Study. Minnesota, 1969. 968p. (DA 30:3700-B)
The study of human migration is a multi-disciplinary endeavor involving locational and motivational variables; areal contrasts are generators of migration streams, while individual movement is a perceptual phenomenon. Information flow and the ability to move are basic determinants of movement decisions; research measures and evaluates their occurrence indirectly in terms of distance, connectivity, and differential mobility rates of various population strata, such as age, sex, income, and occupation. (A)

998. Aldana, Manuel S. The International Responsibility of States for Injuries to Aliens in Recent International Law. Minnesota, 1966. 507p. (DA 27:2583-A)
Several factors have contributed to the renascence of the topic of the international responsibility of states for injuries to aliens. The increasing trend to accord to entities other than states the status of "subjects" of international law opens the way toward the express recognition that in matters of diplomatic protection, it is the right of the alien that is being vindicated. The separate, scholarly drafts prepared by Garcia-Amador and by the Harvard Law School demonstrate the practicability and the convenience of such recognition. Although it may not be disputed that as a consequence of the decision of the International Court of Justice in the Reparations case the theoretical obstacle toward the recognition of entities other than states as bearers of international rights and duties and, consequently, as subjects of international responsibility, may now be said to have been overcome, the express recognition of the rights of the alien in matters of diplomatic protection has met with reluctance among states.

999. Alexander, Norman. Rights of Aliens Under the Federal Constitution. Columbia, 1931. 153p.

1000. Alvarez, Gabriel C. Permanent Migration and Some Structural Correlates: A Comparative Analysis of Recent International Migration. Chicago, 1975. 240p. (DA 36:4789-A)
The study is an attempt at doing a comparative assessment of the out-migration of high-level manpower, as seen within the

perspective of recent international migration. Its primary concern is to evaluate how certain factors are related with recent migratory movements. It contends that some structural correlates are relevant in explaining the migration of highly qualified persons, and recent international migratory movements, in general. The analytical framework adopted considers the following as relevant structural correlates: (1) the level of education; (2) the level of manpower utilization, and (3) the level of socioeconomic development of sending countries.

1001. Anderson, Samuel K. A History of Labor in the Inland Empire During the Early Frontier Period. Washington State, 1960. 222p. (DA 21:2254)

This is a study of the emergence of a laboring force in an American frontier region, the Inland Empire of the Pacific Northwest. The region is defined as the area between the Rocky Mountains and the Cascades, and between the northern Great Bend of the Columbia and the plateaus of central Oregon. Until the 1840s the primary economic activity of the region was the fur trade, and Part I deals with the fur-trade laborer. The trade was dominated by three great corporations, one succeeding another, the last and most powerful, the Hudson's Bay Company, having monopolized the Inland Empire trade after 1821. Like its predecessors this company exercised great power over its employees. It was able, for example, to recruit an extremely cosmopolitan labor force, especially of French Canadians and Iroquois from Quebec, Scots, and Hawaiians. Only during the period of decline did it need to rely heavily upon local labor.

1002. Arafat, Ibtihaj S. The Foreign Stock and the Native Stock in the United States: A Demographic Profile. Oklahoma State, 1970. 138p. (DA 31:6171-A)

The study was a comparative analysis of the differences and similarities in demographic characteristics between the native-born with native-born parents (third-generation Americans), the native-born with foreign-born or mixed parentage (second-generation Americans), and the foreign-born with foreign-born parents (first-generation Americans). In the 1960 Census the Bureau of the Census combined the first- and second-generation Americans in a single category termed "foreign stock." For the purpose of this study a control sample composed of all of the third-generation Americans in the United States, and a study sample composed of all of the first- and second-generation Americans, namely, the foreign stock, in the United States were taken from the 1960 Census 1-in-a-1,000 sample tape.

1003. Avery, D. H. Canadian Immigration Policy and the Alien Question, 1896-1919: The Anglo-Canadian Perspective. Western Ontario, 1973. 310p.

1004. Bactel, D. L. A Comparative Analysis of Recent In-Migrants from Urban Areas and Long-Term Rural Residents' Attitudes Towards Rural Industrial Development: A Multi-

County Study in Southeastern Ohio. Ohio State, 1978. 180p.
This research analyzes the attitudes toward rural industrial development held by recent immigrants from urban areas and longterm rural residents within a five-county area located in the Appalachian region of Ohio. The social-scale theoretical perspective created for this study views the changes taking place within rural areas as one component of the gradual urbanization of less complex social structures. Special emphasis within the theory is placed upon increasing societal interdependence and its contribution to the gradual elimination of many of the previous identifiable differences that have existed between rural and urban groups.

1005. Baldwin, D. O. Political and Social Behavior in Ontario, 1879-1891: A Quantitative Approach. York, 1973. 276p.
Parts of this dissertation deal with political power among Irish immigrants, and the delineation of a measurable Irish Catholic vote, which shifted to the Conservative party in this period.

1006. Becker, Sarah. The Attack on Aliens in the United States, 1917-1921. Wisconsin, 1935. 167p.

1007. Bernard, William S. Naturalization in Its Social Setting in the United States. Yale, 1934. 143p.

1008. Bicha, Karel D. Canadian Immigration Policy and the American Farmer, 1896-1914. Minnesota, 1963. 206p. (DA 25:6559)
The last three decades of the nineteenth century witnessed a rapid decline in agricultural opportunity in the Middle West and Plains states. The long agricultural depression of 1873-1896 dispossessed many farmers, while the rapid increase in land prices after 1896 and the scarcity of virgin land put farm ownership out of the reach of many farmers. For many rural residents of the Middle West and Plains states life on the farm was synonymous with a heavy mortgage burden or permanent tenant status. To improve their economic position farmers resorted to economic organization, political protest, and migration to marginal areas in the Southwest, the Great Basin, and the cutover portion of the Lake states. Many abandoned the farm for the city. Others chose a final alternative: migration to the vast, unexploited Canadian prairie region. (A)

1009. Bigelow, Bruce L. Ethnic Stratification in a Pedestrian City: A Social Geography of Syracuse, New York in 1860. Syracuse, 1978. 445p. (DA 40:459-A)
Syracuse, New York, has been chosen for a case study of the social geography of an early industrial pedestrian city. Syracuse was appropriate because it was of common size (about 30, 000 in 1860), had both an industrial and commercial economic base, and had about the same number of Irish Catholics and German Christians, the two largest immigrant minorities in antebellum America. The native population, mainly New Yorkers of Yankee (New Eng-

Emigration/Immigration 241

land) heritage, and the German Christians created extensive residential districts, while the Irish lived in small pockets about the city. Two small minorities, the Jews and blacks, also clustered near their houses of worship, although they did not numerically dominate any blocks. Congregation by occupational status was much weaker than by ethnic group. Congregation by family-status variables, such as age of household head, household size, and number of children, was even weaker than for status. Domestics per household was an excellent index of upper-class areas. (A)

1010. Billington, Ray A. The Origins of Nativism in the United States, 1800-1844. Harvard, 1933. 436p. Published under the same title (New York: Arno, 1974); also published as Protestant Crusade, 1800-1860: A Study of the Origins of American Nativism (New York: Macmillan, 1938). The arrival of large numbers of Irish Catholic immigrants during the 1830s and 1840s touched off fears, propaganda onslaughts, and eventually riots, which would perhaps have led to more open and widespread conflicts had not the conflicts over Mexico and then slavery intervened. In this richly documented manuscript Billington tells the story of the burning of the Ursuline Convent outside cultured Boston and of Bishop Hughes's battle for an equitable share of the monies allotted to non-Catholic schools and his adventure into municipal politics in New York City. He describes the drive of the American Native Association to repeal the naturalization acts, the rise of the American Republican Party, and the bloody riots in Philadelphia. Billington shows how--a decade before the Know Nothing Party--the impending religious conflict had moved "from fantasies of propagandists' pens to an important place in the sun of American political life."

1011. Booker, Henry M. Efforts of the South to Attract Immigrants, 1860-1900. Virginia, 1965. 157p. (DA 26:6430) The unwillingness of the immigrant to come to the South can be explained by the divergence of wage rates between the North and South for this period. Wages, both on a nominal and real basis, were higher in the North than the South from 1860 to 1900. The thesis shows that a great deal of effort was put forth by the Southerners to turn the immigrants toward the South. All the southern states established immigration bureaus, advertised in Europe extensively, and sent agents to Europe to recruit settlers. Counties, cities, and private organizations and individuals also joined in the promotion effort of the South. Yet, immigrants refrained from coming to the South in any large numbers throughout the period under study.

1012. Brite, John D. The Attitude of European States Toward Emigration to the American Colonies and the United States, 1607-1820. Chicago, 1938. 143p.

1013. Buckland, Roscoe L. Anglo-Saxonism in America, 1880-1898. Iowa, 1955. 231p. (DA 15:1618) This study examines the belief in the superiority of those people called "Anglo-Saxons" and their institutions as that belief was expressed between 1880 and the outbreak of the Spanish-American War. Writings and speeches of public figures, work of scholars, and literature of the period were studied to discover the pattern of thought and to determine the relation between Anglo-Saxonism and some problems of the period.

1014. Cannon, M. Hamlin. The "Gathering" of British Mormons to Western America: A Study in Religious Migration. American, 1950. 265p.

1015. Carey, John J. Progressives and the Immigrant, 1885-1915. Connecticut, 1968. 180p. (DA 29:2634-A)
Within the urban-reform spectrum welfare-type organizations, such as social settlements, charitable societies, and allied groups in such major immigrant centers as New York City, Chicago, and Boston, had the most prolonged and intimate contact with the foreign-born. To identify the reform element concerned with immigrants the careers of several hundred individuals associated with social work were inspected. This investigation yielded a reform cadre of 60 individuals--mostly directors and long-time workers in welfare-type agencies--who invested a major part of their lives to bettering the lot of the immigrant. In creating reform programs related to the immigrant social workers were influenced in a significant way by reform spokespeople who created the intellectual case for betterment activities. (A)

1016. Carino, Ledivina V. Structural Conditions and Professional Migration: A Study of the Movement of Scientists, Engineers, and Medical Personnel into the United States, 1965-1967. Indiana, 1970. 284p. (DA 31:6728-A)
The central hypothesis of this study is that certain structural properties of sending countries served as push factors for migration. Within the fields of natural science, social science, engineering, and medicine, as well as a summary field involving all four, the author tested how two sets of factors affected the migration rate to the United States in 1965 to 1967. The first set was called "primary" because the factors were expected to provide the initial push. The secondary group included factors that affected the choice of destination. Specifically, it was posited that American professional immigration would be high only where both factor-sets were strong. The findings tended to support the central hypothesis in both its general and specific forms.

1017. Cavanaugh, Francis P. Immigration Restriction at Work Today: A Study of the Administration of Immigration Restriction by the United States. Catholic, 1928. 116p.
Published under the same title (Washington, D.C.: Catholic University Press, 1928). Emphasis is on 1924 law then in operation. Includes introductory chapters on the origins and development of sentiment for restriction of immigration into the United States, and a major attention to the administrative aspects of immigration legislation.

1018. Chandler, Clarence W. The Rhetoric of Exclusion: Arguments of "The People" on Behalf of Immigration Restriction. Florida, 1977. 141p. (DA 38:6394)
This study considers a rhetorical movement as a function of four elements: (1) a goal, (2) collective effort striving toward the goal often resulting in (3) drama, and (4) a resolution of the movement, be it denial or confirmation of the goal. With respect to the movement to limit immigration this thesis notes that all elements have been studied by historians, but that resolution has often been viewed by students of public communication as a mere counting of votes, or an examination of election results. It is held here that resolution might be viewed in a more meaningful manner by students of public communication.

1019. Clark, Jane P. Deportation of Aliens from the United States to Europe. Columbia, 1931. 240p.
Published under the same title (New York: Columbia University Press, 1931).

1020. Cochran, Mary E. A History of Restriction of American Immigration, 1607-1820. Chicago, 1930. 294p.

1021. Comay, Peter Y. International Migration of Professional Manpower: The Canada-United States Case. Princeton, 1969. 209p. (DA 31:525-A)
Geographic mobility of labor is only one of several dimensions of mobility; on the whole labor displays least flexibility in its willingness to change geographic location. This may help to explain why so little has been done until recently to place geographic mobility within a theoretic structure. The re-emergence of the notion of "human capital" has given a new perspective on migration in general and highlighted migration of high-level manpower in particular. Such people have been shown to embody vast amounts of capital, the creation and maintenance of which requires the investment of scarce resources both by the individual and by the nation. The human-capital approach has also changed attitudes toward study abroad. (A)

1022. Curran, Thomas J. Know Nothings of New York. Columbia, 1963. 366p. (DA 24:4645)
In New York State in the middle of the nineteenth century, industrialism, urbanism, and immigration upset the older residents of the state. Many conservative New Yorkers turned to political nativism--that is, restrictions upon the political rights of the foreign-born--to provide an escape from the unwanted changes that they faced. Since the Democrats catered to the foreign-born, especially the Irish Catholics, the earlier political nativists found their chief support among the Whigs.

1023. Davis, Lawrence B. The Baptist Response to Immigration in the United States, 1880-1925. Rochester, 1968. 341p. (DA 29:1490-A)
Published under the title Immigrants, Baptists, and the Protes-

tant Mind in America (Urbana: University of Illinois Press, 1973). The years from the 1880s, when the Chinese problem of California led Congress to pass the first major restrictive immigration legislation in the United States, to the passage of the National Origins Act in 1924 were marked by an increasing attention to the influx pouring into America from the Old World. Many of the reactions of white Protestant America at this time are revealed in microcosm in the literature of the Northern Baptists. This dissertation traces their social and intellectual response to the newcomers through the use of the denominational records of the American Baptist Home Mission Society, the Northern Baptist Convention, and other Baptist organizations, along with the various independent Baptist weekly newspapers.

1024. Delkay, Della L. From Melting Pot to Cultural Pluralism: An Examination of the "New" Immigrants As Treated in Secondary American History Textbooks, 1950-1978. Columbia (Teachers College), 1979. 330p. (DA 40:1919-A)
Beginning in the mid-sixties cultural pluralists became increasingly critical of social-studies instruction in secondary schools. These educators charge that the social-studies curriculum has traditionally used the melting-pot concept to characterize American nationhood. In their opinion, by advocating this notion the schools have failed to reflect the importance and reality of ethnicity in American society. They levy four major charges against secondary American-history textbooks that emphasize the melting-pot concept of nationhood. In their opinion these works (1) promote prejudice against members of minority groups; (2) ignore the contributions that minority-group citizens have made to American society; (3) de-emphasize the social and economic oppression suffered by many ethnic groups; and (4) ignore the persistence of ethnicity in American society. This dissertation investigates the validity of these charges and the effectiveness of the cultural pluralists' efforts to reform these textbooks. (A)

1025. Dimmitt, Marius A. The Enactment of the McCarran-Walter Act of 1952. Kansas, 1970. 297p. (DA 31:5980-A)
The purpose of this study is to explore and narrate the events leading to the enactment of the McCarran-Walter Act, more properly known as the Immigration and Nationality Act of 1952.
The Act of 1952 codified existing policy, reaffirming the national-origins quota system and the general restrictive nature of the law. World War II and the Cold War created a number of conditions that seemed to necessitate a comprehensive reconsideration of this policy. The policy was broadened, on the one hand, by legislation granting small quotas to Orientals, admitting war brides and fiancées of American servicemen, and admitting displaced persons from Europe. On the other hand, postwar frustrations and Cold War anxieties intensified and were projected against "subversive" and "foreign" elements in the form of internal-security legislation. This legislation strengthened immigration and nationality policy by giving officials more authority in excluding and deporting "undesirable" aliens.

Emigration/Immigration

1026. Divine, Robert A. American Immigration Policy, 1924-1952. Yale, 1954. 264p.
Published under the same title (New Haven, Connecticut: Yale University Press, 1957). A comprehensive review of immigration-restriction policy across the nineteenth century through the National Origins Quota Act, displaced-persons legislation, and the McCarran-Walter Act.

1027. Egelman, William S. The Debate over Ethnicity, 1900-1924: A Sociohistorical Analysis. Fordham, 1979. 196p.
This study examines the intellectual conflict that took place over the concept of ethnicity and the maintenance of ethnic identities in the United States. It aims to fulfill the following objectives: (1) to explain why groups of scholars living in the same society can come to have perceptions of the world that are diametrically opposed to one another; and (2) to utilize the concept of ideology and insights drawn from the sociology of knowledge in order to add to the clarity and understanding of the reasons behind the debate over ethnicity.

1028. Erickson, Charlotte J. The Recruitment of European Immigrant Labor for American Industry, 1860-1885. Cornell, 1952. 269p.
Published under the title American Industry and the European Immigrant, 1860-1885 (Cambridge, Massachusetts: Harvard University Press, 1957). Deals mainly with the immigrants and the general problem of contract labor. Shows that those few immigrants who came to America under contract were skilled craftspeople. A less formal system of contract labor involved mortgage-secured loans provided to immigrants needing fare to America by steamship companies.

1029. Falk, Gerhard. The Immigration of the European Professors and Intellectuals to the United States and Particularly the Niagara Frontier During the Nazi Era, 1933-1941. State University of New York (Buffalo), 1970. 301p. (DA 31:1584-A)
This dissertation is intended to describe the assimilation process with reference to the German-speaking academicians who settled in the United States between 1933 and 1941. It is, of course, understood that scholars from many other countries have entered the United States since colonial days and that the German contribution is not the only example of academic assimilation. However, it is contended here that the German-speaking professors who assimilated successfully in American culture subsequently made numerous contributions to higher education and scholarship in America and that those German-speaking professors unable to make a contribution were also unable to assimilate successfully and vice versa.

1030. Feingold, Henry L. The Politics of Rescue: A Study of American Diplomacy and Politics Related to the Rescue of Refugees, 1938-1944. New York, 1966. 500p. (DA 27:3793-A)

Published under the title The Politics of Rescue: The Roosevelt Administration and the Holocaust, 1938-1944 (New Brunswick, New Jersey: Rutgers University Press, 1970). The purpose of this dissertation is to examine the Roosevelt administration's rescue policy during the Nazi holocaust. It falls logically into four chronological subdivisions: first is the period from March 1938 to September 1939, when the war broke out; the next period ends with the attack on Pearl Harbor in December 1941, when the United States became an active belligerent; the following period stretches to November 1943; and the final period takes us to the end of 1944.

1031. Foley, Allen R. From French Canadian to Franco-American: A Study of the Immigration of the French Canadian into New England, 1650-1935. Harvard, 1939. 364p.

1032. Fought, John P. News and Editorial Treatment of Alleged Reds and Radicals by Selected Newspapers and Periodicals During 1918-21. Southern Illinois, 1970. 248p. (DA 31: 5345-A)
This study examined certain newspapers and journals of opinion for evidence of bias in news and editorial treatment of events concerning radicals in the post-World War I period. Five major topics were isolated for study: (1) the trial, conviction, and imprisonment of Eugene V. Debs, Socialist candidate for President; (2) the trial and conviction of Victor L. Berger, Socialist U. S. Representative from Milwaukee, Wisconsin; (3) the steel strike of 1919; (4) the coal strike of 1919; and (5) the so-called Red scare, which culminated in the deportations of undesirable aliens to Russia.

1033. Franklin, Frank G. Naturalization in the United States with Especial Reference to Its Legislative History from the Declaration of Independence to the Civil War. Chicago, 1900. 261p.
Published under the title The Legislative History of Naturalization in the United States: From the Revolutionary War to 1861 (Chicago: University of Chicago Press, 1906).

1034. Friedman, Saul S. Official United States Policy Toward Jewish Refugees, 1938-1945. Ohio State, 1969. 425p. (DA 30:4370-A)
Published under the title No Haven for the Oppressed: United States Policy Toward Jewish Refugees, 1938-1945 (Detroit: Wayne State University Press, 1973). This study indicates that throughout the Hitler epoch American anti-Semitism, repeatedly expressed in public-opinion surveys, combined with self-concern born of the Depression and anti-alienism rampant in the halls of Congress, prevented President Roosevelt from inaugurating changes in this country's immigration policies. America's entry into World War II provided the additional convenient rationalization for restrictionism--the priority of winning the war. The United States government, in a series of conferences designed more for propaganda

Emigration/Immigration

effect than action, elected to treat the Jewish question in circuitous euphemisms rather than with decisive planning.

1035. Frye, Robert J. Deportation of Aliens: A Study in Civil Liberties. Florida, 1959. 552p. (DA 20:2876)
The problem of deportation of aliens is the problem of reconciliation of two competing concepts. One concept is based on the idea that the power to deport arises from the same source as the power to exclude aliens: namely, the inherent authority of a sovereign nation to protect itself from the presence of undesirable aliens. This principle was expounded in 1892 in Fong Yue Ting v. United States, the landmark decision of the Supreme Court. A corollary of this concept is the principle that deportation is a civil proceeding. Thus, the constitutional principles, guarantees, and remedies applicable to criminal proceedings do not prevail. The second concept is based on the idea that aliens enjoy certain residual rights under the Constitution that may not be denied them without affording them the same guarantees as those available to citizens. (A)

1036. Garis, Roy L. Immigration Restrictions: A Study of the Opposition to and Regulation of Immigration into the United States. Columbia, 1927. 327p.
Published under the same title (New York: Macmillan, 1927).

1037. George, Neil J. The Interplay of Domestic and Foreign Considerations in United States Immigration Policy. Case Western Reserve, 1975. 268p. (DA 36:3980-A)
This is a study of the process of United States immigration-policy formulation. It examines the issue from its historical origins to the most recent attempt by formal representatives of the United States government to establish an acceptable, lasting, public policy. Elsewhere limited attention has been given to immigration from the perspective of public-policy analysis. Existing studies, viewed collectively, suggest an ambiguous understanding of the domestic and foreign interrelationships of immigration policy. Some consider immigration to be a domestic issue; others classify it as foreign policy. This research sought to determine if United States immigration-policy formulation regularly defied such a sharp policy classification.

1038. Glidden, William B. Casualties of Caution: Alien Enemies in America, 1917-1919. Illinois (Urbana), 1970. 431p. (DA 31:6496-A)
There were 4 million aliens in the United States who had come from Germany or Austria-Hungary and were technically classified as "alien Enemies" during the First World War. Under an old statute the federal authorities exercised summary powers over them. The Justice Department regulated the domestic and foreign travel of German men and women, confiscated their guns, demanded respect for the flag and at least outward political conformity and support for the war effort, restricted their places of residence and employment, and caused them to register with local

police departments or postmasters. People believed to be potentially dangerous were quietly and swiftly arrested, without knowing their accusers or the reason for their arrest, and subsequently were either paroled on bond and under strict supervision or sent to an internment camp for the duration of the war. Austro-Hungarian aliens were less constrained in their activities and movements, but they too were subject to summary arrest and internment. (A)

1039. Gragg, Larry D. Migration in Early America: The Virginia Quaker Experience. Missouri, 1978. 190p. (DA 39:6297-A)
Students of pre-industrial populations have long been frustrated by an inability to examine the migration of any sizable group of people. Consequently little is definitely known about why preindustrial people moved or who among them was likely to be a migrant. The Quakers living in eighteenth-century Virginia provide the first good opportunity to examine a significant migration stream in early America. They not only participated in the large-scale migration to America's backcountry, but they also maintained the best demographic records of any group in their era. The data collected on the lives of 2,445 Quaker migrants provided the information needed to develop a profile of those Friends most likely to move, to determine from where they moved and to what destinations, and to explain why they chose to move.

1040. Gutman, Herbert G. Social and Economic Structure and Depression: American Labor in 1873 and 1874. Wisconsin, 1959. 245p. (DA 20:130)
Considerable attention is paid to the role of immigrants in the labor force.

1041. Hamilton, Bertha. Colonization of Pennsylvania, 1681-1701. Wisconsin, 1932. 240p.

1042. Hansen, Marcus L. Emigration from Continental Europe 1815-1860, with Special Reference to the United States. Harvard, 1924. 306p.
The dissertation forms the basis of the author's The Atlantic Migration, 1607-1860: A History of the Continuing Settlement of the United States (Cambridge, Massachusetts: Harvard University Press, 1940).

1043. Hartmann, Edward G. The Movement to Americanize the Immigrant. Columbia, 1948. 276p.
Published under the same title (New York: Columbia University Press, 1948). A detailed history of the "Americanization" movement as developed by social agencies and federal and state governments, and largely supported by the greater society.

1044. Hassencahl, Frances J. Harry H. Laughlin, "Expert Eugenics Agent" for the House Committee on Immigration and

Naturalization, 1921 to 1931. Case Western Reserve, 1970.
441p. (DA 32:576-A)
Studies by Ralph Huitt, David N. Farnsworth, and David Truman show that often Congressional committees hold hearings to justify a decision already made rather than to formulate legislation. Members of a committee sometimes act as interest groups for a particular piece of legislation and select witnesses to buttress their ideas. This study examines one such witness, Harry H. Laughlin, who was appointed "Expert Eugenics Agent" for the House Committee on Immigration and Naturalization for the years 1921 to 1931.

1045. Heald, Morrell. Business Attitudes Toward European Immigration, 1861-1914. Yale, 1951. 509p. (DA 30:1957-A)
In the economic crisis of the closing decades of the nineteenth century business support for the free immigration policy faltered. Depression, unemployment, and falling wages reduced reliance on Europe for masses of cheap labor. Reappearing during the depression of the seventies, hostility toward immigration grew rapidly in business circles after 1882. Many businessmen held that immigration was making the problem of recovery more difficult. Some feared that the immigrants were responsible for the spread of radicalism among the working classes. Others believed that the low wages of European labor subjected American workers to unfair and degrading competition. Many came to feel that unregulated immigration was bringing more and more undesirable aliens to our shores. For such reasons businessmen supported the rising movement for immigration restriction, approving even such drastic measures as the literacy test.

1046. Henderson, Julia J. Foreign Labor in the United States, 1942-1945. Minnesota, 1945. 246p.

1047. Hendrickson, Homer O. The Religious Element in the Native American Movement in the North, 1835-1855. Northwestern, 1933. 240p.

1048. Herrick, Cheesman A. White Servitude in Pennsylvania: Indentured and Redemptive Labor in Colony and Commonwealth. Pennsylvania, 1899. 326p.
Expanded in 1926, and published in that year. (Reprint, Freeport, New York: Books for Libraries, 1970). Every example of colonial indentured servitude is examined, with particular reference to German immigrants. The information was gathered from contemporary official documents, such as the proceedings of the Pennsylvania legislature, and records of indentures, many of which are disclosed in the appendix. In addition, recourse was made to private papers and secondary works, listed in the 180-item bibliography. Facsimiles of types of documentary materials and a list of indentured servants with relevant data complement the work.

1049. Higham, John W. European Immigration in American Patriotic Thought, 1885-1925. Wisconsin, 1949. 330p.

The dissertation forms the basis of the author's Strangers in the Land: Patterns of American Nativism, 1860-1925 (New Brunswick, New Jersey: Rutgers University Press, 1955). Deals with the nativist response to immigration and restrictionist themes; includes an appraisal of the effects of the Immigration Act of 1924, which severely restricted immigration into the United States.

1050. Hill, Peter J. The Economic Impact of Immigration into the United States. Chicago, 1970. 276p.

1051. Horton, Billy D. The Ideology of Equal Opportunity and the Sociological Study of Race and Ethnic Relations: A Critique of the Relationship Between Liberal Ideology and Social Science. Kentucky, 1977. 482p. (DA 38:4519-A)
In the past decade American sociology has come under considerable criticism for its role as legitimator of and apologist for the dominant institutions and values of American society. One of the places where this ideological role of sociology has been apparent is in the sociological investigation of race and ethnicity in American society. With the racial explosions of the 1960s the inherited theoretical models and empiricistic methods of mainstream sociology proved inadequate to explain the black challenge to the white cultural hegemony. This thesis begins with the assumption that the failure of sociologists to foresee and explain adequately those radical events of the 1960s was largely due to their adherence to the central tenets of American liberalism. This dissertation is, consequently, both a critical analysis of the liberal hegemony and of the ideological role that sociology plays in its maintenance. (A)

1052. Hough, Leslie S. The Turbulent Spirit: Violence and Coaction Among Cleveland Workers, 1877-1899. Virginia, 1977. 212p. (DA 39:4446-A)
This study explores the development of working-class unrest, primarily in the iron, steel, and street-railway industries of Cleveland, Ohio, during the late nineteenth century. A model, or theoretical framework, drawn from the Tillys' Turbulent Century, serves as a basis for analyzing a series of protest events during the period. The changing attitude of Cleveland's workers toward the ownership class is understood as part of the economic and social changes that the city was undergoing, including increases in the size and scale of the urban setting and the factory workplace and the increasing heterogeneity of the city's work force.

1053. Irons, Peter H. America's Cold War Crusade: Domestic Policies and Foreign Policy, 1942-1948. Boston University, 1973. 406p. (DA 33:6842-A)
The post-World War II period of Cold War hostility between the United States and Soviet Union had many of the characteristics of a quasireligious crusade. This dissertation studies the formative years of this conflict, tracing it from the beginning of U.S.-Soviet

military alliance in 1942 and ending with the enactment of the Marshall Plan legislation and the Presidential election in 1948. The focus is upon the domestic roots of the Cold War, as reflected in the activities of several of the crucial domestic-interest groups with foreign-policy concerns.

1054. Jaffe, Erwin A. Passage of the McCarran-Walter Act: The Reiteration of American Immigration Policy. Rutgers, 1962. 354p. (DA 23:680)
At each stage in the adoption of restrictionist immigration policies Congress's central concern has been the problem of selectivity. By 1924 a complex qualitative system had been enacted that denied admission and citizenship to, and provided for the deportation of, physical, moral, and racial "undesirables." In passing the McCarran-Walter Act in 1952 Congress for the most part confirmed past policies.

1055. Jaffe, Julian F. The Anti-Radical Crusade in New York: 1914-1924, A Case Study of the Red Scare. New York, 1971. 643p. (DA 32:1443-A)
Published under the title Crusade Against Radicalism: New York During the Red Scare, 1914-1924 (Port Washington, New York: Kennikat, 1972). Previous historical studies have dealt with the Red Scare from a national viewpoint. This work approaches the subject from the vantage point of a single state: New York. It covers a time span of a decade. The material is arranged topically and includes developments on the local, state, and national levels. After a preliminary analysis of leftist groups on the eve of the Red Scare it explores the origins of the movement during the First World War. Subsequent chapters pertain to the work of the Lusk Committee, the expulsion of the Socialist Assemblyman, the Palmer Raids, the struggle against alleged subversive teachers, the activities of municipal governments, and cases of criminal anarchy. To probe the existing climate of opinion the author discusses attitudes toward the Left held by significant interest groups, in business, labor, and the church.

1056. Jaros, James A. The Gospel of Americanization: The Influence of the Protestant Economy of Salvation in Defining the Ideal of Immigrant Experience. Case Western Reserve, 1973. 297p. (DA 34:5062-A)
This study attempts to explore and evaluate the way the Protestant economy of salvation was used as a basis for defining and understanding the process of Americanization. The author examines the influence of the Protestant economy in the thinking and writing of a number of prominent exponents of immigrant Americanization who wrote during the years 1880 to 1920. His interest specifically centers on a number of home missionaries, particularly Josiah Strong, and three immigrant autobiographers, Jacob Riis, Edward A. Steiner, and Mary Antin.

1057. Keely, Charles B. The Immigration Act of 1965: A Study of the Relationship of Social Science Theory to Group In-

terest and Legislation. Fordham, 1970. 247p. (DA 31: 2513-A)
The study focuses on the relationship of social-science theories of assimilation to immigration legislation. There are two aspects to the problem. The first is the role of scientific theory in the process of adopting legislation and, second, the use of the results of legislation to test scientific propositions. Antecedents and consequences of the most recent major immigration legislation, the Immigration Act of 1965, are used for a case study of the problem.

1058.   Kelly, Mary G.   A History of Catholic Immigration Colonization Projects in the United States, 1815-1860.   Illinois (Urbana), 1939.   290p.
Published under the title Catholic Immigrant Colonization Projects in the United States, 1815-1860 (New York: United States Catholic Historical Society, 1939).

1059.   Kessler, James B.   The Political Factors in California's Anti-Alien Land Legislation, 1912-1913.   Stanford, 1958.   221p.   (DA 19:2380)
This study of the role of groups, personalities, and other factors in the enactment of legislation of international interest by a state, notwithstanding the opposition of the federal government, is based on materials in the Gubernatorial Papers of Hiram W. Johnson, the State Department Papers, and the papers of Woodrow Wilson, William Jennings Bryan, Theodore Roosevelt, Chester H. Rowell, William Kent, Franklin Hichborn, John P. Irish, John Randolph Haynes, James Duval Phelan, David Starr Jordan, Meyer Lissner, and others. These materials were supplemented by interviews with persons who were actively interested in the legislation and who were in Sacramento during the Fortieth Session of the California Legislature in 1913.   (A)

1060.   Killeen, Charles E.   John Siney: The Pioneer in American Industrial Unionism and Government.   Wisconsin, 1942.   211p.

1061.   Kimball, Clark D.   Patriotism and the Suppression of Dissent in Indiana During the First World War.   Indiana, 1971.   235p.   (DA 32:4747-A)
Determined to quash all signs of disloyalty, chauvinists drove suspected disloyalists from schools, churches, and places of employment; suppressed offensive publications; interfered with public meetings of Socialists and Peoples Council of America; harassed German churches and conscientious objectors; and threatened to make public examples of slackers. Patriots ousted German from the schools and forced all but one major German newspaper to cease publication. Banded together as protection or vigilance committees, they assumed the power of courts by summoning, interrogating, and even punishing recalcitrants. The Miami County Loyal Citizens Vigilance Committee terrorized the Peru area. Some members assaulted suspicious persons by beating

Emigration/Immigration 253

them, painting them, or forcing them to make superficial displays of loyalty through kissing the flag or contributing to a fund drive. Although denouncing such acts, Indiana defense and law-enforcement officials imposed no sanctions against those who used physical intimidation. (A)

1062. King, D. T. Speculative Adjustment and Market Efficiency: A Generalized Model of Labor Migration. Tulane, 1976. 316p.
This dissertation is an outgrowth of recent theoretical developments in economic theory that take account of the fact that economic agents usually operate largely on the basis of their forecasts of future developments that might affect their costs and returns, but always hold these forecasts with significant--though varying--levels of uncertainty. The recognition of this microeconomic behavior and the incorporation of it into the theory of individual economic choice quickly lead to clearly derivable and testable implications with respect to price behavior and resource usage and allocation.

1063. Kinzer, Donald L. The American Protective Association: A Study of Anti-Catholicism. University of Washington, 1954. 557p. (DA 14:970)
Published under the title An Episode in Anti-Catholicism: The American Protective Association (Seattle: University of Washington Press, 1964). Expressions of anti-Catholicism appeared from time to time in the years following the Civil War. Suspicious anti-Catholics generally pointed to three developments as the basis for their fears: (1) the appearance of a so-called Catholic vote; (2) the continuing controversy over the public schools, which involved discussions of the teaching of morality and the use of tax money in support of nonpublic institutions; and (3) a so-called Catholic influence over organized labor. The Democratic Party was usually regarded as subservient to Catholics, illustrated most often by references to the Irish-Democratic control of several large cities. President Grant's action in recommending a constitutional amendment to forbid use of public money for any sectarian purpose gave to the Republicans a reputation for favoring the anti-Catholic position. Numerous nationalistic and patriotic societies were organized in this same period. Many of them included anti-Catholicism as one of the planks in their platforms. The American Protective Association, an oath-bound, secret, anti-Catholic organization with a membership open to both men and women, was organized on March 13, 1887, in Iowa. It was intended to have a nationwide appeal and to take an active part in politics.

1064. Kling, Merle. The Tenability of Isolationism and Internationalism as Designations of the Foreign Policy of the United States. A Case Study of Senator Arthur H. Vandenberg and Representative Vito Marcantonio. Washington, 1949. 608p.

1065. Klug, H. G. An Ecological Analysis of Migration Patterns in North Dakota and South Dakota. South Dakota State, 1976. 144p.

Presents an analysis of socioeconomically defined ecological areas through the replication of the patterned factorial design developed by Loebl at the University of Missouri/Columbia. The major emphases of the study were to: (1) delineate homogeneous, although not necessarily contiguous, social areas using the patterned factorial design; (2) determine the capability of the previously delineated social areas to account for significant amounts of variation in residually measured net migration; and (3) compare the procedures and results of the present study with those of Loebl's work.

1066. Knittle, Walter A. The Early Eighteenth Century Palatine Emigration: A British Government Redemptioner Project to Manufacture Naval Stores. Pennsylvania, 1931. 320p.

Published under the same title (Ithaca, New York: Cayuga, 1937). Gives the background of the British government's effort to settle a large number of Palatine emigrants in New York and North Carolina in the early 1800s. The list containing 12,000 names of Palatine emigrants is important for genealogical research. The arrangement is by ship, and the textual material is accompanied by 25 maps, illustrations, and portraits.

1067. Kocolowski, Gary P. Louisville at Large: Industrial-Urban Organization, Inter-City Migration, and Occupational Mobility in the Central United States, 1865-1906. Cincinnati, 1978. 212p. (DA 39:5680)

This urban study analyzes migration patterns to and from Louisville, Kentucky, between 1865 and 1906. The principal sources are biographical sketches for 229 native white and 33 black in-migrants, naturalization records for 1,533 foreign in-migrants, and city-directory out-migrant destinations for 3,319 native and foreign whites. A comparison is also made with 787 native white in-migrations in Ohio and Kentucky taken from biographical sources, 219 foreign in-migrations to Cincinnati from naturalization records, and 336 and 204 out-migration destinations from Nashville and Cincinnati city directories.

1068. Korman, Adolf G. A Social History of Industrial Growth and Immigrants: A Study with Particular Reference to Milwaukee, 1880-1920. Wisconsin, 1960. 500p. (DA 20:2776)

Published under the title Industrialization, Immigrants, and Americanizers: The View from Milwaukee, 1866-1921 (Madison: State Historical Society of Wisconsin, 1967). An attempt has been made to explore some of the social relationships between immigrants and American industrial growth from 1880 to 1920. Since certain of the problems involved could not be readily handled in detail for the national scene, the first part of this study deals with Milwaukee. Here an attempt has been made to describe and analyze some aspects of the relationship: the local labor market, occupations and residence, and internal factory life. Other as-

Emigration/Immigration

pects of the relationship required moving out from the local community; for such matters as protective labor legislation, welfare work, the industrial safety movement, and the Americanization crusade were of national scope.

1069. Kramer, George N. A History of the "Know-Nothing Movement." Southern California, 1936. 273p.

1070. Lagerquist, Walter E. Causes and Effects of Immigration from 1815 to 1860. Yale, 1911. 211p.

1071. Lang, Elfrieda W. H. Immigration to Northern Indiana, 1800-1850. Indiana, 1950. 180p.

1072. Leinenweber, Charles R. Immigration and the Decline of Internationalism in the American Working Class Movement, 1864-1919. California (Berkeley), 1969. 257p. (DA 30: 1257-A)
Because the impact of immigration was felt most directly by the working class it was inevitable that the working-class movement itself developed perspectives on immigration--perspectives that took into account the sectional interests of American workers. In broad outline, the perspectives that emerged closely paralleled the level of trade union development: during the early years of the "old" immigration the trade-union movement was characterized by the predominance of pre-industrial craft unions. These unions--represented by the National Labor Union and later by the Knights of Labor--considered only one aspect of immigration, imported contract labor, to be a problem. They neither felt threatened by nor opposed free immigration, and their perspective was moderately internationalist. (A)

1073. Leonard, Henry B. The Open Gates: The Protest Against the Movement to Restrict European Immigration, 1896-1924. Northwestern, 1967. 306p. (DA 28:3608-A)
Although American policy toward European immigration between 1896 and 1917 became steadily more restrictive, this trend was not unopposed. Following the war the desire for restriction reached new heights, and severe quota laws were enacted in 1921, 1922, and 1924. The ranks of the opposition had thinned, and their morale had deteriorated. Many social workers, businessmen, and even immigrant and Jewish-Americans now approved or passively accepted the death of an American tradition.

1074. Leonard, Ira M. New York City Politics, 1841-1844: Nativism and Reform. New York, 1965. 488p. (DA 27: 731-A)
By late 1843 significant numbers of New Yorkers had become thoroughly disillusioned with the Democratic and Whig administration of the city government, and in April 1844 they turned to political nativism. Most serious students of the nativist phenomenon during the period 1841-1844 have viewed the rise of the Native American Party as a prime example of the influence of religious and ethnic prejudice upon the play of local politics.

1075. Ligouri, Mary. The Impact of a Century of Catholic Immigration in Nova Scotia, 1750-1850. Ottawa, 1961. 263p.
Defines three eras of immigration. From the first to the last, the nature and size of the Irish Catholic immigration population changed drastically. The end result in the 1840s was an influx of poorer Irish Catholics whose numbers forced the elite governing the province to grant greater rights in social, political, economic, and religious areas.

1076. Liptak, Dolores A. European Immigrants and the Catholic Church in Connecticut, 1870-1920. Connecticut, 1979. 459p. (DA 40:420-A)
The growth of the American Catholic Church in the nineteenth century resulting from increased European immigration greatly concerned American Catholic leaders. This concern intensified, especially after the 1880s, when the accommodation of hundreds of thousands of "new immigrants" from southern and eastern Europe confronted the predominantly Gaelic-American hierarchy. As the Catholic population of the country doubled between 1880 and 1900, and reached nearly 20 million by the 1920s, the problems became more pressing. Because American Catholic bishops did not generally promulgate joint policies, procedures for incorporating immigrants remained the province of the individual bishop. The Diocese of Hartford was one of the first dioceses to develop an immigrant policy. This study seeks to clarify three issues having to do with such a policy: the degree to which one diocese worked to adapt itself to the American environment; the manner in which it answered the needs of its members, especially those of the immigrants; and the extent to which its actions were found acceptable to the Church in general and to American society. (A)

1077. London, Herbert I. The Nativist Movement in the American Republican Party in New York City During the Period 1843-1847. New York, 1966. 248p. (DA 28:569-A)
This study considers primarily two hypotheses: (1) nativism in the American Republican Party was hastened by the influx of Catholic immigrants, and (2) the nativist movement in the American Republican Party accelerated the assimilation of immigrants. Neither the nativists nor the Irishmen were capable of a modus vivendi. Popular instinct in the 1840s favored Anglo-American conformity and a homogeneous body politic. American Republicans, as overexuberant advocates of this idea, would allow nothing else. The impossibility of accommodation preserved the Irish culture and increased the ire of American Republicans.

1078. Lorimer, M. Madeline. America's Response to Europe's Displaced Persons, 1945-1952. A Preliminary Report. St. Louis, 1964. 361p. (DA 25:4672)
Early in World War II the Allies made plans to repatriate approximately 10 million persons dislocated by Hitler's population policies. By September 1945 these procedures had proved outstandingly successful, but nearly one million Poles, Ukrainians,

Emigration/Immigration 257

and Balts refused repatriation to their Soviet-dominated homelands. There was also the "surviving remnant" of European Jewry, in addition to thousands of Jews from Poland who infiltrated the American Occupied Zones.

1079. Mann, Ralph E. The Social and Political Structure of Two California Mining Towns, 1850-1870. Stanford, 1970. 206p. (DA 31:4091-A)
The bulk of this work deals with the relation of the miners in the two towns to the rest of the population. The society of the two towns in 1850 was a homogeneous group of placer miners, and traders indistinguishable from miners, who were young, native-born, highly mobile, and overwhelmingly male. Ten years later this had been changed by the growth of corporate mining, which made most miners into wage workers rather than independent prospectors. This movement toward more and more industrialization continued through 1870. Industrial quartz-mining created a social stratification, reinforced by the concentration of the American-born in professional and business positions, leaving the mining to the foreign-born.

1080. Margulies, Herbert F. Issues and Politics of Wisconsin Progressivism 1906-1920. Wisconsin, 1955. 264p.
Published under the title The Decline of the Progressive Movement in Wisconsin, 1890-1920 (Madison: University of Wisconsin Press, 1968).

1081. Marhoefer, Gilbert L. Background and Economic Aspects of Immigration to the United States and the World Refugee Problem. Pittsburgh, 1961. 273p. (DA 21:2140)
Even though this dissertation does treat immigration in general, its specific emphasis is on refugees. It is essential that we keep in mind the distinction between immigrants per se and refugees; refugees constitute a special type of immigrant. The history of the United States demonstrates experience with voluntary, involuntary, and refugee immigration. Three periods are discernible: (1) the Colonial period to 1882, characterized by economic need for immigrants as a part of the policy of economic growth and development; (2) 1882 to World War II, marked by a growing fear of immigrants as an economic threat; and (3) the decade of the 1950s, in which immigration has been linked to foreign economic policy. (A)

1082. Matthias, Ronald F. The Know Nothing Movement in Iowa. Chicago, 1966. 283p.

1083. McConville, Mary. Political Nativism in the State of Maryland, 1830-1860. Catholic, 1928. 137p.
Published under the same title (Washington, D.C.: Catholic University of America Press, 1928).

1084. McGann, Agnes G. Nativism in Kentucky to 1860. Catholic, 1944. 146p.

Published under the same title (Washington, D. C.: Catholic University of America Press, 1944).

1085. McGrath, Sister Paul of the Cross. Political Nativism in Texas, 1825-1860. Catholic, 1930. 158p.
Published under the same title (Washington, D. C.: Catholic University of America Press, 1930).

1086. McKinley, Blaine E. "The Stranger in the Gates": Employer Reactions Toward Domestic Servants in America, 1825-1875. Michigan State, 1969. 319p. (DA 31:1203-A)
This dissertation explores the attitudes and responses of northern employers toward their servants during the middle years of the nineteenth century. Domestic service affords an especially valuable opportunity to study class relationships because in their roles as master and servant the middle and upper classes and the lower class came together in an unusually close association. This investigation therefore provides a case study of the class consciousness of the upper levels of society through focusing on their responses toward a specific group of lower-class persons with whom their relations were especially close.

1087. Meldrum, George W. The History of the Treatment of Foreign and Minority Groups in California, 1830-1860. Stanford, 1949. 186p.

1088. Mellinger, Philip J. The Beginnings of Modern Industrial Unionism in the Southwest: Labor Trouble Among Unskilled Copper Workers, 1903-1917. Chicago, 1978. 245p. (DA 39:6298-A)
The unskilled southwestern copper-industry workers were as organizable as were their skilled brethren. Members of the Western Federation of Miners, the Industrial Workers of the World, and other American Federation of Labor and railway brotherhood unionists all together were only a minority of the copper camps' labor force. Most of the unskilled men at southwestern copper facilities were Mexican immigrants, Mexican-Americans, and Italian, Greek, and Slavic immigrants. Many of them were relatively transient. But neither their ethnicity nor their transiency rendered them especially difficult to organize; nor were they especially "poor unionists" once they had been organized.

1089. Meighan, Cecilia. Nativism and Catholic Higher Education, 1840-1860. Columbia (Teachers College), 1972. 138p. (DA 33:2130-A)
The purpose of Catholic institutions of higher education in the United States is under current debate. Catholic education seems to be at a turning point in its history, as Catholic colleges move out of the Catholic ghetto and into the mainstream of American culture. An understanding of the current problems in Catholic colleges necessitates an examination of the evolution of modern Catholic institutions. The historical context of this study is the 20-year period preceding the Civil War, a period that witnessed

Emigration/Immigration 259

a burgeoning of Catholic college foundations, and an unprecedented movement to discredit and intimidate the Catholic Church. This crusade of anti-Catholic bigotry was called Nativism. (A)

1090. Menatian, Steve. Political and Ethnic Influence As It Affects the Providence School System: A Field Study. Pennsylvania State, 1972. 125p. (DA 33:6626-A)
It was the specific purpose of this paper to identify and analyze political-ethnic influence as it affects the Providence, Rhode Island, public school system. With political scientists and others having already established that ethnicity is a salient source in politics, and astute educational administrators having recognized the existence of the politics of education, this study sought to discover if there existed a marriage between these two forces, the ethnic politics of education. This objective was met by the researcher's inquiries into the Providence school system, a system located in a political-ethnic urban setting.

1091. Meyerhuber, Carl I. Henry Cabot Lodge, Massachusetts, and the New Manifest Destiny. California (San Diego), 1972. 188p. (DA 33:6282-A)
This study is principally concerned with Senator Henry Cabot Lodge's development as an expansionist, and the reaction of his constituents to his involvement in jingoist politics. It traces the Senator's transition from naval expansionist and belligerent nationalist to imperialist and attempts to reach some conclusions concerning the evolution of his thinking on foreign-policy matters. This work also deals at length with the responses of Massachusetts business interests, press, intellectual community, and political parties to jingoism and war, and details their efforts to bring pressure upon Lodge to cease his activities on behalf of those causes.

1092. Mikolji, Boris H. Race, Nationality, and Politics in an Urban Community. Case Western Reserve, 1971. 391p. (DA 32:5361-A)
In view of current political developments, the question is being asked whether or not ethnicity represents a significant line of cleavage in the United States. Seen as a specific, specialized instance of a social system, the polity is characterized by recurrent issues of power, rule, and authority. Polarization here may follow any of the four basic social-structural differences: kinship, territorial communities, social stratification, and ethnic grouping. In America, where the assimilative process does not appear complete, the fourth of these bases for differentiation is postulated as influencing alignments in political contests involving normative pre-eminence, power, and the distribution of values and costs. To study the phenomenon a northeastern metropolitan community was surveyed, covering a five-year span from 1958 to 1962. The community had two major ethnic subcommunities, the Italians and Negroes, and at least one political contest for elective posts on local, state, and federal level took place during the period. (A)

1093. Miley, Elizabeth F. The National Origins Clause in the Immigration Act of 1924. Boston College, 1933. 148p.

1094. Mooney, Peter J. The Impact of Immigration on the United States Economy, 1890-1920. North Carolina (Chapel Hill), 1971. 268p. (DA 32:650-A)
The primary objective of this thesis is to measure the levels and rates of change of several crucial economic indicators that would have prevailed during the period 1890-1920 if the influence of the foreign stock (i.e., the immigrants and their children) were effectively and comprehensively eliminated. A model is constructed to deal with the actual impact of the following labor force characteristics of the foreign stock on overall labor productivity--occupational preferences, sex composition, skill levels, and age distribution. The conclusion is drawn that the combined effect of these particular characteristics of the labor force of foreign stock was to increase the annual levels of total labor productivity in the United States during the relevant period.

1095. Morrow, Rising L. Citizenship in Anglo-American Diplomacy from 1790 to 1870. Harvard, 1932. 156p.

1096. Mueller, Charles F. Labor Force Migration: A Behavioral Approach. Boston College, 1978. 270p. (DA 39:3708)
The interrelationship between migration and regional economic conditions is a recognized concern for regional economic policymakers. This study examines one aspect of that interrelationship: the worker's decision to migrate. The migration decision is considered in isolation of possible effects migration may have upon economic conditions. The study reviews much of the recent literature on migration. The methodological and empirical shortcomings of earlier works are noted as a base for the development of a behavioral model of the migration decision that addresses the shortcomings.

1097. Mulkern, John R. The Know-Nothing Party in Massachusetts. Boston, 1963. 340p. (DA 24:2448)
Most students of the Know-Nothing or American Party attribute its political successes to its superb organization; to popular discontent with existing parties; to the social and economic problems created by the massive influx of foreigners into the country in the generation preceding the Civil War; and to the general outlook prevailing in many sections of the country that favored limiting the numbers and political influence of foreigners and Roman Catholics. In Massachusetts the fact that two out of three voters in 1854 cast their ballots for Know-Nothing candidates shows clearly that such explanations are insufficient. Certain conditions, peculiar to the Commonwealth, made possible this secret organization's winning every state office, the 11 Congressional seats, every seat in the state senate, and all but three in the lower house. (A)

1098. Mullaly, Harry F. United States Refugee Policy: 1789-1956: A Study of the Traditional Policy of Asylum for

Emigration/Immigration 261

Political, Racial, or Religious Refugees. New York, 1959. 367p. (DA 20:4158)
Four factors were found to have affected policy: economic, sociocultural (racial), security (loyalty, nationalism), and foreign policy. Five principles were derived for the formulation and execution of policy: (1) adaptability to foreign-policy requirements; (2) conformability to international law, commitments made by the United States or the purposes of international bodies of which it is a member; (3) flexibility of immigration controls to reflect changing needs of refugee policy; (4) insurability of the defense, economy, and health of the nation and the equal treatment of refugees; and (5) practicability in administration by centralization of policy decision and operations in one agency, with dual functions within and without the nation, and provision for appeal from administrative decisions. (A)

1099. Murray, Robert K. The Great Red Scare of 1919-20. Ohio State, 1949. 260p.
Published under the title Red Scare: A Study in National Hysteria, 1919-1920 (Minneapolis: University of Minnesota Press, 1955). An investigation of the causes and a description of events in which anti-immigrant feeling was a powerful factor.

1100. Nanjundappa, C. Migration and Occupation: Relationship Between Migration and Occupational Status Among Employed Males in the United States, 1967. Georgia, 1976. 128p.
This dissertation examines the relationship between migration and occupational status among employed males 17 years old and over in the United States and in the South and the non-South by race, age, region, and residence of origin. In addition, the impact of cross-regional migration upon the working force in the South and the non-South was examined.

1101. Nava, Alfonso R. A Political History of Bilingual Language Policy in the Americas. Claremont Graduate School, 1977. 191p.
An overview of the controversy surrounding bilingual policies. In the early colonies maintenance of mother tongues was encouraged, but in the nineteenth century opposition was increasingly encountered, and this trend continued into the twentieth century.

1102. Neff, Andrew L. The Mormon Migration to Utah. California, 1918. 214p.

1103. Nelson, Dale C. Ethnicity and Political Participation in New York City: A Theoretical and Empirical Analysis. Columbia, 1977. 289p. (DA 38:6292-A)
The thesis of this study is that ethnicity has a causal influence on whether individuals become active in local-level politics. The author has developed a theory to explain the causal connection between ethnicity and political participation and collected survey data on six ethnic groups (Jews, Irish, blacks, Cubans, Dominicans, and Puerto Ricans) in the Washington Heights-Inwood section

of Manhattan. Our theory is essentially a cultural one stressing the effects of ethnicity on levels of participant political culture (e.g., attitudes of political involvement, efficacy, cynicism, civic awareness, and community political knowledge), which in turn affects the likelihood that an individual will become active in community political affairs.

1104. Nelson, Mary C. The Influence of Immigration on Rhode Island Politics, 1865-1910. Radcliffe College, 1955. 243p.

1105. Nelson, Ronald E. The Role of Colonies in the Pioneer Settlement of Henry County, Illinois. Nebraska, 1970. 255p. (DA 31:2052-B)
Various organized groups, or colonies, founded no less than 38 pioneer settlements in Illinois, the greatest concentration being in Henry County, where Yankee colonies attempted settlements during 1835-1836 at Andover, Geneseo, LaGrange, Morristown, and Wethersfield; a Swedish religious sect established a communal settlement in 1846 at Bishop Hill. The Yankee schemes were fostered by two contemporary movements in the Northeast during the 1830s, the Congregational-Presbyterian "Great Revival" and speculation in western land. The Swedish group, persecuted for separating from the Established Church, emigrated to Henry County in search of religious freedom. The purposes of this study are to determine the effectiveness of the Henry County colonies as agencies of frontier settlement, analyze the role of the colonies in the pioneer settlement and development of the county, and determine temporary and lasting occupance patterns and other areal variations resulting from the colony endeavors. (A)

1106. Nizami, Saeed A. The Law of Immigration in the United States. Southern Illinois, 1968. 288p. (DA 29:3659-A)
This dissertation deals with the public policy in regard to immigration in the United States and also studies certain problems in immigration law.

1107. Noonan, Carroll J. Nativism in Connecticut, 1829-1860. Catholic, 1938. 136p.
Published under the same title (Washington, D.C.: Catholic University of America Press, 1938).

1108. Norris, Martha R. Adoption of Children from Overseas: A Study of the Process Involved in the Intercountry Adoption Placement of 145 Children Conducted Under the Auspices of the Catholic Committee for Refugees - National Catholic Welfare Conference, 1961-1964. Catholic, 1967. 361p. (DA 28:2783-A)
Since World War II intercountry adoption has become an integral part of the fabric of adoption practice and child-welfare services in the United States. This dissertation was designed to explore and describe the intercountry-adoption process and the program under Catholic auspices whereby homeless children from overseas

were placed in United States adoptive homes. The focus of the study was on the adoptive placements made from 1961 to 1964 through the collaborative efforts of Catholic Relief Services-- NCWC (CRS) and an indigenous agency overseas, Catholic Committee for Refugees--NCWC (CCR) in New York City, and a network of United States voluntary and public agencies.

1109. Nugent, Walter T. K. Populism and Nativism in Kansas, 1888-1900. Chicago, 1961. 242p.
Published under the title The Tolerant Populists: Kansas Populism and Nativism (Chicago: University of Chicago Press, 1963). Presents the view that Populism and Nativism included immigrant adherents and that the movements were primarily directed against landlords and financiers.

1110. Oberlander, Barbara J. American Immigration Restriction as a Problem in American Foreign Relations, 1882-1906. Brandeis, 1974. 273p. (DA 34:3650-A)
This dissertation is an analysis of how American immigration restriction from 1882 to 1906--the first 25 years of federal legislation designed to bar objectionable European immigrants--contributed to the nation's expanding external involvements and concerns at the turn of the century. Several areas were examined: the nature of American diplomatic attempts to enforce restriction; the interpretive questions caused by statutory provisions; the effect of the actions of other nations on the operation of American laws; and the role of American consuls abroad in executing restriction.

1111. O'Connell, Lawrence W. The Reform Group in Central City School Politics: The Boston Experience, 1960-1965. Syracuse, 1968. 343p. (DA 30:378-A)
The politics of city school reform has drawn increasing attention from political scientists as public education has become a controversial issue in central cities. As the needs of urban populations are more clearly articulated, the ability of public education systems to meet those needs becomes important. This study examines school reform in Boston. The subject is the role of the Citizens for the Boston Schools, the most recent reform group that has systematically attempted to effect a major change in Boston school policy.

1112. Oder, Irwin. The United States and Palestine Mandate, 1920-1948: A Study of the Impact of Interest Groups on Foreign Policy. Columbia, 1956. 592p. (DA 16:2507)
This dissertation presents the following views: the influence of Zionists on policy-making has been exaggerated. They were able to achieve surprisingly little, although they had available a well-organized and well-financed lobby. In the last analysis, the actions of the United States were taken in what was regarded as the overall national interest.

1113. Orthman, William G. Implications of the Brain Drain: Verdict of Educated Immigrants in the Puget Sound Area.

University of Washington, 1971. 270p. (DA 32:1127-A)
Called the "brain drain" by a report of the British Royal Society, the migration of scientists, engineers, physicians, and other highly educated specialists from one country to another, which began after World War II, reached the stage of a worldwide controversy by the early 1960s. The complaints of the British over the loss of university degree-holders to North America were soon being shunted to one side as the controversy centered on the loss of highly educated talent by the developing countries of Asia, Africa, and Latin America to the advanced industrial nations of Europe and North America. The present study, made to fill some of the gaps in the information available, uses the United Kingdom for purposes of studying the advanced nations that have lost talent to the United States, and India as an example of the effects of the brain drain on a developing nation.

1114. Palamiotis, Alexander A. The Citizen and Alien in American Constitutional Law. Utah, 1959. 262p. (DA 20:3362)
The alien's position in American law is influenced by both federal and state legislation. The federal government's powers to admit, exclude, naturalize, denaturalize for cause, and deport aliens are absolute and unqualified as incidents of sovereignty. The state governments on their part have extensive powers that may limit the alien's rights to own property, share in the natural resources, or to be engaged in a gainful occupation. The development of the law of citizenship and alienage during the past 50 years is characterized by the introduction of political tests in the body of otherwise purely legal tests in the field of admission into the country, acquisition and loss of nationality, and deportation. (A)

1115. Palmer, Earle S. Peopling the Trans-Mississippi Northwest. Chicago, 1942. 246p.

1116. Parmet, Robert D. The Know-Nothings in Connecticut. Columbia, 1966. 376p. (DA 27:442-A)
As the 1850s approached, Connecticut was introduced to industrialization and immigration. The largely Irish newcomers were Roman Catholic. However, by tradition Connecticut was not an especially welcome land for religious minorities. As religious settlement had frequently followed a geographical pattern, various conflicts, usually involving Congregationalists, Baptists, and Episcopalians, had produced sectional tension within the state. When huge numbers of Catholics came in the 1840s and 1850s new antagonisms resulted.

1117. Parsons, Stanley B. The Populist Context: Nebraska Farmers and Their Antagonists, 1882-1892. Iowa, 1964. 352p. (DA 25:2477)
Published under the title The Populist Context: Rural versus Urban Power on a Great Plains Frontier (Westport, Connecticut: Greenwood, 1973). The history of the Populist Movement has been chronicled on the state and sectional level, but no historian has attempted to study the movement as it occurred in its local

context. It is at this level of investigation that cultural antagonisms, rural-urban conflicts, or struggles for political and economic leadership are most evident. These conflicts influenced different groups of people either to defend or attack the farmers' movement. It is the delineation of these groups, together with their point of view, that is the major subject of this dissertation.

1118. Pavlak, Thomas J. Ethnic Identification and Political Behavior. Illinois (Urbana), 1971. 140p. (DA 32:5860-A)
Political scientists have paid little attention to the ethnic factor in American politics. Although there has been some investigation of ethnic voting behavior and political attitudes, there has not been a comprehensive study of the impact of ethnicity on the political perspectives and behavior of ethnic-group members. The present study has attempted to narrow this gap in existing political science research. The study was undertaken with a twofold purpose: (1) to clarify the nature of ethnic identification by testing Dahl's assimilation and Parenti's persistence theories; and (2) to explore the effect of ethnicity on selected aspects of ethnic political behavior, including party affiliation and voting preference, political alienation, and racial antagonism. Data were obtained from interviews with a sample of 354 respondents of Mexican, Irish, Polish, Lithuanian, and Slovak backgrounds in an ethnic community in Chicago. A measure of ethnic identification was developed using items reflecting Parenti's conceptualization of ethnicity in terms of its cultural, social, and identificational components.

1119. Perry, Joseph M. The Impact of Immigration on Three American Industries, 1865-1914. Northwestern, 1966. 210p. (DA 27:3207-A)
Generalizations have been made to the effect that immigration: tended to depress wages and exert competitive pressures on native labor, as low-wage, unskilled immigrant workers swelled the labor force; stimulated the growth of industry and national product, through foreign-born influence in both the factor and the product markets; and prompted technical progress and mechanization, since declining interest rates, contrasted with the stable wages of immigrant labor, made labor relatively more expensive than the capital used in new techniques. This study was designed to test the foregoing generalizations at the industry level. Three American industries that employed relatively large numbers of immigrants during the interwar period were chosen for examination: the New England cotton-goods industry, the basic iron and steel industry, and iron-ore mining.

1120. Petersen, Albert J. German-Russian Catholic Colonization in Western Kansas: A Settlement Geography. Louisiana State, 1970. 232p. (DA 31:4771-B)
The German agriculturalists who colonized the Russian-Volga under the invitation of Catherine the Great immigrated to the Western Kansas steppe during the decade of the 1870s. Conditioned by a century of life on the Volga steppe, the German-Russian

colonists attempted to re-establish that rural-village settlement that they best understood. As a result, elements of German-Russian material culture have created a unique settlement situation that in both form and function has remained as a visible imprint on the local landscape.

1121. Petersen, Roger D. The Reaction to a Heterogeneous Society: A Behavioral and Quantitative Analysis of Northern Voting Behavior, 1845-1870, Pennsylvania: A Test Case. Pittsburgh, 1970. 322p. (DA 31:6526-A)
The dissertation examines voting behavior in 13 northern states via county-level voting returns and federal Census demographic data for the years between 1836 and 1872. It also more intensely explores voting behavior in Pennsylvania through use of minor civil-division voting returns and demographic data from the manuscript federal Census for the years between 1848 and 1870. The pivotal election in these years was the election of 1854. It destroyed the Democrats' position as the nation's majority party and highlighted a full decade of political confusion. The election of 1854 and those succeeding it centered around Protestant hostility toward their society becoming heterogeneous because of the influx of several million Irish and German Catholic migrants. The issue of slavery was not a major force in the voter upheavals of the 1850s. The election of 1854 receives the major focus of attention.

1122. Pinola, Rudolph. Labor and Politics on the Iron Range of Northern Minnesota. Wisconsin, 1957. 237p. (DA 17:999)
Historically, one can note that a fair amount of cooperation between the mining interests and the people prevailed during the early years. This is largely explained by the exploratory and small-scale nature of the operations. The nature of the labor force and a feeling that the mining industry should have every opportunity to develop delayed the outbreak of social conflict. Factors that contributed to the break were the migration to the ore fields of a class-conscious Finnish element; bad conditions in the mines; the need for civic improvements; and the disclosure of the true value of the iron ore deposits, which set off the fight for control of local government. There followed 30 years of struggle between the mining interests and the people, which promoted the union of labor and political-reform groups. When the Farmer-Labor Party appeared on the Range with its own brand of radicalism labor served as a nucleus around which to carry out organizational activity. (A)

1123. Purdy, Virginia Cardwell. Portrait of a Know-Nothing Legislature: The Massachusetts General Court of 1855. George Washington, 1970. 299p. (DA 31:3482-A)
Ninety-eight percent of the 1855 Massachusetts legislature were members of the Know-Nothing or American Party. Contemporary observers and subsequent historians have considered them typical of the self-seeking, bigoted, and xenophobic participants in the national Know-Nothing movement. As a group they have been

characterized as property-less, transient, lacking in legislative experience, only briefly in office, and largely representative of the laboring classes instead of the usual agricultural and legal occupations. Because of their record of reform in office they have been described as the successors of a reform Coalition of liberal Democrats and part of the Free Soil Party, which formed a majority in the 1851-1852 legislatures. The explanation offered for the curious combination of reform with religious and ethnic proscription among Massachusetts Know-Nothings has been that reform-minded Coalitionists became nativist and anti-Catholic and joined Know-Nothing lodges when Irish Catholics supported Old Line Whigs to defeat a revised state constitution promulgated by the Coalition in 1853. This study attempts to test these assertions by statistical means where possible and reach some conclusions about the character of the Know-Nothing legislature. (A)

1124. Quay, William L. Philadelphia Democrats, 1880-1910. Lehigh, 1969. 375p. (DA 30:5393-A)
During the Cleveland-Bryan era the Democratic Party in Philadelphia experienced an almost phenomenal decline in both leadership strength and grass-roots support. At a time when the Democrats built strong and successful organizations in other eastern cities like New York and Boston, Philadelphia Democrats recorded constant losses, which resulted in the collapse of the party in 1910. This study traces the events and analyzes the factors that contributed to this prodigious decline. The major changes in the ethnic fabric of the city also weakened the Democratic Party at the grass-roots level. In the eighties the old Irish and German neighborhoods were solidly Democratic, but when the Russian Jews and the Italians moved into these areas the Republicans gained control of these wards. Hence, both political and ethnic factors contributed to the sharp decline of the Democracy during the Bryan years.

1125. Rawson, Donald M. Party Politics in Mississippi, 1850-1860. Vanderbilt, 1964. 330p. (DA 25:439)
Traces the organization and activities of political parties in Mississippi during the decade preceding the American Civil War. At a time when sectional interests were becoming more pronounced party allegiance on a local level as well as on a national level proved to be rather tenuous. Party membership was unstable, and political doctrines were short-lived. Therefore, this study has been divided into several well-defined periods. Any hopes the Nativists may have harbored for overpowering their Democratic opponents, however, were obliterated in the Presidential election of 1856. The following year saw the demise of the Know-Nothing Party in Mississippi and the termination of the last major effort to wrest political control of the state from the hands of the fire-eaters.

1126. Reich, Max. The Mental Selection of Immigrants to the United States. New York, 1930. 168p.

1127. Reuter, William C. Anglophobia in American Politics, 1865-1900. California (Berkeley), 1967. 290p. (DA 27: 3821-A)
It is a commonplace that a political candidate's chances are reduced if the opposition can associate him in the minds of the voters with some generally disliked or feared agency. This truism helps explain the repeated intrusion of Anglophobia into American politics in the period 1865 to 1900. For millions of Americans in these years England was both the traditional foe of the Republic and a dangerous contemporary rival as well. It is not surprising, therefore, that when circumstances permitted, political strategists attempted to undercut their opponents by labeling them "pro-British." (A)

1128. Risch, Erna. Encouragement and Aid to Immigrants, 1607-1830. Chicago, 1931. 214p.

1129. Ristuben, Peter J. Minnesota and the Competition for Immigrants. Oklahoma, 1964. 305p. (DA 24:5349)
Despite the fact that their campaigns have received only scant attention, territorial and state immigration agencies actively promoted immigration to the West for three-quarters of a century following the Civil War. Minnesota was among the first to accept the responsibility of promoting settlement, with the appointment of an immigration commissioner in 1855. Although this position existed for only two years, the state resumed promotion in 1864. It continued its immigration program until 1927, when the Board was permanently abolished. Between 1864 and 1927 Minnesota spent over $550,000 to promote the settlement of its lands. The methods used by Minnesota to attract immigrants included the employment of honorary and salaried agents, displays at fairs and exhibits, advertising in American and foreign newspapers, and the publication and distribution of more than 3 million pieces of promotional literature. (A)

1130. Rivers, Richard R. American Biological Opposition to Southeastern European Immigration, 1900-1924: Ideas, Policies, and Implications for Teaching. Illinois State, 1978. 179p. (DA 39:5682)
This dissertation examines the specific biological concerns that were crucial in reviving the dormant nativist feelings of Americans in the period 1900-1924. Scientific publications, books, newspaper articles, and popular magazines contributed a wealth of information on this topic. House and Senate Documents and the Congressional Record for the same period were also searched for relevant data. The evidence conclusively proves that substantial numbers of America's scientific community were imbued with feelings of Nordic racial superiority.

1131. Robbins, Richard H. The Immigration Act of 1952: A Case Study in Political Sociology. Illinois (Urbana), 1959. 247p. (DA 20:403)
The Immigration and Nationality Act of 1952, the McCarran-

Walter Act, is an effective case study since its subject matter is as much sociological as political. By treating this case in terms of such social factors as public opinion, regionalism, urbanism, class and ethnic divisions, and formal group interests, the group basis of the political process is affirmed more concretely. The material is based on historical analysis, literature on private organizations and legislative hearings, and selected interviews with group representatives. (A)

1132. Rockett, I. R. H. Immigration, Ethnicity, and Occupational Mobility: The Experience of Recent Male Immigrants to the United States. Brown, 1978. 272p. (DA 40:6349-A)
As part of the effort to enhance understanding of the process of immigrant adjustment this research focuses on the relationship between immigration and ethnicity on the one hand, and occupational mobility on the other. The actual subjects under investigation are adult males of white (non-Spanish), black, Spanish, and Asian extraction who attained permanent immigrant status in the United States between 1960 and 1970. The 1970 United States Census serves as the primary data source. More specifically, the data derive from two Public Use Samples based on the 1970 Census 5-percent schedule.

1133. Rosenblum, Gerald. Modernization, Immigration, and the American Labor Movement. Princeton, 1968. 488p. (DA 29:340-A)
Published under the title Immigrant Workers: Their Impact on American Labor Radicalism (New York: Basic Books, 1972).
This study seeks partially to account for the unique form that the American labor movement has taken when compared with labor movements in other societies that underwent modernization relatively early. It is noted that substantial increments to the nonagricultural labor force during the course of American modernization came from increasingly higher levels of immigration.
The central problem asks what influence immigration exerted on the American labor movement. The course of modernization, immigration, and labor relations in the United States is examined, with particular emphasis on the interval between 1880 and World War I. It is argued that immigration muted a potential radicalism in American labor and positively contributed to the inception of business unionism at the industrial as well as the craft-union level.

1134. Rossi, Ernest E. The United States and the 1948 Italian Elections. Pittsburgh, 1964. 426p. (DA 26:467)
This study attempts to answer the following questions: (1) What activity, both governmental and private, was undertaken by the United States in order to influence the Italian election of 1948? (2) What was the Italian reaction to this activity? (3) What was the influence of American activity on the election results? (4) What does this affair show concerning certain theories of democracy, U. S. foreign policy, and international politics?

1135. Rubin, Ernest. Unemployment of Aliens in the United
States, 1940. Columbia, 1949. 80p.
A study of the alien in the American labor market. The study
concentrates on the high unemployment rate of aliens; special
factors limiting labor demand for aliens; employment as it affects
alien labor; and the occupational distribution of aliens.

1136. Saveth, Edward N. American Historians and European Immigrants, 1875-1925. Columbia, 1948. 244p.
Published under the same title (New York: Columbia University
Press, 1948). An analysis of the development of racist historiography in the United States, with special reference to immigrants.

1137. Schachter, Joseph. Capital Value and Relative Wage Effects of Immigration into the United States, 1870-1930.
City University of New York, 1969. 136p. (DA 31:44-A)
The dissertation presents an estimate of the capital value of net
immigration into the United States from 1870 to 1930. This was
done by valuing an immigrant as a productive asset with earnings
over time. In addition, this dissertation also presents evidence
on the relative wage effects of immigration from 1870 to 1910.
The capital value of net immigration into the United States from
1870 to 1930 is found to be equal to $109.7 billion. This figure
was obtained on the basis of the occupations that immigrants
adopted after settling in the United States. These occupations
were derived from the decennial Census data on the occupations
of the foreign-born population of the United States. If we take
into account the maximum effect of skill upgrading of the occupational distribution of immigrants that took place after they entered
the United States, then the capital value of net immigration from
1870 to 1930 is reduced by 15.2 percent to $93 billion. An examination of the occupational distribution of both the foreign-born
population and immigrants shows that, contrary to the widely held
belief, the "old immigration, " i.e., immigration from northern
and western Europe, was less skilled than the "new immigration, "
i.e., immigration from eastern and southern Europe.

1138. Schmeckebier, Laurence F. History of the Know Nothing
Party in Maryland. Johns Hopkins, 1899. 107p.

1139. Scisco, Louis D. Political Nativism in New York State.
Columbia, 1901. 204p.
Published under the same title (New York: Columbia University
Press, 1901).

1140. Serene, Frank H. Immigrant Steelworkers in the Monongahela Valley: Their Communities and the Development of a
Labor Class Consciousness. Pittsburgh, 1979. 302p.
(DA 40:2843)
This dissertation focuses on the southern and eastern European
unskilled immigrant steelworkers who began to come into the
Monongahela Valley in the 1880s. By the close of the second
decade of the twentieth century four themes characterized the

immigrant experience in this valley. A nascent labor class consciousness, most discernible at its apex during the steel strike of 1919, underlaid the comradeship among the immigrant steelworkers. Except for a brief period during the organizing campaign and the strike, persistence of ethnic identity and concerns for ethnic heritages overshadowed this consciousness. Attempts were made, through Americanization programs, to harmonize immigrant behavior with work rules in the mills and the social mores of American society. Civic, social, economic, and political affairs of the valley were monitored by the United States Steel Corporation, and the gulf between the English-speaking residents and the immigrants enhanced the corporation's control over the mill towns.

1141. Sewrey, Charles L. The Alleged "Un-Americanism" of the Church as a Factor in Anti-Catholicism in the United States, 1860-1914. Minnesota, 1955. 412p. (DA 16:111)
This study deals with the relationship between anti-Catholicism in the United States and the belief that the Church was a threat to American institutions. The sources used include a variety of Catholic and non-Catholic publications, ranging from popular periodicals and tracts to scholarly journals for the clergy.

1142. Shafir, Shlomo. The Impact of the Jewish Crisis on American-German Relations, 1933-1939. Georgetown, 1971. 1,050p. (DA 32:3934-A)
This study deals with the impact of the Nazi persecutions of the German Jews on American-German relations in the context of the policy of isolation up to 1937 and the subsequent challenge to isolation. It attempts to explore the attitude of different layers of the Administration, the interaction between public opinion and policy-makers, the influence of social and economic pressure groups, and the reactions of German authorities. Special attention has been paid to American Jewry, which was deeply involved both because of its unique links with coreligionists in Europe and because of the global anti-Jewish Nazi thrust.

1143. Shannon, James P. Colonization by Catholic Immigrants in Minnesota, 1876-1881. Yale, 1955. 243p.
Published under the title Catholic Colonization on the Western Frontier (New Haven, Connecticut: Yale University Press, 1957).

1144. Shaughnessy, Gerald. A Study of Immigration and Catholic Growth in the United States: 1790-1920. Catholic, 1925. 289p.
Published under the title Has the Immigrant Kept the Faith? A Study of Immigration and Catholic Growth in the United States, 1790-1920 (New York: Macmillan, 1925).

1145. Sheridan, Peter B. The Immigrant in Philadelphia, 1827-1860: The Contemporary Published Report. Georgetown, 1957. 246p.

1146. Simon, Roger D. The Expansion of an Industrial City:
Milwaukee, 1880-1910. Wisconsin, 1971. 412p.
(DA 32: 3226-A)
This study focuses on two aspects of the "city building" process:
the movements of population and the quality of the environment
that results from urban expansion. The German population is
the major ethnic group studied.

1147. Sinkler, George. The Racial Ideas of American Presidents:
From Lincoln to Theodore Roosevelt. Columbia (Teachers
College), 1966. 480p. (DA 27:1307-A)
Published under the title The Racial Attitudes of American Presidents: From Abraham Lincoln to Theodore Roosevelt (New York: Doubleday, 1971). The purpose of this investigation was to ascertain the racial ideas of American Presidents as reflected in
their writings during a selected period of history. This study
also sought to determine the extent to which Gunnar Myrdal's
thesis that the core of the Negro problem in America is the
Caucasian fear of amalgamation, was supported in the expressions
of the Presidents covered in this study. A final aim was to obtain additional insight into the dynamics of race adjustment and to
decide the extent to which ideas of race influenced the general
thinking and political behavior of these Presidents. Published
and unpublished papers of the Presidents were exploited chronologically.

1148. Sipher, Roger E. Popular Voting Behavior in New York,
1890-1896: A Case Study of Two Counties. Syracuse,
1971. 202p. (DA 32:5722-A)
The study focuses on popular voting behavior in two rural New
York counties, upstate Tompkins and downstate Rockland, during
the period 1890-1896. These counties were selected because they
were dissimilar in certain crucial respects. Although both were
rural, dairy-farming counties, they differed in cultural composition and political behavior. Tompkins was basically a nativeborn Protestant county with only a tiny Irish Catholic community
in the city of Ithaca. Rockland's foreign-born Catholic community
was much larger and played a more significant role in the political life of the county. During the 1890s voting patterns in Tompkins, a Republican county, remained largely the same as in the
past while in Rockland, a Democratic stronghold, they underwent
considerable change.

1149. Smith, Geoffrey S. A Social and Diplomatic History of
American Extremism, 1933-1941. California (Santa Barbara), 1969. 773p. (DA 31:5998-A)
Nativist extremism constitutes an important theme in American
history. It has usually appeared in uncertain social situations
when a group of persons feels itself threatened by incomprehensible, external forces. Although such episodes as the Salem
Witch Trials, the anti-Catholicism of the 1830s and 1840s, and
the "Red Scare" of 1919-1920 exhibit individual differences, they
also suggest patterns of behavior that break the surface of Amer-

Emigration/Immigration

ican politics periodically. During the years 1933-1941 the most notable of the American extremists were Father Charles E. Coughlin, a Catholic priest from Royal Oak, Michigan; William Dudley Pelley, leader of the American Silver Shirts; and Fritz Kuhn, Bundesfuehrer of the German-American Bund. The study analyzes the careers of these men, and others, to present a balanced description of extremism during the era. The early chapters concentrate on factors such as leadership, organization, clientele, use of propaganda, revolutionary potential, and ideological and status considerations. The latter chapters deal with the effect of the American extremists upon the debate on American foreign policy between 1937 and 1941. (A)

1150. Snetsinger, John G. Truman and the Creation of Israel. Stanford, 1970. 191p. (DA 31:1742-A)
Although since 1948 Truman has been lauded for his contribution in assisting in the creation of Israel, much of the adulation has been misplaced. The President had no commitment to the Zionist program. For example, when Truman agreed to a reversal of the American policy favoring implementation of the United States partition plan in March 1948 some observers believed that his action was the deathblow for any hope of establishing a Jewish state. When the President's policies were in accord with the Zionists' program his motivation was based primarily, if not solely, on political considerations. With all its contradictions and vacillations Truman's Palestine-Israel policy offers an extraordinary example of conducting foreign policy in line with short-range political expediency rather than long-range national goals. (A)

1151. Solomon, Barbara M. New England Pride and Prejudice: A Study in the Origins of Immigration Restriction. Harvard, 1953. 210p.
Published under the title Ancestors and Immigrants: A Changing New England Tradition (Cambridge, Massachusetts: Harvard University Press, 1956). A detailed analysis of the effect of immigration into New England, and the movement for immigration restriction.

1152. Spletstoser, Frederick M. Back Door to the Land of Plenty: New Orleans as an Immigrant Port, 1820-1860. Louisiana State, 1978. 466p. (DA 40:6923-A)
During the 40 years before the Civil War over 550,000 immigrants entered the United States through the Port of New Orleans. Though that number amounted to only 10 percent of all passengers who traveled to this country by sea and was but 14 percent of those who landed at New York, the Crescent City, rather than Boston or Philadelphia, was the nation's second antebellum port of entry. Furthermore, it was an almost perfect microcosm of the nation's paramount immigrant port and of the entire pattern of human movement into the United States prior to 1860. The people who uprooted themselves and made the voyage to New Orleans, like the overwhelming majority of other antebellum immi-

grants, were primarily from Ireland and the German states. Although they came from all stations of society, most were less than prosperous. Many were famine victims and paupers. As in all other times they left their homes to better their lives by improving their economic status, and the bounty that the United States potentially offered them was their most important incentive for taking all of the risks inherent in moving halfway around the world. (A)

1153.   Stauffer, Alvin P. Anti-Catholicism in American Politics, 1865-1900. Harvard, 1933. 210p.

1154.   Stewart, Barbara M. United States Government Policy on Refugees from Nazism, 1933-1940. Columbia, 1969. 613p. (DA 33:262-A)
The United States government gave little help to refugees from 1933 to 1940, but it did as much as most Americans wanted it to do and more than many desired. Because of the severity of the Depression, the strength of nationalism and isolationism, the waves of anti-Semitism, and the general preoccupation with internal problems, few pressured the government to change its restrictive policy. American Jews, the most deeply concerned, feared to arouse antagonism that might shut the gates entirely. Nevertheless, many of them urged the Administration to adopt a more liberal interpretation of the laws and exert more influence internationally to help settle the refugees. On the other hand, most Gentiles, except for a few individuals and organizations, gave only lip service to Christian charity and looked upon the refugees as a Jewish problem. As a result President Roosevelt, preoccupied by matters of more immediate need, allowed the Department of State to chart its own timid course and determine the extent to which the United States would aid the victims of Nazi persecution. (A)

1155.   Stickle, Warren E. New Jersey Democracy and the Urban Coalition: 1919-1932. Georgetown, 1971. 664p. (DA 32:2624-A)
Although social, cultural, religious, economic, and political cleavages tended to divide Newer Americans from the earlier waves of immigrants, these cleavages were submerged in the Garden State during the twenties because of common enemies and causes that stimulated ethnic pluralism and cultural liberalism. In the twenties the divisive issues of 100 percent Americanism, immigration restriction, the Ku Klux Klan, the Anti-Saloon League, anti-Catholicism, and especially Prohibition bridged the gaps between the Irish and Newer American communities and polarized the Garden State into old-stock and Newer American areas. These social, cultural, and ethnic cleavages transformed Garden State politics and fostered the growth of New Jersey Democracy. (A)

1156.   Stoessinger, Lewis G. The Refugee and International Organization. Harvard, 1954. 163p.

Emigration/Immigration

1157. Suggs, George G. Colorado Conservatives Versus Organized Labor: A Study of the James Hamilton Peabody Administration, 1903-1905. Colorado, 1964. 485p.
Includes considerable material on immigrant labor strife in Colorado and Utah.

1158. Tangwall, Wallace F. Immigrants in the Civil War: Some American Reactions. Chicago, 1962. 74p.
An overview of changing attitudes toward immigrants during the Civil War. Neither the South or the North understood the role of the immigrant in the war; the South attributed its defeat to "foreign mercenaries" and blamed its immigrants for not supporting the South's cause; the North only partially accepted and applauded the role of the immigrant in its armies.

1159. Taylor, Joseph H. The Restriction of European Immigration, 1890-1924. California (Berkeley), 1936. 237p.

1160. Thomas, Mary E. Nativism in the Old Northwest, 1850-1860. Catholic, 1936. 140p.
Published under the same title (Washington, D.C.: Catholic University of America Press, 1936).

1161. Thompson, John. The Settlement Geography of the Sacramento-San Joaquin Delta, California. Stanford, 1957. 210p. (DA 19:295)
The Sacramento-San Joaquin Delta is the floodplain segment of the Central Valley, where arterial rivers converge before discharging into the easternmost of the bays that breach the California Coast Ranges near San Francisco. This study traces the complex continuing physical and cultural processes that have transformed the peat and alluvium accumulating fresh-water tidal swamp into a landscape so surcharged with the cultural imprint that it may be labeled essentially "man made."

1162. Tomaske, John A. An Economic Inquiry into the Causes of International Migration. University of Washington, 1969. 123p. (DA 30:476-A)
The purpose of this study is to formulate and test statistically a general model of international migration into the United States prior to World War I. The 70-year period prior to 1913 witnessed a historically unprecedented mass movement of people out of Europe to the United States and to the other regions of recent settlement. This mass movement of people played a large role in the growth of the population and labor force of the United States. In spite of its importance there is no basic agreement as to the relevant model or of the relevant variables to be included in a model of nineteenth-century international migration.

1163. Tracy, Arthur L. The Social Gospel, "New" Immigration, and American Culture: An Analysis of the Attitudes of Charles Ellwood, Shailer Mathews, and Graham Taylor Toward the "New" Immigration. American, 1975. 282p.

(DA 36:5476-A)
This dissertation examines the attitudes of three Social Gospel leaders toward the new immigration from southern and eastern Europe. The three leaders are Charles Ellwood (1873-1946), sociologist at the University of Missouri and at Duke University; Shailer Mathews (1863-1941), church historian and Dean of the Divinity School of the University of Chicago; and Graham Taylor (1851-1938), social-settlement pioneer and professor of sociology at Chicago Theological Seminary. Each of the three individuals took a different stance toward the new immigration: Ellwood strongly opposed such immigration throughout the period, and at times he used a biological argument for the inferiority of such immigrants. Taylor took a consistently positive stance toward unrestricted immigration and immigrants and argued that they contributed to American life. Mathews took a middle position between the opposites of Ellwood and Taylor.

1164. Treble, J. G. On the Theory of Interregional Migration. Northwestern, 1978. 141p.

1165. Tsiang, I-Mien. The Question of Expatriation in America Prior to 1907. Johns Hopkins, 1942. 141p.
Published under the same title (Baltimore: Johns Hopkins University Press, 1942).

1166. Turner, Albert L. The Deportation of Alien Communists. Michigan, 1943. 240p.

1167. Waldron, Gladys H. Anti-Foreign Movements in California, 1919-1929. California (Berkeley), 1955. 304p.

1168. Wang, Peter H. Legislating "Normalcy": The Immigration Act of 1924. California (Riverside), 1971. 235p. (DA 32:2626-A)
The Immigration Act, or Johnson Bill, of 1924 marked the culmination of a crusade to restrict permanently the entry of central and southeastern Europeans into the United States. After a long legislative battle congressional forces successfully mustered sufficient support to stem the ingress of Italians, Poles, Slavs, and Jews, who, they believed, had inundated the country. Moreover, the measure prohibited Japanese immigration by abrogating the Gentlemen's Agreement, which subsequently produced a major diplomatic crisis. Opponents of restriction charged that the Act was un-American and discriminatory and that its basis rested on the anthropological theory of Nordic superiority. Proponents, on the other hand, hailed the new law as "the longest step forward ever taken in stabilizing the economic and political future" of the country and as representing "the greatest piece of constructive legislation which has come out of Washington in a generation. " (A)

1169. Wetzel, Charles J. The American Rescue of Refugee Scholars and Scientists from Europe, 1933-1945. Wisconsin, 1964. 446p. (DA 25:1180)

There is still insufficient monographic material upon which to base generalizations concerning the "influence" of this immigration of European scholarship and teaching, but the author has attempted to chronicle discussions of influence up to the present. Although the contributions of the refugees have been critically debated, there is general agreement that the new arrivals added a cosmopolitan component to American teaching drawn from their non-American backgrounds and that in some fields, such as nuclear physics, their contributions to American science and scholarship cannot be minimized. (A)

1170. Wood, Katherine D. K. The Question of International Regulation of Migration. Wisconsin, 1929. 210p.

1171. Wood, Samuel E. The California State Commission of Immigration and Housing: A Study of Administrative Organization and the Growth of Function. California (Berkeley), 1942. 265p.

1172. Wyman, David S. American Policy Toward Immigration of Refugees from Nazism, 1938-1941. Harvard, 1966. 243p. Published under the title Paper Walls: America and the Refugee Crisis, 1938-1941 (Amherst: University of Massachusetts Press, 1968).

1173. Young, Clarence K. Rights of Aliens in the United States. Princeton, 1924. 210p.

V. MISCELLANEA

1174. Adler, Norman M. Ethnics in Politics: Access to Office in New York City. Wisconsin, 1971. 247p. (DA 32:4669-A)
This is a study of the pattern of access to public office by ethnic groups in New York City between 1910 and 1960. The nomination and election of six major groups (Irish, Germans, Jews, Italians, Negroes, and Puerto Ricans) to two legislative offices (New York State Assemblyman and New York City Alderman) and eight executive offices (Mayor, Comptroller, President of the Board of Aldermen, and five Borough Presidents) are analyzed.

1175. Ali, Agha A. Theories of Americanization Operative in Gary, Indiana Schools. Ball State, 1964. 167p. (DA 26:6494)
The author studies changing theories of Americanization, giving particular attention to the period 1907 through 1917, and evaluates their effect on school policies, programs, and attitudes. When American independence came of age in the realm of culture and philosophy toward the end of the nineteenth century it found a typical manifestation in the schools of Gary. The educational philosophy of William A. Wirt, reflected also in the thought of Dewey expressed in the Gary schools, was tested in the changed urban conditions. These conditions led him inevitably to expand the role of the school in proportion to the diminishing role of the home, church, and neighborhood. The school day became longer and the school curriculum diversified and permeated by democratic, egalitarian tendencies. (A)

1176. Allen, James P. Catholics in Maine: A Social Geography. Syracuse, 1970. 400p. (DA 32:1013-B)
This study is a historical geographic interpretation of what has been the most fundamental dimension of Maine society. Maine people have been especially conscious of the distinction between Protestant and Catholic, and the most important contrasts and similarities among Maine communities are usually reflections of the varying size, character, and proportion of the Catholic population. Such features provide the basis for this study of the social geography of the state.

1177. Allswang, John M. The Political Behavior of Chicago's
Ethnic Groups, 1918-1932. Pittsburgh, 1967. 320p.
(DA 28:1026-A)
Published under the title A House for All Peoples: Ethnic Politics in Chicago, 1890-1936 (Lexington: University of Kentucky Press, 1971). This dissertation studies the voting and general political behavior of nine Chicago ethnic groups over the period 1918 to 1932. Included are Czechoslovakian-, Polish-, Lithuanian-, Yugoslavian-, Italian-, German-, and Swedish-Americans, and Jews and Negroes. The study is particularly concerned with two related problems: (1) the means, interests, and effects of ethnic political involvement; and (2) the rise of the Democratic Party to unprecedented power. It was found that changing ethnic political behavior was very closely connected with the rise of the Democratic Party. Ethnic voting and party membership became increasingly Democratic from 1928 on and comprised the great part of emergent Democratic strength.

1178. Andrews, Bruce R. Religious and Ethnic Influences on Voting Behavior: A Study of the Syracuse Electorate from 1918 to 1957. Syracuse, 1961. 715p. (DA 22:4395)
Based upon a sampling of empirical and impressionistic findings, this study identifies a variety of conceptions of motivational sources of voting having a direct or indirect basis in Catholic affiliation, along with some of the subsequent political effects, grouped, respectively, into hypotheses of "motivation" and "direction." One of the motivational hypotheses, focusing upon ethnicity as the real source of much that has been identified as "religious," was selected for intensive investigation.

1179. Angus, Jack D. Social Aspects of Aging Catholics in the Deanery of South Bend, Indiana. Notre Dame, 1967. 271p. (DA 28:3773-A)
This study is primarily a social survey of a 25-percent systematic file sample of the Catholics aged 65 and over listed on the rolls of 28 parishes in the South Bend Deanery, which, along with the Fort Wayne Deanery, constitutes the Fort Wayne-South Bend Diocese.

1180. Annakin, Virgil D. The Missionary, An Agent of Cultural Diffusion. Ohio State, 1941. 617p.

1181. Appel, John J. Immigrant Historical Societies in the United States, 1880-1950. Pennsylvania, 1960. 448p. (DA 21: 859)
Published under the same title (New York: Arno, 1980). Appel studies selected historical societies founded by Scotch-Irish, Irish, Jews, Germans, and Scandinavians in the United States, giving particular attention to their origins, founders' ideologies, and the history produced or neglected by them. Drawing on their publications and on accounts of the societies and their members, Appel concludes "that national immigrant societies dating from before 1910 were organized by an ethnic elite promoting immigrant

history to challenge established historical theory and to influence social, religious and political issues closely related to ethnic group interests. " Equally challenging in this provocative study is the conclusion that the decline of national immigrant historical societies was attributable to the loss of ethnic consciousness and consequent dwindling monetary support from ethnic elites, to the emergence of specialized ethnico-religious propaganda and defense agencies, and to the professionalization of historical scholarship.

1182. Arden, Gothard E. The Interrelationships Between Culture and Theology of the Lutheran Church in America. Chicago, 1945. 143p.

1183. Aurand, Harold W. The Anthracite Mine Workers, 1869-1897: A Functional Approach to Labor History. Pennsylvania, 1969. 245p. (DA 30:2932-A)
Published under the title From Molly Maguires to the United Mine Workers: The Social Ecology of an Industrial Union, 1869-1897 (Philadelphia: Temple University Press, 1971). The anthracite mine workers confronted two sets of occupational problems: one concerned wages and the other dealt with the high accident rates of the mines. The organization of work precluded any meaningful response by individuals and compelled the mine workers to act collectively. The failure of violence during the Molly Maguire episode and the strikes of 1877 prompted the mine workers to institutionalize their responses through the labor union.

1184. Babow, Irving P. Secular Singing Societies of European Immigrant Groups in San Francisco. California (Berkeley), 1954. 142p.

1185. Bachman, James R. Theodore Lothrop Stoddard: The Bio-Sociological Battle for Civilization. Rochester, 1967. 276p. (DA 28:3593-A)
The years immediately following World War I were marked by an excess of public tension, confusion, and "free-floating" fear. This condition was reflected in the plethora of "doom" literature that was so voraciously devoured. No writer did more to enrich this literature than Theodore Lothrop Stoddard, whose volumes dramatically set forth the dire perils of the colored races, biological degeneration, and the revolutionary movements that supposedly organized the immense residue of inferior humans into a grand assault against civilization. Stoddard was a journalistic sounding-board for the eugenics movement and scientific racism, which reached an apex in the early nineteen-twenties. (A)

1186. Baker, Gladden W. Race, Nativity, and Parentage as Factors in Adult Mortality in the United States. Yale, 1922. 147p.

1187. Baker, Gwendolyn C. The Effects of Training in Multiethnic Education on Preservice Teachers' Perceptions of Ethnic Groups. Michigan, 1972. 183p.

1188. Ballis, Barbara. Robert E. Park on Race, Ethnicity and
Urbanization: A Study of the "Chicago School" of American
Sociology, 1914-1936. California (Berkeley), 1975. 364p.
(DA 37:647-A)
This study is a reconstruction of a tradition that flourished before
the publication of Talcott Parsons's The Structure of Social Action
in 1937, and the subsequent predominance of systemic perspectives and quantitative methods in sociology in the United States.
This earlier tradition, referred to as the "Chicago school" of
American sociology, was rooted in the scholarly activities of
members of the Department of Sociology at the University of
Chicago from 1914 to 1936, during which time it was regarded
as the most influential center of sociological thought in the United
States, if not the world. The fundamental contribution of the
Chicago sociologists was the development of methods of empirical
research that corresponded to the nature of social processes and
thus captured the reality of human group life. The empirical
thrust of social research was expressed in the methodological injunction that the city of Chicago itself be treated as "a social
laboratory."

1189. Barta, Russell. The Concept of Secularization as a Social
Process. Notre Dame, 1959. 172p. (DA 20:4451)
An examination of the sociological literature on the subject indicates that "secularization" has at least two different meanings,
each meaning suggested by its own tradition in social science.
It can refer to the general, historic movement whereby tradition
as such loses its power to influence social action. The author
prefers to refer to this trend as "rationalization" in the Weberian
sense. Secularization can also refer to that social process
whereby religion ceases to be a constitutive element of inclusive
social systems. It is in this sense that the author prefers to
use the term.

1190. Bauman, John F. The City, The Depression, and Relief:
The Philadelphia Experience, 1929-1939. Rutgers, 1969.
496p. (DA 30:5367-A)
In this study the defeat of the social worker's image of relief in
Philadelphia is analyzed from the perspective of the city's several
centers of organized pressure, namely, labor unions, business
organizations, civic groups, and the city's political parties.
Furthermore, considerable attention is given to the political
significance of unemployment relief, with the conclusion reached
that, in the case of Philadelphia, New Deal relief did not alter
the basic political complexion of the city. Philadelphia, as the
study shows, was a Republican stronghold before the Depression,
and the GOP remained the dominant party during and after the
Depression. Essentially, therefore, by 1937 the city of Philadelphia remained a work-oriented society, and all groups, including labor and the unemployed themselves, in the face of still-
overwhelming unemployment, opted for the older and more reassuring view of poverty, unemployment, and relief.

Miscellanea 283

1191. Beck, Nicholas P. The Other Children: Minority Education in California Public Schools from Statehood to 1890. California (Los Angeles), 1975. 216p.

1192. Bell, Digby B. The Variations for Piano, op. 27 of Anton Webern and the Quaderno Musicale di Annalibera of Luigi Dallapiccola. A Lecture Recital. North Texas State, 1973. 60p. (DA 34:1949-A)
The lecture recital was given on November 20, 1972. The discussion of Webern's Variations and Dallapiccola's Quaderno Musicale consisted of an analysis of the two works followed by a comparison of stylistic and performance aspects. The two works were then performed. In addition to the lecture recital four other public recitals were given. Two of these consisted entirely of solo literature for the piano. The third recital was a vocal chamber music recital and the fourth consisted of a piano concerto performed with an orchestra.

1193. Berman, Hyman. Era of the Protocol: A Chapter in the History of the International Ladies' Garment Workers' Union, 1910-1916. Columbia, 1956. 467p. (DA 16:1245)
This study traces the organization of the labor force of the ladies' garment industry into effective and stable trade unions during the early decade of the twentieth century and then examines the workings of a pioneering trade agreement, known as the Protocol, which was in effect in many branches of the industry from 1910 to 1916. The first two chapters give the reader an economic bird's-eye view of the industry and relate the faltering attempts of the Union to organize the labor force from 1900 to 1910. Chapters III-V, dealing with the Waistmakers' Strike of 1909, the Cloakmakers' Strike of 1910, and the strikes in the women's trades in 1913, relate the successful efforts at trade-union organization. Union and manufacturer tactics are explored and the role of the socially conscious outsiders, such as Brandeis, Filene, Marshall, Schiff, etc., is examined. Without the interference of the social workers and progressives it is doubtful whether trade-union organization would have been successful as early as 1910 in the ladies'-garment industry.

1194. Binstock, Robert H. Ethnic Politics and the Reform Ideal. Harvard, 1965. 276p.

1195. Birnbaum, Lucia D. Behaviorists, Protestants and Progressives, 1913-1933. California (Berkeley), 1964. 183p.

1196. Bischoff, Henry C. The Reformers, the Workers and the Growth of Positive Government: A History of the Labor Legislation Movement in New York State, 1865-1915. Chicago, 1964. 140p.

1197. Bixler-Marquez, D. A School-Community Sociolinguistic Assessment for Decision-Making in Bilingual Education. Stanford, 1978. 97p.

1198. Bodger, John C. The Immigrant Press and the Union Army. Columbia, 1951. 427p. (DA 12:42)
Finds that the immigrant press generally supported the Union cause, but with reservations. Immigrant journals that had supported Douglas in 1860 criticized Lincoln's handling of the war and the recruitment of immigrants in Europe and Canada; Radical Republican German papers supported Fremont over Lincoln in 1864 and criticized Union army treatment of some Germans; and Conservative Republican journals never criticized Lincoln or the army but devoted space to the achievements of immigrant soldiers in the war.

1199. Borowiec, Walter A. The Prototypical Ethnic Politician: A Study of the Political Leadership of an Ethnic Sub-Community. State University of New York at Buffalo, 1972. 286p. (DA 33:1791-A)
A survey of the scholarly writings concerning ethnic politics reveals a relative absence of research that deals with important aspects of this field. Of particular significance is the lack of quantitative interview-based data that assesses the possible changes in contemporary ethnic political behavior that might be attributed to the "melting pot." Ethnic political leaders, and in general the political behavior and characteristics of certain "neglected" groups, such as Polish-Americans, also represent topics that require greater research interest. Accordingly, this study attempts to analyze the possible effects that variables associated with the melting-pot thesis (specifically class and generation) have had upon the traditional form of ethnic political leadership. The term "prototypical ethnic leader" was utilized to refer to the traditional leadership pattern. A review of the literature suggests five dimensions as relevant to the prototypical pattern. The author's hypotheses state that upward class mobility and the passage of time have made contemporary ethnic leaders more "middle class" and less prototypical on each of the dimensions studied. (A)

1200. Bosse, Richard C. Origins of Lutheran Higher Education in Ohio. Ohio State, 1969. 434p. (DA 30:4242-A)
This study traces the origins of Lutheran higher education in Ohio from the American experience of the Lutheran Church, through the frontier adaptations of a missionary objective and the nineteenth-century development of Lutheran theological schools and colleges.

1201. Bradley, Harold C. Frank P. Walsh and Post War America. St. Louis, 1966. 251p. (DA 27:2978-A)
Frank P. Walsh, joint chairman with ex-President William Howard Taft of the War Labor Board, resigned his position as soon as the Armistice was signed. Walsh expected some employers to attempt to lower wages, lengthen hours of labor, and try to weaken the labor organizations that had gained strength during the war. He resigned from the War Labor Board to be free to represent organized labor during the period of reconstruction.

Walsh was in favor of government intervention in the economy to
prevent unemployment and the other social and economic evils
that could be expected to result from the conversion of the nation's economy from war to peacetime production. He thought
the President should grant amnesty to political prisoners because
the war was over. At first an advocate of the League of Nations,
he soon began to oppose the plans for international organizations
when it became obvious that nothing was going to be done to
guarantee the "right of self-determination" of those small nations
that were outside the Austro-Hungarian Empire. (A)

1202. Brody, David. The Steel Makers: A Labor History of the
American Iron and Steel Industry to 1929. Harvard, 1958.
302p.
Published under the title Steelworkers in America: The Non-
Union Era (Cambridge, Massachusetts: Harvard University
Press, 1960).

1203. Brostowin, Patrick R. John Adolphus Etzler: Scientific-
Utopian During the 1830's and 1840's. New York, 1969.
394p. (DA 31:864-A)
The story of John A. Etzler is relevant to American literature
and ideology, for he is a synecdoche of America in the 1830s
and 1840s. In his writings, alternately crude and inspired, awkward and lilting, repetitive and terse, but always impassioned
and sincere, he symbolizes the revolutionary prophet and the revivalist preacher. With equal facility he wrote poetic dream visions, propaganda tracts, and engineering descriptions. Nothing
is known of his early and later life, but the productiveness of
his middle years justifies his rescue from oblivion. German-
born around 1796, he emigrated to the United States in 1831 as
coleader with John A. Roebling (the Brooklyn Bridge builder) of
the Muhlhausen Emigration Society. (A)

1204. Brown, Julia S. Factors Affecting Union Strength: A Case
Study of the International Ladies' Garment Workers Union,
1900-1940. Yale, 1942. 273p.

1205. Browne, Henry J. The Catholic Church and the Knights of
Labor. Catholic, 1949. 210p.
Published under the same title (Washington, D.C.: Catholic University of America, 1949).

1206. Buccheri, John S. An Approach to Twelve-Tone Music:
Articulation of Serial Pitch Units in Piano Works of Schoenberg, Webern, Krenek, Dallapiccola, and Rochberg. Rochester, 1975. 349p. (DA 37:679-A)
The purpose of the dissertation is to develop an approach to
twelve-tone music that focuses on a variety of serial pitch units
(the row, segments, groupings, and permutations of the row) in
context. The extent to which such units are articulated by non-
pitch aspects is the central preoccupation, although potentials of
the pitch set that are realized in the music are also examined.

Each of Chapters II-VI deals with music by one composer, and begins with a comprehensive and comparative discussion followed by analyses of the individual pieces contained in each opus. The works examined are: Schoenberg's Op. 25, Op. 33a, Op. 33b; Webern's Piano Variations, Op. 27; Krenek's Twelve Short Piano Pieces; Dallapiccola's Quaderno Musicale di Annalibera; and Rochberg's Twelve Bagatelles.

1207. Burns, Robin B. A Critical Biography of Thomas D'Arcy McGee. McGill, 1966. 285p.

A multifaceted portrait of a Canadian Irish leader who believed that immigrants had to adapt themselves to their new land to prove that they belonged to the new society.

1208. Burns, Warren T. The Plays of Edward Green Harrigan: The Theatre of Intercultural Communication. Pennsylvania State, 1969. 214p. (DA 30:3130-A)

This research is centered upon 19 unpublished plays written and produced by Edward Green Harrigan between the years 1879 and 1891. His characters and his subject matter were drawn chiefly from the immigrant Irish and Germans, and the native New York Negroes, as well as the newly arriving Italians, Slavic Jews, and Chinese. For these people, Harrigan's rancor comedies and simple melodramas became, in effect, a kind of school for integration into the mainstream of life in their newly adopted homeland.

1209. Burrows, Robert N. The Image of Urban Life As It Is Reflected in the New York City Novel, 1920-1930. Pennsylvania, 1959. 466p. (DA 20:2796)

This study is an examination of the representation of life in New York during the period between 1920 and 1930 by contemporary novelists. The study attempts to report the fullness and character of the view given in these novels of (1) the physical city, (2) urban man, (3) the jazz age, and (4) the major themes developed by these novelists, including "Migrant and Immigrant; Negro and Jew, " "Success and Failure, " "Marriage and Divorce, " and "Religion. "

1210. Butosi, J. Church Membership Performance of Three Generations in the Hungarian Reformed Churches of Allegheny County, Pennsylvania. Pittsburgh, 1961. 265p.

1211. Cale, Edgar Barclay. The Organization of Labor in Philadelphia, 1850-1870. Pennsylvania, 1940. 207p.

1212. Caliandro, Gloria G. B. The Visiting Nurse Movement in the Borough of Manhattan, New York City, 1877-1917. Columbia, 1970. 256p. (DA 32:1680-B)

The emergence and development of visiting nursing is treated in the context of the social forces and factors that influenced the practice of visiting nursing. In the latter part of the nineteenth and early twentieth centuries New York City was coping with the problems of inadequate housing, inadequate facilities for the care of the sick poor, and a population that was growing rapidly from immigration. Visiting nursing began as a response to the health needs of the people of New York City. These health needs were not being met by the medical profession, as they extended beyond the scope of medical practice, and they were not being met by philanthropic workers, who lacked the necessary skills to cope with varied medical and social problems. Finally, the health needs were not being met by institutional care, as approximately 90 percent of the sick poor remained at home during illness.

1213. Candeloro, Dominic L. Louis Freeland Post: Carpetbagger, Singletaxer, Progressive. Illinois (Urbana), 1970. 283p. (DA 31:6509-A)
This study is a biography of Louis Freeland Post, who lived from 1849 to 1928. Post was a reformer and journalist who at various times became involved in radical reconstruction in South Carolina, the Henry George single-tax movement, and various phases of progressivism. Post's finest hour came in early 1920 during the Red Scare. Attorney-General A. Mitchell Palmer and his men had rounded up thousands of alien radicals for deportation. Since the Labor Department had jurisdiction over deportation proceedings and since circumstances left Post as the highest-ranking officer in the Department, it was up to Post to decide on the deportations. Post's perusal of the cases convinced him that Palmer and his young assistant, J. Edgar Hoover, had grossly overstepped the bounds of due process. He therefore canceled most of the deportation warrants. Post's action was a key factor in bringing the excesses of the Red Scare into check.

1214. Cary, Lorin L. Adolph Germer: From Labor Agitator to Labor Professional. Wisconsin, 1968. 288p. (DA 29: 4416-A)
Adolph Germer was born in 1881 and died in 1966 after more than 60 years in the labor movement. Successively active in the United Mine Workers, the Socialist Party, and the CIO, Germer never reached the pinnacles of union power. Yet, Germer's active years illuminated in microcosm the transformation of trade unions from a peripheral element in the nation's life to a powerful bloc. Specifically, his career reflected the declining importance of ideology in the unions, the labor movement's quest for equilibrium, and the implications of that search.

1215. Casmus, Mary I. Gian-Carlo Menotti: His Dramatic Techniques. A Study Based on Works Written 1937-1954. Columbia, 1962. 168p. (DA 23:1118)
The purpose of the study is to analyze Gian-Carlo Menotti's dramatic techniques and to determine the principles of libretto-writing employed in his works. The materials selected for the analysis are the librettos of the eight operas produced by Menotti from 1937 through 1954: Amelia Goes to the Ball, The Old Maid and the Thief, The Island God, The Telephone, The Medium, The Consul, Amahl and the Night Visitors, and The Saint of Bleecker

Street. The librettos are grouped according to the media for which the operas were written, i.e., the traditional opera house, the theater, and the special media of radio and television.

1216. Castellanos, Diego A. The History of Bilingual Education in New Jersey: Its Implications for the Future of Educational Equity for National Origin Students. Fairleigh Dickinson, 1979. 676p. (DA 40:2525-A)
This study chronicles the first decade of bilingual education in New Jersey, 1967-1977. The author provides as background bilingual practices in the United States to the mid-twentieth century and a review of the Hispanic experience in New Jersey schools since World War II. Research for the historical overview revealed that bilingual education is not a new phenomenon. The United States has always had a polyglot population (collectively).

1217. Cavendish, Thomas. Folk Music in Selected Twentieth Century American Operas. Florida State, 1966. 209p. (DA 28:1093-A)
Some 15 operas are studied, including Gian-Carlo Menotti's The Old Maid and the Thief and Marco Bucci's Sweet Betzy from Pike. The operas have been categorized into three groups, based upon the extent to which folk music has been employed: those in which folk sources constitute a major portion of the musical material; those in which the folk music is recessive, but the recurrence of folk themes throughout the work gives the indigenous material some stylistic significance; and those in which occasional reference is made to folk music, but references are not frequent enough to influence the composer's style.

1218. Chalmers, Leonard. Tammany Hall and New York City Politics, 1853-1861. New York, 1967. 258p. (DA 29: 199-A)
In 1853 Tammany Hall, the popular name for the New York City Democratic Party, was the strongest political party in the city. The spokesman for the party was the General Committee, chosen, ostensibly in democratic fashion, in primary elections in the wards. The party owed its strength to: (1) its continuity (manifested in monthly meetings of the Committee, whether or not elections were impending); (2) its use of the immigrant voter; (3) the stamp of authority given it by the sachems of the Tammany Society, which owned Tammany Hall, as a result of which the Committee had the exclusive right to make nominations for the party; and (4) the patronage received by party members from state and national governments.

1219. Chassé, Paul. Les Poètes Franco-Américains de la Nouvelle-Angleterre, 1875-1925. Laval, 1968. 241p.

1220. Chazanof, William. The Political Influence of Joseph Ellicott in Western New York, 1800-1821. Syracuse, 1955. 270p. (DA 15:2518)
Joseph Ellicott, a surveyor who originally had little thought of

seeking an active political career, was introduced to political life
in western New York by the Holland Land Company. In 1798 he
surveyed the more than $3\frac{1}{2}$-million-acre property owned by the
Company. Impressed by Ellicott's accomplishments, the Dutch
owners promoted him to Resident-Agent of this valuable land.
Thus, in 1800 Ellicott became a realtor, intent upon devoting
himself to business alone. Based on more than 6,000 Ellicott
letters, this study pointed up several conclusions. In western
New York from 1800 to 1821 Joseph Ellicott had considerable
political influence, which grew out of his position as Resident-
Agent. Many of the things that he and the Holland Land Company
did politically to increase their business--the creation of counties, the extension of the canal, the establishment of the bank--
also proved beneficial to the settlers of western New York. Ellicott's industriousness stood out as the key personal characteristic in many of his achievements.

1221. Christiansen, Sigurd O. The Sacred Choral Music of
Richard Felciano: An Analytic Study. Illinois, 1977.
206p. (DA 38:16-A)
The topic of this study is the sacred choral music of Richard
Felciano. This topic is broken down in the body of this study
into two broad divisions or chapters. In each chapter the works
of that division are arranged chronologically by date of composition and treated in an analytical way. Chapter I deals with the
works not accompanied by electronic tape. These include the
composer's very early works (1952), as well as his most recent
choral work (Te Deum, 1974). Chapter II deals with the works
that are accompanied by electronic tape or other electronic media. These include Felciano's first electronically accompanied
choral work (Words of Saint Peter, 1965) and his most recent
choral work with electronic tape (Hymn of the Universe, 1974).

1222. Cinel, Dino. Conservative Adventurers: Italian Migrants
in Italy and San Francisco. Stanford, 1979. 385p. (DA
40:4191-A)
The record of Italian emigration and immigration is complex.
Any effort to package it in a theoretical and comprehensive model
of sociological fabrication is likely to distort the past. Immigrants were perplexed individuals trying at the same time to
break away from their past and to retain their traditions. A
general conclusion, however, is possible. Although active in
seeking solutions to poverty, immigrants were reluctant to let
go of the Old World traditions and embrace innovative and intelligent solutions even when the immigrants' commitment to tradition and regionalism worked against their material advancement.
(A)

1223. Clark, Alex R. Low-Income Housing for the Elderly in
Baltimore: A Spatial Analysis of a Social Policy. Pennsylvania State, 1979. 264p. (DA 40:460-A)
In the planning of housing for the low-income elderly location
analysis has been limited to aspects of site and microscale situ-

ation, whereas larger-scale situational problems have been for
the most part ignored. The present study finds that unpredicted
problems of urban spatial organization may follow from this in-
attention to citywide perspective. The current generation of old-
age housing programs, 1965 to 1975, combines conventional upper
limits on income with large scale in project development. The
effect is to concentrate low-income elderly even more than they
were concentrated before becoming project residents. The increased concentration of low-income households may further erode
the already small purchasing power in the project environs, which
in most cases are already lower-class areas. This means that
the housing projects may serve further to segregate the urban
population by age and class, in direct contradiction to the in-
equality-diminishing goals of public-housing programs. (A)

1224. Cole, Donald B. Lawrence, Massachusetts: Immigrant
City, 1845-1912. Harvard, 1957. 248p.
Published under the title Immigrant City: Lawrence, Massachusetts, 1845-1921 (Chapel Hill: University of North Carolina
Press, 1963). An impressive portrait of immigrant communities
and the industrial growth of an American city, with a detailed
account of the textile strike of 1912.

1225. Connaughton, Mary S. The Editorial Opinion of the Catholic
Telegraph of Cincinnati on Contemporary Affairs and Politics, 1871-1921. Catholic, 1943. 256p.
Published under the same title (Washington, D.C.: Catholic University of America Press, 1943).

1226. Coombs, Gary B. Migration and Adaptation: Indian Mis-
sionization in California. Los Angeles, 1975. 258p.
(DA 36:2938-A)
This is an attempt to explicate the reasons for the success of
Franciscan missionaries in effecting the conversion of the Chumash Indians of California to Christianity and the Spanish colonial
way of life. Particular emphasis is placed on the migration of
Chumash from their native villages to Santa Barbara mission.
This was a process that spanned nearly 20 years during the late
eighteenth and early nineteenth centuries and was of critical importance in the Spanish missionization scheme. Analysis indicates
that the observed pattern of migration to the mission, and hence
the success of the missionaries' activities, may be explained
largely in terms of the changing social, economic, and demographic conditions at both the mission and the aboriginal villages.

1227. Cordasco, Francesco. The Role of Daniel Coit Gilman in
American Graduate Education. New York, 1959. 293p.
(DA 20:1254)
Published under the title Daniel Coit Gilman and the Protean
Ph.D.: The Shaping of American Graduate Education (Leiden:
Brill, 1960; rev. ed., Totowa, New Jersey: Rowman and Little-
field, 1973). The aim of the present study has been to place
Daniel Coit Gilman (1831-1908) in the historical framework of the

development of graduate education in the United States. Although Gilman's importance in the history of graduate education is usually acknowledged in a few lines in the general histories of American education, this study attempts the first comprehensive survey of Gilman, giving historical dimension to all his educational service including his presidence of Johns Hopkins University, 1876-1902. Gilman has been widely acknowledged as a major influence on the development of graduate education in America. His importance has been acclaimed by leaders of both old and new academic institutions. Johns Hopkins University fulfilled a half-century of American graduate aspiration; essentially, it was the culmination of a long indigenous educational evolution. If the German Wissenschaftslehre, the history of whose influence on American education remains to be written, had any influence on Gilman and his Hopkins, it was mainly subordinate to native impulses.

1228. Costello, Lawrence. The New York City Labor Movement, 1861-1873. Columbia, 1967. 598p. (DA 28:1193-A)
Among the labor movement's chief beneficiaries were New York City's many depressed immigrant workers. The new arrivals' adjustment to American life frequently was facilitated by union membership; many immigrant workers either joined English-speaking associations or formed their own bodies. They not only benefited from the labor movement, but made valuable contributions to its development and philosophy. Both immigrant and native-born workers faced the threat of growing industrial consolidation. During the 1860s and 1870s the city's labor movement helped to launch and develop the National Labor Union and many national unions. The New York City workers' main centralizing efforts, however, were directed toward the creation and strengthening of local and regional central labor unions. (A)

1229. Dapogny, James E. Style and Method in Three Compositions of Luigi Dallapiccola. Illinois, 1971. 176p. (DA 32:4648-A)
This study examines three of Dallapiccola's vocal-instrumental works: Goethe-Lieder of 1953, Cinque Canti of 1956, and Preghiere of 1962. The study proceeds movement by movement to investigate the details of compositional technique and structure. One of the main parts of the thesis is the examination of Dallapiccola's very personal harmonic practice, particularly in light of its consistency throughout the varied textures of these three works. The continuity of Dallapiccola's style during the evolution and refinement of his serial technique is the central point of the study. The thesis attempts to show how Dallapiccola, in these three compositions, brings his stylistic aims and technical means into accord with each other.

1230. David, Henry. The History of the Haymarket Affair: A Study in the American Social-Revolutionary and Labor Movements. Columbia, 1936. 264p.
Published under the same title (New York: Farrar & Rinehart, 1936).

1231. Degler, Carl N. Labor in the Economy and Politics of New York City, 1850-1860: A Study of the Impact of Early Industrialism. Columbia, 1952. 360p. (DA 12:733)
Radical workers during the period, prompted by two severe depressions, rested their solutions to unemployment on the proposition that government had a responsibility to find work for the jobless. Echoes of such views of the role of the state were to be found in labor's espousal of minimum-wage laws and laws limiting work to ten and even eight hours a day. Though New York had a large immigrant population, very little animosity between native and immigrant labor was found even under the tensions of an advancing industrialism, for the simple reason that the overwhelming proportion of the labor force was of immigrant origin.

1232. Drescher, Nuala M. The Opposition to Prohibition, 1900-1919: A Social and Institutional Study. Delaware, 1964. 434p. (DA 25:3532)
As a part of the Progressive movement reformers undertook to purge the nation of the blight of drink. Failing to achieve their objective through local option or statewide prohibition, they turned to national legislation. Naturally, opposition to such a radical scheme developed. The years before the adoption of the Eighteenth Amendment saw the German-American community ally itself to the trade associations of the liquor industry in a vain attempt to preserve its cherished traditions. It saw in the Prohibition movement an attack on the German language, family, and the Continental Sunday. The leadership of the vain attempt to prevent submission and ratification of the Amendment was in the hands of the United States Brewers' Association. This organization struggled to overcome the natural rivalry within its own ranks and with the hard-liquor interests and to organize an effective program of defense. (A)

1233. Dubofsky, Melvin. New York City in the Progressive Era, 1910-1918: A Study of Organized Labor in an Era of Reform. Rochester, 1960. 268p.
Published under the title When Workers Organize: New York City in the Progressive Era (Amherst: University of Massachusetts Press, 1968).

1234. Duff, John B. The Politics of Revenge: The Ethnic Opposition to the Peace Policies of Woodrow Wilson. Columbia, 1964. 338p. (DA 28:1369-A)
The political influence of America's immigrant groups reached its height in the years following the First World War. Although nearly every sizable ethnic block in the United States engaged in some type of politicking for or against the Treaty of Versailles or the League of Nations; the Irish-Americans, Italian-Americans, and German-Americans were particularly active. It was an unfortunate historical coincidence for Woodrow Wilson that these peoples--the three largest blocs of so-called "hyphenated Americans" in 1920--became the severest critics of his peace policies.

1235. Edwards, Andrew W. An Investigation of Ethnic Minority Courses/Content in Accredited Master's Level Social Work Curriculum Programs in the United States. Kansas State, 1978. 187p. (DA 40:80-A)
The research problem had as its primary aim the investigation of accredited Master's-level social-work curriculum programs in colleges and universities in the United States regarding their inclusion of ethnic-minority courses and the content of such courses. The research was to: (1) determine the extent to which the most appropriate method of curriculum desegregation was being utilized; and (2) analyze the content of the ethnic minority courses of the schools participating in the study.

1236. Eisler, Paul E. History of the Metropolitan Opera, from 1883 to 1908. Boston, 1965. 340p.

1237. Estabrook, George H. Racial Factors in Intelligence. Harvard, 1926. 127p.

1238. Exoo, Calvin F. Ethnic Culture and the Incentives of Political Party Activists in Two Midwestern Cities. Wisconsin (Madison), 1979. 279p. (DA 40:4209-A)
The suggestion of this dissertation is that a locale's party incentive structure may be partly understood as a product of that locale's ethnic culture. Culture is defined, in Clyde Kluckhohn's elegant prose, as "that part of human life which is learned by people as the result of belonging to some particular group, and is that part of learned behavior which is shared with others ... [it is] a system of related designs for carrying out all the acts of living, for thinking, feeling, and believing." Specifically, then, this dissertation suggests that culture is manifest in the power of an ethnic group to impart to its sons and daughters a way of thinking about politics, and it suggests that the incentives of local party activists originate partly in this surprising power of the nurturant community. The author began to investigate that possibility by choosing two focal cities, Gary, Indiana, and Rockford, Illinois, on the basis of their contrasting ethnic compositions. Their ethnic groups are "contrasting," of course, in the sense that their cultures seem to imply the possibility of contrasting incentive structures. (A)

1239. Fahey, Frank M. Denis Kearney: A Study in Demagoguery. Stanford, 1956. 330p. (DA 17:611)
The political career of Denis Kearney from 1877 to 1880 demonstrates the high potential of demagoguery on the American scene. The discrepancy between aspiration and fulfillment during California's early period of statehood, brought to a clear focus by the depression of the 1870s, enabled Kearney to exert upon his contemporaries an influence completely disproportionate to his merit as a statesman. The interaction of large business enterprise and political democracy, both at a stage of rampant adolescence, in a frontier area of magnificent physical resources, provided a fertile field for the demagogue's art. (A)

1240. Farmer, George L. Majority and Minority Americans: An Analysis of Best Selling American Fiction from 1926-1966. Southern California, 1968. 243p. (DA 28:4457-A)
The objectives of this study were to: (1) review the writing in samples of American novels that bear the title "best seller"; (2) ascertain who are the characters in these novels; (3) find who are the important characters; (4) explore who are the approved characters; (5) investigate, among the role players, who are attributed the high-status characterizations; (6) probe who, among the characters, pursue the "heart" and "head" goals; (7) ascertain who, among the role players, manifest what personality traits; and (8) explore the sociological and educational implications of the study.

1241. Farrell, Lawrence. Vincent Persichetti's Piano Sonatas from 1943 to 1965. Rochester, 1976. 280p. (DA 37:3254-A)
This is a study of the currently published piano sonatas, the Third through the Eleventh Sonatas, by Vincent Persichetti. It was prompted by the quality of these nine works by an important composer of our time, and by the lack of available studies of them. In regard to this music, the scope of the study is defined by two questions: What are the musical materials, and how are they used? The study has a secondary thrust, which is its interest in the process of music analysis itself, and begins with a consideration of matters basic to the observation of music.

1242. Feinstein, Estelle F. Stamford, Connecticut, 1865-1893: A Study of Small Town Politics in the Gilded Age. Columbia, 1971. 427p. (DA 32:1435-A)
During the quarter-century following 1868 the politics of the Town of Stamford, Connecticut, contained within the town-meeting framework, responded to three factors: growth in population from 10,000 to 16,000 and concentration of residents in core areas; rise of the Yale Lock Company and its President to positions of dominance; and increase in numbers and political awareness of the Irish-minority resident in visible downtown enclaves. Under the theory of Connecticut's Constitution, the towns exercised a large degree of autonomy, and the town freemen, assembled periodically in meetings, decided policies. In the Gilded Age the system produced a politics of restraint.

1243. Fiege-Kollman, Maria L. Reading and Recall Among Bilingual and Dialect Speaking Children. California (San Diego), 1975. 237p.

1244. Fine, David M. The Immigrant Ghetto in American Fiction, 1885-1917. California (Los Angeles), 1969. 205p. (DA 31:755-A)
Published under the title The City, The Immigrant and American Fiction, 1880-1920 (Metuchen, New Jersey: Scarecrow, 1977).
This study examines the fictional portrait of European immigrants in their ghetto surroundings during the years of their

greatest impact on the American city. Most of this fiction was written by native-born Americans, sympathetic observers of the ghetto who gained their knowledge of immigrant life from their experience as journalists, settlement workers, and teachers. Part One of the study explores the native-drawn portrait of the urban immigrant; Part Two deals with novels written by immigrants.

1245. Flaherty, Patrick D. The History of the Sixty-Ninth Regiment of the New York State Militia, 1851-1861. Fordham, 1963. 183p.

1246. Flynn, Judith Z. Dress of Older Italian-American Women: Documentation of Dress and the Influence of Socio-Cultural Factors. Ohio State, 1979. 198p. (DA 40:4238-A)
The purpose in the study was to investigate everyday dress of older Italian-American women in relation to sociocultural factors. The theoretical basis for the sociocultural factors was based on Tonnies's (1890) ideal types of Gemeinschaft and Gesellschaft, often discussed as the change of culture from a rural community to an urban society. Dress was viewed in relation to a Gemeinschaft/Gesellschaft continuum with three features of change selected to be analyzed: (1) the movement from family life to individuality; (2) the movement from neighborhood to city; and (3) the movement from religion to rationalities. Methodology was based on field research from an ethnomethodological perspective.

1247. Formisano, Ronald P. The Social Bases of American Voting Behavior: Wayne County, Michigan, 1837-1852, as a Test Case. Wayne State, 1966. 512p. (DA 28:590-A)
Published under the title The Birth of Mass Political Parties: Michigan, 1827-1861 (Princeton, New Jersey: Princeton University Press, 1971). Most studies of political parties in the Jackson Period have been dominated by economic determinism, often implicitly. Historians have usually assumed that most voters chose their party according to their economic interest. Recent studies, with different assumptions, and using multi-variate analysis, have challenged the classes-interpretation and proposed that ethnocultural and religious groups must be studied to understand the most important causes of division in the mass electorate.

1248. Frankfort, Nancy. The English as a Second Language Component of Selected Bilingual Programs in a New York City Community School District. A Descriptive Study. New York, 1975. 223p.

1249. Freda, Robert A. The Role of the New Jersey Coalition for Bilingual Education in the Enactment of the New Jersey Bilingual Education Law. Rutgers, 1976. 278p.
The main portion of this study is devoted to the Coalition's politics. The Coalition's guidelines are intended to serve as a tentative model of community intervention in the arena of educational

politics. The study also provides an overview of New Jersey demographic developments, and of documents related to bilingual and bicultural education.

1250. Fryer, Judith A. A Guide to the Study and Performance of Three Operas of Gian-Carlo Menotti. Columbia, 1974. 527p. (DA 35:6180-A)
The purpose of this study is to provide historical information, analytical material, and practical suggestions for the teaching and performance of selected Menotti operas in secondary schools. Younger children of elementary-school age use much of the material. Three operas were chosen for thorough analysis: The Medium (1946); Amahl and the Night Visitors (1951); Help, Help, The Globolinks! (1968). Selection was based on dramatic and musical consideration, use of the English language, frequency of performance, the difficulty of the opera, and appropriateness for educational use.

1251. Garber, Morris W. The Silk Industry of Paterson, New Jersey, 1840-1913: Technology and the Origins, Development and Changes in an Industry. Rutgers, 1968. 294p. (DA 29:1843-A)
By the 1880s the juxtaposition of skilled labor from Europe, improving machinery, and the raw-silk supply culminated in Paterson's earning the nickname "Silk City." It was first in American silk production. But some of the very factors that contributed to the stellar position of Paterson as the leading American silk manufacturer also led to its decline as the leading producer. Improved machinery did not require skilled labor; therefore, silk manufacturers, in an effort to cut production costs, sought locations where there was an abundant supply of cheap, tractable labor. Paterson workers, reacting to the effects of improving machinery upon their livelihood, climaxed a history of strikes, with the silk strike of 1913. But, rather than improving the lot of the workers, this strike only aggravated their plight, for it forced manufacturers to accelerate their exodus from the city.

1252. Garlick, Richard C. Philip Mazzei; Friend of Jefferson: His Life and Letters. Virginia, 1931. 178p.
Published under the same title (Baltimore: Johns Hopkins University Press, 1933).

1253. Geary, Gerald J. The Secularization of the California Missions, 1810-1846. Catholic, 1934. 204p.

1254. Geiser, Karl F. Indentured Servants in the Colony and Commonwealth of Pennsylvania. Yale, 1900. 264p.
Published under the title Redemptioners and Indentured Servants in the Colony and Commonwealth of Pennsylvania (New Haven, Connecticut: Yale University Press, 1901).

1255. Gerson, Louis. Woodrow Wilson and the Rebirth of Poland, 1914-1920. Yale, 1952. 253p.

Published under the title Woodrow Wilson and the Rebirth of Poland, 1914-1920: A Study in the Influence on American Policy of Minority Groups of Foreign Origin (New Haven, Connecticut: Yale University Press, 1953).

1256. Gohmann, Mary D. Political Nativism in Tennessee to 1860. Catholic, 1938. 137p.
Published under the same title (Washington, D. C.: Catholic University of America Press, 1938).

1257. Goodell, M. Elaine. Walter Damrosch and His Contributions to Music Education. Catholic, 1973. 590p. (DA 33:5763-A)
For approximately 60 years Walter Damrosch (1862-1950) was a prominent figure in musical America. In spite of his lengthy participation and significant contributions only minimal recognition is accorded him in the history of music education for his pioneer work in educational concerts for adults, young people, and children. The purpose of the study is to describe and assess his contributions as: (1) conductor of the Symphony Concerts for Young People and Symphony Concerts for Children; (2) coauthor of the Universal School Music Series; and (3) originator and director of the NBC Music Appreciation Hour. (A)

1258. Gorman, Mary F. Federation of Catholic Societies in the United States, 1870-1920. Notre Dame, 1962. 396p. (DA 23:614)
Catholic societies existed in the United States as early as the 1830s, but the notion of federating societies into a national organization suggested itself only after Pope Pius IX commended the Catholic Union of Belgium in 1871. Struck by the Pope's words, Richard Clarke, a New York lawyer, drafted a constitution for local Unions with the aim of forming a national Catholic Union comprised of the individual sections. One unit in the formation of a successful Union was the Catholic Society. Although Clarke's efforts failed, the notion of a federative movement lingered. It cropped up during the preparation of the First Catholic Congress in 1889 in Baltimore and again before the Second Catholic Congress in 1893. And Catholic societies received much attention in the papers at both Congresses. However, it was Martin Griffin of the ICBU Journal who made a first suggestion for a federation of Catholic societies, which was finally attempted on the diocesan level in Pittsburgh in 1890. (A)

1259. Gorman, Mary J. Tertiary Franciscan Missionary Sisters of the Sacred Heart and Catholic Education in the United States. Fordham, 1946. 383p.

1260. Gottfried, Alex. A. J. Cermak, Chicago Politician: A Study in Political Leadership. Chicago, 1953. 382p.
Published under the title Boss Cermak of Chicago: A Study of Political Leadership (Seattle: University of Washington Press, 1962).

1261. Gould, Glen H. A Stylistic Analysis of Selected Twelve-Tone Works by Luigi Dallapiccola. Indiana, 1964. 271p. (DA 25:6676)

It is the purpose of the present investigation to present an analysis of the stylistic features of seven twelve-tone works by Luigi Dallapiccola: Ciaccona, Intermezzo e Adagio for cello (1945); Due Studi for violin and piano (1946-1947); Due Pezzi for orchestra (1946-1947); Quaderno Musicale di Annalibera for piano (1953); Variazioni for orchestra (1953); Piccola Musica Notturna for chamber orchestra (1954); and Concerto per la notte di Natale dell'anno 1956 for soprano voice and chamber orchestra (1956-1957).

1262. Green, James J. The Impact of Henry George's Theories on American Catholics. Notre Dame, 1956. 377p. (DA 16:2057)

This study traces the spontaneous rise of Irish nationalism among American Catholics that resulted from a threatened famine in 1879-1880 in Ireland. This nationalistic sympathy included a strong criticism of economic conditions of the Irish peasantry based largely on landholding practices of the absentee landlords of Ireland. Through American Land Leagues having general remedial aims, the suffering Irish received monetary and moral support in their struggle to better their conditions. Differences over specific remedies--Michael Davitt's nationalization scheme and Henry George's theories forwarding radical solutions--shattered the unanimity of the agitation.

1263. Griffin, Clifford S. Organized Benevolence in the United States, 1815-1865. Wisconsin, 1957. 290p. (DA 18:215)

In the years between 1815 and 1865 the leaders of eight national benevolent societies tried, from their offices in Boston, Philadelphia, and New York, to mold the vigorous, growing nation. Laypeople and clergy of several Protestant denominations, but mostly Presbyterians and Congregationalists, formed the American Education Society to subsidize poor ministerial students and the American Home Missionary Society to subsidize indigent pastors. They began the American Bible Society to publish and circulate the Holy Writ, the American Sunday School Union to issue religious and moral works for children, and the American Tract Society to guide adults. To stop wars, liquor drinking, and slavery they founded the American Peace Society, the American Society for the Promotion of Temperance, and the American Antislavery Society. At first the leaders attempted to persuade other men and women to be good by ministerial preaching and by millions of books and tracts distributed by thousands of agents and auxiliary societies. But a combination of failure and impatience produced political action. These self-styled stewards of the Lord demanded laws to stop wars, Sabbath profanation, liquor selling, and slavery's expansion. They tried to get Bibles and other religious books into common schools. Because all the leaders feared the political and religious power of Catholics and other immigrants, they called for discriminatory ordinances. (A)

Miscellanea 299

1264. Gutierrez, Lorraine P. Attitudes Toward Bilingual Education: A Study of Parents with Children in Selected Bilingual Programs. University of New Mexico, 1972. 180p.
A 63-item questionnaire was given to both parents (in 110 pair) and the responses showed that there were few significant differences between socioeconomic groups. Those under 35 were more positive in their attitudes than the older parents. This sample showed parents strongly in favor of a bilingual society.

1265. Hargrove, Erwin C. The Tragic Hero in Politics: Theodore Roosevelt, David Lloyd George, and Fiorello La Guardia. Yale, 1963. 889p. (DA 25:1313-A)
This is the study of three political leaders from the standpoint of a theory of personality. Common motivations that led to similar styles of leadership are delineated and the political consequences are assessed. These three men felt strong inner demands for attention and power. It is postulated that these demands were compensatory reactions against inner fears of weakness. The winning of attention from others brought increased self-esteem and the wielding of power provided a feeling of mastery and prowess. The genesis of these demands is not discussed.

1266. Harkavy, Ira R. Reference Group Theory and Group Conflict and Cohesion in Advanced Capitalist Societies: Presbyterians, Workers, and Jews in Philadelphia, 1790-1968. Pennsylvania, 1979. 627p. (DA 40:4193-A)
This study examines the history of Presbyterians, workers, and Jews in Philadelphia with the aim of contributing to the development of a credible theory of group behavior and consciousness in advanced capitalist societies. The case study of Jews provides an overview of Philadelphia Jewish history from the late eighteenth century to 1968. From that overview it is asserted that Philadelphia and American Jewish history have not been characterized by shallow and momentary instances of unity. To the contrary, the Jewish experience in Philadelphia is conceptualized as a continuous struggle to preserve Jewish unity, consciousness, and identity. The significance of outgroup hostility in maintaining Jewish group survival and of legal equality in producing group fragmentation is emphasized. Attention is also focused on the particularly intimate connection that exists between capitalist development and Philadelphia and American Jewish history. (A)

1267. Harmond, Richard P. Tradition and Change in the Gilded Age: A Political History of Massachusetts, 1878-1893. Columbia, 1966. 418p. (DA 27:2965-A)
As this study seeks to show, Massachusetts confronted a dual set of challenges in the post-Reconstruction era. In the first place, the Irish-Americans and workers, provoked by their marginal status, united in a political revolt to obtain greater recognition and benefits for themselves. From 1878 to 1883 this ethnic-labor insurrection, led by Benjamin F. Butler, was the focus of Massachusetts politics. Secondly, the accelerated tempo of industrial

and technological changes spawned a spirit of onrushing materialism that threatened the Commonwealth's traditional business and political mores.

1268. Harney, Paul S. A History of Jesuit Education in American California. Berkeley, 1944. 194p.
A detailed overview of Italian Jesuit influence in the development of Catholic higher education in California.

1269. Harrell, Kenneth E. The Ku Klux Klan in Louisiana, 1920-1930. Louisiana State, 1966. 388p. (DA 27:1318-A)
Representatives of the Invisible Empire arrived in Louisiana in November 1920. Chapters of the Klan were established in New Orleans and Shreveport before the year ended. During 1921 approximately 73 other units were chartered. Organization of the Klan in the Bayou State was accomplished with considerable secrecy. Klan organizers utilized the whole spectrum of national Klan themes in recruiting Louisiana Knights; however, the secret society's potential as a counterforce to postwar lawlessness, Catholicism, and petty moral violations was the most appealing feature of the Invisible Empire to Louisianians. (A)

1270. Harrison, Barbara E. Foreign Doctors in American Hospitals: Sociological Analysis of Graduate Medical Education. Columbia, 1968. 474p. (DA 30:1649-A)
The study focuses on socialization and learning experiences of a marginal group--foreign-trained interns and residents in the United States. These graduates' experiences and reactions during graduate medical training are described and related to several themes characterizing both foreign medical graduates in particular and the problems encountered by marginal groups in socialization settings in general.

1271. Hecht, David I. Russian Radicals and America. Harvard, 1945. 215p.

1272. Himmelein, Frederick T. Walter Damrosch, A Cultural Biography. Virginia, 1972. 666p. (DA 33:3540-A)
Walter Damrosch was born in Breslau, Poland, on January 30, 1862. He died in New York City on December 22, 1950. Damrosch was a musician, conductor, impresario, composer, educator, and perpetual enthusiast. He was born into a musical family in which economics and esthetics permeated daily life. His father, a fervent disciple of Richard Wagner and "the Music of the Future," brought his beliefs and family from Europe to the United States and labored to make his Wagnerian faith triumphant in the chaos of American concert life. Walter Damrosch inherited his father's faith and dedication; he supplied his own shrewdly gregarious social sense. (A)

1273. Hinrichsen, Carl D. The History of the Diocese of Newark, 1873-1901. Catholic, 1962. 453p. (DA 24:1997)
This study covers the administrations of Michael Augustine Cor-

rigan (1873-1880) and Winand Michael Wigger (1881-1901), the second and third bishops of Newark. The period was chosen because it was so eventful for the Church in the diocese and the nation. The main purpose of the work is to describe the developments in the diocese that reflect the problems and trends of the Church in the United States. The most important and enduring work of Wigger's administration was the effort to provide for the numerous immigrants of various nationalities. Particularly in regard to the Germans, Italians, and Poles do the developments during these decades shed light on the problems facing the Church from foreign nationalism and immigration. (A)

1274. Hoffman, George J. Catholic Immigrant Aid Societies in New York City from 1880 to 1920. St. John's, 1947. 193p.
Includes information on a number of ethnic immigrant-aid societies, including the Mission of Our Lady of the Rosary (Irish), the St. Raphael Society (German), the St. Raphael Society (Italian), the St. Joseph Society for Polish Immigrants, the Mission of Our Lady of Guadalupe (Spanish-speaking), and French and Belgian immigrant-aid societies.

1275. Holden, Randall. I: The Seattle Production of "The Telephone" by Gian-Carlo Menotti. II: The Six Extant Operas of Antonio Lotti (1667-1740). III: The American Premier of "Jupiter in Argos" by Antonio Lotti. Washington, 1970. 468p. (DA 32:1551-A)
All of the elements that comprised the production are discussed in detail: the design of the sets and costumes, the planning of abstract lighting effects, the question of appropriate dramatic and visual style, the problems encountered in preparing the score and the libretto. Also included in the paper are the Italian and French librettos and a complete orchestral score of the performing edition (approximately one-third of the music was cut for the production).

1276. Holt, Michael F. Forging a Majority: The Formation of the Republican Party in Pittsburgh, Pennsylvania, 1848-1860. Johns Hopkins, 1967. 539p. (DA 28:566-A)
Published under the title Forging a Majority: The Formation of the Republican Party in Pittsburgh, 1848-1860 (New Haven, Connecticut: Yale University Press, 1969). American politics in the 1850s and especially the rise of the Republican Party have traditionally been interpreted in terms of national events. By focusing on the city of Pittsburgh, Pennsylvania, this dissertation attempts to go beneath the surface of national issues, to examine the relationship between social and economic conditions and political behavior, and to assess the influence of local factors in shaping political coalitions before the Civil War.

1277. Hood, Edmund L. The Greek Church in America. New York, 1899. 142p.

1278. Hopkins, Thomas W. Educational Standardization and the "Foreign Child." New York, 1933. 276p.

1279. Howe, Claude L. The Theology of William Newton Clarke. New Orleans Baptist Theological Seminary, 1959. 203p. Published under the same title (New York: Arno, 1980). One of the most prominent theologians among modern Baptists, William Newton Clarke (1841-1912) exercised a broad influence well beyond the confines of his own congregation. Reared in the context of "a mitigated form of Calvinism, " Clarke departed from this heritage as his theology "became increasingly ethical and experiential. " His Outline of Christian Theology (1898) has been hailed as "the first systematic American treatise based on acceptance of biblical criticism, historical change, and scientific knowledge of the natural world. " This work scientifically examines the men, events, and movements that led to the development of Clarke's theological thought. This dissertation offers a look at the man who was perhaps the first systematic theologian of theological liberalism in America.

1280. Huff, Robert A. Frederic C. Howe: Progressive. Rochester, 1967. 301p. (DA 28:175-A)
The dissertation describes in detail the public career of Frederic C. Howe from his early years in Cleveland to his resignation as United States Commissioner of Immigration at the Port of New York in September 1919. Prior to World War I he was sustained by the evidences of progress and he partook of the general optimism. American participation in the war provided the setting for his own personal tragedy. As a public servant he was pained by the self-imposed restraints on his freedom of speech and association; as Immigration Commissioner he was unable to prevent injustice at home; and as an adviser to the Administration he was unable to promote justice in the world. These failures reactivated a feeling of despondency that had been temporarily quieted by a sense of progress during the Progressive years. After 1919 he persisted, intermittently, as an activist, but his faith in the appropriateness of government as a vehicle of reform was seriously weakened. (A)

1281. Hunt, Thomas C. Catholic Educational Policy and the Decline of Protestant Influence in Wisconsin's Schools During the Late Nineteenth Century. Wisconsin, 1971. 475p. (DA 32:4389-A)
Churches, as well as governments, have sought to control the education of the young. Since the educational goals of Church and State are sometimes incompatible, conflicts have occurred between the "City of God" and the "City of Man. " Educational policy of the Catholic Church in Wisconsin in the late nineteenth century had two major aims: (1) to rid the public schools of mainstream Protestant influence; and (2) to achieve substantial independence from the state in the schools that the Church operated. This second goal was felt to be more important by the Wisconsin Catholic Bishops, since the parochial schools were thought to be the instruments by which the faith of Catholics was preserved. (A)

1282. Hunter, Diane M. The Cultural Communication Factor in ABE-TESOL Programs. Georgetown, 1975. 141p.

1283. Irizarry, Richard. The Relationship Between Creativity and Bilingualism. Texas (Austin), 1979. 139p. (DA 40: 3841-A)
The purpose of the study was to isolate, explore, probe, and discuss the possible variables in the relationship that exist between creativity and bilingualism. The study offered cognitive and affective attributes that were characterized as belonging to either bilinguals or to creative persons. If, on an empirical basis, bilingualism and creativity share certain factors, traits, or characteristics unique to humanity, then the possibility exists that these attributes are correspondingly shared by individuals that are characterized as either bilingual or as creative. The study supported the idea that an early bilingual-bicultural experience may have cognitive implications for problem-solving and creative expression.

1284. Iverson, Robert W. Morris Hillquit: American Social Democrat, A Study of the American Left from Haymarket to the New Deal. Iowa, 1951. 248p.

1285. Jackson, Kenneth T. The Ku Klux Klan in the City, 1915-1930. Chicago, 1967. 276p.
Published under the same title (Chicago: University of Chicago Press, 1967).

1286. Jaffee, Irma B. Joseph Stella: An Analysis and Interpretation of His Art. Columbia, 1966. 526p. (DA 27:716-A)
Joseph Stella is recognized by most scholars as an important figure in American art. However, no scholarly work devoted to him has been published, and he is all but forgotten by the art-interested public since his death in 1946. The present dissertation brings to light a large body of previously unknown handwritten manuscripts by Stella. Presented in their original Italian in an appendix, large sections are translated and incorporated into the text, serving to make Stella's art and personality more understandable; these texts are also related to many of the 142 works discussed and illustrated. There is also a documented checklist of 758 oils and drawings. (A)

1287. Jensen, Richard J. The Winning of the Midwest: A Social History of Midwestern Elections, 1888-1896. Yale, 1967. 402p. (DA 27:4194-A)
Published under the title Winning of the Midwest: Social and Political Conflict, 1888-1896 (Chicago: University of Chicago Press, 1971). In 1889 the prohibition issue shook the Republican loyalty of many Germans and defeated the once invincible Iowa GOP. Prohibition was decisive because it brought to boil a simmering conflict between the two basic religious cultures, the pietism of the old-stock Yankees and Scandinavians, and the liturgicalism of Catholics and German Lutherans. Pietistic and

liturgical tendencies existed in all economic and ethnic groups, but the crusading moralism of the pietists, strongest in the small towns and rural areas, created a dilemma for the professional politicians of the GOP. In 1890 the cultural conflict erupted in Wisconsin over the issue of foreign languages in the schools. Combined with popular dissatisfaction with the high McKinley tariff and the political blunders of President Harrison, the cultural conflict produced a massive victory for the Democrats in 1890. (A)

1288. Kalangis, George P. The Sociocultural and Religious Ethos of the Greek Parochial Schools in the American Southeast. Florida State, 1979. 408p. (DA 40:3742-A)
The conceptual framework of this research was that the sociocultural, ethnolinguistic, and religious triad of the Greek Orthodox Ethos is primarily transmitted by the Greek Orthodox Parochial School to second- and third-generation Greek-Americans in the Southeastern United States. A combined total of 428 subjects-- 288 fifth- and sixth-grade students, 111 parents, 17 teachers and 12 clergymen--were included as subjects in this research. For the purpose of this study a battery of questionnaires was developed and validated.

1289. Kim, Yong-Kwon. Alfred Stieglitz and His Times: An Intellectual Portrait. Minnesota, 1970. 162p. (DA 31: 3096-A)
At the turn of the twentieth century a number of American artists and intellectuals suffered from a sense of alienation in American Society. This was largely a result of the discrepancy between intellectual pursuits and ordinary life, which was marked by vast social and technological change. The typical conflicts were between the urban and the rural, the collective and the individual, the industrial-technological and the agrarian, the artistic and the commercial. The life of Alfred Stieglitz exemplifies this ambivalence. Alfred Stieglitz was born in a liberal Jewish-German family and brought up in the metropolitan milieu of New York City. He combined a basic urban orientation with a minority consciousness. Throughout his life Stieglitz struggled to reconcile urban and rural values.

1290. La Gumina, Salvatore J. Vito Marcantonio, Labor and the New Deal, 1935-1940. St. John's, 1966. 265p. (DA 27: 4196-A)
Published under the title Vito Marcantonio, The People's Politician (Dubuque, Iowa: Kendall-Hunt, 1969). It is hoped that this study will bring some justice and balance to the role Marcantonio played in the New Deal era. He was active on many fronts-- civil liberties, civil rights, Communism, and issues of war and peace--but he was most consistent and his truest role can best be detected in his untiring efforts in behalf of labor. Marcantonio's record demands that he be given a significant place in the saga of American labor. (A)

Miscellanea 305

1291. Lambert, Byron C. The Rise of the Anti-Mission Baptists: Sources and Leaders, 1800-1840. Chicago, 1957. 240p. Published under the same title (New York: Arno, 1980). This dissertation treats the origins of the Primitive Baptists and the social, theological, and political milieu out of which that major movement in Baptist history arose. Thus, it serves as an essay in American intellectual history as well as a study in American religious individualism. Many other denominations shared the Baptists' fear that national church organizations might lead to a national religion. The Baptists, however, are the "single most important heirs of the original larger movement" known as Antimissionism. This movement sought to stem the tide of national religion. The author has worked with and quotes extensively from rare periodical material.

1292. Lane, James B. Bridge to the Other Half: The Life and Urban Work of Jacob A. Riis. Maryland, 1970. 362p. (DA 31:4090-A)
In the spring of 1870 the 21-year-old Jacob Riis, restless with the languid pace of life in his rural birthplace of Ribe, Denmark, emigrated to the United States. After seven years of drifting from job to job and living in semi-poverty, he became a police reporter in the heart of New York City's slums. His imaginative, sensitive, and contentious personality was well suited to the requirements of journalism. He poignantly described and realistically photographed the life and habits of the impoverished immigrants of New York's East Side. His aim was to awake affluent Americans to the political, economic, and moral necessity of combatting urban decay. His book How the Other Half Lives (1890) generated great interest and spurred a variety of humanitarian efforts to prevent the dehumanization of the individual caught in the maelstrom of the slum. (A)

1293. Lawrence, Elwood P. The Immigrant in American Fiction, 1774-1830. Case Western Reserve, 1944. 243p.

1294. Leclair, Paul J. The Francis Scala Collection: Music in Washington, D. C. at the Time of the Civil War. Catholic, 1973. 166p. (DA 34:7268-A)
In order to demonstrate the artistic growth that took place the author explored three specific areas of importance: the growth of musical activities in Washington, the development of the United States Marine Band in the city, and the music that this band performed. An exposition of these areas shows a relationship between the influx of European music and the growing cosmopolitan nature of the city. There was an assimilation of traits found in European music, notably opera, and in the band music performed, usually for patriotic purposes. The resultant assimilation of national styles paved the way for the thoroughly American style of John Philip Sousa. The discussion is concerned with the music from the Francis Scala Collection. This is the music library of the Marine Band during the years of Scala's leadership, and is located in the Music Division of the Library of Congress. (A)

1295. Lothrop, Gloria R. Father Gregory Mengarini, an Italian Jesuit Missionary in the Transmontane West: His Life and Memoir. Southern California, 1970. 376p. (DA 31:2286-A)

Before mid-nineteenth century the star of empire had coursed across the continent, leading American settlers to the Pacific shore. Among the vanguard of the pioneer caravan that followed close upon the heels of the fur trapper was a significant minority who came in response to the repeated request for Blackrobes made during the 1830s by Indian tribes of the Interior Plateau, particularly the Flatheads. Among these missioners was a young Roman Jesuit, Gregory Mengarini (1811-1886). This study traces Mengarini's life along the frontier in a biographical introduction that accompanies the translated edition of his Flathead memoirs. Also included is a brief history of Jesuit missionary activities and a summary of the Protestant response to the Indian plea for religion, as well as a sketch of Mengarini's later life in California at the University of Santa Clara.

1296. Madden, Henry M. [John] Xantus, Hungarian Naturalist in the Pioneer West. Columbia, 1950. 187p.

1297. Martin, James J. Individualist Anarchism in the United States: A Survey of Native Anti-Statist Thought and Action, 1827-1908. Michigan, 1949. 284p.

1298. Mathisen, Robert R. An Historical Model of the Interaction of Religion with American Society. Illinois State, 1978. 227p. (DA 39:5680-A)

The research consisted of two distinct yet related components. The first was concerned with the development of a historical model that would illustrate the interaction of religion with specified factors in American society during the period 1865 to 1900. The second component was the production of a teaching unit for an undergraduate introductory American history course that would demonstrate the viability of the historical model and would enable the writer to determine if any changes took place in students' perceptions of the model while studying the teaching unit.

1299. Maxwell, William J. Frances Kellor in the Progressive Era: A Case Study in the Professionalization of Reform. Columbia (Teachers College), 1968. 307p. (DA 29:3561-A)

Kellor, a younger contemporary of Jane Addams, Lillian Wald, and Florence Kelley, was both a lawyer and a University of Chicago-trained sociologist. Operating out of Hull House in Chicago and the Rivington Street College Settlement House in New York, she helped to lead the Progressive attack on the problems of the new immigrant and the Negro. Her efforts to halt the exploitation of Negro household workers in New York culminated in 1906, when she founded the National League for the Protection of Colored Women, one of three organizations that consolidated in 1911 to form the National Urban League of today.

1300. McBeth, H. Leon. English Baptist Literature on Religious Liberty to 1689. Southwestern Baptist Theological Seminary, 1961. 263p.
Published under the same title (New York: Arno, 1980). In this work McBeth examines and explains the writings of the early English Baptists Smyth, Helwys, Murton, and Busher. His survey begins with the early Stuart era. As Baptists increased in number during the last years of the reign of King Charles and under the regime of the Puritans their writings became more diffuse. In addition to an analysis of these early Baptist works McBeth continues his study to encompass Baptist writings after the Restoration and the passing of the Test Act to the Act of Toleration. As the author points out, many of the seventeenth-century writings are "ill-arranged, repetitious and cumbersome." Nonetheless, as records of Baptist history and the development of the Baptist theological point of view, they cannot be ignored.

1301. McColgan, Michael D. Individual Role in Educational Change and a Framework for Its Analysis, with Particular Reference to the Establishment of a Bilingual Sub-School in an Urban School System. Columbia (Teachers College), 1972. 521p.

1302. McCourt, Kathleen. Women and Grass-Roots Politics: A Case Study of Working-Class Women's Participation in Assertive Community Organizations. Chicago, 1975. 340p. (DA 36:2440-A)
The problem under investigation here is what leads working-class women to become involved in assertive community organizations and what effects such participation has on the active women, both politically and personally. We have seen in the late 1960s and early 1970s the rise of urban community groups that are assertively making demands on the political system. These demands, characteristically, center on integration, housing, schools, and pollution. This research was carried out on the Southwest Side of Chicago, a residential area made up of white, predominantly working-class neighborhoods. In recent years a number of grass-roots organizations have formed there and women have been notably active in them, providing not only large numbers for demonstrations and picket lines but also speaking, organizing, and providing leadership.

1303. McGovern, George S. The Colorado Coal Strike, 1913-1914. Northwestern, 1953. 307p. (DA 13:1166)
On September 23, 1913, 9,000 coal miners of southern Colorado launched one of the most bitter strikes in American history. Striking for recognition of the United Mine Workers' Union, the miners were convinced that their political and social freedom, as well as their economic welfare, had for too long rested upon an industrial despotism--a despotism that was not always benevolent and seldom very wholesome. (The strikers included immigrant Italian workers.)

1304. McGrath, William J. History of Vocational Education. New York, 1913. 154p.

1305. McKay, Ernest A. Henry Wilson: Practical Radical. New York, 1969. 407p. (DA 30:3139-A)
Published under the title Henry Wilson: Practical Radical, A Portrait of a Politician (Port Washington, New York: Kennikat, 1971). This is the biography of a native of New Hampshire, born in Farmington in 1812, who served as United States Senator from Massachusetts from 1855 to 1873 and as Vice President during the second term of Ulysses Grant. He died in office in 1875. In the forties and fifties Wilson was a leading participant in the transformation of political parties in Massachusetts. Bolting the Whig National Convention in 1848 when Zachary Taylor was nominated for President, Wilson helped to form the Free Soil Party, and in 1851 he organized a coalition of Free Soilers and Democrats to elect Charles Sumner to the United States Senate. An opportunist, even though remaining true to the antislavery cause, Wilson used the popularity of the Know-Nothing Party in 1854 and 1855 to win election to the Senate. (A)

1306. McKevitt, Gerald. The History of Santa Clara College. A Study of Jesuit Education in California, 1851-1912. California (Los Angeles), 1972. 372p. (DA 33:1654-A)
The subject of this study is the development of Santa Clara College, in California, from its founding in 1851 to its transformation into a university in 1912. This Catholic institution was established as the outcome of a visit to California in 1849 by two Jesuit priests from their order's Indian missions in the Pacific Northwest. Invited by Bishop Joseph Alemany to help meet the educational and religious needs of his mushrooming frontier diocese, the Jesuits founded the school in May 1851, in the adobes of the former Franciscan Mission of Santa Clara.

1307. McSeveney, Samuel T. The Politics of Depression: Voting Behavior in Connecticut, New York, and New Jersey, 1893-1896. Iowa, 1965. 727p. (DA 20:5985)
The analysis of political behavior rests on a detailed examination of ward and town-level returns from national and state elections in the three states from 1892 through 1896. These returns were studied in the light of information on the socioeconomic, occupational, ethnic, religious, and racial composition of the population that was derived from official (i.e., federal and state censuses, the reports of public commissions) and unofficial (i.e., county and town histories, gazetteers, atlases, and newspapers) sources.

1308. Medina, Amelia C. A Comparative Analysis of Evaluative Theory and Practice for the Instructional Component of Bilingual Programs. Texas A & M, 1975. 283p.
Published under the same title (New York: Arno, 1978). In this study Medina sought to compare general evaluation theory, bilingual-education evaluation theory, federal regulations and guidelines for the evaluation of bilingual programs, and a local educa-

tional audit to determine if there were significant differences among requirements and practice.

1309. Mejia, Raynaldo D. Bilingual Education: An Analysis of Local District Commitment and Development of an Index of Critical Requirements. University of Southern California, 1976. 139p.

1310. Messbarger, Paul R. American Catholic Dialogue, 1884-1900: A Study of Catholic Fiction. Minnesota, 1969. 325p. (DA 30:1506-A)
The process of Catholic Americanization, both institutional and social, proceeded with greatest intensity during the years 1884 and 1900. The attitudes of the American hierarchy toward this change produced two well-defined factions within the American Church, the Americanists and the traditionalists. The public debate of this issue culminated in the condemnation by Pope Leo XIII of the heresy of Americanism, in 1899. Well below the level of that public debate, however, changes were taking place among American Catholics as they adjusted to the native culture. These changes are reflected in the fiction written by Catholics for a Catholic audience. The purpose of this study is first to discover the ways in which imaginative literature was used as a conscious instrument of institutional influence; and second to trace out the covert values and attitudes of the Catholic subculture during a period of rapid change.

1311. Miceli, Mary V. The Influence of the Roman Catholic Church on Slavery in Colonial Louisiana Under French Domination, 1718-1763. Tulane, 1979. 233p. (DA 40: 4196-A)
Religious history as an area of study and research must be examined in the wider context of world history. Concomitantly, study of the influence of the Roman Catholic Church on slavery in colonial Louisiana under French domination necessitates the involvement of demographic, economic, political, social, and psychological factors to measure with some accuracy the bearing of religion upon that particular segment of Louisiana's history from 1718 to 1763. It is precisely that time period that is subjected to inquiry by this dissertation. The search for an authentic influence of the Catholic Church on the institution of slavery as it existed in the eighteenth century includes a discrete inquiry into the attitudes, motivations, and characteristics of both the Catholic Church and, specifically, the French nation with its strong orientation toward Gallicanism and individualism. (A)

1312. Mikkelsen, Michael A. The Bishop Hill Colony: A Religious Communistic Settlement in Henry County, Illinois. Johns Hopkins, 1892. 143p.
Published under the same title (Baltimore: Johns Hopkins University Press, 1892).

1313. Miller, Sally M. Victor L. Berger and the Promise of Constructive Socialism 1910-1920. Toronto, 1966. 276p.

(DA 27:2993-A)
Published under same title (Westport, Connecticut: Greenwood, 1973). The Socialist Party of America in 1910, a decade after its birth, showed significant promise of becoming a permanent political party in the United States. More than the major parties, it played a daily role in the lives of its members; they read its newspapers, attended meetings, collected funds, and spread its propaganda. Although only in some areas was there organization in depth, it was in outline a national party. Under the guidance of reformist-minded leaders, such as Victor L. Berger, who could both maintain fundamental theories and operate political machines, the Socialist Party offered its supporters a bright future. By 1920, however, the promise turned out to be hollow. The problem of why and how such potential proved empty and to what extent failure was the responsibility of the party leaders has been examined through manuscript collections and party documents. (A)

1314. Moll, Dianne-Lynn. A Comparative Study of the English Language Proficiency of Monolingual and Bilingual Children. Pittsburgh, 1978. 272p. (DA 40:829-A)
This study was designed to determine if a bilingual second-grade population compared favorably with their monolingual peer group on a battery of tests measuring their English-language proficiency. The research was based on the position that there is a necessary level of linguistic attainment for satisfactory academic achievement in a second-grade population. The subjects were 130 children attending second grade in American schools, located on military bases in southwest Germany.

1315. Moll, Luis C. Bilingual and Cross-Cultural Referential Communication. California (Los Angeles), 1978. 119p. (DA 39:2839-A)
The results indicated differences in communication accuracy (as measured by correct listener selection of target referents) due to the ambiguity of the messages given by the speakers. The children designated as speakers performed competently in a variety of situations. However, in two specific contexts, with (1) younger Anglo (English-monolingual) listeners and (2) older Hisplanic Spanish-speaking listeners, these otherwise competent communicators performed comparatively poorly. Since the children's performance was significantly better in some contexts than in others, the possibility was considered that some sort of contextual interference affected the communication.

1316. Morrison, John W. Social Polity and Ethnic Classification in Hawaii. Illinois (Urbana), 1978. 265p. (DA 40:7410-A)
Ethnic categories are social categories defined in terms of putative descent of their current extensions from ancestral "groups" with unique histories. It is argued, however, that these categories and the concomitant histories are cultural properties of the whole population, which is organized in terms of them.

Therefore, the proper study of ethnic categories must take place
in the context of the ethnically complex population as a whole,
and cannot be done properly through comparative studies of particular "ethnic groups." It is shown that in Hawaii, people of all
ethnic identities share substantially the same system of ethnic
categories.

1317. Morrow, Victoria P. Bicultural Education: An Instance of
Cultural Politics. Colorado, 1978. 435p. (DA 39:5161-A)
The thesis is an exploration of cultural politics, the way in which
dominant and subordinate groups characterize their own and each
others' cultures. It includes, first, a conceptual framework for
the understanding of cultural politics, in which it is distinguished
from stereotyping. Based on the literature on stereotyping and
cultural politics, a paradigm for the way in which powerful and
powerless groups seem to use characterizations of both routine
and rhetorical culture is proposed.

1318. Mulkey, Young J. Reactions of Parents of Different Ethnic
and Socioeconomic Groups to Instruction in Values Education
in a Metropolitan Area. Texas (Austin), 1979. 122p. (DA
40:3746-A)
In recent years there has been a resurgence of interest in teaching values in the schools, and as a result school districts have
given consideration to the addition of a values-education component to the school curricula. Due to the personal nature of values,
plus the increase of parental involvement in decisions affecting
school policy, the implementation of values education could be
positively, or negatively, affected by the parents' attitudes toward
it. This study was designed to determine whether parents wanted
values education in the public schools. (A)

1319. Mulvey, Mary D. French Catholic Missionaries in the
Present United States (1604-1791). Catholic, 1936. 184p.
Published under the same title (Washington, D. C.: Catholic University of America Press, 1936).

1320. Murphy, John C. An Analysis of the Attitudes of the American Catholics Toward the Immigrant and the Negro, 1825-
1925. Catholic, 1941. 158p.
Published under the same title (Washington, D. C.: Catholic University of America Press, 1941).

1321. Murphy, Mary C. Bishop Joseph Rosati, C. M. and the
Diocese of New Orleans, 1824-1830. St. Louis, 1960.
245p. (DA 21:3079)
Joseph Rosati, born in Sora, Italy, January 30, 1789, entered
the Congregation of the Priests of the Mission in 1807. While
a seminarian he gave much thought to serving God on the foreign
missions. Therefore, when Bishop DuBourg went to Rome, in
1815, seeking laborers for his vast diocese of Louisiana, Rosati
volunteered. He came to America in 1816 and was named Superior of the diocesan seminary by Bishop DuBourg in 1818.

During his term as administrator Rosati performed many creditable duties for the diocese. The explanation of these activities forms the core of this dissertation. Among his various achievements were a decisive blow to lay trusteeism in New Orleans, the clearing of the great debt of the diocese, obtaining needed priests, and the raising of a renewed interest in the question of a seminary for New Orleans.

1322. Nelson, Mally. The First Italian Opera Season in New York City: 1825-1826. North Carolina, 1976. 240p. (DA 38:1048-A)

1323. Newell, James S. A Critical Analysis of the Development and Growth of the Kenneth Sawyer Goodman Memorial Theatre and School of Drama, Chicago, Illinois, 1925-1971. Wayne State, 1973. 306p. (DA 34:3603-A)
The Kenneth Sawyer Goodman Memorial Theatre and School of Drama has been in continuous operation behind the Art Institute of Chicago for some 47 years. In those long years of service it has contributed much to the cultural life of the city of Chicago as well as to the country at large. The Goodman Theatre became one of the first examples of the professionalization of the amateur theater, a culmination of the desire for dramatic self-expression that swept this country in the early years of the twentieth century. Since its idealistic beginning the Goodman Theatre has gone through a number of changes. In 1931 the professional company was disbanded due to economic and administrative pressures. From 1932 to 1957 the Theatre was maintained solely as a vehicle for student productions of the School of Drama. During this period the School was run by Dr. Maurice Gnesin, a contemporary of Stanislavsky, and by David Itkin, a former member of the Habima Theatre of Moscow. (A)

1324. Norton, Mary A. Catholic Missionary Activities in the Northwest, 1818-1864. Catholic, 1930. 154p.
Published under the same title (Washington, D.C.: Catholic University of America Press, 1930).

1325. Nur, Fazel. Language Maintenance Efforts of Several Ethnic Groups in Allegheny County, Pennsylvania. Pittsburgh, 1978. 104p. (DA 40:829-A)
Language-maintenance efforts, operationally defined as instruction of the ethnic language by religious, fraternal, and cultural organizations and the usage of the ethnic language in the various activities and services of these institutions, of eight ethnic groups in Allegheny County, Pennsylvania, are investigated. The relationship between these two variables and some organizational features, such as size, homogeneity, percentage of foreign-born membership, and leader's nativity, and some attitudinal characteristics of the organizational leaders, such as their belief in the maintenance of ethnic language, their belief in the future prospects of the ethnic language, and so forth, have been examined. Fifty-three interviews, 40 of them with national parish pastors and 13

Miscellanea 313

of them with leaders of ethnic fraternal and cultural organizations, have been completed.

1326. Offenbach, Lilly. The Anatomy of an Ethnic Organization. Brandeis, 1970. 212p.

1327. Olson, Frederic I. The Milwaukee Socialists, 1897-1941. Harvard, 1952. 237p.

1328. Owens, Mary L. The History of the Sisters of Loretto in the Trans-Mississippi West. St. Louis, 1925. 171p.

1329. Pahorezki, M. Sevina. The Political and Social Activities of William James Onahan. Catholic, 1942. 143p. Published under the same title (Washington, D.C.: Catholic University of America Press, 1942).

1330. Palm, Mary B. The Jesuit Missions of the Illinois Country, 1673-1763. St. Louis, 1931. 138p.

1331. Panchok, Frances. The Catholic Church and the Theatre in New York, 1890-1920. Catholic, 1976. 606p. (DA 37: 1733)
During the transition from the largely artificial drama of the nineteenth century to the realistic problem-oriented drama of the twentieth century some prominent New York Catholic laity and clergy involved themselves in movements to influence the stage. The nature of this involvement has never been clearly defined.
The Catholic Theatre Movement, founded by Eliza O'Brien Lummis in 1912, and the Catholic Actors Guild, founded by John Talbot Smith in 1914, together form the total organizational response of the New York Archdiocese toward the theater before 1920.
By examining the rise of these organizations, their founders, supporters and publications, this study has attempted to delineate the Catholic Church's evolving reaction to the drama in the theater capital of the United States.

1332. Parsteck, Bennet J. A Rhetorical Analysis of Fiorello H. La Guardia's Weekly Radio Speeches: 1942-45. New York, 1969. 236p. (DA 30:3127-A)
The purpose of this study was to make a rhetorical analysis of selected weekly radio speeches delivered by Mayor Fiorello H. La Guardia to the people of New York City from 1942 through 1945. This analysis was achieved through a consideration of: (1) the development of La Guardia as a speaker; (2) the milieu in which his weekly radio speeches were presented; (3) the manner in which La Guardia prepared his radio speeches; (4) a description of La Guardia's oral delivery; (5) the construction and the style of these radio addresses; and (6) the basic appeals he used in the content of these speeches.

1333. Passi, Michael M. Mandarins and Immigrants: The Irony of Ethnic Studies in America Since Turner. Minnesota,

1972. 248p. (DA 33:258-A)
The dissertation argues that ethnic studies in America have been "ironic" in that they have ignored the persistence of ethnic consciousness in American society and instead have sought to demonstrate the process by which white ethnic communities have been, or are being, absorbed into a homogeneous American culture. This, in turn, results from deeply rooted assumptions about American society that center on the belief that in the New World people were freed from the history, traditions, and institutions of the Old World to recover the ancient freedoms of the "natural man." This view shaped interpretations of American nationality from Crèvecoeur to Fredrick Jackson Turner. Urbanization, industrialization, and mass immigration in the late nineteenth century, in the minds of many American intellectuals, seemed to preclude the possibility of further assimilation of immigrants and threatened to shatter the presumed homogeneity of American culture. Professional social scientists in the emerging universities, however, offered a new synthesis that would make the traditional view of American society compatible with urbanization and industrialization. Drawn largely from the rural and small-town, old-stock, Protestant middle class, these professional academics did not challenge the normative assumption that the society ought to be culturally homogeneous. As new members were recruited into the academic profession, many of them from ethnic backgrounds, the assimilationist position remained unchallenged. In part this resulted from the fact that the concept of assimilation tended to rationalize the upward mobility of ethnic Americans, in part because the socialization process in the universities compelled students to adopt the intellectual framework of the profession. In the years following World War II the work of two scholars from immigrant backgrounds, Louis Wirth and Oscar Handlin, crystalized the assimilationist perspective in ethnic studies.

1334. Petrello, Barbara A. The New York-New Jersey Bilingual Job Market: Its Implications for Foreign Language Education. Rutgers, 1977. 179p.
Although 11 languages were cited in the survey, Spanish, French, and German were requested most frequently, with Spanish accounting for 44 percent of all job openings. Statistical evidence supports the need for a career-oriented component in foreign-language education.

1335. Pfau, John M. Economic Relations Between the United States and Italy, 1919-1949. Chicago, 1952. 247p.

1336. Piedmont, Eugene B. An Investigation of the Influence of Ethnic Group Differences in the Development of Schizophrenia. Buffalo, 1962. 369p. (DA 23:2235)
The purpose of this study was to show that ethnicity is a significant variable that must be considered in searching for the cause of a particular functional mental disorder--schizophrenia. Genetic and organic causes of schizophrenia are not dealt with in this study. Their influence and perhaps even determinativeness in

particular cases is not denied, however. Examining the ethnic variable, the author outlines the overall cultural pattern of the two groupings selected--Polish and German. Those aspects of the normative culture most relevant to personality development (socialization) were stressed. Different problems were encountered for each grouping. The disorganization that followed the rather recent shift from a peasant society to an urban society was significant for the Poles. For the Germans factors that sustained ethnic solidarity were pointed out.

1337. Poague, Leland A. The Cinema of Frank Capra. Oregon, 1973. 384p. (DA 34:5986-A)
Critics of Frank Capra have generally attacked him for being too popular, too American, and too politically naive to warrant recognition as a major figure in cinema history. They most often describe him as a "populist" filmmaker, a man who makes movies for and about the "little people" of America, cataloging their simple aspirations, painting with the heavy brush of caricature the fat-cat villains who oppose their individualistic ethic, and finally demonstrating the wished-for but seldom-believed victory of this democratic ethic over the realpolitik of the Robber Barons.

1338. Pyros, John A. Morris Gest, Producer-Impresario in the American Theatre. 279p. (DA 34:3604-A)
The problem of this research was to help ascertain the place of producer-impresario Morris Gest (1881-1942) in the American theater. In the main, the methodology entailed the study and scrutiny of Gest's New York productions. Brief consideration was given to Gest's biography and to his related activities in the theater. Especially during his most brilliant period, the early 1920s, Gest was associated with such international theater luminaries as Constantin Stanislavsky, Charles Cochran, David Belasco, Max Reinhardt, Sergei Diaghilev, Vladimir Nemirovitch-Danchenko, Eleonora Duse, Norman Bel Geddes, and Alexander Moissi. The study includes the biography, his early heyday, and final theater productions and attendant critical reactions. Finally, there is a consideration of his entire work and its overall place in the American theater.

1339. Reaman, George E. A Method of Teaching English to Foreigners. Cornell, 1920. 110p.

1340. Rendell, Harry J. Application of Calculus to Assimilation of Immigrants. Chicago, 1950. 211p.

1341. Ring, Jennifer B. Illusions of Success: The Uncertainty About Class and Ethnicity in American Politics. California (Berkeley), 1979. 353p. (DA 40:4214-A)
This study treats class identification and ethnic heritage in the American personality. It offers a theory about class, grounded in American political thought from the first founding to the present. The middle class is a recent rhetorical construct, masking

unwillingness to acknowledge any class structure at all. Rather than an economic grouping or traditional social class, the American middle class describes a psychological state in which aspirations to personal distinction are obscured by an ideological commitment to equality. The middle class functions to inhibit public discussion of the private agony of American ambition.

1342. Roddy, Edward. The Catholic Newspaper Press and the Quest for Social Justice. Georgetown, 1961. 115p.

1343. Romano, Louis A. Manual and Industrial Education at Girard College, 1831-1965: An Era in American Educational Experimentation. New York, 1975. 414p. (DA 36: 2073-A)
Published under the same title (New York: Arno, 1980). The purpose of this study was to describe and analyze the history of manual and industrial education at Girard College, founded in Philadelphia in 1831 as a privately endowed free boarding school for white, indigent, fatherless boys between the ages of six and 18, and to relate this history to the mainstream of manual and industrial education in the United States, 1831-1965. Overwhelmingly, the boys it served were the progeny of the Irish and Italian immigrant poor. Girard College is of particular interest to the historian of education because it was founded in that period of United States history when formal, carefully structured, and organized instruction of a practical nature was almost nonexistent for a major portion of the citizenry and for the lower classes. The school was founded in Philadelphia in 1831 by the testament of Stephen Girard and opened on January 1, 1848. It is a privately endowed, free boarding school for fatherless boys, and maintains and educates free of charge as many boys as the income from the endowment will permit.

1344. Rowley, William E. Albany: A Tale of Two Cities, 1820-1880. Harvard, 1968. 260p.

1345. Rubin, Sharon G. Alfonso Iannelli: The Career of an Artist in the American Social Context, 1906-1965. Minnesota, 1972. 321p. (DA 33:6256-A)
Historically, American artists have occupied three positions in relation to their society. They have tried to find support for their aesthetic ideals through wealthy connoisseurs; have withdrawn from society into themselves, accepting the art-for-art's-sake dictum; or have accepted the idea of social art, built on national character and needs, in order to obtain a broad audience interested in making art serve democracy as a medium of communication. Alfonso Iannelli was one of the small group of nineteenth- and twentieth-century artists, architects, and critics who took the third position. Although Iannelli would be worthy of study even if he had only defined his role as an artist in a democracy philosophically, he also attempted to express his philosophy in his works. (A)

Miscellanea 317

1346. Russo, Joseph L. Lorenzo da Ponte, Poet and Adventurer. Columbia, 1922. 166p.
Published under the same title (New York: Columbia University Press, 1922).

1347. Ryan, Leo R. Old St. Peter's, the Mother Church of Catholic New York (1785-1935). Fordham, 1936. 114p.

1348. Safier, Gwendolyn S. Jessie Bernard: Sociologist. Kansas, 1972. 366p. (DA 33:3040-A)
This dissertation is designed as a contribution to the sociology of knowledge especially as it is related to the sociology of science. The study gives a detailed account of one American female sociologist, Jessie Bernard. Bernard's recognized success as a sociologist, and her extensive publications over more than a 50-year span in a predominantly male profession and a young discipline are factors that demand careful scrutiny. The main question of the study is what, if any, is the effect of ethnicity (Jewish background) and gender (female) on the subject's work? Bernard's choice of topics for research, her methods and style, and the general reception of her work are the focus of the analysis.

1349. Salazar, Teresa A. Bilingual Education Bibliography. Northern Colorado, 1975. 127p.

1350. Samora, Julian. Minority Leadership in a Bicultural Community. Washington, 1953. 130p. (DA 15:2177)
This dissertation reports an investigation of the leadership of a minority group in a bicultural setting involving dominant-subordinate group relationships. The locale for the study is a community in southern Colorado whose population is 58 percent "Spanish" and 42 percent "Anglo." The populations are distinguishable both ethnically and culturally. The theoretical framework is borrowed primarily from G. C. Homans's The Human Group, which states essentially that leadership is the function of a specific situation and emerges from the group context. The elements involved in leadership are interaction, social rank, embodiment of norms, and social control. These elements are interrelated and reinforce one another.

1351. Sanchez, Gilbert. An Analysis of the Bilingual Education Act, 1967-1968. Massachusetts, 1973. 274p.
The author gathers data from the literature, from government documents, and from in-depth interviews with some of those involved with the passage of the act.

1352. Santerre, Richard. Le Roman Franco-Américain de la Nouvelle-Angleterre. Boston College, 1974. 283p.

1353. Scarangelo, Anthony. Church and State in Italian Education. Columbia, 1966. 325p. (DA 27:1247-A)
Of value in understanding educational backgrounds of some Italian

immigrants. For its own part, the Italian State, whether monarchical, totalitarian, or republican, has sought to limit the Church's influence in education, permitting the Church to supervise and administer religious instruction in the public schools, but under the overall supervision of the State through the Ministry of Education. Thus, the State permits the Church certain privileges, remaining on guard at the same time lest it lose its own.

1354. Sarna, Jonathan D. Mordecai M. Noah: Jacksonian Politician and American Jewish Communal Leader--A Biographical Study. Yale, 1979. 595p. (DA 40:4199-A)
Mordecai Manual Noah (1785-1851) has long been considered the most important American Jew of his time. A leader of the several-thousand-member Jewish community in New York, he was active in Congregation Shearith Israel and director of innumerable Jewish organizations. He was equally involved in the general community. He edited several important New York newspapers, and filled a variety of political and government posts, including consul at Tunis, sheriff of New York, surveyor of the New York port, judge, chairman of the John Tyler Central Committee, and Grand Sachem of Tammany Hall. Finally, he was a successful playwright, speaker, and author. (A)

1355. Schaffer, Alan L. Caucus in a Phone Booth. The Congressional Career of Vito Marcantonio: 1934-1950. Virginia, 1962. 275p. (DA 23:3339)
Published under the title Vito Marcantonio, Radical in Congress (Syracuse, New York: Syracuse University Press, 1966). Intended as a study of the political career of Vito Marcantonio (1902-1954), Representative from the East Harlem (New York City) district, largely Italian-American and Puerto Rican.

1356. Scharnau, Ralph W. Thomas J. Morgan and the Chicago Socialist Movement, 1876-1901. Northern Illinois, 1970. 361p. (DA 31:1739-A)
This study was undertaken to probe the influence of Thomas J. Morgan (1847-1912) on the Chicago socialist movement in the last quarter of the nineteenth century. Born into a poor working-class family in Birmingham, England, Morgan emigrated to the United States in 1869. He settled in Chicago and was employed as a machinist and brass finisher. His conversion to socialism came as a result of his bitter experiences during the panic of 1873. A few years later he became the leading figure in the local Socialist Labor Party.

1357. Schonback, Morris. Native Fascism During the 1930s and 1940s: A Study of Its Roots, Its Growth and Its Decline. California (Los Angeles), 1958. 89p.
A study of native fascism during the 1930s and 1940s, with particular attention given to its genesis, growth, and decline.

1358. Schneider, Susan G. The 1974 Bilingual Education Amendments: Revolution, Reaction or Reform. Maryland, 1976.

519p.
Published under the title Revolution, Reaction or Reform: The
1974 Bilingual Education Act (New York: Las Americas, 1976).
This study concerns itself with such topics as the history and
legislative background of bilingual and bicultural education, the
developing positions of the U.S. House and Senate, and the position of the federal administration. Lau v. Nichols substantially
influenced the positions of the legislative bodies.

1359. Schutzengel, Tirzah G. The Effects of Bilingualism on
Concept Formation: A Comparative Study of Monolingual
and Bilingual Elementary School Students. Clark, 1974.
227p.

1360. Seetharaman, Arumbavur N. Peter V. Karpovich, M.D.:
His Life and Contributions to Physical Education. Boston
University, 1972. 344p. (DA 33:1494-A)
The purpose of the study was to investigate the life and the nature and influence of the contributions of Peter Vasilievich Karpovich to physical education in his various roles within the profession. Karpovich was born in Louga, Russia, on April 6, 1896.
He was the sixth of nine children and was very attached to his
family. In spite of inadequate financial resources Karpovich
successfully completed school and was admitted to the Imperial
Military Medical Academy, Petrograd, where he began to specialize in physiology under the direction of Professor Ivan Pavlov. Circumstances encouraged him to leave Russia, and he
came to the United States in 1925.

1361. Sellmeyer, Francis M. The Southern Province of the
School Sisters of Notre Dame, 1925-1965. St. Louis,
1967. 310p. (DA 28:3125-A)
The Congregation of the School Sisters of Notre Dame was founded
in Germany in 1833, by Reverend Mother Teresa of Jesus Gerhardinger, for the education of youth. In 1847 the Congregation
established its first mission in the United States. As the Congregation grew in America a division of the territory into provinces became necessary. The Southern Province was formed
in 1895, with the motherhouse, Sancta Maria in Ripa, at Saint
Louis, Missouri. The early history of the Southern Province to
1924 has been described in other works. The purpose of this
dissertation is to discuss the work of the sisters in the Southern
Province from 1925 to 1965.

1362. Sheridan, Peter B. The Immigrant in Philadelphia, 1827-
1860: The Contemporary Published Report. Georgetown,
1957. 246p.

1363. Shradar, Victor I. Ethnic Politics, Religion, and Public
Schools of San Francisco, 1849-1933. Stanford, 1974.
240p. (DA 35:3481-A)
This dissertation demonstrates how different models of school
governance affected the political linkages between the schools of
San Francisco and the city's multitude of religious and ethnic

communities from 1849 to 1933. A number of significant changes
occurred over time in the relationships between politics, religio-
ethnicity, and school governance.

1364. Shurden, Walter B. Associationalism Among Baptists in
America, 1707-1814. New Orleans Baptist Theological
Seminary, 1967. 268p.
Published under the same title (New York: Arno, 1980). Prior
to 1814 the center of any Baptist cooperative life lay in the association. "In influence and importance ... early Baptist associations in America were comparable to national Baptist conventions at the present." The author discusses the historical development of this movement, the logical and biblical bases for it,
and finally its significance. For any understanding of Baptist
church polity, both its shibboleths and its realities, the role of
the association must be examined. Shurden's study makes this
possible.

1365. Siegel, Morton. The Passaic Textile Strike of 1926.
Columbia, 1962. 412p. (DA 13:85)
This dissertation discusses the ten-month strike of 15,000 textile
workers employed in the woolen and worsted mills of Passaic,
New Jersey, that took place in 1926. The strike was under the
leadership of members of the Communist Party and attracted
widespread public attention. In order that the various phases of
this incident in the labor history of the nineteen-twenties be adequately treated, the book is subdivided into three sections: "The
Passaic Community," "The Strike," and "In Retrospect."

1366. Smith, Ross H. Development of Manual Training in the
United States. University of Pennsylvania, 1913. 90p.
Published under the same title (Lancaster, Pennsylvania: Intelligence Printing, 1914). Includes materials on the education of
immigrant children.

1367. Smith, William B. The Attitude of American Catholics
Toward Italian Fascism Between the Two World Wars.
Catholic, 1969. 329p. (DA 31:2470-A)
This study was initiated to answer a need for a more complete
understanding of the historical development of the American
Catholic community in the twentieth century, especially where
that development is indicated along intellectual lines. The subject in question is an investigation of the reaction on the part of
American Catholics to the phenomenon of the Fascist seizure of
the government in Italy in 1922, and the years of that party's
power up to the time when it was obvious to all that it had allied
itself with the Nazi party of Germany and its international aims.
Therefore, the study concludes in 1939.

1368. Solberg, Curtis B. As Others Saw Us: Travelers in
America During the Age of the American Revolution.
Santa Barbara, 1968. 351p. (DA 30:4356-A)
The primary purpose of this study is to describe the kind of

eighteenth-century American society that colonial travelers recorded in their journals, diaries, and letters during the age of the American Revolution. Although the author has liberally used sources from the early eighteenth century, his emphasis has been on travelers who described America in the second half of the century. Their observations form a unique record of the growth and development of America and help us to understand how the Revolution became a social movement. Although there are serious problems in evaluating the information given in travel literature, the best accounts nevertheless are an invaluable source for the student of social and cultural history. In the course of the past five years research for this study has included the examination of approximately 500 travel accounts.

1369. Spergel, Irving A. Types of Delinquent Groups. Columbia, 1960. 352p. (DA 21:2034)
In this exploratory study anomie theory and opportunity-systems theory constituted the framework for the development of a typology of delinquent groups. The conditions of disjunction between aspirations and expectations by young people located in neighborhoods with varying opportunity structures, legitimate and illegitimate, were offered as explanation for the genesis of different types of delinquent subcultures. In the racket subculture the delinquent group was oriented to participation in limited racket activities and characterized by a pervasive criminal-value outlook. In the conflict subculture the delinquent group was oriented to involvement in a system of gang-fighting activities. Here, gang fighting was conceived as the development of an alternate and temporary opportunity system. In the theft subculture the delinquent group was oriented to participation in a great deal of burglary and car-theft activity. Generally, the theoretical formulation and the empirical findings in relation to the theft subculture were of an ad hoc nature.

1370. Stachowski, Floyd J. The Political Career of Daniel Webster Hoan. Northwestern, 1966. 230p. (DA 27:2124-A)
Daniel W. Hoan (1881-1961), son of German immigrants, served as City Attorney of Milwaukee, 1910-1916, and as Mayor of that city, 1916-1940. Throughout his career Hoan was a member of the Socialist Party and the party's most successful candidate. He is generally recognized as the leader in establishing Milwaukee's reputation for good government.

1371. Stanford, Robert M. The Patriot in Exile: A Study of Heinrich Mann's Political Journalistic Activity, 1933-1950. Southern California, 1971. 323p. (DA 32:986-A)
The study treats Heinrich Mann's political journalistic activity during the 17 years of his exile. A brief introduction discusses the definitions of exile literature and reviews the works on the subject. It is followed by a presentation of the controversy, in the early years of exile, among writers and critics about the nature and purpose of exile literature. It was chiefly a question as to whether literature in exile was a vital force in the battle

against National Socialism or, as one critic saw it, an ineffective perpetuation of mediocre literature sustained by a lack of constructive criticism from within.

1372.   Steinberg, Salem H.   Reformer in the Marketplace: Edward W. Bok and "The Ladies' Home Journal." Johns Hopkins, 1971. 245p.

1373.   Surace, Samuel J.   The Status Evolution of Italian Workers, 1860-1914. California (Berkeley), 1962. 343p. (DA 24:1280)

Published under the title Ideology, Economic Change and the Working Classes: The Case of Italy (Berkeley: University of California Press, 1966). Major economic transformations generate pressures on social structure that tend toward a reconstitution of relations between social classes. The manner in which these pressures are developed, exerted, and resolved cannot be predicted by a simple theory of economic interests. Ideological perspectives play an important role in intensifying pressures and in facilitating their transformation into programs of action. Evolution in the status of the Italian working classes supplies a research problem and an opportunity to examine the interaction between ideological perspectives and social structure under the impact of economic change.

1374.   Swanson, Charles G.   The Social Backgrounds of the Lower West Side of New York City.   New York, 1934. 141p.

1375.   Tarr, Joel A.   William Lorimer of Illinois: A Study in Boss Politics.   Northwestern, 1963.   398p.   (DA 24:3721)

Published under the same title (Urbana: University of Illinois Press, 1971). William Lorimer is best known to historians because of his expulsion from the United States Senate in 1912 on the grounds that he had bought his way in. Actually, this event occurred several years after the period of his greatest strength and influence, the years from 1896 to 1904, when he was the most powerful and the most controversial politician in Illinois. Boss of the Republican Party in that state, he held power over the nominations for Chicago, Cook County, and state offices, and even United States Senators and Representatives.

1376.   Taylor, Mary C.   A History of the Foundations of Catholicism in Northern New York.   St. Louis, 1967. 455p.   (DA 28:3128-A)

It is the purpose of this study to trace the growth of Catholicism in northern New York from the days of early Iroquois missions to the end of the first episcopate. Based primarily on correspondence, deeds, diaries, and church documents, the narrative revolves around the priests laboring in the area over these centuries, although it is interwoven with salient points of parish histories and with geographical and historical notes of interest. It is intended both as a historical record of the Church in the North Country and as an inspiration to succeeding generations of Catholics there.

1377. Thompson, Horace R. A Study of the Sociological Backgrounds of Manhasset Valley School Children. New York, 1933. 193p.

1378. Thurner, Arthur W. The Impact of Ethnic Groups in the Democratic Party in Chicago, 1920-1928. Chicago, 1966. 243p.

1379. Tilley, Margaret C. The Boy Scout Movement in East Harlem (New York). New York, 1935. 215p.

1380. Titus, Matthew F. A Study of Protestant Charities in Chicago: History, Development, and Philosophy. Chicago, 1939. 264p.

1381. Tull, James E. A History of Southern Baptist Landmarkism in the Light of Historical Baptist Ecclesiology. Columbia, 1960. 212p.
Published under the same title (New York: Arno, 1980). The Landmark Movement was a major influence in the Baptist tradition, especially powerful in the nineteenth century but by no means impotent in the twentieth. In this dissertation the Landmark Movement is described as "an extremely sectarian movement which ... attempted to call Baptists back to what were conceived to be the historical tenets (the 'old Landmarks') of their faith." Tull sets the ideas of the Landmark Movement into their historical context. He examines the tenets of the Landmark system and follows the course of the Southern movement as it permeated the lifestyle of the Southern Baptist denomination.

1382. Tweedie, Stephen W. The Geography of Religious Groups in Ohio, Pennsylvania, and Upstate New York: Persistence and Change, 1890-1965. Syracuse, 1969. 315p. (DA 31: 1347-B)
Comparative study of the locational aspects of religious groups has long been hindered by the lack of comparable membership statistics, resulting from varying membership definitions and data-gathering procedures. The available statistics have been adjusted in order to produce a series of maps for Ohio, Pennsylvania, and upstate New York that are suitable for comparisons both through time and between groups. The persistence of religious patterns established during the initial settlement is evident, as indicated by stable German Protestant, native Protestant (Methodists, Baptists, and Disciples of Christ) and Presbyterian areas. Subsequent Roman Catholic immigration has generally overlaid, rather than displaced, the original patterns, and has itself displayed marked stability.

1383. Underwood, Gary N. The Dialect of the Mesabi Iron Range in Its Historical and Social Context. Minnesota, 1970. 291p. (DA 31:5384-A)
This thesis is a study of the English of the oldest generation of residents of the Mesabi Iron Range region of Minnesota. Through standard linguistic-atlas interviewing techniques, 17 informants

representing 13 ethnic backgrounds were interviewed using a questionnaire that is a slightly modified form of the one used for the Linguistic Atlas of the Upper Midwest. The data for 97 lexical items, 68 phonological items, and 66 verb-form items are compared with evidence from Minnesota fieldrecords of the Linguistic Atlas of the Upper Midwest and with evidence for the eastern U. S. summarized in Hans Kurath, A Word Geography of the Eastern United States; E. Bagby Atwood, A Survey of Verb Forms in the Eastern United States; and Hans Kurath and Raven I. McDavid, Jr., The Pronunciation of English in the Atlantic States.

1384. Valentine, Foy D. A Historical Study of Southern Baptists and Race Relations 1917-1947. Southwestern Baptist Theological Seminary, 1949. 320p.
Published under the same title (New York: Arno, 1980). The author of this study had for many years played the major role in guiding Southern Baptists through the complexities of Christian ethical responsibility. In this work he uncovers major trends of Southern Baptist thought and practice in the area of race relations. He also examines these trends with a view to discovering reasons for reaction and progression. Extensive research was made into the Baptist weekly papers in Texas, Mississippi, Kentucky, and North Carolina. In the early part of the 30-year period investigated in this volume Southern Baptists talked "about the training of Negro religious leaders." Toward the end of that period, however, "they gave less attention to endless pious platitudes about training Negro preachers--a task at which they never enjoyed any notable measure of success--and more attention to overcoming race prejudice, to helping the needy brother ... and to actually improving race relations."

1385. Vaswani, Hari V. A Study of the Problem of Foreign Students at the Berkeley Campus of the University of California. California (Berkeley), 1950. 318p.

1386. Venettozzi, John T. Band Works of Tommaso Venettozzi, Edited and Rescored. Florida State, 1954. 294p. (DA 14:1233)
Among the most musically productive of Italo-American bandleaders was one Tommaso Venettozzi, who, from 1911 to 1930, was conductor of the Banda Bianca of Utica, New York. Venettozzi's unpublished scores were acquired shortly after his death in 1940. The scoring of these compositions ranges from a mere basic guide to a carefully worked out instrumentation. It is the purpose of this study to rescore and edit the representative band works of this pioneer in the development of band music in America; to present a history of the Italo-American band movement as a background to the music of the period; and to explain the editing procedures and problems encountered in preparing the music for modern bands.

1387. Ventry, Lance T. The Impact of the United States Committee on Public Information on Italian Participation in the

First World War. Catholic, 1968. 164p. (DA 30:1123-A)
The Committee on Public Information was established 17 days after President Wilson asked for and received a declaration of war against the Central Empires. Its purpose abroad was to facilitate the explanation of American policy in the war to America's allies. The American Ambassador to Italy, Thomas Nelson Page, initially welcomed the new agency as a vital but subordinate adjunct to his own efforts in Italy since 1913. It is the contention of this study that the Committee on Public Information played a vital role in the mitigation of Italian territorial ambitions but that its supradiplomatic status paralyzed the normal channels through which such solutions are implemented.

1388. Vloutidis, Nicholas E. Some Effects of Bilingualism upon Intelligence and Reading Test Performance of American-Born Children: A Comparative Study. Delaware, 1972. 84p. (DA 22:625-A)
The purpose of this study was (1) to investigate some effects of bilingualism upon intelligence-test and reading-test performance of American-born children of different language groups; and (2) if such effects exist, to analyze and compare them by school grades and language groups. A sample of 160 children of Greek, Italian, Polish, and American parentage was randomly selected from a population of private and public schools in Wilmington, Delaware. All the subjects were administered (1) the California Short-Form Test of Mental Maturity (levels 1, 2, 3); (2) the Comprehensive Test of Basic Skills (sections: reading vocabulary and reading comprehension); and (3) the Hoffman Bilingual Schedule to measure the extent of the subjects' bilingual background or environment.

1389. Wack, John T. The University of Notre Dame Du Lac: Foundation, 1842-1857. Notre Dame, 1967. 378p. (DA 28:1777-A)
The University of Notre Dame du Lac (the present University of Notre Dame) suffered from most of the problems that brought failure to 80 percent of the American colleges founded before the Civil War. Yet the University managed to survive this ordeal of birth and to enter the period of the Civil War as a viable organism, capable of growing to reach some of the lofty aims with which its founder had endowed it.

1390. Wacker, Roland F. Race and Ethnicity in American Social Science, 1900-1950. Michigan, 1975. 185p. (DA 36:1735-A)
The manner in which social scientists have approached the ideas of race and ethnicity in America has been shaped by movements within the various disciplines as well as within the wider society. Yet, few discussions of the alleged "racism" and "assimilationism" of American social scientists, and of sociologists in particular, have taken these internal and external forces into account. This present-mindedness has led to serious distortions of the work of men like Robert Park and W. I. Thomas, who played

significant roles in the development of the study of racial and
ethnic movements in Europe and America. This study is, in
part, a critical analysis of the ideas and attitudes of Park,
Thomas, and other social scientists and an attempt to place those
ideas within their intellectual and cultural context.

1391.   Walkowitz, Daniel J. Working Class Culture in the Gilded
Age: The Iron Workers of Troy, New York, and the Cotton
Workers of Cohoes, New York--1855-1884. Rochester,
1972. 317p. (DA 33:264-A)

This study begins to examine the ways in which the achievements
and aspirations of the working class influenced their behavior.
Two communities are studied between 1855 and 1884: the iron-
worker community of Troy, New York, and the cotton-worker
community of Cohoes, New York. In the first part census data
are used to identify the workers in the community, to trace their
social and occupational mobility, and to investigate their family
patterns. The Irish dominated the mills in both cities before the
Civil War and quickly gained prominence in the skilled trades as
well. By 1880 French Canadians shared much of the work load
in the Cohoes Harmony Company cotton mills. Although approximately a quarter of the cotton-worker families were headed by a
woman, most cotton-worker families were nuclear. Troy and
Cohoes factories provided the Irish and French Canadian workers
with regular employment and many skilled positions, and the
workers had been able to hold families together. For immigrants used to the famines in Ireland, for example, these achievements were significant.

1392.   Walters, Joel. Variation of Language Use in the Language
Acquisition of Bilingual Children. Boston, 1978. 192p.
(DA 39:5377-A)

This investigation deals with the social and pragmatic competence
of bilingual children. It utilizes structural aspects of language
(the requesting strategies a speaker uses) as a window to social
knowledge in the same way Vygotsky conceived of language as a
window to the mind. The notion of a requesting strategy is defined by the semantic form (e.g., can, could, will, would, do).

1393.   Waltz, Waldo E. The Nationality of Married Women. Illinois (Urbana), 1936. 289p.

Published under the title The Nationality of Married Women: A
Study of Domestic Policies and International Legislation (Urbana:
University of Illinois Press, 1937).

1394.   Waniek, Marilyn R. N. The Schizoid Nature of the Implied
Author in 20th Century American Ethnic Novels. Minnesota,
1979. 124p. (DA 40:3305-A)

The thesis of this study is that the implied authors, or literary
selves, of American ethnic novels tend to be schizoid and that by
examining the larger rhythms, interplaying themes, symbols, and
characters of this class of novels the qualitative nature of their
implied authors can be identified. The study further demonstrates

Miscellanea 327

that examination of the conflicts between the values of the particular ethnic groups to which the historical authors belong and the values of the more powerful majority clearly establishes the existence of a fictionalized schizoid self at the moral center of novels as diverse as Cahan's The Rise of David Levinsky, Rölvaag's Giants in the Earth, Johnson's The Autobiography of an Ex-Colored Man, Wright's Native Son, Ellison's Invisible Man, Potok's The Chosen, Malamud's The Assistant, Roth's Portnoy's Complaint, DiDonato's Christ in Concrete, and Puzo's The Godfather.

1395. Ward, Robert J. Europe in American Fiction: The Vogue of the Historical Romance 1890-1919. Missouri, 1967. 213p. (DA 28:2224-A)
Between 1890 and 1910 historical romances using European settings reached their peak of popularity in America. This study examines some 118 of these books that were written by American authors. It also analyzes the contemporary reviews and criticism of such fiction. As sources of reliable information about European history, the stories are practically useless. But their popularity reflects an increased interest in Europe on the part of large numbers of Americans. England and France are the most often used countries as settings for the stories, and the Renaissance period provides the most popular time. The stories reveal little anti-European prejudice. Only the Italian figures are consistently depicted in a biased light, usually emerging as cowardly, treacherous, and violent figures.

1396. Weinbaum, Marvin G. A Minority's Survival: The Republican Party of New York County, 1897-1960. Columbia, 1965. 393p. (DA 26:4783)
Data on the social and ethnic backgrounds of several hundred Republican candidates, district and county leaders, together with parallel information about Democrats, permit a comparison of the characteristics and qualifications of their respective memberships. Particular interest is taken in the changing ethnic composition of Republican and Democratic nominations and district leaderships. The statistics demonstrate relatively freer access to places of prominence in the Republican ranks. But the overall picture is one of competing parties staffed by individuals with generally similar backgrounds--in residence, age, education, and occupation. This two-party correspondence is believed to be closely related to the Republicans' ability to sustain their party-system role.

1397. Weinberg, Daniel E. The Foreign Language Information Service and the Foreign Born, 1918-1939: A Case Study of Cultural Assimilation Viewed as a Problem in Social Technology. Minnesota, 1973. 277p.
The Foreign Language and Information Service and its related educational program reflected the values of its leaders. They were the professional technocrats who wanted to redesign society in the direction of a harmonious and dependent relationship with the emerging corporate society.

1398. Welch, Charles E. The Philadelphia Mummers Parade: A Study in History, Folklore, and Popular Tradition. Pennsylvania, 1968. 164p.
The early customs in the city of Philadelphia, at least those connected with mummery, resemble those found in Great Britain in connection with the Mummers' Play, the Plough Play, and the Sword Dance. These were always performed by the less well-to-do. The average parade participant was most certainly not one to keep a diary or leave any account of his social activities. The major source of information about this social order is from outsiders, people who did keep diaries; the public records, newspapers, magazines; and the people themselves. (A)

1399. Westhues, Kenneth L. The American Catholic World: Its Origins and Prospects. Vanderbilt, 1970. 159p. (DA 31: 3064-A)
This research project was prompted by certain limitations of the Greeley-Rossi approach to predictions of the future of Catholic education. Instead of a survey method utilizing attitudes of individuals, the dissertation offers an organizational model, the variables in which relate to characteristics of the Roman Catholic Church as an organization and of its environment.

1400. White, Charles M. The Socialist Labor Party, 1890-1903. Southern California, 1959. 311p. (DA 20:2239)
Daniel De Leon joined the party in 1890; he quickly became its "boss" and ran the organization until his death in 1914. A political party based on one-man leadership with followers of foreign birth, a union based on the coming revolution, and tactics based on rigid party discipline--all these were elements that tended to doom the Socialist Labor Party in America to well-deserved oblivion. (A)

1401. White, James A. The Era of Good Intentions: A Survey of American Catholics' Writing Between the Years 1880-1915. Notre Dame, 1956. 377p. (DA 17:2985)
The purpose of this study is to review the works of 53 American Catholic authors who wrote during the years 1880-1915. This writer is convinced that these men and women, through their writings, hoped to inspire their coreligionists to achieve higher standards of education and culture. Almost every literary form was used in recording their impressions of life in the United States.

1402. White, James D. The Needs and Problems of Girard College Graduates. University of Pennsylvania, 1949. 122p.

1403. White, John F. Thomas Mann in America: The Rhetorical and Political Experiences of an Exiled Artist. Minnesota, 1971. 486p. (DA 32:2832-A)
This study of Thomas Mann considers the public-address experiences during the years of American exile. Historical and rhetorical methodologies combine for a descriptive study of public-

speaking activity between 1934 and 1950. All of the known addresses, whole or in part, were assembled for the study, and an authenticated chronology was established. Divided into three parts, the thesis considers Mann's basic themes, the crosscountry lecture experiences, and his rhetorical encounters with American academia.

1404. White, William B. The Military and the Melting Pot: The American Army and Minority Groups, 1865-1924. Wisconsin, 1968. 422p. (DA 29:4443-A)
This study was undertaken because of two existing gaps in historical scholarship. First, the social and intellectual exploration of military thought has in the main been left to the sociologists, who should not be permitted unchallenged dominion. More specifically, existing studies of minority groups and of the theory and practice of assimilation in American culture have largely ignored the role of the military, probably because most authors have assumed that, as admitted social and economic conservatives, military men have not offered any innovative solutions to racial problems.

1405. Wilhelm, Clarke L. William B. Wilson: The First Secretary of Labor. Johns Hopkins, 1967. 288p. (DA 28:4587-A)
Before 1913 William B. Wilson already had fashioned two important careers in the labor movement. As a mine-union leader he had been one of the founders of the United Mine Workers of America and had served as that union's Secretary-Treasurer during its most crucial period of growth. Then, from 1907 to 1913, he had acted as the American Federation of Labor's main representative in Congress, sponsoring a large number of labor measures. When Woodrow Wilson took office as President the unions eventually persuaded him to appoint William B. Wilson as the first Secretary of Labor. Wilson played a major role in standing against the war and reconstruction hysteria over radicals. He prevented a massive attack against alien members of the Industrial Workers of the World and also blunted the efforts of Attorney-General A. Mitchell Palmer to deport thousands of radical aliens during the "Red Scare." (A)

1406. Williams, Arthur W. Democracy in Colonial America: A Study with Particular Reference to Its Treatment in Historiographic Source Materials, and to Its Educational Implications. Middle Tennessee State University, 1975. 174p. (DA 36:3971-A)
The study addresses itself to certain basic educational problems occasioned by the increased interest in the nature of American democracy and especially in its roots in colonial America. Specifically, the study is concerned with the nature of the treatment of the theme and concepts of democracy in colonial America in high school and college textbooks. Also of concern are the interrelationships between treatment of colonial democracy in primary and secondary sources and its treatment in various schools of historical interpretation in the wider academic historical literature.

1407.   Williams, James M. An American Town: A Sociological
        Study. Columbia, 1906. 284p.
        Published under the same title (New York: Columbia University
        Press, 1906).

1408.   Wilson, M. Debora. Benedictine Higher Education and the
        Development of American Higher Education. Michigan,
        1969. 353p. (DA 30:1839-A)
It is the purpose of this dissertation to study this group of Benedictine colleges within the context of other Catholic, denominational, private and public institutions of higher education in America. The study is both chronological and topical, tracing the development of the schools through the nineteenth-century period of denominational college-founding and twentieth-century expansion. It focuses particularly on developments in organization and administration, faculty quality and composition, curriculum and extracurricular activities, student life and discipline, and academic freedom in the Benedictine colleges.

1409.   Wyman, Roger E. Voting Behavior in the Progressive
        Era: Wisconsin as a Case Study. Wisconsin, 1970.
        1118p. (DA 31:722-A)
The Progressive Era is a transitional period in the history of American politics and voting behavior. Between 1900 and 1914 in Wisconsin, new issues raised by Robert M. La Follette and the Progressives transformed a politics of cultural division, which had characterized Wisconsin politics since the Civil War, into a new politics of ideology and factionalism. The transformation was evident in both the character of political campaigns and the behavior of the state's voters. The issues of Progressivism began the erosion of the primacy of ethnic and religious factors in voting in Wisconsin, a transformation that did not reach completion until the New Deal. Although ethnicity and religion remained as the primary determinants of voter choice through the First World War, these forces were weakened by issues of an economic nature that elicited division along economic lines and by the institution of the direct primary, which removed the crucial factor of party identification in primary elections. (A)

1410.   Yang, Charlotte Shiang-Yun Wang. The Influence of Residence and Migration on Socioeconomic Achievement. Wisconsin, 1976. 265p. (DA 37:1250-A)
This study examines the direct and indirect influences of place of origin, place of current residence, and migration on the socioeconomic careers of a large random sample of 1957 Wisconsin high school male seniors who have been followed over the years. This is done by adding these variables to the Sewell-Hauser (Education, Occupation, and Earnings: Achievement in the Early Career, Academic Press, 1975) basic model of the socioeconomic-achievement process.

1411.   Ziff, Ruth. Ethnic Penetration into Managerial Positions
        in Advertising Agencies (of New York City). City Univer-

sity of New York, 1975. 599p. (DA 36:1125-A)
The study examines the changes occurring during recent decades in the religious composition of occupants in top managerial positions in New York advertising agencies. It analyzes current ethnic patterns in these top echelons. It reviews the experiences and adaptation of minority members who were "actors" during the period of change. Three types of research were involved: a historical study of persons in managerial positions in the top 20 New York agencies; a mail survey among selected personnel in New York agencies billing $10 million or more; depth interviews with a subsample of Jewish executives.

1412. Zinn, Howard. Fiorello La Guardia in Congress. Columbia, 1958. 228p. (DA 18:1782)
Published under the same title (Ithaca, New York: Cornell University Press, 1959).

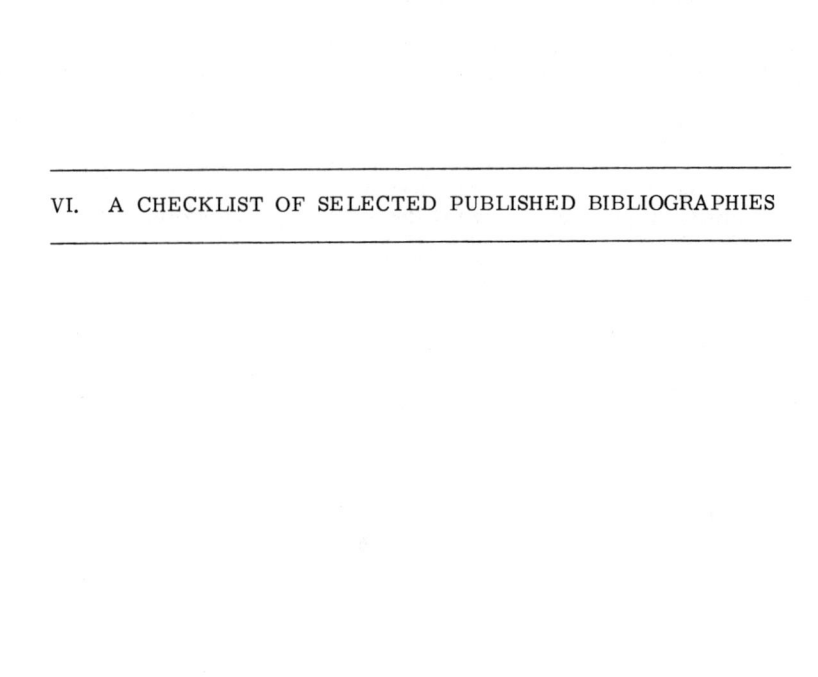

VI. A CHECKLIST OF SELECTED PUBLISHED BIBLIOGRAPHIES

American Council for Nationalities Service. The Ethnic Press in the United States: Lists of Foreign Language, Nationality and Ethnic Newspapers and Periodicals in the United States. New York: 1974.

Baden, Anne L. Immigration in the United States: A Selected List of Recent References. Washington, D.C.: Library of Congress, 1943.

Balch Institute. The Balch Institute Historical Reading Lists. Nos. 1-31. Philadelphia, 1974-1976. (Brief commentaries and bibliographies on European American ethnic groups.)

Balys, Jonas. Lithuania and Lithuanians: A Selected Bibliography. New York: Praeger, 1961.

Barton, Josef J. An Annotated Guide to the Ethnic Experience in the United States. Cambridge, Massachusetts: Press of the Langdon Associates, 1976.

Beers, Henry P. The French in North America: A Bibliographical Guide to French Archives, Reproductions, and Research Missions. Baton Rouge: Louisiana State University Press, 1957.

Bengelsdorf, Winnie. Ethnic Studies in Higher Education: State of Art and Bibliography. Washington, D.C.: American Association of State Colleges and Universities, 1972. Reprint, New York: Arno, 1978.

Briani, V. Italian Immigrants Abroad: A Bibliography on the Italian Experience Outside Italy in Europe, the Americas, Australia, and Africa. Edited and with a Supplementary Bibliography by F. Cordasco. Detroit: Blaine Ethridge, 1979.

Brickman, William W. The Jewish Community in America: An Annotated and Classified Bibliographical Guide. New York: Burt Franklin, 1976.

Buenker, John D., and Nicholas C. Burckel. Immigration and Ethnicity: A Guide to Information Sources. Detroit: Gale, 1977.

Buttlar, Lois, and Lubomyr R. Wynar. Building Ethnic Collections: An Annotated Guide for School Media Centers and Public Libraries. Littleton, Colorado: Libraries Unlimited, 1977.

Catsumbis, Michael N. A Bibliographical Guide to Materials on Greeks in the United States, 1890-1968. New York: Center for Migration Studies, 1970.

Chartier, Armand B. A Selected and Thematic Checklist of Publications Relating to Franco-Americans. Kingston: Department of Languages, University of Rhode Island, 1975.

Cohen, D. Multi-Ethnic Media: Selected Bibliographies in Print. Chicago: American Library Association, 1975.

Cordasco, Francesco. Immigrant Children in American Schools: A Classified Annotated Bibliography with Selected Source Documents. Fairfield, New Jersey: Augustus M. Kelley, 1976.

_____. The Italian American Experience: An Annotated and Classified Bibliographical Guide. With Selected Publications of the Casa Italiana Educational Bureau. New York: Burt Franklin, 1974.

_____. Italian Americans: A Guide to Information Sources. Detroit: Gale, 1978.

_____. Italians in the United States: A Bibliography of Reports, Texts, Critical Studies, and Related Materials. New York: Oriole, 1972.

_____, ed. A Bibliography of American Immigration History. The George Washington University Project Studies. Fairfield, New Jersey: Augustus M. Kelley, 1978.

Deodene, Frank, Comp. The Origins of Ethnicity: Immigrants in America, Including the Immigrant in Fiction. Chatham, New Jersey: Chatham Bookseller [c. 1978]. (A catalogue of 623 items.)

Diodati, C. M., et al. Writings on Italian Americans. Bicentennial Bibliography. New York: Italian American Center for Urban Affairs, 1975.

Doezema, Linda P. Dutch Americans: A Guide to Information Sources. Detroit: Gale, 1979.

Eager, Alan R. A Guide to Irish Bibliographic Materials. London: Library Association, 1964.

Erickson, E. Swedish-American Periodicals: A Selective and Descriptive Bibliography. New York: Arno, 1979.

Eterovich, Adam S. A Guide and Bibliography to Research on Yugoslavs in the United States and Canada. San Francisco: R & E Research Associates, 1975.

_____, ed. Jugoslav Immigrant Bibliography. San Francisco: R & E Research Associates, 1968.

Glanz, Rudolf. The German Jew in America: An Annotated Bibliography Including Books, Pamphlets and Articles of Special Interest. New York: Ktav, 1969.

Greene, Amy Blanche, and Frederic A. Gould. Handbook-Bibliography on Foreign Language Groups in the United States and Canada. New York: Council of Women for Home Missions, 1925.

Gregorovich, Andrew. Canadian Ethnic Groups Bibliography: A Selected Bibliography of Ethno-Cultural Groups in Canada and the Province of Ontario. Toronto: Department of the Provincial Secretary and Citizenship of Ontario, 1972.

Groennings, Sven. Scandinavia in Social Science Literature: An English Language Bibliography. Bloomington: Indiana University Press, 1970.

Herman, Judith M. White Ethnic America: A Selected Bibliography. New York: American Jewish Committee, 1969.

Horecky, Paul. East Central and Southeast Europe: A Handbook of Library and Archival Resources in North America. Santa Barbara, California: American Bibliographical Center, 1975.

Inglehart, Babette F., and Anthony R. Mangione. The Image of Pluralism in American Literature: An Annotated Bibliography on the American Experience of European Ethnic Groups. New York: Institute on Pluralism and Group Identity of the American Jewish Committee, 1974.

_____, and _____. Multi-ethnic Literature: An Annotated Bibliography on European Ethnic Group Life in America. New York: American Jewish Committee, Institute of Human Relations, 1974.

Janeway, William Ralph. Bibliography of Immigration in the United States, 1900-1930. Columbus, Ohio: Hedrick, 1934. Reprint, San Francisco: R & E Research Associates, 1972.

Jerabek, Esther. Czechs and Slovaks in North America: A Bibliography. New York: Czechoslovak National Council of America, 1976.

Juliani, Richard N. Immigration and Ethnicity. (Balch Institute Historical Reading Lists, No. 1) Philadelphia: Balch Institute, 1974.

Keresztesi, Michael, and Gary R. Cocozzoli. German-American History and Life: A Guide to Information Sources. Detroit: Gale, 1980.

Koivukangas, O., and S. Toivonen. Suomen Iürrtolais uuden ja Maasamuuton Bibliografia: A Bibliography on Finnish Emigration and Internal Migration. Turku, Finland: Migration Institute, 1978.

Kolehmainen, John I. The Finns in America: A Bibliographical Guide to their History. Hancock, Michigan: Finnish American Historical Library, Suomi College, 1947.

Kolm, Richard. Bibliography of Ethnicity and Ethnic Groups. Rockville, Maryland: National Institute of Mental Health, Center for Studies of Metropolitan Problems, 1973.

Kuehl, Warren F. Dissertations in History: An Index to Dissertations Completed in History Departments of United States and Canadian Universities, 1873-1960. Lexington: University of Kentucky Press, 1965.

Long, J. The German-Russians: A Bibliography. Santa Barbara, California: American Bibliographical Center, 1978.

Meyen, Emil. Bibliography on German Settlements in Colonial North America. Leipzig, Germany: Otto Harrassowitz, 1937.

Miller, Wayne C., ed. Comprehensive Bibliography for the Study of American Minorities. 3 vols. New York: New York University Press, 1976.

Mortensen, E. Danish-American Life and Letters: A Bibliography. Des Moines, Iowa: Committee on Publications of the Danish Evangelical Lutheran Church in America, 1945. Reprint, New York: Arno, 1979.

Pap, Leo. The Portuguese in the United States: A Bibliography. New York: Center for Migration Studies, 1976.

Pochmann, Henry A., and Arthur R. Schultz, eds. Bibliography of German Culture in America to 1940. Madison: University of Wisconsin Press, 1953.

Prpic, George J. Croatia and Croatians: An Annotated and Selected Bibliography in English. Cleveland: John Carroll University, 1972.

Pula, J. S., and M. N. Pula. An Index to Polish American Studies, 1944-1973. Chicago: Polish American Historical Association, 1977.

Rischin, Moses. An Inventory of American Jewish History. Cambridge, Massachusetts: Harvard University Press, 1954. (Al-

Published Bibliographies

so, the author's "Since 1954: A Bicentennial Look at the Resources of American Jewish History." Immigration History Newsletter, Vol. 7 [November 1975], pp. 1-6.

Rose, Walter R. A Bibliography of the Irish in the United States. Afton, New York: Tristram Shandy, 1969.

Roucek, Joseph S., and Patricia N. Pinkham. American Slavs: A Bibliography. New York: Bureau of Intercultural Education, 1944.

Social Science Education Consortium. Materials and Human Resources for Teaching Ethnic Studies: An Annotated Bibliography. Boulder, Colorado: 1975.

Tolzmann, Don H. German-Americana: A Bibliography. Metuchen, New Jersey: Scarecrow, 1975.

Tomasi, Silvano M., and Edward C. Stibili. Italian Americans and Religion: An Annotated Bibliography. New York: Center for Migration Studies, 1978.

Vlachas, Evangelos. An Annotated Bibliography of Greek Migration. Athens: Social Sciences Centre, 1966.

Vollmar, Edward R. The Catholic Church in America: An Historical Bibliography. 2nd edition. New York: Scarecrow, 1963.

Wasserman, Paul, and Jean Morgan. Ethnic Information Sources of the United States. Detroit: Gale, 1976.

Weed, Perry L. Ethnicity and American Group Life: A Bibliography. New York: Institute of Human Relations, 1972.

Wertsman, Valdimir. Romanians in the United States: A Guide to Information Sources. Detroit: Gale, 1980.

Wynar, Lubomyr R. Encyclopedic Directory of Ethnic Newspapers and Periodicals in the United States. 2nd edition. Littleton, Colorado: Libraries Unlimited, 1976.

_____. Encyclopedic Directory of Ethnic Organizations in the United States. Littleton, Colorado: Libraries Unlimited, 1975.

_____, and Lois Buttlar. Guide to Ethnic Museums, Libraries and Archives in the United States. Preliminary edition. Kent, Ohio: Program for the Study of Ethnic Publications, Kent State University, School of Library Science, 1978.

Zurawski, Joseph W. Polish American History and Culture: A Classified Bibliography. Chicago: Polish Museum of America, 1975.

INDEX OF NAMES

Abraham, S. Y. 785
Abrahamson, H. J. 786
Adams, R. B. 997
Adams, W. F. 1
Adler, N. M. 1174
Agocs, C. 787
Alatis, J. E. 388
Aldana, M. S. 998
Alexander, N. 999
Ali, A. A. 1175
Alissi, A. S. 389
Allen, J. P. 1176
Allswang, J. M. 1177
Alper, M. 589
Alvarez, G. C. 1000
Andeen, G. K. 153
Ander, O. F. 154
Anders, J. O. O. 155
Anderson, A. W. 156
Anderson, B. L. 157
Anderson, M. D. 89
Anderson, N. 390
Anderson, R. J. 242
Anderson, S. K. 1001
Anderson, V. D. 158
Andrews, B. R. 1178
Angus, J. D. 1179
Annakin, V. D. 1180
Antonovsky, A. 590
Appel, J. J. 1181
Arafat, I. S. 1002
Arden, G. E. 1182
Arsenian, S. 788
Athearn, R. G. 2

Atzman, E. 591
Aurand, H. W. 1183
Avery, D. H. 1003
Avery, E. H. 90
Avoruch, K. E. 592
Axelrod, H. C. 789

Babb, W. C. 91
Babcock, K. C. 159
Babics, W. V. 507
Babow, I. P. 1184
Bachelis, F. G. 593
Bachman, J. R. 1185
Bactel, D. L. 1004
Baden, J. A. 508
Badgley, R. F. 3
Baiamonte, J. V. 391
Bailey, D. T. 790
Baker, G. C. 791
Baker, G. C. 1187
Baker, G. W. 1186
Baker, L. C. 243
Baldridge, E. R. 92
Baldwin, D. O. 1005
Bales, R. F. 792
Ballis, B. 1188
Balogh, J. K. 244
Bander, C. J. 245
Barba, P. A. 246
Barcio, R. G. 4
Barendse, M. A. 509
Baretski, C. A. 510
Barry, C. J. 247

Index of Names

Barta, R. 1189
Barton, J. J. 793
Baskauskas, L. 511
Bauer, B. G. 392
Bauer, J. 393
Bauland, P. M. 248
Bauman, J. F. 1190
Bayer, A. E. 794
Bayor, R. H. 795
Beadles, J. A. 5
Beck, N. P. 1191
Becker, S. 1006
Bek, W. G. 249
Belgum, G. L. 160
Bell, D. B. 1192
Bell, L. V. 250
Bellemarre, M. 796
Bender, J. E. 251
Bender, T. W. 252
Benjamin, G. G. 253
Benkart, P. K. 254
Bennett, E. 594
Bennett, L. A. 512
Bennion, L. C. 255
Benson, O. A. 161
Benynon, E. D. 258
Bere, M. 797
Berger, M. D. 513
Berger, M. I. 798
Berger, S. L. 595
Bergquist, J. M. 256
Berkson, I. B. 596
Berman, B. A. P. 597
Berman, H. 1193
Berman, N. 598
Bernard, W. S. 1007
Berrol, S. C. 799
Berthoff, R. T. 6
Betz, G. A. 257
Bianco, C. D. 394
Bicha, K. D. 1008
Biesele, R. L. 259
Biever, B. F. 7
Bigelow, B. L. 1009
Bilik, D. S. 599
Billington, R. A. 1010
Bin-Nun, D. 600
Binstock, R. H. 1194
Biondi, L. H. 395
Birnbaum, L. D. 1195
Bischoff, H. C. 1196
Biskar, H. M. 601
Bixler-Marquez, D. 1197

Bjorgan, G. R. 162
Blake, N. M. 8
Bleda, S. E. 800
Blegen, T. C. 163
Bloomberg, P. 260
Bloore, S. 602
Bodger, J. C. 1198
Bodnar, J. E. 801
Bogusas, J. 514
Bohme, F. G. 396
Bole, J. A. 261
Bolger, S. G. 9
Boody, B. M. 802
Booker, H. M. 1011
Born, D. O. 803
Borowiec, W. A. 1199
Bosse, R. C. 1200
Boxerman, B. A. 603
Bradley, H. C. 1201
Bratt, J. D. 93
Bratt, J. H. 94
Brede, C. F. 262
Bressler, M. 604
Breton, R. J. 804
Brickner, B. R. 605
Bridger, D. 606
Briggs, J. W. 397
Brite, J. D. 1012
Brody, D. 1202
Brostowin, P. R. 1203
Brown, J. A. 805
Brown, J. S. 1204
Brown, L. G. 806
Brown, T. N. 10
Browne, H. J. 1205
Bruins, E. J. 95
Buccheri, J. S. 1206
Buch, A. T. 607
Buckland, R. L. 1013
Buckley, J. P. 11
Buell, C. C. 807
Burns, R. B. 1207
Burns, W. T. 1208
Burrows, R. N. 1209
Burstein, A. N. 808
Butosi, J. 1210
Buxbaum, E. C. 398

Cable, J. N. 515
Cabral, S. L. 96
Cale, E. B. 1211
Caliandro, G. G. B. 1212

Campisi, P. J. 809
Candeloro, D. L. 1213
Cannon, M. H. 1014
Capponi, G. 399
Capps, F. H. 164
Carey, J. J. 1015
Carino, L. V. 1016
Carlin, M. B. 810
Carlson, C. E. 165
Caroli, B. B. 400
Carr, H. G. 608
Carter, J. B. 401
Cary, L. L. 1214
Casmus, M. I. 1215
Cassimates, L. P. 402
Castagnera, J. O. 811
Castellanos, D. A. 1216
Castelli, J. R. 97
Castiello, K. R. 403
Cavanaugh, F. P. 1017
Cavendish, T. 1217
Cazden, R. E. 263
Cerase, F. P. 404
Chalmers, L. 1218
Chammou, E. 609
Chandler, C. W. 1018
Chassé, P. 1219
Chazanof, W. 1220
Chevalier, F. M. 98
Child, I. L. 405
Childs, F. S. 99
Chiodo, J. J. 100
Chock, P. P. 406
Chrismas, N. J. 166
Christensen, T. P. 167
Christiansen, S. O. 1221
Chudacoff, H. P. 812
Churchill, C. W. 407
Chyet, S. F. 610
Cinel, D. 1222
Cink, K. 516
Clark, A. R. 1223
Clark, J. D. J. 12
Clark, J. P. 1019
Clinchy, E. R. 813
Cochran, A. L. 13
Cochran, M. E. 1020
Cohen, B. 612
Cohen, B. L. 611
Cohen, J. L. 814
Cohen, M. J. 408
Cohen, N. W. 613
Cohen, S. I. 614
Cohen, S. M. 815
Colakovic, B. M. 517
Cole, D. B. 1224
Coleman, J. W. 14
Coleman, M. R. 816
Collins, D. M. 409
Comay, P. Y. 1021
Condon, T. J. 101
Connaughton, M. S. 1225
Consistre, M. J. 410
Constantakos, C. M. 411
Coombs, G. B. 1226
Cordasco, F. 1227
Correa-Zoli, Y. 412
Costello, L. 1228
Covello, L. 413
Cozen, K. 264
Cressey, P. F. 817
Crispino, J. 414
Crocker, B. 15
Cronin, H. C. 16
Crowder, D. L. 615
Cuddy, H. 17
Curran, T. J. 1022

Dahlie, J. 168
Damm, J. S. 265
Danesino, A. 818
Danielson, L. W. 169
Dann, M. E. 819
Dapogny, J. E. 1229
Dapp, C. F. 266
Darcy, N. 820
D'Arcy, W. 19
David, H. 1230
Davidson, H. C. 821
Davis, J. D. 518
Davis, L. B. 1023
De'ath, C. E. 822
De Bileo, F. D. 415
Decroos, J. F. 102
Degler, C. N. 1231
DeGroot, D. E. 823
DeJong, J. B. 103
Delkay, D. L. 1024
Dell, R. M. 824
De Marr, M. J. 519
Dempsey, A. D. 825
Dennis, H. K. 104
Dexter, R. C. 105
Deye, A. H. 20
Dickinson, J. Y. 416

Index of Names

Diggins, J. P. 417
Dillon, M. F. 21
Dimmitt, M. A. 1025
Dimock, A. B. 267
Dinin, S. 616
Dinnerstein, L. 617
Dinsky, S. H. 618
Di Pietro, R. J. 418
Divine, R. A. 1026
Dobbert, G. A. 268
Dobkowski, M. N. 619
Doby, H. R. 170
Dolan, J. P. 826
Dollin, N. 269
Donnelly, D. J. 270
Donovan, G. F. 22
Doroshkin, M. 620
Douglas, M. I. 621
Dowie, J. I. 171
Doyle, D. N. 23
Drachler, J. 827
Drescher, N. M. 1232
Dreyer, J. R. 106
Drummond, R. R. 271
Dube, N. C. 107
Dubofsky, M. 1233
Duff, J. B. 1234
Duke, F. J. 419
Dushkin, A. M. 622

Earl, J. L. 108
Easterly, F. J. 420
Easum, C. V. 272
Eckstein, N. T. 172
Edson, C. H. 828
Edwards, A. W. 1235
Efron, D. 829
Eftink, E. M. 24
Egelman, W. S. 1027
Eisler, P. E. 1236
Eklund, E. E. 173
Eller, D. B. 273
Eller, P. H. 274
Emmons, C. F. 520
Engerrand, G. C. M. 275
Engleman, U. Z. 623
Erickson, C. J. 1028
Ernst, R. 830
Esslinger, D. R. 831
Estabrook, G. H. 1237
Everest, K. A. 276
Exoo, C. F. 1238

Fahey, F. M. 1239
Fairchild, H. P. 421
Falconer, J. O. 277
Falk, G. 1029
Fallon, J. 422
Fandetti, D. V. 832
Farmer, G. L. 1240
Farrar, R. D. 833
Farrell, J. J. 834
Farrell, L. 1241
Fauman, S. J. 624
Feibelman, J. B. 625
Feierstein, M. 626
Feingold, H. L. 1030
Feinstein, E. F. 1242
Feinstein, M. 627
Feldberg, M. J. 25
Feldon, V. B. 835
Femminella, F. X. 423
Fenton, E. 424
Fernandez, R. L. 109
Fernberg, B. G. 628
Ferroni, C. D. 425
Fevold, E. L. 174
Fiege-Kollman, M. L. 1243
Fierman, F. S. 629
Fine, D. M. 1244
Finestone, H. 836
Fingerhut, E. R. 26
Fiore, A. T. 426
Fishman, J. A. 837
Flaherty, P. D. 1245
Fleishaker, O. 630
Flouris, G. 427
Flynn, A. 27
Flynn, J. Z. 1246
Foerster, R. F. 428
Fogarty, G. P. 28
Fogel, E. M. 278
Foley, A. R. 1031
Fonkalsrud, A. O. 175
Ford, M. L. 838
Ford, R. W. 839
Formisano, R. P. 1247
Forrester, J. R. 840
Fortenbaugh, R. 279
Fought, J. P. 1032
Fowler, M. E. 841
Fox, H. C. 280
Francher, J. S. 429
Frank, B. B. 631
Frankfort, N. 1248
Franklin, F. G. 1033

Index of Names

Franzblau, A. N.   632
Franzblau, R. N.   842
Freda, R. A.   1249
Freedman, S.   633
Freeman, S. D.   634
Freund, M. K.   635
Frey, J. W.   281
Friedman, S. S.   1034
Frye, R. J.   1035
Fryer, J. A.   1250
Fuchs, L. H.   636
Funchion, M. F.   29
Furio, C. M.   430

Gabert, G. E.   30
Gabriel, R. A.   843
Galford, J. B.   844
Galitzi, C. A.   521
Gallo, P. J.   431
Galush, W. J.   522
Garber, M. W.   1251
Garfinkle, H. G.   637
Garlick, R. C.   1252
Garis, R. L.   1036
Garner, J. P.   282
Garrido, A. R.   845
Gartner, C. B.   846
Garvey, W. P.   847
Gaspar, S.   283
Geary, G. J.   1253
Gedicks, A. J.   176
Gehring, C. T.   110
Geiser, K. F.   1254
Gelzer, D. G.   284
Gemorah, S.   177
Genen, A.   31
George, N. J.   1037
Georges, R. A.   432
Gerber, S. N.   523
Gersman, E. M.   848
Gerson, L.   1255
Gerstein, A. A.   638
Giannotta, R. O.   433
Gibson, F. E.   32
Giese, J. R.   639
Gilbert, G. G.   285
Gilkey, G. R.   434
Ginsburgh, S. A.   640
Giordano, P.   435
Gitin, L.   641
Gittlen, A. J.   642
Glad, D. D.   849

Glasco, L. A.   850
Glatfelter, C. H.   286
Gleason, J. P.   287
Glidden, W. B.   1038
Gobetz, G. E.   524
Gohmann, M. D.   1256
Golab, C. A.   525
Goldberg, G. J.   643
Goldberg, M. F.   644
Golden, L.   851
Goldenweiser, E. A.   526
Goldman, H.   645
Goldstein, J.   646
Goldstein, P. R.   647
Gollin, G. G.   288
Golovensky, D. I.   648
Golub, J. S.   649
Good, P. K.   852
Good, W. A.   289
Goodell, M. E.   1257
Goodside, S.   650
Gordon, A. I.   651
Gordon, N. K.   652
Gorelick, S.   653
Goren, A. A.   654
Gorman, M. F.   1258
Gorman, M. J.   1259
Gottfried, A.   1260
Gottlieb, M.   655
Goudeau, J. M.   111
Gould, G. H.   1261
Gould, K. H.   527
Govorchin, G. G.   528
Grabowski, J. J.   853
Graebner, A. N.   290
Gragg, L. D.   1039
Graham, I. C. C.   33
Grand, S.   656
Graves, N. B.   854
Gray, M. P.   112
Green, J. J.   1262
Green, R. B.   436
Greenberg, A. H.   657
Greenberg, D. W.   658
Greenberg, M.   659
Greene, V. R.   529
Gregg, C. E.   855
Grenke, A.   291
Griffin, C. S.   1263
Griffin, J. A.   113
Grinstein, H. B.   660
Groen, H. J.   292
Gross, M. B.   661

Index of Names

Grossberg, S. H. 662
Grossfield, A. J. 663
Grove, C. L. 114
Gudelunas, W. A. 35
Guignard, M. 856
Guillet, E. B. 115
Gustafson, W. W. 178
Gutierrez, L. P. 1264
Gutierrez, M. 116
Gutman, H. G. 1040
Guysenir, M. G. 664

Haas, J. H. 857
Haebler, P. 858
Hakimian, L. E. 665
Hale, F. 179
Halich, W. 530
Hall, R. L. B. 531
Hall, R. M. R. 666
Halley, H. 437
Halperin, S. 667
Halpert, M. 668
Hamilton, B. 1041
Hamre, J. S. 180
Handelman, S. 669
Handlin, O. 859
Haney, J. L. 293
Hannon, J. U. 860
Hannon, T. J. 861
Hansen, J. F. 181
Hansen, M. L. 1042
Hargrove, E. C. 1265
Harkavy, I. R. 1266
Harlow, J. E. 862
Harmond, R. P. 1267
Harney, L. 36
Harney, P. S. 1268
Harper, R. C. 863
Harrell, K. E. 1269
Harris, A. K. 670
Harrison, D. E. 1270
Hartmann, E. G. 1043
Hartwell, E. A. 864
Hasselmo, N. 182
Hassencahl, F. J. 1044
Haug, H. R. 294
Haussman, C. F. 295
Haussmann, W. A. 296
Hayes, M. 117
Head, V. 297
Heald, M. 1045
Hecht, D. I. 1271

Heckman, S. B. 298
Heimonen, H. S. 183
Heinrich, D. L. 865
Helling, R. A. 299
Helling, R. A. 866
Hemdahl, R. G. 184
Hendel-Sebestyen, G. 671
Henderson, J. J. 1046
Henderson, T. M. 867
Hendrickson, H. O. 1047
Henthorne, M. F. 37
Herman, H. V. 532
Herrick, C. A. 1048
Herrmann, E. M. 118
Hertz, R. C. 672
Hewitt, W. P. 533
Higham, J. W. 1049
Hill, H. S. 438
Hill, P. J. 1050
Hill, R. F. 534
Himmelein, F. T. 1272
Himmelfarb, H. S. 673
Hinrichsen, C. D. 1273
Hirst, A. H. 119
Hirst, D. W. 300
Hoffman, G. J. 1274
Hoffman, M. N. H. 868
Hoglund, A. W. 185
Holden, R. 1275
Holland, J. B. 869
Holt, M. F. 1276
Holte, J. C. 870
Hood, E. L. 1277
Hoover, K. E. 186
Hopkins, T. W. 871
Hopkins, T. W. 1278
Horak, J. 535
Hornberger, M. A. 872
Horton, B. D. 1051
Hosay, P. M. 873
Hough, L. S. 1052
Houston, G. 187
Houtman, L. H. 874
Hove, H. L. 188
Howe, B. J. 38
Howe, C. L. 1279
Huber, D. L. 301
Huff, E. D. 674
Huff, R. A. 1280
Hulston, R. F. 39
Hummasti, P. G. 189
Hunt, T. C. 1281
Hunter, D. M. 1282

343

Index of Names

Hustvedt, L. M.   190
Hutchens, N. C.   439

Ianni, F. A.   440
Iorizzo, L. J.   441
Irizarry, R.   1283
Irons, P. H.   1053
Irvine, W. B.   875
Isaacman, D.   675
Iverson, N.   302
Iverson, R. W.   1284

Jackson, K. T.   1285
Jackson, S. G.   40
Jaffe, E. A.   1054
Jaffe, I. B.   1286
Jaffe, J. F.   1055
Jamison, E. A.   41
Janson, F. E.   191
Jaros, J. A.   1056
Javetz, S.   876
Jebsen, H. A. A.   877
Jensen, R. J.   1287
Jick, L. A.   676
Jirak, I. L.   878
Johannes, M. E.   536
Johnson, A.   192
Johnson, G. E.   193
Johnson, N. M.   303
Johnston, B. V.   537
Johnston, W. M.   879
Jokinen, W. J.   194
Jonas, F. L.   677
Jonassen, C. T.   195
Jonitis, P. P.   538
Jordahl, L. D.   304
Jordan, A. C.   305
Jordan, L. W.   442
Jordan, R. H.   880
Jordan, T. G.   306
Joseph, S.   678
Joyce, W. L.   42
Juhnke, J. C.   307
Juliani, R. N.   443
Juroczak, C. A.   539
Jursa, P. E.   444
Jutronic, D.   540

Kabakoff, J.   679
Kachuck, R. S.   680
Kaganoff, N. M.   681
Kahn, R. I.   682
Kalangis, G. P.   1288
Kallassay, L. A.   308
Kamesis, F. S.   541
Kamman, W. F.   309
Kane, J. J.   43
Kaplan, B.   683
Karlin, J. A.   445
Karni, M. G.   196
Katz, S. G.   684
Kaups, M. E.   197
Keely, C. B.   1057
Keim, J.   310
Keller, K. W.   881
Keller, P.   311
Kelly, M. G.   1058
Kelly, R. J.   446
Kelso, T. J.   312
Kennedy, R. E.   44
Kenneson, S. R.   882
Kenney, A. P.   120
Kent, D. P.   313
Kercher, L. C.   198
Kernaklian, P.   542
Kerstan, R. J.   883
Kessler, C.   447
Kessler, J. B.   1059
Kessner, T.   884
Killeen, C. E.   1060
Killen, D. P.   45
Kim, Y. K.   1289
Kimball, C. D.   1061
Kimmerle, M. M.   199
King, D. T.   1062
Kinzer, D. L.   1063
Kiriazis, J. W.   448
Kirk, G. W.   885
Kirkpatrick, C.   886
Kitay, P. M.   685
Klaperman, G.   686
Kling, M.   1064
Klug, H. G.   1065
Knauss, J. O.   314
Knights, P. R.   887
Knittle, W. A.   1066
Knoche, C. H.   315
Knuth, H. E.   46
Koch, J. B.   316
Kocolowski, G. P.   1067
Koenning, A. R.   317
Koepplen, L. W.   888
Kogut, A. B.   889

Index of Names

Kolasa, B. J. 543
Kolehmainen, J. I. 200
Kolivosky, M. E. 890
Kolm, R. 891
Komjathy, A. 318
Korman, A. G. 1068
Korn, B. W. 687
Koslowe, I. 688
Kovacik, C. F. 892
Kovacs, M. L. 689
Kovacs, S. B. 544
Krall, D. N. 893
Kramer, G. N. 1069
Kranzler, G. C. 690
Krassowski, W. 894
Kraus, H. P. 895
Kraybill, D. B. 319
Kremling, H. J. 320
Kristufek, R. 896
Krueger, N. M. 897
Krzywkowski, L. V. 545
Kuntz, L. I. 691
Kutak, R. I. 546
Kutzik, A. J. 692
Kuznicki, E. M. 547

Labovitz, S. 899
Lagerquist, W. E. 1070
La Gumina, S. J. 1290
Lakeberg, A. P. 201
Lambert, B. C. 1291
Landis, P. H. 202
Lane, F. E. 900
Lane, J. B. 1292
Lang, E. W. H. 1071
Langley, S. 901
Lannie, V. P. 47
La Piere, R. T. 548
Larralde, C. M. 693
Larson, R. V. 203
Lasby, C. G. 321
Laurie, B. G. 902
Lawrence, E. P. 1293
Lawson, E. B. 204
Lazar, R. J. 694
Lazerson, M. 903
Leaf, H. 695
Leclair, P. J. 1294
Leder, H. H. 121
Lehrman, I. 696
Lehtinen, M. K. T. 205
Leifer, A. 904

Leinenweber, C. R. 1072
Leonard, H. B. 1073
Leonard, I. M. 1074
Leonard, S. J. 905
Leuca, M. 549
Leuchs, F. A. H. 322
Levinger, L. J. 697
Levinson, R. E. 698
Levy, B. H. 699
Lewis, C. A. 906
Lewis, C. S. 907
Lewis, O. F. 323
Lewis, R. G. 908
Lewin, R. G. 700
Lichtenstein, J. H. 909
Licon, L. L. 910
Lieberson, S. 911
Liemohn, E. T. 324
Ligouri, M. 1075
Lindberg, D. R. 206
Lindberg, P. M. 207
Lindenthal, J. J. 701
Linkh, R. M. 912
Liptak, D. A. 1076
Loffredo, C. A. 48
London, H. I. 1077
Lopata, H. Z. 550
Lopreato, J. 449
Lorimer, M. M. 1078
Lothrop, G. R. 1295
Lovell-Troy, L. A. 450
Lovoll, O. S. 208
Lovrich, F. M. 551
Lovrich, N. P. 913
Loxley, W. A. 914
Leubke, F. C. 325
Luidens, J. P. 122
Luke, O. S. 915
Lund, G. 209
Lyman, K. C. 49

Maas, E. H. 702
MacArthur, M. S. 326
Machado, D. A. M. 123
Mackun, S. 552
Macris, J. 451
Madden, H. M. 1296
Maguire, E. J. 50
Mahoney, J. M. 51
Maiale, H. V. 452
Major, M. I. 327
Malaska, H. O. 210

Index of Names

Mamchur, S. W.   553
Mamone, J. R.   916
Mancuso, A.   453
Manfra, J. A.   52
Mann, R. E.   1079
Mannion, L. J.   53
Marcuson, L. R.   917
Margolis, I.   703
Margulies, H. F.   1080
Marhoefer, G. L.   1081
Mariano, J. H.   454
Marjoribanks, K. M.   918
Markovitz, E.   704
Markus, D.   554
Marquardt, C. E.   328
Marsh, M. C.   919
Martens, H.   329
Martin, J. J.   1297
Marty, M. A.   920
Marzolf, M. T.   211
Massman, J. C.   330
Mathias, E. L.   455
Mathisen, R. R.   1298
Matthews, M. F.   456
Matthias, R. F.   1082
Mattis, M. C.   54
Matulich, L. K.   921
Mavelshagen, C.   331
Maxwell, W. J.   1299
Mayer, J. D.   923
Mayer, J. E.   922
Mazur, A. C.   705
McAvoy, T. T.   924
McBeth, H. L.   1300
McBride, P. W.   925
McColgan, M. D.   1301
McConville, M.   1083
McCord, S. J.   332
McCourt, K.   1302
McDonald, M. J.   55
McGann, A. G.   1084
McGivern, E. P.   56
McGovern, G. S.   1303
McGowen, O. T. P.   124
McGrath, (Sister Paul of the Cross)   1085
McGrath, W. J.   1304
McKay, E. A.   1305
McKay, R. Y.   926
McKevitt, G.   1306
McKinley, A. E.   125
McKinley, B. E.   1086
McLaughlin, V. Y.   457
McLeod, J. A.   927
McManamin, F. G.   57
McSeveney, S. T.   1307
Meade, R. D.   706
Medina, A. C.   1308
Meighan, C.   1089
Meister, R. J.   928
Meixner, E. C.   212
Mejia, R. D.   1309
Meldrum, G. W.   1087
Mellinger, P. J.   1088
Menatian, S.   1090
Merwick, D. J.   58
Messbarger, P. R.   1310
Messinger, J. S.   707
Metraux, G. S.   333
Meyer, H. J.   708
Meyer, L. R.   334
Meyerhuber, C. I.   1091
Meyerstein, R. G.   555
Miceli, M. V.   1311
Mikkelsen, M. A.   1312
Mikolji, B. H.   1092
Milano, F. A.   458
Miley, E. F.   1093
Millard, W. E.   929
Miller, A. H.   930
Miller, J. A.   709
Miller, M. D.   931
Miller, S. M.   1313
Minard, R. D.   932
Minshall, C. W.   710
Mirak, R.   556
Mitchell, A. G.   59
Mitchell, W. E.   711
Mizner, J. S.   712
Moe, T.   213
Moehlenbrock, A. H.   335
Mol, J. J.   933
Moll, D. L.   1314
Moll, L. C.   1315
Mondello, S. A.   459
Monos, D. I.   460
Mooney, P. J.   1094
Moore, D. D.   713
Moore, W. H.   336
Morawska, E. T.   557
Mormino, G. R.   934
Morrison, J. W.   1316
Morrison, K. M.   935
Morrow, R. L.   1095
Morrow, V. P.   1317
Mossberg, C. L.   214

Index of Names

Mostwin, D. 558
Mowshowitz, I. 714
Mueller, C. F. 1096
Mulder, W. 215
Mulhern, J. 936
Mulkern, J. R. 1097
Mulkey, Y. J. 1318
Mullaly, H. F. 1098
Mulligan, J. S. 937
Mulvey, M. D. 1319
Murphy, J. C. 938
Murphy, J. C. 1320
Murphy, M. C. 1321
Murray, J. E. 126
Murray, R. K. 1099
Myers, J. K. 461

Nair, M. D. 939
Nam, C. B. 940
Nanjundappa, C. 1100
Natelson, H. 715
Nathan, M. 716
Nau, J. F. 337
Nava, A. R. 1101
Neff, A. L. 1102
Neidle, C. S. 941
Nelli, H. S. 462
Nelson, C. L. 216
Nelson, D. C. 1103
Nelson, E. C. 217
Nelson, F. C. 218
Nelson, H. 559
Nelson, L. M. 219
Nelson, M. 1322
Nelson, M. C. 1104
Nelson, R. E. 1105
Nettinga, J. Z. 127
Neubauer, R. 717
Neuringer, S. M. 718
Neve, P. E. 338
Newander, M. C. 942
Newell, J. S. 1323
Newman, D. R. K. 943
Newton, L. W. 128
Nicholson, M. 944
Niehaus, E. F. 60
Niemi, T. J. 220
Nizami, S. A. 1106
Nolle, A. H. 339
Noonan, C. J. 1107
Norman, J. 463
Norris, M. R. 1108

Norton, M. A. 1324
Nugent, W. T. K. 1109
Nur, F. 1325
Nussenbaum, M. S. 719

Oberlander, B. J. 1110
Obidinski, E. E. 560
O'Brien, T. J. 464
O'Connell, L. 561
O'Connell, L. W. 1111
O'Dowd, W. G. 61
O'Dea, J. K. 720
Oder, I. 1112
Offenbach, L. 1326
O'Grady, J. P. 62
Okazaki, G. D. K. 945
Ollila, D. J. 221
Olson, A. L. 340
Olson, F. I. 1327
Onesto, S. F. 465
O'Reilly, C. T. 946
Orthman, W. G. 1113
Osborne, W. A. 947
Ostafin, P. A. 562
Ostyn, P. 129
Overmoehle, M. H. 341
Owens, M. L. 1328
Ozolins, K. L. 342

Pahorezki, M. S. 1329
Palamiotis, A. A. 1114
Palisi, B. J. 466
Palm, M. B. 1330
Palmer, E. S. 1115
Palmer, H. C. 467
Panchok, F. 1331
Papaiovannu, G. 468
Parenti, M. J. 469
Parmet, R. D. 1116
Parot, J. J. 563
Parsons, S. B. 1117
Parsteck, B. J. 1332
Passero, R. L. 470
Passi, M. M. 1333
Patterson, G. J. 471
Paul, D. L. 948
Paulsen, F. M. 222
Paulson, A. C. 223
Pavlak, T. J. 1118
Pedersen, H. A. 949
Peebles, R. W. 472

Perry, J. M.   1119
Person, P. P.   224
Petersen, A. J.   1120
Petersen, R. D.   1121
Petrello, B. A.   1334
Petropoulos, N. P.   473
Pfau, J. M.   1335
Phillips, B. A.   721
Piedmont, E. B.   1336
Pieper, E. H.   63
Pieters, A. J.   130
Pike, R.   131
Pinola, R.   1122
Pinsker, S. S.   722
Pioppi, I. R.   474
Poague, L. A.   1337
Pogue, F. G.   950
Polish, D.   723
Pollock, T. M.   724
Polsky, H. W.   725
Pomerantz, I. C.   726
Portis, B.   951
Post, E. H.   132
Potts, H. N.   133
Powell, J. H.   952
Pozetta, G. E.   475
Prewitt, T. J.   343
Prpic, G.   564
Punch, T.   953
Purcell, R. N.   954
Purdy, V. C.   1123
Pyros, J. A.   1338

Qualey, C. C.   225
Quay, W. L.   1124

Ragucci, A. T.   476
Rammelkamp, C. H.   134
Raphael, M. L.   727
Rappaport, J.   728
Raun, J. J.   226
Rawson, D. M.   1125
Reader, W. A.   955
Reaman, G. E.   1339
Reed, C. F.   344
Reed, D.   477
Reese, J. L.   956
Reich, M.   1126
Reigstad, P. M.   227
Reimer, T. T.   478
Rendell, H. J.   1340

Renkiewicz, F. A.   565
Renoff, R. M.   566
Reuter, W. C.   1127
Reynolds, C. J.   957
Ribardy, F. X.   479
Ring, J. B.   1341
Rink, O. A.   135
Risch, E.   1128
Rischin, M.   729
Ristuben, P. J.   1129
Rivers, R. R.   1130
Robbins, R. H.   1131
Robbins, W. L.   345
Robinson, T. P.   64
Roche, J. P.   480
Rockaway, R. A.   730
Rockett, I. R. H.   1132
Roddy, E.   1342
Rodechko, J. P.   65
Rodgers, H. R.   346
Roemer, T.   347
Rogoff, A. M.   731
Romano, L. A.   1343
Roohan, J. E.   66
Rosen, P.   958
Rosenberg, S. E.   732
Rosenblum, G.   1133
Rosenblum, H.   733
Rosenquest, C. M.   228
Rosenstock, M.   734
Rosenthal, E.   735
Ross, J. M.   736
Ross, M.   67
Rossi, E. E.   1134
Rothan, E. H.   348
Rothfuss, H. E.   349
Rothkoff, A.   737
Rowley, W. E.   1344
Rubin, E.   1135
Rubin, S. G.   1345
Rubin, V. D.   481
Rubinger, N. J.   738
Rudavsky, D.   739
Rudisill, A. S.   350
Russo, J. L.   1346
Russo, N. J.   482
Rutman, H. S.   740
Ryan, L. R.   1347
Ryskamp, H. J.   136

Saalberg, H.   351
Sabey, R. H.   567

Index of Names

Sable, J. M. 741
Safier, G. S. 1348
Salazar, T. A. 1349
Samora, J. 1350
Sanchez, G. 1351
Sandberg, N. C. 568
Santerre, R. 1352
Sarna, J. D. 1354
Sarrell, R. S. 137
Saveth, E. N. 1136
Scanlan, W. G. 68
Scarangelo, A. 1353
Scarpaci, J. A. 483
Schachter, J. 1137
Schaefer, L. L. 353
Schaefer, M. R. 69
Schaffer, A. L. 1355
Schanin, N. 742
Scharnau, R. W. 1356
Schaumann, H. F. 354
Schelbert, L. 355
Scherini, R. D. 484
Schersten, A. F. 229
Schmeckebier, L. F. 1138
Schmidt, W. E. 356
Schnackenberg, W. C. 230
Schneider, C. E. 357
Schneider, S. G. 1358
Schoem, D. L. 959
Schoenfeld, E. 743
Scholnick, M. L. 744
Schonback, M. 1357
Schrag, L. D. 358
Schreiber, E. S. 745
Schrier, A. 70
Schuchat, M. G. 359
Schuler, P. J. 960
Schultz, S. K. 961
Schutzengel, T. G. 1359
Scisco, L. D. 1139
Scott, G. S. 746
Scott, W. W. 962
Scourby, A. 485
Seaman, P. D. 486
Seder, D. L. 963
Seetharaman, A. V. 1360
Seifert, L. W. J. 360
Seiger, M. L. 747
Seipt, A. A. 361
Seller, M. S. 748
Sellmeyer, F. M. 1361
Selvan, I. C. 749
Sengstock, M. C. 964

Serene, F. H. 1140
Serino, G. R. 487
Servaitis, C. P. 569
Sessler, J. J. 362
Sewrey, C. L. 1141
Shafir, S. 1142
Shanabruch, C. H. 965
Shannon, J. P. 1143
Shapira, R. N. 750
Shapiro, M. A. 751
Shapiro, Y. 752
Sharfman, I. H. 753
Shasteen, A. E. 966
Shaughnessy, G. 1144
Shaw, D. V. 71
Shea, M. M. 72
Shea, W. S. 570
Shepardson, F. W. 73
Shepperson, W. S. 74
Sheridan, P. B. 1145
Sheridan, P. B. 1362
Shlonsky, H. R. 754
Shoemaker, A. L. 363
Shradar, V. I. 1363
Shurden, W. B. 1364
Sidlofsky, S. 488
Siegel, M. 1365
Silver, A. M. 755
Silverman, S. S. 756
Simirenko, A. 571
Simon, R. D. 1146
Singer, D. F. 757
Sinkler, G. 1147
Sipher, R. E. 1148
Sirota, D. 967
Skardal, D. B. 231
Skeute, B. M. 232
Sklare, M. 758
Skrabanek, R. N. 572
Slocum, W. L. 968
Sluiter, F. 138
Smith, G. S. 1149
Smith, H. 364
Smith, R. H. 1366
Smith, W. B. 1367
Snetsinger, J. G. 1150
Snow, C. E. 759
Sokoll, C. A. 352
Solberg, C. B. 1368
Solomon, B. M. 1151
Soltes, M. 760
Soviv, A. 761
Spalding, T. W. 75

Spanheimer, M. E. 365
Spengler, P. A. 969
Spergel, I. A. 1369
Spiegel, J. A. 970
Spletstoser, F. M. 1152
Spurgeon, J. H. 139
Srole, L. 971
Stachowski, F. J. 1370
Stack, J. F. 972
Stack, R. F. 76
Stanford, R. M. 1371
Stauffer, A. P. 1153
Stegenga, P. J. 140
Steigelfest, A. 762
Stein, H. F. 573
Stein, R. F. 973
Steinberg, A. H. 763
Steinberg, S. H. 1372
Steininger, R. F. 366
Stellos, M. H. 489
Stephanides, M. C. 490
Stern, H. D. 764
Stern, M. H. 765
Stevens, R. L. 233
Stevens, R. P. 766
Stewart, B. M. 1154
Stibili, E. C. 491
Stickle, W. E. 1155
Stine, C. S. 367
Stipanovich, J. P. 574
Stivers, R. A. 77
Stob, G. 141
Stoessinger, L. G. 1156
Stofflet, E. H. 974
Stolarik, M. M. 575
Strong, D. S. 767
Stuart, I. R. 975
Sturm, R. 576
Suggs, G. G. 1157
Sullivan, M. J. 976
Supervielle, A. F. 977
Surace, S. J. 1373
Sutker, S. 768
Svendsbye, L. 368
Swain, B. M. 978
Swanson, B. R. 235
Swanson, C. G. 1374
Swansen, H. F. 234
Swidersky, R. M. 492
Sypek, S. T. 577
Syrjamaki, J. 979
Szamek, P. F. 369
Szarnicke, H. A. 78

Taft, D. R. 142
Taggart, G. L. 578
Tait, J. W. 493
Tanzwall, W. F. 1158
Tarpey, M. V. 79
Tarr, J. A. 1375
Tarshish, A. 769
Tavuchis, N. 494
Taylor, J. H. 1159
Taylor, M. C. 1376
Teitelbaum, S. 770
Temkin, S. D. 771
Ten Zythoff, G. J. 143
Ter Maat, C. J. 144
Terwilliger, M. P. 980
Thacker, C. M. 981
Thatcher, Mary A. 982
Theriault, G. F. 145
Thernstrom, S. A. 983
Thomas, M. E. 1160
Thompson, B. 495
Thompson, H. R. 1377
Thompson, J. 1161
Thorson, G. H. 236
Thurner, A. W. 1378
Tilley, M. C. 1379
Titus, M. F. 1380
Todes, D. U. 772
Tomasi, S. M. 496
Tomaske, J. A. 1162
Townsend, A. J. 370
Tracy, A. L. 1163
Treble, J. G. 1164
Tregoe, B. B. 984
Trelease, A. W. 146
Trutza, P. G. 579
Tsiang, I. M. 1165
Tsushima, W. T. 985
Tucker, M. T. 371
Tull, J. E. 1381
Turner, A. L. 1166
Tweedie, S. W. 1382

Uhlendorf, B. A. 372
Ulin, R. O. 497
Ulrich, R. J. 373
Umbeck, S. G. 374
Underwood, G. N. 1383
Urbanski, A. 580

Valentine, F. D. 1384

Index of Names

Valletta, C. L. 498
Van De Luyster, N. 375
Vander Hill, C. W. 147
Varbero, R. A. 499
Vaswani, H. V. 1385
Vecoli, R. J. 500
Veidemanis, J. 581
Venettozzi, J. T. 1386
Ventry, L. T. 1387
Vicero, R. D. 148
Vinyard, J. M. 80
Vlachos, E. C. 501
Vloutidis, N. E. 1388
Von Raffler, W. 502
Vrga, D. J. 582

Wack, J. T. 1389
Wacker, R. F. 1390
Wagman, M. 149
Waldron, G. H. 1167
Walker, M. 376
Walker, M. G. 81
Walkowitz, D. J. 1391
Wall, M. F. 986
Walsh, F. R. 82
Walsh, J. P. J. 83
Walters, J. 1392
Waltz, W. E. 1393
Wang, P. H. 1168
Wangler, T. E. 84
Waniek, M. R. N. 1394
Ward, R. J. 1395
Warzeski, W. C. 583
Waschek, B. 584
Wayland, J. W. 377
Weber, S. E. 378
Webster, J. A. 503
Wechman, R. J. 773
Wefald, J. M. 237
Weinbaum, M. G. 1396
Weinberg, D. E. 1397
Weinberger, A. L. 774
Weinstock, S. A. 379
Weintraub, H. 238
Weisz, H. R. 987
Weitz, M. 988
Welch, C. E. 1398
Weng, A. G. 380
Wenger, M. R. 381
Wentz, A. R. 382
Werb, M. R. 775
Wess, R. C. 150

Wessel, B. B. 989
Westhues, K. L. 1399
Wetzel, C. J. 1169
Wheeler, W. L. 239
White, C. M. 1400
White, G. C. 990
White, G. L. 240
White, J. A. 1401
White, J. D. 1402
White, J. F. 1403
White, J. P. 585
White, W. B. 1404
Whyman, H. C. 241
Whyte, W. F. 504
Wilhelm, C. L. 1405
Wilhelm, H. G. H. 383
Williams, A. R. 85
Williams, A. W. 1406
Williams, D. J. 86
Williams, H. P. 384
Williams, J. M. 1407
Willie, C. V. 991
Willigan, W. L. 87
Wilson, C. F. 151
Wilson, M. D. 1408
Winfield, O. A. 385
Winograd, L. 776
Winsey, V. R. 505
Wirth, J. B. 386
Wirth, L. 777
Wisse, R. R. 778
Wolf, R. C. 387
Wolniewicz, R. 586
Wood, K. D. K. 1170
Wood, S. E. 1171
Woodland, L. A. 992
Worden, V. J. 152
Wozniak, P. R. 993
Wu, C. L. 994
Wyman, D. S. 1172
Wyman, R. E. 1409

Yang, C. S. W. 1410
Yapko, B. L. 779
Yearley, C. K. 88
Yeretzian, A. S. 587
Yodfat, A. Y. 780
York, L. F. 781
Young, C. K. 1173
Young, K. 995
Young, W. L. 996
Youngerman, L. M. 782

Zeitlin, J. 783
Zerin, E. 784
Ziegler, S. G. 506
Ziff, R. 1411
Zinn, H. 1412
Zivich, E. A. 588

SUBJECT INDEX

References are to entry numbers.

Addams, J., 1299
Albany (N. Y.): Dutch in, 120
Alcohol, Addiction: Irish and Jewish social norms, 792; drinking patterns among ethnic groups, 908
Alexander, M., 615
Aliens: injuries and international law, 998; rights of, 999, 1173; attack on in U. S., 1006; deportation of, 1019, 1035, 1165, 1166; as enemies in U. S. (1917-1919), 1038; anti-alien land legislation, 1059; in American constitutional law, 1114; unemployment of in U. S., 1135
American Bible Society, 1263
American Protective Association, 1063
Americanization, 1043; gospel of, 1056; theories of, 1175
Amish: school controversy in Iowa, 346
Anderson, R. B., 190
Anglo-Americans: upper-class activities, 38
Anglo-Saxonism, 46
Arizona: ethnic groups, 825
Armenians: ethnicity, 542; in California, 548, 559; history of in U. S. (1890-1915), 556; emigration to U. S., 587
Assimilation: of American family patterns by immigrants, 794, 963; in southern Illinois, 803; cultural conflict, 806, 891, 893, 925, 943; measurement of acculturation, 809, 897, 921; immigrant autobiography as document of, 821, 941; rate of social assimilation, 855, 911, 940, 955; in rural Christian congregations, 861; and persistence of cognitive style, 864, 914; naturalization and, 894; theology and Americanization, 933; survey of public opinion (1882-1914), 990; and Pan-Catholicism, 993
Atlanta (Ga.): Leo Frank Case, 617; assimilation of immigrants, 823
Atterdag College, 187

Augustana Synod, 171, 173, 207
Augustana Theological Seminary, 153

Baltimore (Md.): Italian and Polish immigrants, 832; low-income housing, 1223
Bancroft Naturalization Treaties, 334
Baptists: and racial and ethnic minorities, 927
Basel Foreign Mission Society, 284
Basques: in Western U.S., 97; assimilation of, 102; family life in Idaho, 112
Bay Ridge (Brooklyn): Norwegian community, 195
Belgians: and Catholic Church in America, 113
Bennett Law (1889), 373
Bergendoff, C., 235
Berger, V. L., 1313
Bernard, J., 1348
Bilingualism: and mental development, 788; and elementary school children, 789; and intelligence, 820, 995, 1388; measurement, 868; and bicultural communities, 977; political history of bilingual language policy in U.S., 1101; school-community assessments, 1197; history of in New Jersey, 1216, 1249; reading in, 1243; English as a second language, 1248; attitudes toward, 1264; cultural communication, 1282, 1315; creativity and, 1283; in urban schools, 1301; instructional components of, 1308; index of critical requirements, 1309; and monolingualism, 1314; and cultural politics, 1317; job-market, 1334; bibliography, 1349; minority leadership, 1350; Bilingual Education Act, 1351, 1358
Bintl Brief, 604
Bishop Hill Colony, 1312
Bok, E. W., 1372
Boston: acculturation of immigrants, 859, 972; demographic and social study, 887
Boston Pilot, 42, 57, 82
Boyesen, H. H., 172
Bucci, M., 1217
Buffalo (N.Y.): Irish and German immigrants, 850

Cahan, A., 652, 724
California: treatment of foreign groups (1830-1860), 1087; anti-foreign movements, 1167; Commission of Immigration and Housing, 1171; minority education, 1191
Canadians: in Michigan, 892
Cape Verdeans, 123
Capra, F., 1337
Carpatho-Ruthenians: loss of religious community in U.S., 566; national consciousness, 583
Catholic Church: in Erie (N.Y.), 4; Irish Catholicism in America, 7; Catholic press, 39, 42, 57, 82, 1225, 1342; episcopacy, 52; Boston clergy, 58; and social questions, 66; in Chicago, 69, 83; and Belgians in U.S., 113; colonization projects in U.S., 1058, 1120, 1143, 1144; anti-Catholicism in U.S., 1063, 1141, 1153;

Subject Index 355

and European immigrants, 938, 1076, 1320; and Progressive Education, 1906; role in Americanization, 965, 1310; immigrant-aid societies, 1274; influence on slavery, 1311; and theater in New York City, 1331
Catholic Education: in Missouri, 24; history of, 30; common-school controversy (1840-1842), 27, 47; and diocesan boards of education, 68; future of, 1399
Catholic Telegraph, 1225
Cermak, A. J., 1260
Chicago: Irish nationalists, 29; Catholic Church, 69, 965; succession of cultural groups, 817; ethnics and politics, 1179; socialist movement in, 1356
"Chicago School" of American Sociology, 1188
Christiansen, F. M., 219
Churgin, P., 695
Civil War: immigrants in, 1158; immigrant press during, 1198
Clan-na-Gaelers, 29
Clarke, W. N., 1279
Cleveland (Ohio): ethnic groups in, 793; Hiram House, 853
Clinton, G., 134
Colorado Coal Strike, 1303
Control-Verein, 287
Covello, L., 472
Crime: in foreign-born, 862; national and cultural differences, 974
Croats: ethnic identity among, 512; occupations in U.S., 532; in Pennsylvania, 540; history of in U.S., 564; political activities, 570; in Indiana, 588
Cultural pluralism: in American social thought, 952, 1024
Czechs: radicalism, 516; in Texas, 533; in Chicago, 535; in Virginia, 544; acculturation, 546; in Texas, 572; in Wisconsin, 578; folk music, 584

Dallapiccola, L., 1192, 1206, 1229, 1261
Dalton, Henry, 40
Damrosch, W., 1257, 1272
Danes: ethnic voluntary associations, 166; in Iowa, 167, 234; social interactions, 181; folk high schools, 187; Lutheranism, 226; and Poles, 949
daPonte, L., 1346
DeJong, D. C., 144
Demography: foreign and native stock in U.S., 1002
Denver (Colo.): immigrants (1859-1910), 905
Detroit (Mich.): ethnic neighborhoods, 787; voluntary associations, 805; acculturation of immigrants, 866, 906; public schools and immigrants, 874
DeVries, P., 144
Diekema, G. J., 147
Domestic servants, 1086
Dutch: Calvinism, 93; Christian Reformed Church, 94, 103, 122, 127, 132, 140, 141, 143; diplomacy in North America, 100; New Netherland, 100, 101, 125, 126; language in colonial New York, 110; in upper Hudson Valley (N.Y.), 120; settlements in Michi-

gan, 130, 136, 139, 147; schools in North America (1620-1750),
133; in New York, 134, 135; on Pacific Coast, 138; novelists,
144; rural settlements in Washington State, 157

East Harlem (New York City), 1379
Ellicott, J., 1220
Ellis Island: immigrant children at, 802
Emmet, T. A., 64
English: immigrants in industrial America, 6; views of emigration,
74; in American labor movement (1860-1895), 88
Erie (N. Y.), 4; ethnic politics, 847
Ethnicity: and political behavior, 930, 1103, 1118, 1121, 1174,
1194, 1199, 1238, 1341, 1378; education and ethnic attitudes,
951; ethnic communal systems, 971, 1326; and Alienage, 982;
in current education newsletters, 986; debate over (1900-1924),
1027, 1390; and ideology of equal opportunity, 1051; and occupational mobility, 1132; ethnic studies, 1333
Etzler, J. A., 1203
Eugenics: and immigrants, 1044, 1126

Fall River (Mass.): Portuguese in, 124; ethnic factor in, 876
Felciano, R., 1221
Felician Sisters, 547, 898
Fenian movement, 17, 19, 51, 63, 81
Fenwick, B. J., 36
Finns: rural communities, 170, 183, 197, 198; immigrant radicals,
176, 196; in America (1880-1920), 185; sociological interpretation,
194; in Western Reserve, 200; in Michigan, 202; Trade Union
Movement (1890-1920), 203; language, 205; adult education, 210;
language press, 211; Lutheranism, 220, 221; folk traditions, 222
Fitzpatrick, J. B., 34
Flemish: study of language loss, 129
Ford, P., 65
Frank, W., 652
French: and political history of United States, 90; in southern U.S.
(1791-1810), 91; French National Societies, 98; refugees (1790-
1800) in U.S., 99; teaching French to Franco-Americans, 107;
in Holyoke (Mass.), 115; in Woonsocket (R.I.), 137; assimilation
in Louisiana, 128; bilingual programs for, 118
French Canadians: in New England, 104, 105, 1031; in Holyoke
(Mass.), 115, 858; in Woonsocket (R.I.), 137; in Nashua (N.H.),
145; integration of, 148; poets, 1219; novel, 1352
Fur trade: in New France and New Netherland, 126; Indian relations with, 146
Furuseth, A., 238

Gaelic American, 11
Gallego-Spanish speakers, 116
Gamoran, E., 773
Gary (Ind.): and immigrants, 928

Subject Index 357

Genoese: in Seville and opening of New World, 131
George, D. L., 1265
George, H., 1262
Germans: in Milwaukee, 242, 264, 315; drama, on N. Y. stage, 243, 248, 322, 328: on Cleveland stage, 320: in Philadelphia, 323; exiled writers, 245; intellectuals, 313; Catholicism, 247, 282, 287, 348; in Philadelphia, 249, 261, 271; German-American Bund, 250, 352; language, 251, 257, 270, 281, 285, 305, 332, 336, 344, 354, 360, 363; in Texas, 253, 275, 306, 383; emigration, 255, 260, 375, 376; in Illinois, 256, 370, 371; German-American press, 263, 266, 292, 315, 317, 331, 342, 351; Lutheranism, 265, 274, 279, 286, 289, 290, 293, 294, 295, 301, 304, 316, 317, 338, 342, 350, 353, 356, 357, 366, 368, 380, 385, 386, 387; in Cincinnati, 268, 292; Baptist settlements, 273, 883; in Wisconsin, 276, 341, 356, 373; in Pennsylvania, 278, 314, 367, 378, 936; Presbyterianism, 280; in Winnipeg, 291; hymnology, 296, 324, 338, 361; in Detroit, 299; in Toronto, 299; propaganda in U. S., 300, 303; in Minnesota, 302, 330, 349; socialism, 309; political relations, 310, 312; and World War I, 311; scientists, 321; in Nebraska, 325; in Colorado, 326; in Rochester (N. Y.), 329; in Louisiana, 332, 334, 335; in St. Louis, 339, 340; in Oklahoma, 343; in North Carolina, 345; in Chicago, 370, 374; in Virginia, 377; in New York, 382; the Russian-German, 384; in Reading (Pa.), 839
Germer, A., 1214
Gest, M., 1338
Ghetto: immigrant fiction of, 846, 1244, 1293
Gilman, D. C.: and American graduate education, 1227
Girard College, 1343, 1402
Goodman Memorial Theatre, 1323
Grand Rapids (Mich.): Dutch subculture in, 93
Greeks: language, 388, 451, 486; in Florida, 398, 437; Greek-American relations, 402; ethnicity, 406; in Texas, 409; acculturation, 411, 450, 501; emigration to U. S., 421; and American schools, 427, 1288; folk beliefs, 432; in Los Angeles, 446; social mobility, 460, 473, 494; Greek Orthodox Church, 468, 1271; in Denver (Colo.), 471; attitudes toward Jews and blacks, 473; in Columbus (Ohio), 478, religious attitudes, 485; in St. Louis, 489; in Detroit, 490; in Indiana, 501
Greenfield (Mass.): immigrant social mobility, 955
Gronlund, L., 177
Gypsy-Andalusians: ethnography of, 151

Harmony Society, 261
Harrigan, E. G., 1208
Hasselquist, T. N., 154
Hawaii: ethnic classification in, 1316
Hayes, P. (Cardinal): and Catholic charities, 72
Haymarket Affair, 1230
Hebrew Technical Institute, 645
Hedstrom, O. G., 204
Herbst, J., 277

Hillquit, M., 1284
Hoan, D. W., 1370
Holland (Mich.): Dutch community, 147; immigrant social mobility, 885
Holyoke (Mass.): French culture in, 115
Hope College, 140
Howe, F. C., 1280
Hughes, J., 47
Huguenots: in South Carolina novel, 89; in South Carolina, 119
Hungarians: in Pittsburgh, 244; migration to American cities, 254; occupational adjustments, 258; travelers in America, 283; 1956 revolt, 297; Reformed Church, 308, 318, 1210; American-Hungarian relations (1918-1944), 327; refugees, 359; eastern American dialect, 369; acculturation, 379
Hutterites: political ethnography, 508

Iannelli, A., 1345
Immigrant historical societies, 1181
Immigration: migration geography, 997; international migration, 1000, 1162, 1164, 1170; Canadian policy, 1003, 1008; attitudes of European states to emigration, 1012; professional migration, 1016, 1021, 1029, 1113; restriction, 1017, 1018, 1020, 1036, 1110, 1130, 1151; protest against, 1073, 1163; Baptist response to, 1023; McCarran-Walter Act (1952), 1025, 1054, 1131; American policy, 1026, 1030, 1037; history of, 1042, 1070, 1071, 1136; business attitudes toward, 1045; economic impact of, 1050, 1094, 1137; Immigration Act of 1965, 1057; Catholic colonization projects, 1058; Immigration Act of 1924, 1093, 1168; law of, 1106; immigrant aid, 1128; and American labor movement, 1133
Indiana: immigration to, 1071
International Ladies' Garment Workers' Union, 1193, 1204
Ireland: emigration, 21, 44, 70; Irish revolution (1914-1922), 8; marriage and fertility in, 44
Ireland, J., 84
Irish: emigration, 1, 21, 44, 70; in Syracuse (N. Y.), 5; and Catholicism, 7; in American fiction, 9; Irish-American nationalism (1870-1890), 10; in New York (1914-1921), 11; adjustment to urban life, 12; Fenian movement, 17, 19, 51, 63, 81; and national isolationism, 18; in Massachusetts, 22; during decade of expansion (1890-1901), 23; in Chicago, 29, 83; and the Irish question, 41; Irish-American press, 42, 65, 87; Irish drama on New York stage, 1900-1958, 49; and foreign policy of the United States, 1865-1872, 51; in Buffalo (N. Y.), 54; in Wisconsin, 55; in Pittsburgh, 56; in Lowell (Mass.), 59; in New Orleans, 60; and urban planning, 61; and Anglo-American relations, 1880-1888, 62; in California gold fields, 76; and drinking, 77; on urban frontier (Detroit, 1850-1880), 80; and humor, 85; and Jews, 792, 849, 917; and Italians, 818, 843, 879, 917, 970, 985, 987; in Toronto (1840-1900), 944; in Halifax (1815-1867), 953; in Ottawa (1825-1870), 992
Irish Colonization Association, 37
Irish Emigrants Guide For the United States, 50

Subject Index

Irish National League of America, 29
Irish World, 11
Irving, W. , 150
Italians: family patterns, 389, 397, 408, 457, 477, 1246; in East Harlem (N. Y.), 390, 410; in Louisiana, 391, 435, 445, 483; writers, 392, 436; in Pennsylvania, 394, 440, 443, 452, 498, 499; language, 395, 412, 418, 419; in New Mexico, 396; as depicted in early American periodicals, 399; repatriation, 400, 404, 444; Italian Fascism, 401, 417, 442, 463, 1367; sculptors, 403; acculturation, 405, 414, 423, 429, 455, 481, 498, 505; in Newark (N. J.), 407; and American schools, 413, 438, 447, 456, 465, 474, 493, 497; Protestant mission work among, 415, 919: women in labor force, 416, 430, 453; Catholicism, 420, 422, 464, 482, 496; and organized labor, 424, 470; in Cleveland, 425; in Nebraska, 426; emigration, 428, 434, 444, 449, 505; in politics, 431, 452, 469, 487, 879; in eighteenth-century America, 433; bilingualism, 438, 447, 502; in Brooklyn (N. Y. C.), 439; and Padrone system, 441; in New York City, 454, 475; in Buffalo (N. Y.), 457; and Vietnam era, 458; and contemporary periodical press, 459; in New Haven (Conn.) 461; Italian-American press, 462; in Chicago, 462, 500; voluntary associations, 466; in California agriculture, 467; health practices, 476; crime, 479, 836; in Rhode Island, 480; in San Francisco, 484, 1222; in Toronto, 488, 506; protection of Italian immigrants, 491; in Massachusetts, 492, 495; social structure of Italian slum, 504; in Rome (N. Y.), 810; and Jews, 814, 828, 829, 865, 917, 956, 980; and Irish, 818, 843, 917, 970, 985, 987; and blacks, 822, 879, 1092; and Poles, 832, 836; and Puerto Ricans, 870, 916; in St. Louis, 934; and Swedes, 969

Jersey City: making of immigrant city, 71
Jesuits, 1268, 1330
Jewish Daily Forward, 597
Jews: ideologies of, 590; acculturation, 591, 596, 616, 661, 689, 716, 717, 720, 721, 765; in Israel, 592, 665; attitudes toward, 750; day schools, 593, 606, 641, 648, 650, 756; Yiddish theater, 595, 709, 747; immigration, 598, 676, 678, 718, 1030, 1034; in Los Angeles, 600, 601, 609, 611; literature, 599, 602, 612, 628, 633, 642, 644, 652, 657, 679, 680, 684, 722, 726, 746, 763, 778, 781; in St. Louis, 603; anti-Semitism, 603, 619, 697, 714, 741, 744, 767; in Cincinnati, 605; in Scranton (Pa.), 607; in Washington (D. C.), 608; Sephardic, 609, 671; education, 614, 618, 622, 626, 629, 634, 637, 653, 669, 673, 703, 715, 739, 759, 770, 772, 779, 837, 959; Yiddish language, 620, 666, 760; agricultural communities, 621, 647; population trends, 623; in Detroit, 624, 662, 708, 730; in New Orleans, 625; Zionism, 627, 656, 667, 674, 752, 754, 766; in Illinois-Iowa, 630; housewife, 631; adolescents and youth, 632, 640, 649, 663, 675, 742, 750, 784; in Colonial America, 635; and politics, 636, 646, 658, 664, 755, 1142; Reform Judaism, 638, 641, 672, 699; in Denver, 639; in Minneapolis, 651, 700, 740; in New York, 654,

660, 668, 670, 688, 690, 711, 713, 729, 755; anti-Nazi boycott movement, 655; in Fairfield (Conn.), 658; in Chicago, 664, 735; in Louisiana, 683; and Civil War, 687, 706; in Pittsburgh, 691, 749; philanthropy, 692; in Texas, 693, 702; in North Dakota, 694; in Florida, 696; in California, 698; in Middletown (Conn.), 701; social scientists, 705; in Syracuse (N.Y.), 707; in Columbus (Ohio), 710; Orthodox Judaism, 719, 725, 762; in Brookline (Mass.), 721; nationalism, 723; intra-Jewish conflict, 727; and World War I, 728; and labor movement, 731; in Rochester (N.Y.), 732; United Synagogue, 733; in Albany (N.Y.), 738; small town, 743; religious textbooks, 751; Conservative Judaism, 758; social workers, 764; in Atlanta (Ga.), 768; in New Jersey, 775; and American-Russian relations, 780; American rabbis, 782, 783; and Irish, 792, 849, 917; and Italians, 814, 828, 829, 865, 917, 956, 980; and blacks, 899, 988; intermarriage, 922

Kaplan, M. M.: and Jewish education, 589
Karpovich, P. V., 1360
Kearney, D., 1239
Kellor, F., 1299
Kelly, John, 31
Knights of Labor: and Catholic Church, 1205
Koehler, J. P., 304
Ku Klux Klan, 1269, 1285

Labor market: and ethnic discrimination, 860; white ethnic and black assimilation, 909; intergroup conflict, 975, 1004, 1052; and social mobility, 983; in Pacific Northwest, 1001; recruitment of European immigrant labor, 1028; and economic depression, 1040; foreign labor in, 1046; labor migration, 1062, 1096, 1100; industrial unionism, 1088, 1157, 1183, 1211; impact of immigration, 1119, 1140; labor-legislation movement, 1196; iron and steel industry, 1202
La Guardia, F., 1265, 1332, 1412
Landmarkism, 1381
Latvians: value-systems, 581
Laughlin, H. H., 1044
Lawrence (Mass.): immigrants and industrial growth, 1224
League of Nations: and 1920 presidential election, 18
Leboffe, E., 503
Leeser, I., 594, 626, 748
Lewisohn, L., 652, 757
Lindsborg (Kan.): Swedish community, 169, 239
Lithuanians: refugees in Los Angeles, 511; family in America, 514; in Pennsylvania, 538; cooperation among in U.S., 541; folkways, 569; in Chicago, 585
Lodge, H. C., 1091
London, M., 643
Lopez, A., 610
Lorimer, W., 1375
Los Angeles: and ethnic churches, 835

Subject Index

Louisiana: early libraries and Creole influence, 111; assimilation of French, 128; French bilingual programs, 118
Louisville (Ky.): occupational mobility, 1067
Lowell (Mass.): Irish immigrants, 59
Luther Academy, 171

Mack, A., 298
Magazines: ethnic content analysis, 978
Manfred, F., 144
Mann, H., 1371
Mann, T., 1403
Marcantonio, V.: and A. H. Vandenberg, 1064; and New Deal, 1290; congressional career of, 1355
Marriage: interethnic, 815, 827, 890, 922
Marshall, L., 734
Mazzei, P., 1252
McGarrity, J.: and Irish independence, 79
McGee, T. D., 1207
Meagher, T. F., 2
Medical education, 1270
Melting-pot idea: history, 863; and cultural pluralism, 1024; and the military, 1404
Mendes, H. P., 704
Mengarini, G., 1295
Mennonites: health movement, 252; in Kansas, 307, 358; in Lancaster (Pa.), 319; school controversy in Iowa, 346; Swiss Mennonites, 355; in Pennsylvania, 364
Menotti, G. C., 1215, 1217, 1250, 1275
Metropolitan Opera, 1236
Miller, J. H., 266
Milwaukee (Wis.): ethnicity and occupations, 923; industrial growth and immigrants, 1068, 1146
Minnesota: labor and politics on the northern iron range, 1122; and competition for immigrants, 1129
Missionaries: Franciscans in California, 1226; secularization of, 1253; and education, 1259, 1361; French Catholic, 1319; in the Northwest, 1324; in trans-Mississippi West, 1328
Molly Maguires: in eastern Pennsylvania, 14, 35; and industrial unions, 1183
Morais, S., 719
Moravians: congregations in New York City, 267; Bishop Johannes Herbst, 277; in Pennsylvania, 288, 362
Morgan, T. J., 1356
Mormons: from Scandinavia (1850-1905), 215; migration to western U. S., 1014; migration to Utah, 1102
Motherhood: cultural concepts of in America (1830-1916), 937
Mullanphy, John: descendants of, 13
Mullen, T.: and Erie Diocese, 4

Nativism: and Catholic press, 39; origins of in U. S., 1010, 1149; Anglo-Saxonism in U. S., 1013; in New York, 1022, 1074, 1077,

1139; religious element in, 1047; and American patriotic thought, 1049; history of, 1069, 1149; in Iowa, 1082; in Maryland, 1083, 1138; in Kentucky, 1084; in Texas, 1085; and Catholic higher education, 1089; in Massachusetts, 1097, 1123; in Connecticut, 1107, 1116; in Kansas, 1109; in Mississippi, 1125; in Tennessee, 1256

Naturalization: in its social setting in U. S., 1007; legislative history, 1033

Nelson, K., 162

Newark (N. J.): Roman Catholic schools, 48; history of Diocese, 1273

New Bedford (Mass.): Portuguese in, 96

New Brunswick Theological Seminary, 95

New England: French National Societies in, 98; French Canadians in, 104, 105, 115, 856, 1031, 1219, 1352

New Haven (Conn.): English immigrants in, 3

New Netherland, 100, 101, 125, 126, 133, 134, 135, 149

New Orleans: Irish (1803-1862), 60; as immigrant port, 1152

New Sweden (Del.), 192

New York City: school controversy (1840-1842), 27, 47; Irish drama in, 49; Friendly Sons of St. Patrick, 54; Catholic charities, 72; Dutch language in Colonial, 110; Gallego-Spanish speakers in, 116; as a Dutch colony, 134, 135, 149; ethnic conflict in, 795; immigrant children, 799, 819, 834; representation of immigrant on stage, 824; Catholicism, 826; intermarriage in, 827; immigrant life, 830; Settlement House, 873; immigrant nobility in, 884, 981; and urban novel, 1209; visiting nurse movement, 1212; labor movement, 1228, 1231, 1233

New York (State): assimilation of immigrants (1764-1776), 26; Irish, 32

Noah, M. M., 1354

North Dakota: Norwegians, 206; migration patterns, 1065

Norwegian Synod: in America (1853-1890), 160

Norwegians: and American public affairs (1840-1872), 156; English-language hymnals, 158; immigration before Civil War, 163; after Civil War, 225, 237; writers, 172, 223, 236; Lutheranism, 174, 180, 217, 230; ethnicity, 186; immigrant press, 188; in Brooklyn (N.Y.), 195; surnames, 199; in North Dakota, 206; the Bygdelag, 208; economic growth in Norway, 213; school controversy, 218; political conservatism, 273

Notre Dame University, 1389

Nova Scotia: Catholic immigration, 1075

O'Connell, D. J., 28
O'Connor, M., 78
O'Hanlon, J., 50
Omaha (Neb.): residential mobility, 812
Onahan, W. J., 1329
O'Neill, Eugene: and Irish-American Catholicism, 16
O'Reilly, J. B., 57

Subject Index 363

Palatine emigrants: in New York and North Carolina, 1066
Palestine Mandate: interest groups and, 1112
Park, R. E., 1188
Passaic (N. J.) Textile Strike, 1365
Paterson (N. J.): silk industry, 1251
Pennsylvania: Molly Maguires, 14, 35; colonization (1681-1701), 1041; white servitude in, 1048, 1254
Persichetti, V., 1241
Philadelphia: riots of 1844, 25; immigrants, 43, 808, 1145; working people of, 902, 1190; ethnic politics, 1124; worker mobility, 1266; Mummers Parade, 1398
Pittsburgh (Pa.): public schools and immigrants, 896
Poles: Polish-American press, 510, 580; and Polish Question (1939-1948), 515; in Chicago, 520, 563; in Cleveland, 522; in Utica (N. Y.), 522; ethnicity, 527, 534, 568; in Philadelphia, 525; health practices, 539; bilingualism, 543; Catholicism, 545, 547, 563, 898; voluntary associations, 550; in Detroit, 552; in Boston, 557, 577; social adjustment of immigrant family, 558, 562; in Buffalo (N. Y.), 560; philanthropic facilities for immigrants, 561; in Indiana, 565; in Los Angeles, 568; independent church movement, 570; in Minneapolis, 586; in Rome (N. Y.), 810; and Italians, 832, 836; and Danes, 949
Policemen: ethnic backgrounds, 950
Portuguese: in New Bedford (Mass.), 96; in Somerville (Mass.), 106; in Fall River (Mass.), 124, 142; in Montreal (Canada), 109; in California, 121; bilingual programs for, 114; in Portsmouth (R. I.), 142; education of youth, 152
Post, L. F., 1213
Prohibition: German community opposition, 1232
Providence (R. I.): political and ethnic influences, 1090
Purcell, J. P. (Archbishop), 20

Quakers: migration in early America, 1039

Radicals: immigrant, 1032; crusade against, 1055; and American working class, 1072; Red Scare of 1919-1920, 1099; Russian radicals in U. S., 1271; Anarchism, 1297; socialists, 1327, 1400
Rattermann, H. A., 365
Rauschning, H., 260
Reading (Pa.): immigrants in, 839
Reconstructionism: and Jewish education, 589
Refugees: U. S. policy toward, 1034, 1078, 1098, 1154, 1169, 1172; economic aspects of immigration to U. S., 1081; Catholic Committee for, 1108; and international organization, 1156
Reinhold, H. A., 282
Revel, B., 737
Rhodians, 448
Riis, J. A., 1292
Rölvaag, O. E., 172, 227, 233
Rome (N. Y.): Italian and Polish immigrants, 810
Roosevelt, T., 1265

Rosati, J., 1321
Roseto (Pa.): Italian community, 394
Rumanians: assimilation, 521; in Indiana, 549; in Chicago, 579
Russians: language, 513; in U.S., 518; literature by Russian-Jewish immigrants, 519; in American Midwest, 523; emigration to the U.S., 526; in Oregon, 531, 567; Russian-German settlements in Kansas, 536; social mobility, 537, 571

St. Louis (Mo.): colonial government, 117; immigrant education, 848; cultural heritage of, 942; "hyphenism" in, 976
St. Raphael Society, 491
San Pedro (Calif.): ethnic groups in, 913
Santa Clara College, 1306
Santa Fe (N.M.): ethnic differentiation, 790
Scala Collection, 1294
Schizophrenia: ethnic differences, 1336; in ethnic novels, 1394
Schurz, C., 272
Schwenkfelders, 269, 361
Scots: emigration to America (1707-1783), 33, 73
Sealsfield, C., 372
Serbs: ethnic identity among, 512; in Pennsylvania, 540; political activities, 574; Serbian Orthodox Church, 582
Settlement House: and the public school, 798; in New York City, 873, 895, 900; in the Progressive Era, 889, 1015
Siney, J., 1060
Sladek, J. V., 576
Slavs: in Pennsylvania anthracite fields, 509, 529; bilingualism, 555; dynamics of Americanization, 573; political movements, 574; immigration and urbanization (1870-1918), 575; folk music, 584
Slovenes: ethnic identity among, 512; assimilation of refugees, 524; political activities, 574
Socialist Party: Jews and Italians, 980; 1327, 1400
Somerville (Mass.): Portuguese in, 106
South (American): efforts to attract immigrants, 1011
South Bend (Ind.): urbanization of immigrants, 831; Catholics, 1179
South Dakota: migration patterns, 1065
Spalding, J. L., 37, 45
Spalding, T. W., 75
Steelton (Pa.): immigrants in industrial community, 801
Stella, J., 1286
Stieglitz, A., 1289
Stoddard, T. L., 1185
Straus, O. S., 613
Strubberg, F. A., 246
Stuyvesant, P.: foreign policy of, 100
Swedes: religious organizations in Minnesota, 155; rural settlements in western Washington, 157; in Northwest, 159; acculturation, 161, 969; Swedish-American press, 164, 229; immigration history, 168, 191, 192; ethnic festivals, 169; Lutheran congregations, 171, 173, 209, 235; Swedish language, 178, 182, 212; in Illinois politics, 184; in Chicago, 193; Methodism, 201, 204, 241; immigrant fiction, 214, 231, 240; sacred and secular music,

216; higher education, 224; in Texas, 228; legends and folk beliefs, 232
Swedish Mission Covenant Church, 179
Swinton, J., 67
Swiss: emigration to U. S., 333, 355; Swiss-German dialect study, 381
Syracuse (N. Y.): ethnic areas, 991; social geography of, 1009; ethnic electorate, 1178

Talleyrand, C. M., 92, 108
Tammany Hall: and immigrants, 867, 1218
Teachers: multi-ethnic education, 791, 1187, 1235; levels of ethnicity in, 838
Textbooks: treatment of minority groups, 851, 852, 907, 926, 957, 958, 1024; high school libraries and ethnic polarization, 857
Truman, H.: and creation of Israel, 1150
Turner, F. J., 1333

Ukrainians: economic activity in U. S., 530; assimilation, 553; ethnic leadership, 554
United Mine Workers, 1183
Urban education, 903, 961

Van Raalte, A. C., 143
Venettozzi, T., 1386
Viereck, G. S., 303
Vladeck, B. C., 677
Vocational education, 1304, 1366

Wahoo (Neb.), 171
Wald, L., 1299
Walsh, F. P., 1201
Welsh: integration in America, 15; in Columbus (Ohio), 86
West Indies: French refugees from, 91
Wilson, H., 1305
Wilson, W.: ethnic opposition to peace policies, 1234; and rebirth of Poland, 1255
Wilson, W. B., 1405
Wisconsin: Catholic education in, 1281
Wise, I. M., 771
Woonsocket (R. I.): French immigrants, 137; social networks in, 796; ethnic survey, 989
Worcester (Mass.): social mobility in, 807

Xantus, J., 1296

Yeshiva University, 686

Yezierska, A., 652
Yiddish Theater: themes of persecution, 595; in Detroit, 709; in New York City, 747
Yugoslavs: in Ohio, 507; migrations to U.S., 517; history of, 528; in Louisiana, 551

Zangwill, I., 712